The
Zapruder
Film

The
Zapruder
Film Reframing JFK's
Assassination
David R. Wrone

University Press of Kansas

Published by the

University Press of Kansas

(Lawrence, Kansas 66049),

which was organized by the

Kansas Board of Regents and

is operated and funded by

Emporia State University,

Fort Hays State University,

Kansas State University,

Pittsburg State University,

the University of Kansas, and

Wichita State University

© 2003 by the University Press of Kansas
All rights reserved

Library of Congress
Cataloging-in-Publication Data
Wrone, David R.
The Zapruder film : reframing JFK's assassination /
David R. Wrone.
p. cm.
Includes bibliographical references and index.
ISBN 0-7006-1291-2 (alk. paper)
1. Kennedy, John F. (John Fitzgerald), 1917–1963—
Assassination. 2. Kennedy, John F. (John Fitzgerald), 1917–
1963—In motion pictures. 3. Zapruder, Abraham. 4. Amateur
films—Texas—Dallas—History—20th century. 5. Conspiracies
—United States—History—20th century. I. Title.
E842.9.W765 2003
364.15′24′097309046—dc21
2003013218

British Library Cataloguing-in-Publication Data is available.
Printed in the United States of America

10 9 8 7 6 5 4 3 2 1

The paper used in this publication meets the minimum
requirements of the American National Standard for
Permanence of Paper for Printed Library Materials
Z39.48-1984.

For

Elizabeth Maliha Wrone, M.D., M.S.

David Alley Wrone, M.D.

CONTENTS

PREFACE

Abraham Zapruder's famous film is key evidence in the investigation of one of the worst crimes that can occur in a representative society, the assassination of the head of state. The film was part of the official evidence assembled by the government in pursuit of its inquiry into President John F. Kennedy's death. What the film actually reveals firmly and definitively refutes the official conclusions.

The President's Commission to Investigate the Assassination of President John F. Kennedy, known as the Warren Commission after its chair, Chief Justice of the United States Earl Warren, conducted its inquiry from November 29, 1963, to September 24, 1964, with unlimited resources and funding. The Commission included the chief justice, a future president, a former director of central intelligence, and powerful senators and congressmen, with a staff and observers that included a future Supreme Court justice, federal judges, senators, esteemed judicial scholars, future deans of law schools, and outstanding attorneys, with the powerful assistance of the Federal Bureau of Investigation, the Central Intelligence Agency, and many other agencies of government.

In the Commission's official account of the crime and in the writings of countless commentators, as well as in the works of numerous critics, the history, importance, and understanding of Zapruder's film is often dimly perceived or crippled by frequent gaps in the record. Thus, to provide a solid history of the film—from its creation to its current resting place—and its relationship to the criminal investigation is the primary purpose of this work, which rests squarely upon a careful analysis of the voluminous evidentiary base of the official investigation.

I appreciate the assistance of many librarians and archivists, especially at the National Archives and the Lyndon Johnson Presidential Library. The Sixth Floor Museum at Dealey Plaza in Dallas provided exceptional assistance from its unique collection. Over the years the University of Wisconsin–Stevens Point library has been consistently helpful. Attorney Jim Lesar, president of the Assassination Records Center in Washington, D.C., counseled me and filed my Freedom of Information Act suit. For three decades he has labored on complex legal suits associated with dissent from the official findings. Many other individuals helped and guided me, including Hal Verb, Ray Marcus, Jerry McKnight, and Clay Ogilvie. Gary Mack provided invaluable insight and commentary from his deep knowledge.

As a friend and associate for thirty years, Harold Weisberg provided inestimable advice. He opened to me, as he did to all who asked, the voluminous records in his private archives in Frederick, Maryland, soon to be transferred to Hood College. These include a third of a million pages of FBI records (better arranged and easier to use than those in federal depositories), indexes, and extensive subject matter files compiled from the documentary base over a lifetime. Since 1965 a principal figure in the community of those who dissented from the official findings of the Warren Commission—known as critics—he possessed unsurpassed knowledge of the crime, insights into the evidence, and perspectives on approach to issues that are unmatched. On the assassination, Weisberg wrote nine published books and thirty-five unpublished book manuscripts now available on CD-ROM. His main concern, indeed passion, was that those who examine the assassination rely only on the evidence in the crime and the facts and eschew theory and speculation, the bane of understanding. I have relied on his files and on his published work.

Mike Briggs of the University Press of Kansas played a principal role in guiding me through the process of publication, and to him I owe my thanks and a debt of enduring gratitude.

My wife, Elaine Alley Wrone, provided advice and help. Without her unfailing assistance and constant encouragement, the book would not have been possible.

For it is a truth, which the experience of ages has attested,

that the people are always most in danger when the means of

injuring their rights are in the possession of those of

whom they entertain the least suspicion.

—Alexander Hamilton, *Federalist No. 25*

INTRODUCTION

As we began the twenty-first century, our nation finally acquired ownership (but not the copyright) of perhaps the most famous home movie of all time—Abraham Zapruder's brief film of the assassination of President John F. Kennedy. After a thirty-five-year odyssey, involving numerous disputes over the rights to and authenticity of the movie, the six-foot strip of film has now found a final home. It is held within a protective case inside a locked cabinet behind the secure doors of the cold storage freezer of the Special Media Archives Services Division of the National Archives and Records Administration at College Park, Maryland, maintained at twenty-five degrees Fahrenheit and 30 percent relative humidity. There it remains, a grim memorial to a tragic day that—like December 7, 1941, and September 11, 2001—forever altered American and world history. Like those other two fateful days, November 22, 1963, exploded the peace and security of the American nation; unlike those days, however, it also robbed the country of its leader by an act so bold and brutal that even now, four decades later, it is hard to comprehend. How could this event have happened in broad daylight on the streets of a major American city? Could it have really been the work of a solitary and crazed gunman, as the government's official investigation declared in pinning the murder on Lee Harvey Oswald?

In fact, the Zapruder film—both by itself and in conjunction with a body of other assassination evidence—convincingly contradicts the government's declaration. A close examination of the Zapruder film leads to the inescapable conclusion that more than one person wielded weapons in Dealey Plaza that day and that, most likely, Lee Harvey Oswald was *not* one of them.

Thus, in effect and by technical definition, John F. Kennedy's murder was the result of a conspiracy. Precisely who the conspirators were this study does not attempt to say because the evidence at this time is insufficient to make such a determination. But there definitely is more than sufficient evidence still available—in the Zapruder film and elsewhere—to determine that a conspiracy killed the president and that the subsequent official investigation at minimum failed miserably in its efforts and at worst appears to have deliberately ignored or distorted evidence to force

Oswald into a Procrustean conclusion reached well before the actual official inquiry had even begun.

With that in mind, the present work is designed both to highlight the Zapruder film's history, content, and controversies and to revisit the flaws and failures of the Warren Commission and its official report on the assassination. By doing so, I hope to encourage other scholars—especially those who continue to defend the Warren Commission—to reconsider the official evidence and conclusions and join with me in a collective march toward a deeper and more accurate understanding of the events of that dark day in November 1963.

Without question the Zapruder film is a crucial piece of evidence for understanding key aspects of the assassination, its investigation, and a wide spectrum of views about both that have emerged during the past forty years. First, the film provides an extraordinarily precise time line for examining what happened second by second from just before until just after the attack—thanks to our knowledge that the film's 486 frames recorded this momentous event at precisely 18.3 frames per second or about one frame every one-eighteenth of a second. Second, the film provides with considerable clarity key information regarding the positions and reactions of the attack's two victims—the murdered president and the seriously wounded Governor John Connally—which, in turn, helps us determine the number and direction of the shots fired that day. It also allows us to locate and identify many of the eyewitnesses to the murder. Third, and most important, it provides compelling evidence for the existence of a conspiracy to murder the president.

A comment about that word: the word "conspiracy" has acquired a lot of emotional baggage over the years, usually in dismissive reference to those who wail about alleged high-level corporate or federal misdeeds or to the overheated paranoia of Hollywood films and television shows like the enormously popular *X-Files*. Indeed, to argue "conspiracy" is to invite direct association with the so-called lunatic fringe, which would be anathema to any serious scholar. But, for those who are well versed in American history, the concept of conspiracy is a familiar one, in part because it represents a common phenomenon in American society, politics, and law—ranging from the revolutionary generation through the cabals of the Federalists, the treason of the Confederacy, the theft of public resources by various robber barons, the rise of organized crime, the plunder of savings and loans institutions, the demise of Enron and Worldcom, and so on.

The word itself has Latin roots—"con," meaning with or together, and "spire," meaning to breathe—and derives from the practice among the Roman legions of soldiers entering or leaving camp to voice the password to guards by whispering into their ears to avoid listening spies. From this curious origin it evolved under Roman and then European and American usage and law to mean two or more persons working together to do what the law says is wrong. Thus, it applies to procedures utilized by the Continental Congress to overthrow the colonial legal establishment, to methods devised and implemented by the railroad capitalists to acquire land for their corporations, to executions of competing mobsters by Mafia capos and hit men, to the cover-up of illegal misadventures by President Nixon and his henchmen, and to the killing of JFK by two or more individuals. All in all, such things have been a more frequent part of the American landscape than most of us might think.

To state unequivocally that the official evidence proves that two or more individuals, and none of them Lee Harvey Oswald, killed JFK does not, however, imply or require that the facts also reveal to us who those individuals were. Because I do not find evidence for such clear identifications, I do not speculate here regarding *who* might have shot JFK. Nor is it incumbent upon me or any other historian to go beyond the available facts to perform such speculations. Indeed, to speculate, to go beyond the evidence, is the antithesis of what a historian must do and what society obligates a genuine scholar to do. The historian, however, is obligated to establish what we actually know with a sizable degree of certainty—that is, a baseline on which all additional intellectual efforts can be built. Without that foundation, the whole edifice of the intellectual enterprise collapses.

America's founding generation firmly believed that honor was the measure of a nation's greatness and that with its quiet presence or loud absence the new American nation would thrive or crumble. In the history of the Zapruder film, however, very little honor or saving grace can be found in the conduct and execution of the profoundly sloppy and thus counterproductive official investigation into JFK's assassination. Indeed, the actions of members of the Warren Commission, Federal Bureau of Investigation, Central Intelligence Agency, and a number of other federal agencies responsible for the original investigation must be viewed with grave disappointment, for those efforts failed the nation in a time of great crisis. To a lesser extent the same must also be said regarding the flawed inquiries that followed, including the 1965 prosecutors review, the 1968 Department of Justice Panel Review, the Schweiker subcommittee of the Church Committee, the Belin-Rockefeller Commission, the House Select Committee on Assassinations, and the Assassination Records Review Board—all of which, despite the best of intentions, produced profoundly unsatisfactory results.

The combined flaws and failures of these investigating institutions and organizations—chief among them the Warren Commission—have exponentially increased the difficulties confronting any scholar who wishes to pursue the complexities, contradictions, and misunderstandings surrounding JFK's assassination. No wonder so many mainstream scholars have collectively abdicated their duty to submit this case to the highest standards of reputable scholarship. As a result the field has been overrun by best-selling popularizers, paranoid conspiracy theorists, and true believers in the Warren Report—none of whom have moved our nation any closer to true understanding and closure in this matter.

There have been exceptions to this sad state of affairs, and for those we should be immensely grateful. Working with average means and outside the halls of academe, individuals such as the late Harold Weisberg have labored against enormous odds to analyze and follow the evidence (no matter where it leads) and to critique the Warren Commission efforts in an investigation that was so flawed it created an *effective*, if not actual, cover-up. These scholars persisted after the truth in the face of gigantic spools of bureaucratic red tape; destruction or disappearance of evidence; the ridicule of government officials, mainstream academics, and media pundits; and the distortions supported or introduced by other less responsible writers on the assassination. One is reminded of the words of Edmund Burke (cited by JFK himself in *Profiles in Courage*): "He well knows what snares are spread about his path, from personal animosity . . . and possibly from popular delusion. But he has put to hazard his case, his security, his interest, his power, even his . . . popularity. . . . He is traduced and abused for his supposed motives. He will remember that . . . calumny and abuse are essential parts of triumph."[1] These individuals deserve our gratitude and respect for helping preserve the evidentiary record and for challenging the often contorted and ultimately unconvincing official conclusions that have denied our rightful access to the truth. Without their efforts this truth would forever be denied to the citizens of this nation.

Americans have always been supremely optimistic about their place in the firmament of nations, about the enduring efficacy of their democratic form of government, and about their ability to triumph over the toughest obstacles. But the assassination of President Kennedy, like the attack at Pearl Harbor and the attacks of September 11, 2001, strongly tempered that previously unabashed optimism and signaled to the nation's citizens that things would never again be the same. And, indeed, things never were. In the decade immediately after JFK's murder, nearly sixty thousand Americans died and many thousands more were wounded in a disastrous war in Southeast Asia, violence erupted in response to black Americans' pursuit of their constitutional civil rights, two more American leaders were assassinated, and yet another American president was removed from office for probable crimes against the state. Would things have been different had JFK not been killed? We will never know. But we do know that the events of November 22, 1963, stole from America both optimism and innocence, losses that succeeding events only deepened, forever framing JFK's death as the doorway to those terrible times.

The chronicle of the world's most famous amateur motion picture, then, goes well beyond the provision of a mere repository of insights into the assassination of an American president, a president after all who has been loved and reviled in equal measure (not unlike the heavy counterwinds that buffeted another assassinated president, Abraham Lincoln). It opens a window on a nation's entire institutional order and demonstrates that those institutions that define and sustain our society can and do sometimes fail us—at a time when they are most needed to perform to the highest standards. In the aftermath of this particular failure, following the terribly tragic "darkness at noon" in Dealey Plaza, even darker times followed. But while we cannot change the past or bring back JFK, we can redeem that past and resurrect our own honor by taking another unflinching look at what actually happened, by following the evidence wherever it takes us, and by fearlessly challenging false reports and fantastic stories.

I

The Film

Abraham Zapruder
Films the Assassination

Early on Friday morning, November 22, 1963, late fall rain fell on Dallas, pushed with gusts of wind. A few hours before noon the rain ended and the sun broke through the clouds, but the erratic wind bursts lingered.

That morning, fifty-nine-year-old Abraham Zapruder drove seven miles from his Dallas home to his office in the Dal-Tex building at 501 Elm Street, the corner of Elm and Houston Street, where he manufactured ladies dresses.[1] Catercorner lay the public park of Dealey Plaza; directly west across Houston at 411 Elm stood the Texas School Book Depository building. A co-owner of Jennifer Juniors, Inc., with his young partner Erwin Schwartz, the heir of his deceased partner, Zapruder managed the factory and Schwartz the sales.[2] In 1905, Zapruder had been born in Russia, where his family had experienced privation, persecution, and sometimes near starvation.[3] He recalled those years as "terrible."[4] America gave him freedom and opportunity and a good life. He spoke with a slight accent.[5]

In midmorning Zapruder, at work in his fourth-floor office, was excited about President John F. Kennedy coming to Dallas and about watching the motorcade that the newspaper had reported was routed along Dealey Plaza's Elm Street just outside his window.[6] But, as he later recalled for a Warren Commission staff attorney, "I didn't have my camera."[7] He had left it at home. The morning had been cloudy and rainy and did not seem suitable for filming. By around ten o'clock the skies cleared and the sun poked through. His clerks and staff urged him to go home to retrieve his camera. Zapruder demurred. "I wouldn't have a chance even to see the President," he told his secretary Lillian Rogers.[8] Rogers finally convinced him with the argument that "the President didn't come through the neighborhood every day."[9] The crowds would be light in the plaza, Rogers added. At around 10:00 A.M. Zapruder drove back home, picked up the camera, and returned to the office.[10]

Zapruder was an avid amateur cameraman. The previous autumn, at the Peacock Jewelry Company in Dallas, he had purchased a Bell & Howell

8mm Director Series movie camera, Model 414 PD, serial no. AS 13486, with case.[11] It had a good zoom telescopic lens, later determined by citizens to be a Varamat 9–27mm f1.8 zoom lens.[12] Federal authorities never recorded the specifics and make.[13]

The camera recorded images on a twenty-five-foot spool of 16mm color film, with a sprocket advancing mechanism,[14] but exposed on only one half of the film.[15] When that half was used up, the user reversed the roll of film in the camera and exposed the other half.[16] After development, the laboratory precision-slit the film down the middle, and the second half of what then emerged as standard 8mm film was cemented to the first half.[17] The lab returned the film to the user as though it had been a single reel of 8mm film rather than a doubled reel that had been split in half and then made into a single reel of twice the original length.[18]

The day of President Kennedy's visit to Dallas, Zapruder had his camera loaded with Kodachrome II Safety Film, a color outdoor film; at his home he had previously taken a few frames of his grandchildren playing.[19] Only by inspecting the film edge of the reproduced frames printed in volume 18 of the Warren Commission's Hearings as Commission Exhibit 885 (CE 885), however, can one identify with certainty the type of film he used, for the official investigation into the assassination never obtained that critical information.[20]

Sometime after noon, Zapruder prepared to film the motorcade. He had first thought he could film JFK from the window of his office, but this proved to be impractical.[21] As the time for the motorcade's arrival drew near, he left the office to walk down to Elm Street on the plaza to find a site where he could "take better pictures."[22] "I tried one place and it was on a narrow ledge," he told the Warren Commission on July 22, 1964, "and I couldn't balance myself very much. I tried another place and that had some obstruction of signs or whatever it was there and finally I found a place farther down near the underpass that was a square of concrete."[23]

While searching near the north grassy knoll for a spot to stand, Zapruder tried the concrete steps of the pergola but was dissatisfied with them. As the scheduled time for the motorcade drew nearer, he checked on the proper functioning of his take-up reel by shooting a few frames of his office receptionist Marilyn Sitzman walking up the small hill, and also captured two persons sitting on the nearby pergola bench, Beatrice Hester, one of his payroll clerks, and her husband, Charles.[24] As he recalled later for the Commission, "I was shooting some of the pictures to start my roll from the beginning. I didn't want to have a blank."[25]

Zapruder explained to Sitzman his problem with the position.[26] She suggested that he stand on a small concrete abutment forming part of the pergola built on the slope of the north hill or knoll of the plaza, half-way between the Texas School Book Depository building and the railroad underpass. But her boss hesitated. He suffered from vertigo and was afraid he could not keep his balance on the abutment. Sitzman offered to hold onto his coat to steady him.[27] Zapruder and Sitzman then scrambled up on the four-foot-high stumpy pillar.[28] Behind them stood the pergola and behind that a tree-lined five-foot-high stockade fence that enclosed and shielded a parking lot.[29] The tree-masked parking lot contained several rows of parked cars stretching back perhaps a hundred feet to the railroad tracks and four hundred feet to the north. Sitzman "was right behind him" holding on to his coat.[30]

Zapruder and Sitzman had some of the best views of the assassination of anyone in Dealey Plaza. They stood about sixty-five feet from the center of Elm Street and about two hundred feet from the seven-story Texas School Book Depository, which loomed to their left or east, the only building on the plaza.[31] On the hill, they were above the street that dipped to enter the triple underpass. Zapruder, peering through the telephoto lens, would prove to be a witness to the president's assassination. The lens magnified what it focused on approximately four times. The Commission failed to define precisely how much.[32]

At 12:30, the president's motorcade arrived from the east off Houston Street, slowly turning left 120 degrees onto Elm Street and led by three motorcycle policemen many feet ahead of the limousines.[33] Elm curved in toward the center of the park and downward to join Main and Commerce Streets to dip beneath the triple underpass of the railroad tracks.[34] Zapruder kept his eye to the telescopic lens, filming the motorcycles. But then, seeing they were not the cars of the presidential party, he stopped.

When the limousines appeared he began filming again, and despite sounds and commotion around him, never took his eye off the viewer or stopped filming until the president's limousine disappeared from view to his right.[35] "I was shooting through a telephoto lens," he later told Warren Commission staff attorney Wesley Liebeler.[36] The lens magnified every-thing he saw, and he focused his eye on JFK.[37]

Federal authorities ignored Sitzman. "I was totally ignored. Absolutely," she recalled thirty years later.[38] Only through the work of reporters and critics did Zapruder's assistant on the abutment eventually find a way to relate what she had seen.

Immediately after the shooting, as Sitzman wandered in shock on the plaza, Darwin Payne, a reporter for the *Dallas Times Herald*, ran up to her and asked what she had seen. As he recorded in hurried notes, she replied: "I heard the first shot . . . he slumped over in seat . . . 2nd shot hit pres right in the temple."[39]

In 1966, three years later, Sitzman recalled the incident for critic Josiah Thompson:

> There was nothing unusual until the first sound which I thought was a firecracker, mainly because of the reaction of President Kennedy. He put his hands up to guard his face. . . . And the next thing that I remembered clearly was the shot that hit directly in front of us, or almost directly in front of us, that hit him on the side of his face . . . above the ear and to the front. . . . And, we could see his brains come out, you know, his head opening.[40]

Sitzman's comments require two observations. Her description of seeing the first shot hit does not fit the Warren Commission's findings. A large street sign on the north side of Elm Street blocked Zapruder's vision for many frames, starting at frame 210.[41] At this same time, the Commission stated that a tree blocked a shot from the Texas School Book Depository and that Lee Harvey Oswald could not have fired his first shot after frame 210.[42] This is a fixed boundary of the federal assassination investigation. Thus, if a shot had been fired before frame 210, as Sitzman claims, it could not have been fired by the alleged official assassin.

The second observation relates to her seeing the next shot "hit him on the side of the face," which also meant Oswald could not have fired it regardless of whether Sitzman heard a sound behind her. The angles and physical constraints of the evidence rule out a shot from the alleged sixth-floor easternmost window of the depository hitting JFK on the side of his face.[43] The official allegations necessitate the death shot entering the back of his head. As the Commission concluded, "A bullet . . . entered the back of his head and exited through the upper right portion of his skull."[44]

Unlike Sitzman's official exclusion as a witness, Zapruder had six brief chances to provide some scraps of information. Two arose when reporters contacted him immediately after the shooting; another came early that afternoon at a television station; the next he revealed during a conversation at the film developing plant; the fifth was recorded that night by a Secret Service agent; and the last occasion came nine months later in his exceptionally brief and cursory pro forma appearance before the Warren Commission.

Zapruder's first opportunity to comment came when reporters asked him questions on Dealey Plaza. Darwin Payne, who had run most of the six blocks from his newspaper office, encountered Sitzman and Beatrice Hester, who told him about their boss and his film. Payne went to Zapruder's office, spoke with him, took notes, and then phoned the *Dallas Times Herald*. At the rewrite desk they recorded his words. Payne said Zapruder "heard three shots. After 1st one pres. slumped over grabbed his stomach hit in the stomach 2 more shots looked like head opened up & everything come out . . . blood splatters everywhere . . . side of face . . . looked like blobs out of his temple . . . for[e]head."[45]

Harry McCormick of the *Dallas Morning News* had sped to Dealey Plaza from the Trade Center, where Kennedy was to have delivered a speech. Zapruder was the first witness McCormick interviewed after leaving his car for a fellow reporter to park. The photographer blurted out, "There were three shots. Two hit the president and the other Gov. Connally. I know the president is dead for his head seemed to fly to pieces when he was hit the second time."[46]

About an hour later, Zapruder was afforded another brief moment to comment when he appeared on television station WFAA, an ABC affiliate, where he had been taken to see if the station could develop his film. The station's program director, Jay Watson, interviewed Zapruder live on the air, and the program was broadcast nationally.[47] Erwin Schwartz, Zapruder's partner, stood off scene holding the camera with the film still enclosed. Watson began by asking Zapruder if he would "tell us your story please, sir?" Zapruder described the scene on Dealey Plaza, then added, "I heard a shot, and he slumped to the side." His use of the word "slumped" seems peculiar, for it indicates no direction, and he never mentioned it in any other instances.

After the introductory comments, Watson and Zapruder were discussing the efforts of WFAA to process Zapruder's film when suddenly the station interrupted them with the announcement that President Kennedy's body had left Parkland Memorial Hospital. It screened some footage of the hearse leaving the hospital driveway.[48] The interruption occurred just after 2:00 P.M. The break also showed a recent photograph of the Texas School Book Depository building. When they returned to the interview, Watson pointed to the sixth-floor window and explained to Zapruder, "This is a picture of the window where the gun was allegedly fired from that killed President Kennedy."[49]

Zapruder interrupted Watson to comment, "I must have been in the line of fire." He repeated, "I say I must have been in the line of fire where I see that picture where it was" and added an observation on the scene.[50] Then Zapruder put his right hand to his right temple with the fingers pointing to where he saw the president's head explode. With that Watson ended the interview. But there is a problem with the phrase "line of fire." Zapruder had been on the knoll or hill. To his far left stood the depository, and to his front was Elm Street. For him to have been in the line of fire from the sixth-floor window, the bullet would have had to traverse a triangle from the window to Zapruder's camera to JFK, which is physically impossible. Was Zapruder perhaps struggling to say that the shots came from behind him?

But in showing and commenting on the photograph of the depository, was it possible that the interviewer, although reflecting the information then coming over the wire in the studio, confused Zapruder by introducing details Zapruder himself did not recall? Zapruder the eyewitness should have been asked where he thought the shots came from without being presented with the memory-filtering photograph.

After the brief television interview, Zapruder traveled to the Kodak plant to have his film developed. As he sat on a bench near the processing machinery, he discussed what he had seen with Jack Harrison, a manager of the firm. Years later Harrison recalled the scene in an oral interview for the Sixth Floor Museum at Dealey Plaza in Dallas: "Zapruder thought he heard gunshots from behind him."[51]

Whereas Harrison's memory is subject to the possible flaws attributable to the passage of many years, Zapruder's statement made on the evening of November 22 was set down while his memories were fresh and confirms the earlier comments. Around 9:30 P.M., at the offices of the Dallas Secret Service, the dress manufacturer arrived to give federal authorities two copies of his film.[52] Agent Max Phillips wrote in a memorandum that accompanied one print of the film to Washington, "Mr. Zapruder was photographing the President at the instant he was shot. According to Mr. Zapruder, the position of the assassin was behind Mr. Zapruder."[53] Since

Oswald was to the far left of Zapruder, sixty-one feet high in the Texas School Book Depository building, he could not have fired that shot.[54]

Having spoken to two reporters, a television interviewer, a film developer, and a Secret Service agent on November 22, Zapruder spoke again on July 22, 1964, when federal officials grudgingly decided to take his testimony in a hurried and truncated session before Commission assistant counsel Wesley J. Liebeler in Dallas. (Until late June, officials had intended not to interview him.) He reiterated for Liebeler, "I saw his head opened up and the blood and everything came out."[55] Regrettably for history, when Zapruder struggled to locate the position of the shooter, Liebeler abruptly shifted topics and cut off his testimony.[56] Regarding the first shot, he testified:

> MR. ZAPRUDER. 'I heard the first shot and I saw the President lean over and grab himself like this (holding his left chest area).[57]

Regarding the shot to the president's head:

> MR. LIEBELER. Do you have any impression as to the direction from which these shots came?
>
> MR. ZAPRUDER. No, I also thought it came from back of me. Of course, you can't tell when something is in line—it could come from anywhere, but being I was here and he was hit on this line and he was hit right in the head—I saw it right around here, so it looked like it came from here and it could come from there.
>
> MR. LIEBELER. All right, as you stood here on the abutment and looked down into Elm Street, you saw the President hit on the right side of the head and you thought perhaps the shots had come from behind you?
>
> MR. ZAPRUDER. Well, yes.
>
> MR. LIEBELER. From the direction behind you?
>
> MR. ZAPRUDER. Yes, actually—I couldn't say what I thought at the moment, where they came from—after the impact of the tragedy was really what I saw . . .
>
> MR. LIEBELER. But you didn't form any opinion at that time as to what direction the shots did come from actually?
>
> MR. ZAPRUDER. No.[58]

Zapruder's perception that JFK received the first shot prior to frame 210 demolishes the official solution to the crime. His view of the death shot hitting the president on the right side of his head makes impossible a shot from the alleged sniper's lair in the depository.

Immediately after Zapruder had filmed the assassination, his receptionist on the abutment with him recalled he lowered his camera from his eye and screamed, "They killed him! They killed him! They killed him!"[59] In his testimony before the Commission staff, Zapruder described himself as wandering "incoherent, in a state of shock":[60]

> And then, I didn't even remember how I got down from that abutment there, but there I was, I guess, and I was walking toward—back toward my office and screaming. "They killed him, they killed him," and the people that I met on the way didn't even know what happened and they kept yelling, "What happened, what happened, what happened?" . . . I kept on just yelling, "They killed him, they killed him, they killed him," and finally got to my office and my secretary—I told her to call the police or the Secret Service—I don't know what she was doing, and that's about all. I was very much upset.[61]

These several strands of information, pieced together from scattered sources, provide an indication of what Zapruder saw through his viewfinder. Federal officials—FBI, Secret Service, Warren Commission staff— never interviewed him properly, although federal conclusions about the assassination often turn on the critical facts held on his film.

After he climbed down from the abutment, for several minutes he wandered dazed around the plaza. Finally he was starting to move toward his office when Harry McCormick of the *Dallas Morning News* found him. On the plaza McCormick had met Beatrice Hester, who told him about what Zapruder had filmed.[62] He approached Zapruder to speak to him, but Zapruder refused, saying he would talk only to federal authorities. McCormick recalled that Zapruder told him, "I got it all on film," to which the reporter replied, after taking down Zapruder's description of the shots, "The Secret Service will want to see those films. Where are you going?" Zapruder said he was going to his office across the street. "Go ahead," McCormick directed him. "I will find Forrest Sorrels, head of the Secret Service here, and we'll be back to talk with you." As an experienced crime reporter, he knew Sorrels well, and he left for the sheriff's office to find him.[63]

In the meantime, Zapruder reached his own office. He had his secretary put the camera, still loaded, on top of a filing cabinet near her desk. Still in a daze, he directed her to telephone the police about his film. The police did not respond; they were so caught up in the events surrounding the murder that the odd phone call from someone claiming that an amateur had filmed the assassination was ignored.[64] Zapruder sat at his desk weeping.[65] The scene had so shocked him that for the rest of his life he suffered recurring nightmares and never got over the horrible sight.[66]

Back on Dealey Plaza, Zapruder's employees continued to tell police and reporters about the film. One of his shipping clerks, probably Beatrice Hester, who had heard him exclaim about his filming JFK's murder, told a policeman that her boss had taken a motion picture of the assassination.[67] The officer got his partner and, carrying their shotguns as was standard practice for the emergency, walked over to Jennifer Juniors to obtain the film.[68] Zapruder refused to give it to the officers. He would hand it over, he said, only to someone in authority.[69] The officers lingered in the outer office, trying to sort out their problem.

After Zapruder went back into his office, two of his employees standing outside the Texas School Book Depository, Beatrice Hester and Marilyn Sitzman, told Darwin Payne about their boss's film.[70] Payne wanted to see it, so they led him across the street and to Zapruder's office. In the office Payne questioned Zapruder about the assassination and then about his film. He attempted to obtain publication rights for the *Dallas Times Herald*. Again, the distraught Zapruder shrugged off the request.[71]

Payne persisted, asking Zapruder if they could take the film to his newspaper's laboratory to have it developed. He told Zapruder that he was certain his paper would pay for the film rights and would "do the right thing." But Zapruder insisted on giving it to the Secret Service or FBI. Next Payne got the president of the *Dallas Times Herald* on the phone, and they had a three-way conversation with Zapruder. If the film was good, James F. Chambers Jr. said, he would pay. The figure of a few hundred dollars was mentioned. Despite entreaties, Zapruder refused. The classic newsman's drive was pushing Payne, who later recalled that for a second he had thought, "The camera was on top of the filing cabinet right there. And in a fleeting moment, I thought, 'Well, I could grab it. Nobody would stop me. I could grab the camera and run.'" As he dallied, Secret Service agent Sorrels arrived with McCormick.[72]

After his initial contact with Zapruder on the plaza, McCormick had been covering the events at the sheriff's building a block away, where he had met Secret Service agent Forrest Sorrels. Sorrels had gone to Parkland

Memorial Hospital with the wounded president but at about 12:45 P.M. had returned to the plaza.[73] Much of our information comes from his January 22, 1964, report on the film to Inspector Thomas J. Kelley, chief of the Secret Service, in which Sorrels explained how he came in contact with Zapruder (see documents 1 and 2 in the appendix).[74]

Many witnesses to the assassination had been taken into the sheriff's office to be interviewed. Soon after returning to the plaza, Sorrels had gone to the sheriff's office to question them. He amplified his account when he testified before the Commission. While in the sheriff's office, he testified, he was approached by McCormick, whom he "had known for many years."[75] McCormick informed Sorrels about Zapruder, telling him, "I have a man over here that got pictures of this whole thing."[76] Sorrels replied, "Let's go see him."[77] Together the two walked the block to Zapruder's office.[78] It appears that it was just after 1:00 P.M.

By the time Sorrels and McCormick entered Zapruder's office at a little after 1:00 P.M., Erwin Schwartz had arrived to join his partner.[79] A few minutes earlier Schwartz had telephoned the office from across town where he was having lunch, only to be told by the secretary, Lillian Rogers, that policemen were in the office with shotguns and wanted the film, which Zapruder had by then placed in the safe directly behind her. "Mr. Z" was in his office, distraught. Thirty years later Schwartz recalled that he had told Rogers to lock the safe.[80]

In the outer office when McCormick and Sorrels entered were Payne, the two officers, Schwartz, Rogers, and apparently other media representatives. In the outer office McCormick, for the *Dallas Morning News*, promptly offered Zapruder $1,000 for the film, which was refused.[81] Sorrels and McCormick headed straight for Zapruder's office, but Payne protested his rival being favored, whereupon Sorrels and Zapruder ejected McCormick.

On May 7, 1964, before the Commission, Sorrels recalled his meeting with Zapruder: "And Mr. Zapruder was real shook up. He said that he didn't know how in the world he had taken these pictures, that he was down there and was taking the thing there, and he says, 'My God, I saw the whole thing. I saw the man's brains come out of his head.'"[82] Sorrels then asked if it would "be possible for us to get a copy of those films."[83] Zapruder said yes, for Sorrels was the person of authority he had sought.

Sorrels related Zapruder's reply in his report to the chief of the Secret Service, providing a glimpse of Zapruder's commercial concerns even at the early critical period, a theme fated to run throughout the history of the film's various owners: "Mr. Zapruder agreed to furnish me with a copy of this film with the understanding that it was strictly for official use of the Secret Service and that it would not be shown or given to any newspapers or magazines as he expected to sell the film for as high a price as he could get for it."[84]

At this point two larger questions arise. One wonders whether Zapruder would have given the original to the government at that time if authorities had asked for it rather than a copy. Richard Stolley, who later purchased the film for *Life*, believed that in his shock Zapruder would have given the film to the government if he had been asked. As Stolley remarked, "If the federal government had not been in such disarray at that moment . . . someone would probably have asked Zapruder for the original film and he probably would have relinquished it."[85] However, Forrest Sorrels's report that Zapruder's expectation less than an hour after the assassination was "to sell the film for as high a price as he could get for it" seems to contradict Stolley's observation.

During the short time Zapruder was in the office, the film remained in the camera. Now Zapruder and Sorrels faced an additional task of developing it and making a copy for the government. McCormick hastily spoke up that the *News* could do it. "Can we go there?"[86] Zapruder answered, "Sure!" They would go to the offices of the *Dallas Morning News*, which were five blocks away. Sorrels commandeered a squad car and ordered the two policemen to drive them.[87] Schwartz retrieved the camera, with its film, from the safe and joined Sorrels, Zapruder, McCormick, and the two police officers.[88] With Schwartz clutching the camera holding the undeveloped film, the six men piled into the police car and left Payne behind.[89] With the car's siren blaring and lights flashing, the men pushed through the crowds on their way to develop the film.[90]

The task they undertook was not an easy one. Over the next nine hours a bedraggled Schwartz and Zapruder would visit seven offices and plants. Then, in the midst of the process being abandoned by officials, they would have to figure out on their own how to deliver their two promised finished copies to a government in profound disorder.

2　Development and Sale of the Film

Sometime after 1:30 P.M. the squad car carrying Abraham Zapruder and his film, Secret Service agent Forrest Sorrels, Erwin Schwartz, Harry McCormick, and two policemen pulled up to the offices of the *Dallas Morning News*. "We took Mr. Zapruder to the Dallas Morning News and to their radio station offices," Sorrels later reported to his chief.[1] The six men quickly went inside to contact someone who might be able to develop Zapruder's film.[2] They discovered that the newspaper was not equipped to process the motion picture film; in the words of Sorrels, "there was no one there that would tackle the job."[3]

The group then decided to walk next door to the newspaper's television station, WFAA-TV, Channel 8, an ABC affiliate, to see if its film lab could assist them. At the station Sorrels explained to Bert Shipp, assistant news director and chief photographer, that they wanted the film processed. When Shipp asked, "What do you have here?" the agent replied, "Well, we think maybe we have the . . . we have some very important film that has to do with the moment that President Kennedy was shot." After Shipp looked at the film camera he said, "Let me tell you something. You have 8mm. We can only process 16mm. Don't you be running around town all over town trying to find somebody to soup this film" (he used the word "soup" because the developing process involves treating the film with a chemical solution).[4] Suggesting that Eastman Kodak Processing Laboratory near Love Field had the facilities and could do the job, he offered to phone someone there. Sorrels agreed, and Shipp telephoned Eastman Kodak but could rouse no one. He tried the company's emergency number and finally reached Jack Harrison, the staff supervisor.[5] The Secret Service agent came to the phone and asked the laboratory to develop the reel of film "right away." It was "official business," said Sorrels, requesting that a line be shut down and made ready, for "we need it now."[6] Kodak agreed.

While Sorrels and McCormick vainly sought to develop the film, the station's program director, Jay Watson, interviewed Zapruder live on the air, broadcast nationally over ABC television (as discussed in the previous chapter).[7] Erwin Schwartz, Zapruder's partner, stood off scene holding the camera with the film still enclosed.

After the interview Sorrels, Zapruder, Schwartz, and McCormick loaded back into the squad car with the two policemen and were driven to the Kodak laboratory.[8] The group arrived at the laboratory around 2:45 P.M., for as they approached the building, the great blue and white Air Force One bearing JFK's body was ascending from Love Field on its way back to Washington.[9]

An emotional Zapruder, carrying his camera, appeared in the second-floor lobby of the large processing facility and announced to receptionist Marilyn Brandon that he had some film to be developed.[10] She phoned the lab's production supervisor, Philip C. Chamberlain Jr., who immediately walked over to the desk, along with Richard Blair, from the service department.[11] "I'm not sure what I've got," Zapruder blurted out to them in words recalled by Chamberlain, "but I think I was taking pictures when the shooting happened."[12]

The Kodak personnel walked the film through the processing. In the initial step Blair removed the exposed film by taking Zapruder and his camera into a darkroom, where he finished running the unexposed portion of the film through to the end of the strip, opened the camera, and removed the spool.[13] Next Blair handed the film over to Kathryn Kirby of the Customer Special Handling Department. She put the film in the processing identification edge printer and on the strip end punched in the perforation identification number 0183.[14] Then Blair delivered the film to Bobby Davis and Bob Willie at machine number 2.[15] Previously, in response to the telephone call from WFAA-TV studios, the machine had been cleared and certified by John "Kenny" Anderson, production foreman, and dedicated to processing only the incoming Zapruder film.[16] Before starting the development sequence, Davis loaded the machine with new leader to guard against splits and splices.[17]

Individuals from the Zapruder party monitored the development procedure. Schwartz recalled years later for interviewers that he "watched the girl" process the film through the glass window on the processing machine.[18] But more authoritative affirmation of monitoring came from Dick Blair, who stated the Secret Service agent remained in the developing darkroom with the workers.[19] Zapruder stayed in the building, talking with employees and with McCormick and phoning his attorney and his home.[20]

As part of the identification elements, the edge print on the strip of the developed film included the letter "D," to show that it had been prepared at Kodak's Dallas plant.[21]

As the men waited for the completion of the process (drying the film, winding it on spools, etc.), Sorrels telephoned his office, which told him the police had arrested a man for the murder of police officer J. D. Tippit and that Sorrels was wanted at the police station.[22] One policeman stayed at Kodak while the other drove Sorrels downtown. Before Sorrels left, he spoke to Zapruder, in words recalled thirty years later by Schwartz: "If it comes out get me a copy."[23] After depositing Sorrels, the police driver returned to the plant to wait.

While they waited at Kodak, McCormick, in contact with his paper, worked hard to acquire the film from Zapruder. In his memoir of the day he wrote:

> We made large cash offers which he refused. He was still excited and agitated, and could not think straight. When I could not get them for the paper, I tried to get them for myself, thinking I could then get them for the paper. I told him he did not know the markets and how to handle this and that if he would turn it over to me I would give him all but 25 and later went down to 10% but still had no luck. He talked with his attorney Sam Donosky a half a dozen times asking what he could do and should do and I believe Sam tried to help me but with no success. Then I agreed to meet him in the morning.[24]

In addition to phoning his attorney repeatedly, throughout the afternoon Zapruder also spoke to his wife and adult daughter at his home.[25]

Processing took about one hour. As soon as the film was ready, Chamberlain and Zapruder reviewed the unslit 16mm-wide, double-perforated film on a Kodak processing inspection projector running at four times normal speed, a standard quality-control practice.[26] At that point, according to Chamberlain, Zapruder asked if he could have three copies made.[27] That was not possible, though, because the Kodak plant did not possess the equipment to duplicate movies.[28] Dick Blair phoned Jamieson Film Laboratory across town to see if it could make copies from the unslit 16mm Zapruder original. As it turned out, the company had the machines and capability but lacked the "duplicating film perforated for 8mm." On behalf of Kodak, Blair gave Zapruder three rolls of Kodachrome Type A film designed to be used with tungsten lights (the more appropriate film for the task would have been duplicating film). After Jamieson manufactured the duplicates in 16mm, they would be returned to Kodak to be developed, processed, slit, and pasted into an 8mm strip.

Then Zapruder permitted the Kodak lab to screen the unslit, 16mm film for himself, Schwartz, McCormick, and Kodak staff in a small projection room, with the machine run by Dick Blair.[29] The assassination sequence appeared on just one half of the screen; the other half of the running film was blank. The film was, in the words of Schwartz, "needle point" clear, and it stunned the viewers. McCormick remarked that Sorrels would want a copy.[30]

Zapruder then asked Chamberlain formally to swear to the work that had been done.[31] In his affidavit Philip Chamberlain says that he was production supervisor and received and processed the Kodachrome II film of "A. Zapruder."[32] The film was "not cut, mutilated or altered in any manner during processing." Further, while in the possession of Kodak, "it was not shown to any person other than employees of said laboratory of known integrity in the ordinary course of handling the same." He also affirmed that at "the end of the processed film and carrier strip" an East-man Kodak Company employee at the time of processing perforated the identification number of 0183. Chamberlain signed and swore before a notary public (see document 3 in the appendix).

News of the film had leaked out to the local press and media. In his book *Tell Me A Story*, Don Hewitt, a news producer for CBS at its national desk in New York City, related his experiences with the film that character-ize the thrust of the press in the breaking story of President Kennedy's assassination. He repeated the description in an interview in Dallas in 2002, in which he read the pertinent pages:

Dan Rather, new to CBS and our correspondent on the scene, phoned me from Dallas and told me that a guy named Zapruder was supposed to have film of the assassination and was going to put it up for sale. . . . In my desire to get a hold of what was probably the most dramatic piece of news footage ever shot, I told Rather, "Go to Zapruder's house, sock him in the jaw, take his film to our affiliate in Dallas, copy it onto videotape, and let the CBS lawyers decide whether it could be sold or whether it was in the public domain. Then, take the film back to Za-pruder's house, give it back to him." That way, the only thing they could get him for was assault because he would have returned Zapruder's property. Rather said, "Great idea. I'll do it." I hadn't hung up the phone maybe ten seconds when it hit me, what in the hell did you just do? I called Rather back. Luckily, he was still there, and I said to him, "For Christ's sake, don't do what I just told you to! I think this day has gotten to me, and thank God I caught you before you left." Knowing Dan to be as competitive as I am, I had the feeling that he wished he'd left before the second phone call. The things you do in the heat of battle.[33]

In his memoirs relating to coverage of the assassination crisis, Dan Rather does not mention this incident, which was, after all, but one of many occurrences in the kaleidoscope of events. He does remark, however, that at the sale of the film the next day in Zapruder's office, the following idea occurred to him: "For a moment I thought, if I have to, I'll just knock him down and grab the film, run back to the station, show it one time and then let him sue us."[34]

On the night of November 22, before leaving the Kodak lab with the un-slit original 16mm double-perforated film, Zapruder thought of the dress business he and Schwartz had walked out on. He remarked to his partner, "Let us close the plant." The police drove Zapruder and Schwartz to their factory and then McCormick to the offices of the *Dallas Morning News*.[35]

The partners found the Elm Street plant deserted and the doors open. They sat down, had a glass of whiskey, and then closed up. Soon they walked the two blocks up Elm to the lot where Schwartz's car was parked, then drove to the Jamieson Film Company, owned by Bruce Jamieson. By then, according to Schwartz's oral history, it was about 6:00 P.M.[36]

They arrived at the Jamieson Company sometime before 6:30. As they approached the building, a man stepped out of the shadows and on behalf of the *Dallas Morning News* offered Zapruder $200 per frame for his film, which Zapruder rejected.[37] Inside Zapruder asked Schwartz if he wanted a copy, too, and he said yes, according to Schwartz. Zapruder had three duplicates made, presumably two for Sorrels and one for Schwartz. Marshall Collier ran the printer and Robert Collier the laboratory, with Jamieson assisting them.[38] Zapruder carefully watched and monitored the processing so only the three copies could be made.[39] Bruce Jamieson noted that "printing with Mr. Zapruder in the dark room" posed some awkward moments.[40]

Jamieson related that it was a complicated task to obtain the correct shades of color and proper degrees of light on the Kodachrome film and then to mate it with his machinery. His staff finally decided what to do, but to be certain they gave each of the duplicates a different setting in processing, one a notch below presumed optimum, one optimum, and one a notch above optimum. Each copy carried its own number; in the end, copy 2 was clearly the best.[41]

The duplicating process at Jamieson could not reproduce the material filmed on the sprocket holes, approximately 22 percent of the images. Zapruder's film captured images from edge to edge of the film, including that around the sprocket holes. Only the original retained the sprocket images.

The firm took about an hour to duplicate the film, finishing between about 7:30 and 7:45. When the Jamieson employees were finished, Zapruder required Frank R. Sloan, the laboratory manager, to swear, depose, and say in an affidavit that he had received the Kodachrome II film from "A. Zapruder" and had made "Three (3) duplicate copies. That the film was not cut, mutilated or altered in any manner during the printing operation" (see document 4 in the appendix). He further swore that the film was not shown to any person other than employees of the lab "of known integrity in the ordinary course of handling the same." In addition he stated that "the end of the processed film carried the identification number: 0183 which was printed onto the said duplicate copies." Sloan swore before Walter Spiro, notary public for Dallas County, and signed his statement.[42] The film was not viewed by anyone at the Jamieson Film Company.[43]

Several factors support the conclusion that only three duplicate copies of Zapruder's film were made. Foremost are the three copies themselves. For the Assassination Records and Review Board, Roland Zavada, the renowned expert from Kodak Company, made an exhaustive technical study and decided on three.[44] In itself this is almost definitive, but the number was also affirmed by the statements of Zapruder, Schwartz, Sloan, and Spiro, three of whom (Zapruder, Sloan, and Spiro) made their statements under oath. Bruce Jamieson is adamant that only three copies were made, and in fact the company had no film available other than the three rolls of Kodachrome Type A supplied by Zapruder, so the plant could not have produced more than three copies.[45] Each roll of film could produce only one duplicate.

Other details uphold the explanation that only three copies were made. Kodak's production supervisor estimated that in an hour's time only three copies could have been duplicated.[46] He would have been aware of the amount of time required to complete the duplication, which involves chemical treatments, transfer processes, drying, and other mechanical and technical procedures. Finally, Zapruder was a sharp businessman who knew almost from the first moment that he owned a valuable property whose value lay in its exclusivity. He and Schwartz carefully monitored the Jamieson procedures so that only three duplicates could be made.

After leaving the Jamieson Film Company, Schwartz and Zapruder immediately drove back to the Eastman Kodak Company laboratory to have the duplicates developed and processed, arriving sometime around 8:00.[47] Kodak took an hour to complete the task. When the lab finished developing the three 16mm films of the duplicates, it perforated identification numbers 0185, 0186, and 0187 to the end of their filmstrips. The number 0183 had already been used to tag the original, with the perforated number also printing on each duplicate. The number 0184 was expended in cocking the mechanism to accommodate the new processing. For each duplicate print, Zapruder had Tom Nulty, production foreman for that shift at Kodak, swear out an affidavit, which was signed and notarized (see document 5 in the appendix).[48]

There were now four 16mm double-perforated films, the original plus three color copies. We can be confident that the original was slit and prepared as 8mm. First, at his home that evening Zapruder showed the film on his 8mm movie projector to his son-in-law and wife, his adult daughter refusing to look at the depiction of the death of President Kennedy, a man she idealized.[49] While not definitive in themselves, Zapruder's actions the next morning in his office sustain the conclusion that the film was slit. Using his 8mm projector, he showed the film to prospective purchasers. Presumably, he would not have tried to sell the original by showing a copy. Finally, Stolley, the purchaser, states it was the original.[50]

Of the three copies, Zapruder permitted an 8mm movie to be shown to the employees of the new shift.[51] Chamberlain used one of the duplicate copies that was slit, which had to be either copy 1 or copy 3, which Zapruder later gave to the Secret Service.[52] An 8mm copy 3 was sent to Washington later that night, leaving copy 1 with the Dallas Secret Service. The next morning, Saturday, Kodak opened its office specially for two FBI agents to view for two hours, "over and over" again, the Zapruder film on its 8mm special projector that would permit frame freeze stops without damage to the film. That would have been copy 1, copy 3 being in Washington and copy 2 at Zapruder's office being sold. They could have only borrowed it from the Dallas Secret Service; it was obviously slit.[53]

Copy 2, sold to Time Inc. the next day, could not have been slit in Dallas. In the materials Time Inc. gave Henry Zapruder in 1975 and turned over to the Sixth Floor Museum twenty-five years later are three excellent black-and-white 16mm double-perforated copies of the Zapruder film made from one of the Jamieson unslit duplicates of November 22.[54] There are no sprocket images.[55]

Having completed the development process at Kodak, Zapruder and Schwartz left with the three duplicates and one original, plus five affidavits, and set out to find Sorrels.[56] It was now after nine o'clock. According to Schwartz (and we possess no other confirmation), they drove downtown to the Dallas police station to search for the Secret Service agent to whom Zapruder had promised a copy of the original, but who had disappeared for the last five hours. Years later Schwartz recalled in an interview that the police station was "like a zoo." People, press, and officers were every-where, some standing on desks, and Zapruder and Schwartz could not find Sorrels. They finally jumped on top of a desk and over on the side of the large room saw Sorrels, to whom they waved. When he came over, they told him they had copies of the film for him.[57]

But, incredibly, he was too busy to accept it. In an extraordinary request he asked them, "Do me a great favor, take it to my office on Ervay Street."[58] They willingly agreed, and the two citizens trudged on. For many hours now, they had scrambled all over town to get the graphic depiction of the assassination into the hands of the federal government, which, to say the least, was casual about it all.

Schwartz and Zapruder drove the few minutes to Ervay Street and even-tually located the small Secret Service office tucked away there.[59] Inside they found agent Max Phillips, in his shirtsleeves and wearing a shoulder hol-ster, waiting for them. Schwartz's reflections on the meeting seem to suggest a casual attitude on Phillips's part. They handed over two copies of the film, the first and third of the copies run off by Jamieson, signed a paper, and left.[60]

The Secret Service dispatched a copy of the film to Washington by com-mercial airplane courier with a covering memorandum dated 9:55 P.M.[61] Phillips wrote, "Enclosed is an 8 mm movie film taken by Mr. A. Zapruder, 501 Elm St., Dallas, Texas (RI8-6071). Mr. Zapruder was photographing the

President at the instant he was shot." Then he added the striking information he had received from Zapruder in his office: "According to Mr. Zapruder, the position of the assassin was behind Mr. Zapruder."

Phillips noted two additional points. First, he addressed possession of the original, a detail that later would become important to some dissenters from the official findings of the Warren Commission: "Mr. Zapruder is in custody of the 'master' film." Zapruder would later affirm this,[62] and Schwartz would independently concur.[63] Independently of both, *Life* magazine's representative, Richard Stolley, would state he possessed the original.[64] It would have been mechanically impossible for the duplicates to be made without the master, and their very existence refutes any conjecture that Zapruder did not have it.

Second, in addition to affirming that Zapruder still had custody of the master, Phillips fixed the number of copies given to the federal government. Zapruder gave "two prints" to "SAIC Sorrels, this date." Phillips introduced slight confusion, showing unfamiliarity with the actual copy numbers by stating, "The third print is forwarded," when he no doubt meant numbered copy 3 of the two copies Zapruder had given him.[65] Zapruder kept the master and a copy, which turned out to be the second of the three copies run off by Jamieson.[66] Sorrels and the Dallas office kept the other print, copy 1.[67] Within a few hours, by about two o'clock in the morning of November 23, a copy of the Zapruder film was in Washington.[68]

Washington headquarters sought help from the CIA to study the film. Just before midnight on Sunday, November 24, the director of the Central Intelligence Agency, John McCone, telephoned at his home Dino Brugioni, the agency's foremost photoanalyst at its renowned National Photographic Interpretation Center and ordered him to "go in" to the NPIC. Two Secret Service men were coming with a photographic emergency. Brugioni went, not knowing what to expect. At midnight two Secret Service agents appeared with a roll of 8mm film, the Zapruder film. Because the NPIC did not possess a projector to show the film, he telephoned the owner of a private film company in the area, got him out of bed, and met him at his store, where he acquired one.

With white gloves on as was typically done for "precious films," Brugioni threaded the film and then screened it, the scene of JFK's death shot at frame 313 stunning them all. The Secret Service wanted the film timed and a selection of prints made for them. With a stopwatch Brugioni timed the film and made two "enormous briefing boards," thirty-six by thirty-six

inches, hinged for display, and a duplicate with twenty or more enlargements of the tiny frames into five-by-seven-inch prints made with absolutely the "world's finest" precision enlarger. The agents were especially
interested in prints that showed the limousine just before it reached the
sign, when it passed behind the sign, and immediately after it emerged
from behind the sign. Each of the mounted prints had attached beneath it
the time down to the split second.

When Brugioni was finished the agents took the film back. He then sent
both copies of his boards to Director McCone who sent one to the Secret
Service. One set ultimately went to the Warren Commission, which set
eventually came back to the NPIC where it was stored in the locked cabinet
of the vault room, until a congressional committee sometime in the 1970s
asked for everything the CIA had done domestically. Then the set was sent
to the then director of the CIA, disposition unknown.[69] These are unrelated
to the documents associated with the Rockefeller Commission discussed
elsewhere.

The account of how the Secret Service acquired copies of the film illustrated a basic characteristic of the federal investigation into the assassination of President Kennedy. It seems that officials took a decidedly indifferent
approach to garnering essential photographic evidence. Conceivably, as far
as Sorrels knew, the film could have shown the actual assassins, making it
possible to identify them. Without Zapruder and Schwartz protecting and
supervising the film, it could have been subjected to willful or chance
destruction; in the extreme, the assassins even could have attacked the
photographer.

The FBI's treatment of Zapruder and its acquisition of a copy was even
more disgraceful than the Secret Service's. The national and local FBI
acquired its copy of the Zapruder film from the Secret Service, although, as
just noted, the local FBI had viewed the Secret Service copy the morning
after the assassination. It, too, displayed a casual disregard for the crucial
evidence. A few hours after the assassination, both Washington headquarters[70] and the Dallas Field Office[71] had independently concluded that
Oswald, alone and unaided, killed JFK.[72] Any evidence contrary to this
premise or any evidence that cluttered the FBI's Procrustean bed of "facts"
was seen as not germane to its primary task of defining Oswald's "guilt."[73]
The Zapruder film fit into this category.

By midmorning of November 23, the Washington headquarters of the
bureau had received numerous telephone calls from the press about the

Zapruder film, including knowledge that *Life* had a copy of the film. It contacted the Dallas special agent in charge of the field office, Gordon Shanklin, for information about the film. Shanklin reported he knew about it and had also received calls about it, but Dallas agents had not yet made contact with Zapruder. Then Shanklin added the striking comment that although he had not seen the movie, "he did not believe the film would be of any evidentiary value"[74]—this after his agents had carefully examined the film for two hours that morning at the Kodak plant.

Media pressure, not evidentiary concern, forced the FBI to seek copies of the Zapruder film, coming up with the Dallas Secret Service's retained copy. Later on November 23 (probably early or midafternoon), Inspector Kelley of the Secret Service lent Sorrels's retained copy of the film (copy number 1) to Special Agent James W. Bookhout of the FBI's Dallas Field Office for the bureau to copy.[75] Bookhout turned it over to Special Agent Robert M. Barrett to have a copy made, but he soon gave it to Shanklin. Incredibly, Barrett had failed to find a local firm to duplicate the processed, developed, split, and spliced film.

In a dilemma over what to do next, at 4:55 P.M. Shanklin telephoned FBI headquarters and explained to C. D. DeLoach that "local film processing houses in Dallas were unable to handle this film."[76] Shanklin added that the Dallas Field Office had no movie projector to show the film, but when he held the film up to the light, he could see it showed both JFK and Connally being hit.[77] He also affirmed Zapruder's account that the dress manufacturer had had three copies made, had given two to the Secret Service, and had sold the other copy plus the original to *Time* and *Life*. DeLoach directed him "immediately" to place the film on the next commercial flight to Washington,[78] whereupon the Dallas FBI delivered the copy to American Airlines Flight 20, which left Dallas at 5:20 P.M.[79] In a cover memorandum Shanklin requested that the FBI laboratory make three copies, retaining one for the bureau and returning two to Dallas "by the most expeditious means possible."[80] Alas, all the hurry was for naught.

The much-praised FBI laboratory lacked the technical equipment necessary to handle the film and could not duplicate it and had to wait until Monday, November 25, to send the film to a commercial developer that was closed over the weekend.[81] The resultant delay in returning the film to Dallas caused the anxious Dallas FBI to phone Washington supervisor George Benjamin, Division VI, at 8:40 P.M. on Monday to ask for the status of the film and request that it be returned for a Tuesday morning "show-up."[82] Benjamin initially claimed not to know anything about the film, but he later advised Dallas that it would be sent via Braniff Airlines to arrive in Dallas at 3:21 A.M. on November 26, and that agents should contact the pilot. Special Agent C. Ray Hall picked up the film at the airport and delivered it to Bookhout, who at 9:00 A.M. brought it to Inspector Kelley.[83] Thus, the FBI received its copies in Washington three days after the assassination.

But Washington sent only the Secret Service copy and one print of it back to Dallas, stating that they would be sufficient. The Dallas office handled the criminal investigation and received one print, and Washington, which supervised, received two copies. Headquarters added to its cover memorandum for Dallas, "You are cautioned that this film is for official use only."[84] Unfortunately, Washington did not follow its own advice and established policy; its agents surreptitiously took a copy home to show to family and friends.[85]

In addition to the Secret Service and FBI obtaining copies, the Dallas Police Department acquired one. On December 5, Shanklin notified FBI headquarters that the Secret Service had requested a copy of the film for the Dallas Police Department. The next day Washington sent a copy for transmittal to the Secret Service and by them to the Dallas Police Department, "if it so desires." A handwritten note by Dallas FBI agent or clerk Charles Brown said that on December 9 the copy was turned over to Secret Service agent Charles Kunkel.[86]

Thus, from the evening of November 23 to the morning of November 26, the original and one copy of the Jamieson duplicates were in either Chicago or New York City, and the other two copies were in Washington. Yet around 4:00 P.M. on Monday, November 25, over Dallas KRLD CBS affiliate television and radio, Dan Rather breathlessly described the film he had just watched.[87] The origin of the film he saw is not covered by any documentation yet discovered.

On the evening of November 22, after depositing the copies with the Secret Service on Ervay Street, Schwartz took Zapruder to his car, and they went home. It was after 10:00 P.M. About 10:30 Schwartz's doorbell rang, and he answered it to find three scruffy photographers from the *Saturday Evening Post* and a local woman who had once worked with him. They offered Schwartz $10,000 to be introduced to Zapruder; he refused and told them to leave.[88]

Around 11:00 the telephone rang at Zapruder's home. It was Richard

Stolley of *Life* magazine inquiring about the film.[89] That phone call initiated the chain of events that would result in *Life* purchasing the film.

Word of the assassination had reached *Life* offices in Beverly Hills by a telephone call. Richard B. Stolley, in charge of the magazine's large West Coast office, phoned the New York office, quickly assembled a team—consisting of himself, reporter Tommy Thompson, and photographers Don Cragvens and Allan Grant[90]—and rushed by automobile to the Los Angeles airport to catch a National Airlines flight to Dallas.[91] On the way the car's radio announced the death of JFK, which occurred officially at 1:33 P.M.

By 4:00 they had reached Dallas, where Stolley quickly established a command post in the Adolphus Hotel. "In an hour or two" he received a phone call from Patsy Swank, a *Life* stringer in Dallas, phoning from her home,[92] who had word from a colleague at the police station that a man with a name starting with Z had made a home movie of the assassination.[93] Soon she phoned again, providing Stolley with a phonetic spelling of the name. With that fragment of a lead, Stolley found Zapruder's name listed in the telephone book and called his home, but no one answered.[94] He continued calling every fifteen minutes until around 11:00 P.M., when, in "a weary voice," Zapruder answered.[95] After introducing himself, Stolley learned that the film existed and that no one else had yet contacted Zapruder about it. He politely asked four questions:

1. Is it true you filmed the assassination? Yes.
2. Have you seen it? Yes.
3. Did you get it from beginning to end? Yes.
4. May I come out and see it? No.[96]

Stolley also learned that Zapruder had made three duplicates and given two to the Secret Service, keeping the original and one copy, which he had in his possession. Zapruder further informed Stolley that federal agents had said he could dispose of the film as he wanted and that "he knew the film was valuable." Zapruder, too tired to talk further, asked Stolley to come to his office at 9:00 A.M. the next day.[97]

But Stolley appeared at Zapruder's office at 8:00 A.M. He wore a suit and was neat, well mannered, calm, and businesslike, in stark contrast to the ragamuffin representatives of the press who flowed into the office over the next hour.[98] Zapruder came out and looked at him, slightly annoyed. "Well," he finally remarked, "you might as well come and see this." Zapruder had contacted the Secret Service and was about to show the movie to several "grim-faced men in dark suits—Secret Service agents" who would see the film for the first time.[99] In a room he set the projector atop a rickety TV table and cast the picture against the wall.[100] Everyone stood to watch. When the film came to the gory head shot at frame 313, all the agents, Stolley recalled, "reacted with a sound like they had been punched in the gut—Ahgh!" Zapruder showed the film two more times. After the screenings, he and Stolley walked into the outer room, and the silent, sad agents left.

The clamoring press had begun to fill the inner room. The group included representatives from Movietone, Associated Press, and United Press International, the three scruffy representatives from *Saturday Evening Post* who had knocked on Schwartz's door the night before, and many others. No television representatives were there. The reporters were gruff, shabbily dressed, unkempt, rude, noisy, and brash as they filed into the room to see the film.

Zapruder showed the film to the packed room four times, according to his partner Schwartz.[101] While the film rolled in the inner room, Stolley stood in the outer office and chatted politely with Lillian Rogers, Zapruder's secretary.[102] Zapruder came out and saw him, commenting, "I see you made friends with Lillian." The *Life* representative's politeness, impeccable dress, and good manners impressed him.[103] The rest of the press straggled out of the room.

Shocked by the images he had seen, Stolley knew that it was "absolutely crucial *Life* got the film."[104] He asked Zapruder if he could speak to him alone. Zapruder replied by turning to the press representatives and saying, "Because he [Stolley] had been the first I will talk to him first." The two walked into Zapruder's office with Schwarz as witness and closed the door. With that move the press went "ballistic," yelling, shouting, and pounding on the door.[105]

Later Schwartz explained to Stolley that Zapruder had selected him for two crucial reasons. First, Zapruder wanted dignity for President Kennedy. He trusted *Life* to handle the film in a proper manner and not exploit the tragedy. Second, Zapruder had formed a deep respect for Stolley's character. The *Life* representative had not pressured him the previous night when he had phoned, and he was the only well-mannered person among the clamoring press.[106] Schwartz would carefully explain to Stolley that in the end these personal factors were the main reasons Zapruder decided to sell the film to *Life*.

Stolley remembers that he opened the negotiations in a calm, detached manner by stating that for photographs outside the usual range of interest, *Life* sometimes went above the normal purchase price, and thus he could offer $15,000.[107] Zapruder smiled. To Stolley that smile meant only one thing: "He knew." Zapruder knew how valuable the film was, and this set the ground rules for the negotiations. They quickly negotiated the sum up to Stolley's top figure of $50,000 for print rights, but not motion picture rights. At that point Stolley remarked that he could not go higher without asking New York headquarters for authorization, at which time Zapruder said, "Let's do it."[108] Zapruder had accepted. Stolley sat at a typewriter in the room and drew up a contract.

Nov. 23, 1963

In consideration of the sum of fifty thousand dollars ($50,000.), I grant LIFE Magazine exclusive world wide print media rights to my original 8 mm color film which shows the shooting of President Kennedy in Dallas on Nov. 22, 1963. I retain all motion picture rights, but agree not to release the film for motion picture, television, newsreel, etc., use until Friday, Nov. 29, 1963. You agree to return to me the original print of that film, and I will then supply you with a copy print.

Abraham Zapruder

Agreed to:
Richard B. Stolley
LIFE Magazine

Witnesses
[Lillian Rogers
Erwin Schwartz][109]

As part of the agreement, Stolley required Zapruder to turn over to *Life* the master print plus the remaining duplicate, leaving Schwartz without his promised copy.[110] Zapruder also provided a sheaf of five affidavits from the processing the day before.

With the negotiations completed and the film in hand, Stolley faced the problem of how to leave with the raucous crowd outside the door. He left through a back way and left Zapruder to face the irate press mob.[111]

Stolley immediately "couriered" the original film to Chicago by commercial plane, where *Life*'s press was located in the massive R. R. Donnelley and Company printing plant. The duplicate eventually continued on to *Life*'s New York City home office.

By approximately early afternoon of November 23, then, the master of the Zapruder film was in Chicago, with the three copies in Washington, D.C., and Dallas, in the control of a commercial organization, commercial printers, and the Secret Service. From then on, the original and each copy would have separate and distinct histories.

When, on November 22, *Life* officers had heard news of President Kennedy's assassination, they stopped the presses in Chicago and flew a special team to that city to recast the forthcoming issue. Mechanical constraints of working on a tight schedule meant there was no time to run color photographs; the photos would have to be black and white. Working almost nonstop, the editors made "scores of eight-by-ten inch prints from the Zapruder film" and "picked thirty-one pictures" that ran in the issue appearing on the morning of Monday, November 25 (bearing the date November 29).[112] As part of their processing, they made a copy of the color original. This job was assigned to a young man just learning the trade, who accidentally broke the film, destroying frames 208 through 211.[113] He spliced frame 207 to frame 212, a routine repair that normally leaves a dark line across the image. He salvaged the top portion of frame 212 and pasted that onto the bottom of frame 208. Here the dark repair line is much cruder than is typical, with the top half of a tree in the background glaringly out of alignment with its bottom half.[114]

In the meantime, sometime on Sunday in New York City, *Life*'s publisher C. D. Jackson viewed with horror the images on the newly arrived film.[115] According to secondhand sources, its shocking scenes convinced him that the magazine should acquire motion picture rights to the film as well to keep its frightful death sequences out of the hands of exploiters and such gruesome images away from the public. Why control of information about a president's murder belonged in the exclusive domain of Time Inc. was never sufficiently explained. After a board meeting with Time Inc. executives on Monday morning, November 25, Jackson directed Stolley to purchase all rights to the film from Zapruder,[116] a telephone call the night before to Stolley in Dallas having put the transaction in motion.[117] As Stolley recalled, Jackson "was so upset by the head-wound sequence that he proposed the company obtain all rights to the film and withhold it from public viewing at least until emotions had calmed."[118]

Stolley had telephoned Zapruder on Sunday evening, November 24, to discuss the possibility of meeting the next day to purchase all the rights. In Stolley's words, "I would like to come and see about additional rights." He recalls Zapruder being "relieved," for he had already gone to an attorney, Sam Passman, to seek assistance (his regular attorney was unavailable). He did, however, decline to meet until after the funeral ceremonies for President Kennedy were concluded.[119]

On the afternoon of Monday, November 25, Stolley and Zapruder met in Passman's office for formal negotiations over purchase of the film and all rights. By late in the afternoon they had worked out a new contract that incorporated the terms and conditions of the earlier agreement.[120]

By the terms of the contract, Zapruder agreed to "sell, transfer and assign to Time Inc. all my right, title and interest (whether domestic, foreign, newsreel, television, motion picture or otherwise) in and to my original and all three (3) copies of 8 mm. color films which show the shooting of President John F. Kennedy in Dallas, Texas, on November 22nd, 1963" (see document 6 in the appendix).[121]

This clause spelled out the number of duplicates that had been made. Of the three copies, one had gone with the original film to *Life*, one had gone to the Secret Service in Washington, and one had gone to the Secret Service in Dallas.

In the lengthiest clause of the contract, Time Inc. agreed to pay Zapruder or his heirs $150,000, in installments of $25,000 a year, the first immediately and the rest in equal sums on the third day of January in 1964, 1965, 1966, 1967, and 1968. In addition to the stipulated cash payment, Zapruder would obtain a source of income for the life of his copyright from any sales of the film by Time Inc., for the company agreed to pay Zapruder one-half "of all gross receipts derived by Time, Inc." for any "use, sale, showing, rental, leasing, licensing, or other publication of any kind or character whatsoever after" that exceeded $150,000 in cash from gross receipts derived from the same sources. Each calendar year, Time Inc. agreed to furnish a certified audited report showing the total gross receipts derived.

The document protected Zapruder's interests in the event Time Inc. sold or otherwise disposed of the film. If Time Inc. sold or transferred its right in the film, the purchaser would be bound by the terms of the contract. An important paragraph for Zapruder stated that Time Inc. would present the film "to the public in a manner consonant with good taste and dignity" and that it would use its "best business judgment" for the "production of gross receipts."

A key paragraph required Time Inc. to defend the copyright. The pertinent part reads, "Time Inc. agrees to obtain, at its expense, such copyright protection, domestic and foreign, as it may deem necessary or proper for its own safety and to prevent any infringement thereof." In 1975 a controversy erupted between the heirs of Zapruder, who had died in 1970, and Time Inc. over efforts to enforce this clause.[122] That bitter conflict would become a key factor in the company's decision to return the film to the Zapruder family. Zapruder provided a statement of authenticity of the original and number of copies plus the affidavits by processors (see document 7 in the appendix).

Years later, when reminiscing about the affair, Stolley recalled two key points about his negotiation with Zapruder and Passman. The first related to the price Time Inc. had paid for the film. He stated that when negotiations ended, "Zapruder asked that we not reveal it at the time."[123] In carrying out this request for silence on the price, Time Inc. would throw a blanket of secrecy over the amount paid to Zapruder. Consequently, the public and critics alike would accept a fiction that he had been paid only $25,000.[124]

Stolley further observed that during the negotiations Passman brought up his concern about the possibility of anti-Semitism intensifying toward Zapruder and Dallas Jews because of the large sum of money Zapruder, a Jew, had received for the film.[125] To Zapruder, Passman made what Stolley called "an inspired" suggestion when he said, "This is not going to go down well, Abe. I think you ought to take the first year's installment and donate it to Tippit's widow."[126] Zapruder replied, "Excellent idea."

Passman worked out a way to have the initial payment of $25,000 donated to the Fireman's Fund set up for the widow of police officer J. D. Tippit, killed on November 22 in a murder alleged to be linked with the assassination events.[127] For many years most Americans, including the critics of the official investigation, believed that Zapruder had donated all the money Time Inc. had paid him to the widow, a generous act that in the eyes of many converted the dress manufacturer into an inspired civic-minded citizen.[128]

With copies of the film now in their custody, federal officials could begin to determine exactly what information the 486 frames held. The evidence contained on the frames would transform the assassination investigation, lead to profound official corruption, and lay down immutable boundaries that dictated many of its findings.

 **The Film**

In the first traumatic days after the assassination, the Zapruder film moved into the hands of federal agencies—the Federal Bureau of Investigation, the Secret Service, the Central Intelligence Agency, and perhaps others. They utilized and studied it in a variety of unconnected ways. But it was not until November 29, when President Lyndon B. Johnson by Executive Order 11130 appointed a commission of seven men to investigate the assassination of President John F. Kennedy, called the Warren Commission after its chair, Chief Justice Earl Warren, that the several efforts received an official focus.[1]

In a dramatic although behind-the-scenes confrontation in the waning days of 1963, as the Commission organized for its task, the members buckled under intense pressure from the FBI and elected to use the bureau for most of its inquiries, data collection, interviews, and scientific tests.[2] Consequently, the commissioners did not develop their own staff of experts in a wide variety of forensic and criminal evidentiary fields (fingerprints, ballistics, medical, photography, and other categories) as one would expect for an inquiry into the violent death of the most powerful man on earth. With that decision, the Commission forsook these indispensable tools of criminal inquiry, with a predictable result.[3] The FBI often clashed with the purposes of the Commission while exerting control over major features of the inquiry.[4] Its agents operated under the bureau's own structural and command system, one dramatically different from the Commission's, with different superiors and procedures, as well as its own agenda and ends.

Along with other tasks performed for the Commission, the FBI assumed primary responsibility for the evaluation of the Zapruder film as evidence in the assassination investigation. The FBI conducted a variety of tests and numerous reenactments using the film as the baseline, answered Commission staff inquiries, prepared exhibits on the film, and testified before the Commission. Of the many bureau examinations, findings, and decisions linked to the Zapruder film, several are essential to understand for any responsible study of the film and the assassination. These include the decision on what portion of each individual frame would be utilized as evidence, the numbering of the frames, determining the speed of Zapruder's Bell & Howell camera, and establishing the minimum speed with which the alleged assassin's rifle could be worked. The last two elements enabled the bureau and the Commission to conclude how many frames would be required between shots alleged to have been fired by the rifle, a critically important fact.

The first major decision about the film made by the bureau, strongly backed by the Commission, excluded a large portion of the evidentiary information available on the sprocket area of each frame. In addition, the FBI numbered the individual frames. Frame numbers are essential to the history, study, and use of the Zapruder film. Knowledge of their origin comes from Special Agent Lyndal Shaneyfelt's June 4, 1964, testimony before the Commission.[5] "I numbered the frames on the Zapruder film," Shaneyfelt told assistant counsel Arlen Specter, "beginning with No. 1 at the assassination portion of his film."[6] Shaneyfelt counted 486 frames, beginning with the first frame to show President Kennedy's motorcycle escort turning from Houston Street onto Elm Street until the limousine disappears into the trees and other growth blocking Zapruder's view as his lens followed the fleeing car into the triple underpass.

A key problem was determining how many frames per second the camera exposed. With the frame speed established, one could address several aspects of the murder as they were recorded. Tests conducted by the FBI laboratory, later confirmed by the Bell & Howell Company, established that on November 22 the camera ran at 18.3 frames per seconds.[7] "Examination of the Zapruder motion picture camera by the FBI," said the Warren Report, "established that 18.3 pictures or frames were taken each second, and therefore, the timing of certain events could be calculated by allowing 1/18.3 seconds for the action depicted from one frame to the next."[8] Since Shaneyfelt numbered 486 frames, the film takes about 26.5 seconds to run (486 divided by 18.3 equals 26.5).

Working with this figure and other evidence, the FBI and the Commission concluded that the first bullet "was not shot before frame 210, since it is unlikely that the assassin would deliberately have shot at him with a view obstructed by the oak tree," and the last was fired at frame 313.[9] This meant that 103 frames, or about 5.9 seconds, were consumed by the official construction of the murder and that all shots had to be accounted for within that short time.[10]

The bureau, with a team of its marksmen, next determined how rapidly the alleged murder weapon could have been fired in order to compare it with the film's record. This step would impose iron conditions on many witness testimonies, on the official timing of shots, including when they could have been fired in the six seconds, and on numerous other conditions of the federal investigation. For this work, important to the Commission's credibility with the public and thus the acceptance of its findings, the Commission supplemented the FBI marksmen with a separate team of army riflemen composed of the best shooters in the nation.

The two groups separately performed a variety of firing tests with a Mannlicher-Carcano rifle that had been found buried under some boxes on the sixth floor of the Texas School Book Depository and was alleged to have been used by Lee Harvey Oswald in committing the assassination.[11] Although both the bureau and the army reported on their tests with scores of shots, out of the many results the Commission accepted an FBI time of 2.3 seconds as the minimum speed with which the bolt-action rifle could be fired.[12] The Commission employed deceptive means to derive this figure. A team of three FBI agents fired time tests with three bullets using Oswald's alleged rifle and produced varied results: 9, 9, 7,[13] 6, 5.9,[14] 6.2, 5.6, 6.5,[15] 4.6,[16] 4.8,[17] and 2.3[18] seconds. On only one of the dozens of attempts at firing the weapon did expert FBI riflemen achieve the time of 2.3 seconds, and that was under quite improved (and artificial) conditions.[19] The FBI, for example, overhauled the rifle to make it function properly, changed the alleged stance of the assassin, and employed a stationary, not moving, target.[20]

Moreover, the FBI time of 2.3 seconds between shots did not correspond even remotely to the times derived by the military shooters in testing the weapon. At Aberdeen Proving Grounds the army used the nation's very best riflemen under greatly improved conditions to test the weapon, and prior to firing, they further repaired the rifle.[21] But even then, not one of the master riflemen was able to duplicate the shooting interval attributed to Lee Harvey Oswald; their times were 8.25, 7, 6.75, 6.45, 5.15, 4.6, and 4.45 seconds as the minimum between shots.[22] Compounding the suspicions that these scores, by America's best marksmen, were in fact much lower than Oswald could have achieved was the Marine Corps evaluation of his ability as a "rather poor shot."[23]

Notwithstanding the varied results produced by the FBI and army marksmen, the Commission accepted the single lowest score as the official established time between shots. Its report states, "Tests of the assassin's rifle disclosed that at least 2.3 seconds were required between shots."[24]

An interval of 2.3 seconds between shots means a minimum of 42 frames (18.3 times 2.3 equals 42.09) must have been exposed between two consecutive shots from the Mannlicher-Carcano rifle. In 2.3 seconds, a shooter using that rifle must remove the eye to avoid the backward-thrusting bolt, work the bolt handle up, pull back the bolt to eject the empty cartridge, ram home into the breech a new spring-fed bullet, lock it into place by working the bolt handle down, aim, and fire.

The Warren Commission concluded, in a text marked by frequent use of "most probably"[25] and similar phrases, that "the weight of the evidence is there were three shots fired."[26] But that conclusion rests exclusively on the discovery of three empty cartridges near the easternmost window on the sixth floor of the Texas School Book Depository building.[27] Moreover, it asserts, an employee in the depository, Lee Harvey Oswald, alone and unaided, fired the shots at President John F. Kennedy. It is an absolute in official dogma that Oswald fired no more and no fewer than three shots.

On the Zapruder film the depository is located to the rear of JFK and high to his right, and thus Oswald would have been firing down to the street. Between frames 166 and 209, a live oak tree blocked a view of the limousine from the depository window.[28] This species, *Quercus virginiana*, keeps its leaves through the winter and was in full leaf on November 22, as seen in the film.

If there were fewer than three shots, then all the shooting could not be accounted for. If more than three shots were fired, Oswald could not have fired them, and the Report's conclusion of a lone assassin is demolished. The Report's language is sometimes ambiguous on the timing of the shots, but its conclusions are constructed on a precise timing. The first official shot came at frame 210, when JFK's limousine passed behind the freeway sign on Elm Street and was hidden from Zapruder's view.[29] It was the first frame in which a person in the depository had a view of the president through a tree that, until then, had blocked the view.[30] As the Warren Report states, "Analysis of his photograph [Willis number 5] revealed that it was taken at approximately frame 210 of the Zapruder film, which was the approximate time of the shot that probably hit the President and the Governor."[31] This first shot wounded JFK. It "entered at the back of his neck and exited through the lower front portion of his neck" and continued on to strike Governor John B. Connally.[32] This shot inflicted two nonfatal wounds on President Kennedy and five on Governor Connally, breaking two of Connally's bones.[33]

The second of the official two shots to strike JFK hit between frames 312 and 313, when he was 230.8 feet west of the curb line of the juncture of Houston and Elm Street, 260.6 feet from the triple underpass, and 265.3 feet from the depository's sixth-floor easternmost window.[34] As the Warren Report describes it, "A subsequent shot entered the back of his head and exited through the upper right portion of his skull. The Zapruder, Nix and Muchmore films show the instant in the sequence when that bullet struck. (See Commission Exhibit No. 902, p. 108.)"[35] Commission Exhibit 902 depicts frame 313.[36]

One shot missed. About two hundred feet south of the limousine, James T. Tague stood near the underpass. A bullet hit the curb at his feet, producing a spray of concrete that very slightly wounded him, as was immediately reported to authorities.[37] As Tague described it for the Commission, "There was a mark. Quite obviously, it was a bullet, and it was very fresh."[38] To account for this shot, the Commission concluded it came from a missed shot.[39] It could only have been fired between the first and second JFK hits.

Reasonable critics have noted many implausible aspects of the official scenario, as well as factual errors, corruption of evidence, and facts that were ignored.[40] Their persuasive evidence requires a careful student of the assassination to employ great caution when considering the Commission's and the FBI's allegations.

A further comment on the type of ammunition supposedly used by the alleged assassin is in order. The official conclusion held that the bullets were traveling at about 1,904 feet per second when they struck JFK,[41] that they bore a jacket or sheath of copper around a lead core,[42] and that they contained metal that had been hardened as is typical of military ammunition.[43] In terms of the Zapruder film, a bullet would have been traveling at about 100 feet per frame (or 100 feet per 1/18.3 seconds), at a time when the president was sitting about five feet from the governor. In convoluted and ambiguous language, the Commission contends the bullet that hit JFK at frame 210 transited his body and hit Governor Connally, but that the governor did not manifest his reaction until about sixteen frames later, a physiological impossibility. As the film vividly shows, the governor was struck by a separate bullet, which is incompatible with the explanation that the shots came from the same rifle.

The film contradicts the Commission's assertion regarding the type of metal in one of the bullets. Military bullets were hardened according to the Geneva Convention to prevent their shattering and the subsequent tearing and mangling of the victim's flesh. On the battlefield this type of injury required other personnel to treat a wounded man, thus rendering the other side less effective. On Zapruder's film the explosion of JFK's head at frame 313 does not conform to the impact of a hardened bullet asserted to have been used by the alleged sole assassin. The bullet that wounded JFK and Connally and the one that slightly wounded Tague, however, corresponded to the Geneva military code. Neither the Commission nor the released FBI records address this evidentiary problem, which poses the profound, un-asked, and unanswered question on the source of the radically different ammunition.

The shooting, of course, occurred as Zapruder filmed the presidential limousine in the motorcade. The presidential motorcade resembled a military maneuver, requiring skilled organization, survey of the route, logistics, and coordination. In Dallas on November 22 the motorcade consisted of the following:[44]

A group of motorcycle police
A pilot car
Another group of motorcycle police
A lead car
The presidential convertible, which had two collapsible jump seats[45]
Four motorcycle police flanking the rear bumper of the president's car, two on each side
A follow-up car, a few feet behind JFK (a 1955 Cadillac convertible with two Secret Service agents in the front seat, two in the backseat, two riding on the left running board, and two riding on the right running board); JFK aides Dave Powers and Kenneth O'Donnell sat on the jump seats
The vice presidential limousine
The vice presidential follow-up car
Five cars of dignitaries
Communication vehicles
Three press cars

Buses

A police car and more motorcycle police bringing up the end

A base station with a radio network linking the various key cars in the
motorcade

President Kennedy rode in a modified 1961 Lincoln convertible. The
Ford Company had worked with the firm of Hess & Eisenhardt of Cincin-
nati to convert a stock Lincoln that had been built in Michigan. They
lengthened the wheelbase to 156 inches and added the most powerful
commercial engine that could be used, a 430-cubic-inch V-8, that was
carefully hot-tested. Structural reinforcements and steel plates, a rear seat
that could be hydraulically raised 10.5 inches (but that was not raised on
November 22), a siren, two radio telephones, auxiliary jump seats that
could be folded when not in use, and other additions increased the weight
of the limousine to 7,800 pounds. With the occupants the car weighed over
four tons.[46]

■ I now provide an unofficial overview of the Zapruder film, noting certain
frames that are important and/or of historical interest. Examination of the
film makes it possible to draw conclusions about the assassination other
than those reached by the Warren Commission.

Snippet At the start of the original film, a few frames of Zapruder family
matter appear along with a few frames of Zapruder's receptionist,
Marilyn Sitzman, and Beatrice and Charles Hester recorded on Dealey
Plaza to test the camera just before the motorcade appeared.

Frames 1–486 Dealey Plaza is a small arena. The scene of the motorcade is
open to easy view from buildings to the south, north, and east, as well
as from structures and shrubs around the north and south hills, or
grassy knolls.

1–166 There would have been a clear view of the motorcade from the
easternmost window of the Texas School Book Depository, the alleged
source of shots.

1–132 The three lead police motorcycles turn from Houston Street onto
Elm Street. After Zapruder filmed for a bit, he stopped until the
limousine bearing the president came into view.

133–153 In these frames the limousine is directly in front of the
depository. President Kennedy waves with his right hand to the crowd.

154–188 President Kennedy, with his hand down, looks to his right. Then he waves.

183 President Kennedy raises his right hand to wave. Governor Connally is facing forward in the limousine.

186 Hugh Betzner snaps the third of his three photographs.

171–334 The Warren Commission printed these frames in black and white in volume 18 of its *Hearings and Exhibits*, pages 1–80, omitting frames 208–211.

183–201 Phil Willis can be seen standing on the south curb of Elm Street with his 35mm camera to his eye.

189 President Kennedy holds his right hand high. This could be the time of the first hit.

190 Blurred.

191 Blurred.

192 Blurred.

193 President Kennedy's hand starts to drop.

198 President Kennedy's hands at throat level.

202 Jacqueline Kennedy turns to face the president.

205 Willis walks with camera down as seen in sprocket margin of the frame.

206 Last frame in which top of President Kennedy's head is visible before the limousine passes behind a sign.

207–212 Damage occurred to these frames.

207 Back of sign appears, with the limousine behind it. Frame is broken and patched.

208 Back of sign. Missing from original film.

209 Back of sign. Missing from original film.

210–313 These frames set the limits for the assassination sequence in the official findings. According to Warren Commission theory, all shots had to be fired during this period, which lasted 5.6 seconds, or 103 frames.

210 According to the Warren Commission, the first shot occurred at this frame. President Kennedy is behind the sign. The original is missing; the copy is in good condition, with only its color off a bit. At this frame authorities state President Kennedy was first visible from the sixth-floor, easternmost window of the depository, the alleged assassin's window.

211 Back of sign. Missing from original film.

212 Back of sign. This is a composite with a crude patch.

224 Limousine begins to appear from behind sign, with Governor Connally visible.

225–312 Jacqueline Kennedy continues turning toward the president. By frame 312 she is fully turned and reaching to him.

225 First frame in which President Kennedy is visible after passing the sign; he obviously has been hit.

226 President Kennedy is fully visible, clutching at his throat. His wife is looking at him.

227 Blurred.

228 President's elbows begin to push out in front of him as he clutches his throat.

230 Shows clearly, as Governor Connally testified, that he had not yet been hit.[47]

232 Governor Connally holds his Stetson.

233 Governor Connally turns to right, shoulder slightly down.

236 Governor Connally with chest front square to the camera, as in process of turning.

238 Governor Connally's cheeks puff out, lips purse, and he reels under the impact of a shot striking and shattering his fifth rib.

239 Governor Connally begins to fall into his wife's lap.

240 Jacqueline Kennedy is turned, looking at the president. Governor Connally is down in his wife's lap, but still holding his hat.

252 According to official findings, this is the first frame in which Governor Connally could have been hit by a separate bullet fired from the alleged assassin's rifle—if President Kennedy was hit by the first bullet fired at frame 210.

255 This frame is simultaneous with the photograph taken by James W. Altgens, an Associated Press photographer, while he stood on the south side of Elm. Governor Connally still clutches his Stetson.

312 President Kennedy's head moves rapidly forward one frame.

313 President Kennedy's head explodes.

314–315 President Kennedy's head moves violently backward and to the left. These frames were misnumbered by the printer for the Warren Commission as a result of an incorrect page layout, imparting the effect of reversing the direction of the head movement. When a critic drew this to the attention of J. Edgar Hoover, the director of the FBI, he acknowledged the mistake and attributed it to a "printing error."[48]

314–381 Secret Service agent Clint Hill jumps from the left running board of the backup car and, in a dangerous move, runs to the limousine. The backup car brushes his leg.

334 Last frame printed by the Warren Commission in Commission Exhibit 885.[49]

343 Hill first places his hand on the presidential car.

345 Jacqueline Kennedy climbs out of rear seat onto trunk lid of the car.

368 Hill places one foot on the bumper of the car. The first time his foot steps on the bumper it slips off, as shown in other assassination films but not the Zapruder film.[50]

381 Hill has both feet on the bumper (3.7 seconds after frame 313).

390–420 Secret Service agent Clint Hill pushes Jacqueline Kennedy back into the rear seat.

486 End.

Most persons viewing the Zapruder film probably have little awareness of its importance to the investigation of President Kennedy's assassination. They have seen it in a number of movies or television shows as colorful background to the larger subject of JFK's trip to Dallas or as a lead-in to a plot line. Oliver Stone's film JFK (1991), for example, used the Zapruder film as part of its depiction of the assassination.[51] Some who have viewed the Zapruder film in its entirety at a lecture or on a videotape are aware of the explosion of the head at frame 313, but little more. But when one becomes critically aware of the information held in the film and its relation to other basic data in the evidentiary base, the film takes its rightful place as a fundamental record of what happened that day in Dallas.

The Zapruder film performs two basic functions, one negative and one positive. Its negative importance lies in the series of hard facts that disprove the official story of what happened to JFK. But in supplying eight crucial evidentiary points, the film establishes that multiple riflemen killed the president. Specifically, I argue the following:

1. The Zapruder film disproves the theory that a single bullet wounded JFK and Governor Connally. The reaction of Governor Connally to a shot at about frame 237 occurred too late for the shot allegedly fired at frame 210 to have caused it. (It is also too late for a shot fired from frame 211 through frame 224.) The timing of his reaction indicates that another shooter had to inflict the wound.

2. The film, studied in concert with other evidence, establishes that a first shot was fired at or just before frame 190. This shot would have been impossible for anyone firing from the Texas School Book Depository because a live oak tree blocked the view of JFK from that building. Thus a second shooter must have fired, which by definition means a conspiracy. This detail also demolishes the single-bullet theory by requiring a separate shot for Connally at about frame 237 and another for the wounding of James Tague.

3. The film shows the back of the president's head intact and not rumpled after the head shot. This clashes with the official assertions that a bullet struck the back of the head.

4. The film depicts Phil Willis taking his fifth photograph that day, just at frame 202 in response to a shot. This alone disproves the official conclusions of the Warren Commission because physical constraints made it impossible for a shot to have been fired prior to frame 210.

5. The film places witnesses and locates physical features of the assassination.

6. The film provides a chronological record of the assassination.

7. The film demonstrates the heroism of Secret Service agent Clint Hill.

8. The explosion of President Kennedy's head at frame 313 is incompatible with the type of injury that would have been caused by the military-hardened ammunition allegedly used by the assassin.

These points, to which I will return later in the book, by no means exhaust the evidentiary matter contained in the film. But, by supporting the theory of a conspiracy, they seriously challenge the Warren Commission's (and thus the government's) official findings, which had begun with the preconception of Oswald's sole guilt.

The Film
and Private
Ownership
of American
History

Ownership, Copyright, and the Zapruder Film, 1963–1975

In midmorning of the tumultuous November 23, as the world's press pounded on his door, Abraham Zapruder sold the print rights for his twenty-six-second movie to *Life* magazine's representative Richard Stolley. With that sale the 8mm color motion picture passed into the private control of one of the most powerful and influential corporations in America, where it would remain under its tightly supervised use for more than eleven years.

Nothing in the published record of *Life* magazine or its parent, Time Inc., nothing set forth in the memoirs of its employees, and nothing presented in the histories of the magazine remotely suggests that the owners and editors saw anything unusual in its purchase and copyright of evidence central to a proper understanding of President John F. Kennedy's assassination.[1] There is certainly not a word in any federal publication associated with the assassination investigation that even hints at the irregularity of permitting definitive evidence in the criminal investigation to be owned and controlled by a private corporation.[2] Nor did the larger ethical and criminal investigative issues associated with this exclusive control find any expression in the federal investigators' records.[3] Among these major questions of social ethics and legal principles are the following:

1. Is private control and copyright of such important primary evidence in the murder of a president not only a violation of legal principles but also contrary to the national interest?

2. Has any wealthy corporation the right in our society to use its wealth to, in effect, control knowledge about the assassination of the nation's chief executive?

3. Has a private corporation the right exclusively to determine the history of the nation? By controlling the Zapruder film, presumably only for profit and effectively making it unavailable to critical scholars and the public, the popular weekly magazine shaped our history to an unprecedented degree.

These questions cloud Time Inc.'s dozen years of ownership. Among critics, they sowed suspicion of collaboration in a cover-up of JFK's murder as an awareness of the federal inquiry's failures spread. Apart from visiting the National Archives to view a copy available to only a few, neither critics nor citizens had access to the film or a way to obtain a print. Critics around the nation were in a similar stymied plight. In Los Angeles some resorted to cutting out the poor black-and-white frame reproductions printed in the twenty-six *Hearings and Exhibits* volumes of the Warren Report to make study booklets.[4]

Time's troubles began on the very day Stolley bought the film. Charges were levied that it had destroyed several key frames in the processing of the film and had, with the connivance of federal authorities, hidden the fact. In addition, critics and citizens tried to force a public viewing of the film. Eventually the combined impact of an increasing awareness of the film's importance and the public's discontent forced Time to abandon ownership and return the film to the Zapruder heirs in 1975.

The frames had an irregular history made even more singular by the determined efforts of critics to obtain replacement copies of them, as well as to see and use the entire original film. On the evening of November 23, *Life*'s Chicago processing facilities ruined five frames. After completing the film purchase, around noon Stolley dispatched the original film plus the copy by commercial airplane to Chicago. In Chicago *Life* experts rushed the original to the massive R. R. Donnelly and Company printing plant, where a special team waited to prepare prints.[5] R. R. Donnelly was a commercial press that printed the magazine, with *Life* maintaining a production office in the building. The high-speed presses ran at eighty thousand copies per hour; on November 22, they had been set up and already had been running the regular November 29 issue when news of the assassination reached Time's New York offices.[6] In preparation for incorporating the breaking assassination story into a new edition, Time executives in New York City had immediately stopped the presses. They scrubbed most of the original material, destroyed the two hundred thousand copies already printed, and held the presses open while an editorial team flew to Chicago to prepare a new issue with whatever incoming information and pictures they could obtain. For two days they would work around the clock to put out the new edition.

At the Chicago plant the special crew in place to make up the revised November 29 edition of the magazine carefully viewed the Zapruder film.[7] With a hand-cranked Movieola projector, they ran the film through several times, looking for frames suitable to be made into prints. Because the limited time available precluded the use of color copies, the prints would have to be published in black and white. To select the frames to print, the Chicago photographic laboratory made "scores of eight-by-ten-inch prints," and the staff laid them out on the floor of the office.[8] They selected thirty-one pictures for the four pages of the edition allotted to them for Zapruder frames, then folded them in with other pages of text and other photos of JFK.

On the evening of November 23 the Chicago plant hurried to make enlargements, in addition to another copy.[9] Managers gave the 8mm original to a film technician.[10] While working on the enlargements, he "broke the film diagonally," ruining frames 208, 209, 210, and 211, tearing 207, and destroying most of 212.[11] Apparently the technician considered the fragments of frames 208, 209, 210, 211, and much of 212 beyond rescue, so he snipped them away "and idly disposed" of them.[12] As mentioned in an earlier chapter, he repaired frame 207, with the patch line running horizontally across it. Frame 212 was also fixed, with its remaining top half spliced with what seems to be the bottom fragment of frame 208.[13] The most conspicuous feature of frame 212 is the crude black horizontal patch line, which runs through a tree.[14] The upper half of the tree's trunk is suspended in air, and beneath the black line and to the right, the misaligned lower trunk reaches from the earth to halt in midair.

The history of the frames then became intertwined with the Warren Commission's viewing of the original. Ninety-two days after the purchase, February 25, 1964, in response to a Commission request, a *Life* specialist carried the original film to Washington—the company refused to let it out of its hands—to show it to some of the Commission staff as well as some agents of the FBI and Secret Service.[15] Knowledge of the screening was disclosed in the afternoon of June 4, 1964, when FBI special agent and photographic expert Lyndal L. Shaneyfelt testified before the Commission and its assistant counsel Arlen Specter in Washington, D.C.[16] Herbert Orth, assistant chief of *Life*'s photographic laboratory, Shaneyfelt said, had run the film through several times for them.

After viewing the film, Orth "volunteered," in Shaneyfelt's sworn testimony,[17] or "at the request of the Commission," in J. Edgar Hoover's words,[18] to prepare three sets of 35mm color slides of the "pertinent [!] frames of the assassination which were determined to be frames 171 through 434 [sic]," counting 160 slides, 171–207 and 212–334; Shaneyfelt did not mention the missing and damaged frames and the reference to frame 434 as a typographical error.[19] But *Life* actually furnished 171–207 and 212–343, or 169 slides in all.[20] The FBI photographic expert further explained the evidentiary importance of the original: "The original had considerably more detail and more there to study than any of the copies, since in the photographic process each time you copy you lose some detail."[21]

There is an unresolved puzzle regarding why *Life* provided a larger number of slides than requested.[22] Nevertheless, the FBI simply ignored the additional nine frames (335–343) and made for the Commission's use poor black-and-white copies of only 160 slides (171–207 and 212–334), bound into an album and printed two to the page, which became Commission Exhibit 885 (CE 885), ultimately printed in the hearings and exhibits volumes.[23] These were actually fifth-generation copies, if one considers the color original the first generation, the color slides the second generation, the black-and-white album copies the third generation, and the published black-and-white copies the fourth generation. The additional weakness of fading detail when an image is transferred from color to black and white could be included as another image-degrading, or fifth, generation.[24] As will be explained in a later chapter, the nine slides that were not printed are of key evidentiary worth, with the startling evidence they hold disproving the official findings.

On the afternoon of June 4, the Commission adjourned, but it returned to its offices at 7:00 P.M. to complete Shaneyfelt's testimony and view the film. That evening, under the direction of Specter,[25] the agent screened the Zapruder movie and other related films to Commission members John J. McCloy, Gerald Ford, and Allen Dulles.[26] Because Specter and Shaneyfelt did not introduce the film properly, both McCloy and Ford thought they were seeing the original.[27] Only when Ford mentioned "the original Zapruder" did the FBI agent inform them that he had shown the FBI's copy of the original.[28] Specter remained quiet. The film they had seen was then "marked with Commission Exhibit No. 904 identifying the Zapruder copy."[29] But this brought up another puzzle.

When critics later examined film CE904, deposited with the Commission records in the National Archives, they found that it was not the copy mentioned by Shaneyfelt but one from a more distant generation, a difference that is left unexplained.[30] The Commission did not view the color slides, which were never assigned an exhibit number.

Two important evidentiary features stamp Specter's taking of Shaneyfelt's testimony. In the first place, most of the FBI agent's testimony is hearsay, without supporting documentary evidence entered to sustain a large part of his observations. In addition to this open violation of one of the main tenets of legal procedure, Specter did not establish the chain of possession of the original film or any of the three first-generation copies.[31]

The Commission's report, published in late September 1964, did not mention the damaged and destroyed frames. The findings, though, rested squarely on a first shot hitting the president at frame 210. Moreover, the Report had included a photograph of frame 210 "from the Zapruder Film" as part of its illustrative evidence.[32] Careful critics first became aware of the damaged and missing frames when they studied the Warren Commission hearings and exhibit volumes.[33] In CE885, reproduced in volume 18, the frames suddenly jump from 207 to 212, and both of these are damaged. Readers found no explanation for this in the published record, and officialdom has remained forever silent.

In the face of increasing public concern, Life seemed rather unperturbed by the claims of careless handling and irreparable destruction of evidence.[34] In late 1966 and early 1967, the third anniversary of President Kennedy's death, dissent from the official findings was welling up across the country. New critical books hit with a punch. These include Mark Lane, Rush to Judgment; Penn Jones Jr., Forgive My Grief; Sylvia Meagher, Accessories after the Fact; Leo Sauvage, The Oswald Affair; Edward Epstein, Inquest; Richard Popkin, The Second Oswald; Ray Marcus, The Bastard Bullet; and Harold Weisberg, Whitewash II.[35] In addition, William Manchester's Death of a President, a controvesial best-seller that supported the government's conclusions about the assassination, roused public interest.[36]

Other forms of criticism swept the nation in this same period. A Berkeley student published a smash play, Mac Bird, that dissented from the official findings and would be performed across the nation.[37] Controversial panels of attacking critics and fumbling defenders were broadcast over many radio and television shows.[38] Questioning articles were published.[39]

In the midst of this national concern, Life underwent a brief spell of modified outlook. It called for a reopening of the federal investigation, permitted a select handful of critics to view the original film in its offices, hired an erstwhile critic to investigate the murder, and then suddenly stopped and retreated. The statement about reopening the investigation followed publication of "A Matter of Reasonable Doubt," an article observing the third anniversary of President Kennedy's death, on November 25, 1966.[40] The article examined the Zapruder film with an interview of John F. Connally, in which the former governor adamantly concluded that he was hit by a separate bullet at frame 234. Then, after proclaiming he had never read anything on the assassination—books, articles, or the Warren Report itself—he upheld the official findings of the Report, not aware that a separate shot meant conspiracy.[41]

Life also permitted a handful of critics to view the film in its offices during this period. Sylvia Meagher, for example, related that she watched it twenty-five times.[42] The company also employed a college professor, Josiah Thompson, to examine the assassination and the surrounding controversies, as discussed in a later chapter. But the magazine still would not provide copies of the missing frames or show the film in public. This issue came to a head when critics pressured the magazine to respond. Harold Weisberg, who had first brought the missing slides to public notice in his book Whitewash (1965),[43] noted the problem again in his second volume, published late the next year, Whitewash II, which, in the changing climate, received more attention.[44] In late 1966, Weisberg tutored a young Baltimore Sun reporter, Richard H. Levine, on the issue of the frames and film. Levine then sought and obtained an interview with Life officials to discuss the missing frames.[45]

While Levine's subsequent December 22, 1966, article on the subject was one of several sources of increased pressure on Life, its description of the damage, which quoted several Time Inc. and Life officials, had an especially strong impact on the public and the corporation.[46] Dick Pollard, the magazine's photographic director, had responded to a query about the damage that the laboratory technicians "were not editorially minded" and had made an "arbitrary decision that at the time seemed to have little significance."[47] Further public concern over Life's control of the film and destruction of the frames originated in readers' reaction to Weisberg's books. Although thousands of individuals had read his works, many thousands more had heard him on clear channel talk radio programs that were common in the evening along the eastern seaboard. Several of his listeners and readers wrote to Life to ask for information or lodge complaints.

Finally, on January 30, 1967, George Hunt, the editor of Life, responded in a public release to the press marked with studied disdain for critics who had brought the loss to the public's attention.[48] He stated for the record that "there had never been any missing frames"; copies of frames from the original intact copy made by Zapruder on November 22 were never de-stroyed and were available.[49]

Unfortunately, he was in error. Even the best of news magazine editors, of which he was no doubt one, are not criminal investigators or experts on the assassination of President John F. Kennedy. This is the province of professional detectives, forensic scientists, and those who have carefully and exhaustively studied the available evidence. Moreover, mere possession of a film by itself has never been known to impart the knowledge and in-sight that are necessary to make sophisticated judgments about the mer-its of primary evidence in a murder. Indeed, when the original Zapruder frames are properly examined, they are found to contain evidence essential to understanding the facts of the murder. In the first place, they offer clearer pictures of the scene than do the copies. Further, they include images captured on the sprocket area, which constituted 22 percent of the exposure and was packed with data now gone forever.

On January 29, 1967, *Life* began an elaborate public charade to keep the frames away from the public and critics. It announced that it would release the four "missing" frames. In a story on the release the next day, the *New York Times* quoted Life's managing editor, George Hunt, as admitting the frames had been destroyed, but only "after the FBI had viewed the film, after the magazine made its own copies, and after the film was made available to the Warren Commission."[50] His reference to the FBI is imma-terial, for it was not the Commission.[51] Only a few members of the Com-mission staff, many FBI agents, and some Secret Service agents saw the original.[52] Three Commission members saw a copy screened for it on the evening of June 4, 1964.[53]

But *Life* did not in fact release the frames. After the public announcement and news reports had circulated on its release of the contested frames, no citizen or critic received copies of them, and neither *Life* nor any other magazine or newspaper printed them. Critics who wrote to the magazine requesting copies did not receive them, or, for that matter, even a reply.[54] When a private investigator called on *Life* officials to obtain copies, they referred him to the National Archives. When critics went to the National Archives, it referred them to *Life*. One set of prints was provided to the Associated Press in New York City, but it did not distribute them or other-wise make them available.[55] On the file folder memorandum the AP had established for the subject was written "For Use Only If Forced to Do So."[56]

Finally, in late 1967, *Life* released the frames to Josiah Thompson, a philosophy professor at Haverford College, when his book *Six Seconds in Dallas* was about to appear. Thompson printed small black-and-white images of frames 207 through 212 on good clay-coated paper along with George Hunt's boilerplate explanation. "In light of the needless controversy surrounding these 'missing frames,'" wrote Thompson, "it is fortunate that we can publish them here for the first time."[57]

Unfortunately, there are problems with Thompson's presentation of the frames. They appeared in a historical vacuum, with no mention of the "release" eleven months earlier or of the repeated futile efforts of critics to obtain copies. In addition to omitting the important historical perspective, he did not cite the sources of discontent leading to the magazine's decision to release the frames. But Thompson did assert that books by Mark Lane and Harold Weisberg had called attention to the missing frames, causing Time to address the issue. He cites Weisberg's two volumes correctly, but his reference to Lane's *Rush to Judgment* was too hastily drawn; Lane's work includes no mention of the missing frames.

During the Warren Commission investigation of the assassination and later in a number of other federal examinations of the murder, officials never admitted the damage to the film and never inquired into the circumstances surrounding the destruction of the frames. The Warren Report and its accompanying hearings and exhibit volumes do not contain any information about the damage, nor is this detail contained in the Commission's archival records. In the course of two federal investigations of the murder, only two references can be found, one made by the President's Commission in 1964, and another by the House Select Committee in 1979. Information about the Commission's explicit knowledge of the missing frame comes from a single remark from a July 1964 questioning of Zapruder by Warren Commission staff counsel Wesley Liebeler, who showed him the FBI album of black-and-white slide prints.[58]

> MR. LIEBELER. And the motorcade comes behind it. Now, what about picture No. 210—however—there is no No. 210 in here.
>
> MR. ZAPRUDER. No.
>
> MR. LIEBELER. How about No. 222?[59]

In its inquiry into the murder in 1976 through 1979, the House Select Committee also avoided the subject; just a single sentence slipped into the hearings in an off-the-cuff comment by Michael Goldsmith, senior staff counsel. In the process of querying a witness about the film, he remarked, "As you know . . . the original Zapruder film is missing four frames between frames 208 and 211."[60] Liebeler's exchange with Zapruder and Goldsmith's remark constitute the sum of the federal published record, from 1963 to 1998, on the damaged and missing frames.

In addition to resisting releasing the questioned frames, Time Inc. also held fiercely to its copyright control of the movie, using it variously for commercial reasons. *Life* continued to publish frames from the film and also sold copies abroad. For example, on December 7, 1963, a special "John F. Kennedy Memorial Edition" printed nine enlarged Zapruder frames in color. On October 2, 1964, the magazine's cover contained enlargements of five frames, and eight frames, enlarged and in color, appeared in the text. *Life* referred to the film as "one of the most important pieces of evidence to come before the . . . Commission," which underscored the fact that it recognized the film was key evidence in the assassination investigation. The November 25, 1966, issue of *Life* featured the frames. And so it continued in other issues of the magazine from time to time.

Many critics circumvented the ownership barrier by obtaining illegal copies of the copyrighted Zapruder film from two sources. The first source of bootleg copies was the unsuspecting owner of the film and copyright, *Life* itself. As the CBS anchorman Dan Rather reported in his memoir *The Camera Never Blinks*, "Their security was so lax as to be almost comical. A major executive in the Time-Life Building who wished to look at the Zapruder film could call down and order a print sent to his office. For years it was not shown on television or in theaters. But, frequently, whenever a *Time-Life* big wheel ordered up a print for himself, offhandedly or otherwise, several bootleg copies would be produced. An underground industry soon developed."[61]

Other bootleg copies came from outside the magazine's corporate structure. The first unauthorized print from the Zapruder film to appear in book format was in Harold Weisberg's *Whitewash*, mentioned earlier, which included black-and-white frames 207 and 212 taken from the Commission volumes.[62] The images in Weisberg's book did not carry a copyright notice and had been reproduced without the permission of *Life* magazine, but the owner of the film has never registered a protest. Numerous other critics have also used slides and prints of those two frames and of other frames in lectures and on local television shows, all without copyright notice. They received no complaint.

When Jim Garrison, the New Orleans district attorney, subpoenaed the Zapruder film for his prosecution of Clay Shaw's trial, he had been explicitly warned by *Life* not to make copies. The magazine made a special print of the film so that in the event copies appeared, they could trace it back to the New Orleans trial.[63] Garrison, however, immediately had bootleg copies made and distributed them to critics and universities.[64]

From the New Orleans copies. additional copies were made and distributed by several critics, including newspaper editor Penn Jones Jr., of Midlothian, Texas, a noted early dissenter from the official doctrines. He sold the copies, showed them at lectures, and in other ways promoted their distribution.[65] Mark Lane showed the film at his numerous lectures around the country and also sold copies in a special Super 8mm format. Out of Boston, a group of young critics called the Assassination Information Bureau promoted the film at hundreds of appearances on the college lecture circuit, earning large lecture fees while promoting conspiracy theories. Other critics and dissenters around the country used copies of the film to present shows and informational lectures on the assassination. These copies were mostly of poor quality, often several generations removed from the master and without the sprocket matter.

Although public showings of the bootleg Zapruder film could take place in such diverse places as the living rooms of the wealthy, the back rooms of taverns, or the meetings of small social clubs, the most typical one was in colleges across the nation. A typical showing of the film in a college lecture hall would occur before an audience of two or three hundred students, a scattering of local people (conservatives and liberals), and representatives of the press.[66] These audiences tended to include few faculty members, who for the most part supported the official findings and refused to question them or even listen to dissent.

A student sponsor typically would introduce the subject with a few words on its importance and then present a second student who was in charge of the meeting. She or he would then explain the credentials of the speaker and how important the subject was to America, often criticizing both the right wing and liberals for permitting a cover-up. Often a few words would be added to remind listeners that in a democracy the people were the government.

The featured presenter would then launch into a speech. In animated terms, he would hammer at the evidence and the cover-up, describe falsities, frauds, and corruption, and then ask for the lights to be dimmed. The Zapruder film typically would be shown several times, at first without explanation, then with comments by the speaker to bring attention to main points.

The film would be the highlight of the evening, the central point in the speaker's argument, and at the end the audience would usually be silent, sensing the profound seriousness of the problem. The lights would go on, and questions would be taken, often for as long as the speaker's formal presentation. After the speech, various books on the subject of the assassination and copies of the film and slides were often sold.

Typically a discussion would continue later in a coffee shop or saloon. Sometimes, with a firebrand speaker like Texas newspaper editor Penn Jones Jr., in his cowboy hat and boots, it would go until three o'clock in the morning. Jones carried his own whiskey in a special suitcase and often continued the discussion in his motel room, " 'til the dawn killed the night." Others might talk until midnight or later, or sometimes even bunk in with students. The student newspaper and sometimes the local and regional press would report on the evening lecture.

Notably, in not one instance of these thousands of illegal public showings of the Zapruder film did *Life* or the film's next owner, LMH Company, protest in defense of its copyright, request fees, or take any action whatsoever to make the users cease. In 1975, when *Life* returned the film to the heirs of Abraham Zapruder, his widow, Lillian, daughter, Myrna, and son, Henry, formed a corporation, LMH, to control the film and attendant matters. Only once, in 1967, would the film's owner attempt to block its use in a book, and that failed spectacularly. As discussed in a later chapter, through a lawsuit, Time Inc. sought to halt the use of charcoal copies of frames in Josiah Thompson's *Six Seconds in Dallas* and lost.

Only once in the years of *Life*'s custody of the film did the actions of the federal government pose a potential threat to its ownership. For a brief moment, November 1, 1966, the date of an executive order published in the *Federal Register*, it seemed the United States attorney general might enforce a new law, Public Law 89-318, and take the original Zapruder film from the office files of *Life*. Then critics read the pages of fine print listing the thousands of items relating to the assassination included in the order under the listings of Commission and FBI evidence and discovered several items not mentioned: the film, for example, and Ike Altgens's photographs and Jack Ruby's pistol. They were dismayed. But upon reading a catchall section 5, they discovered the general statement certainly included the Zapruder film. However, federal authorities did not acquire it.

In 1963 the murder of President John F. Kennedy was punishable only under the laws of Texas.[67] Texas had no law for confiscation of weapons and apparently other key evidence used in prosecuting criminal cases.[68] Moreover, since no prosecution had occurred in President Kennedy's murder, the various weapons and other artifacts of the investigation into the murder could not be forfeited even if a law had been available.[69] Nor did common law permit acquisition. In this state of affairs, in May 1965 a rich Colorado oil man, John King, purchased Lee Harvey Oswald's 6.5-mm Mannlicher-Carcano rifle and pistol from his widow, Marina, contingent upon their return to her from the government.[70] The federal government still held the weapons and fought the purchase.[71]

Judge William J. Doyle of the federal district court remarked on this odd fact in a decision concerned with the private acquisition of the alleged murder rifle, when he opined that "under the peculiar facts of this case, one would suppose that under some principle of common law or at least natural law or natural justice, weapons used in the commission of a crime of this magnitude would be subject to forfeiture by the proper authorities and, certainly, that property of this character would not be subject to commercial traffic. It is, therefore, somewhat astonishing to discover that there is not any such principle and that forfeiture is a matter of statutory regulation."[72]

Under what principle, law, or rule could the federal government acquire title and control over materials utilized in the investigation into the murder of JFK, including the Zapruder film? None seemed to be available.

To overcome this barrier, on June 17 Attorney General Nicholas Katzenbach wrote to the chairmen of the House Judiciary Committee and the Senate Judiciary Committee with a model bill enclosed, asking for its passage.[73] He said in part:

> In my judgment, a failure to retain the critical physical exhibits and [block] the resultant possibility of their loss, destruction, or alteration will serve to encourage irresponsible rumors and allegations designed to destroy the widespread public confidence in the work and conclusions of the President's Commission. Furthermore, retention of these items would permit an accurate and complete reassessment of the con-

clusions of the President's Commission if at any time in the future this was considered desirable.[74]

The House Judiciary Committee did not hold hearings on the bill, which was assigned the number H.R. 9545. On August 19 it submitted its report to the full House as House Report 813, entitled "Preserving Evidence Pertaining to the Assassination of President Kennedy."[75] On September 7 the House suspended rules; the bill was amended, discussed, and passed by voice vote.[76]

On the floor, Chairman Byron Rogers of Colorado argued that the bill was important: "To eliminate questions and doubts the physical evidence should be securely preserved. A failure to do so could lead to loss, destruction or alteration of such exhibits and in time may serve to encourage irresponsible rumors undermining the public confidence in the work of the Warren Commission."[77] Congressman Charles "Mac" Mathias of Maryland strongly supported H.R. 9545, adding to Rogers's remarks, "I agree with the gentleman completely, that this legislation is necessary in the interest of history, and in the interest of any future calm and deliberate reevaluation of the events which surrounded the very tragic occurrence of the assassination of President Kennedy."[78]

At that point Congressman Hale Boggs of Louisiana, a member of the Warren Commission, rose in support of the legislation. With an emotional tinge apparent in his printed remarks, he urged the acceptance of the bill. "As gruesome as it is," he told the Congress, "it would be very tragic, indeed, for [sic] these items—and that is the only word I know of to use in describing them—did not remain the property of the Government of the United States, so that for a great many reasons, the most compelling reason being that they were very vital in the evidence which the Commission used in its deliberations and in its determination."[79]

On September 8 the Senate received H.R. 9545 from the House and referred it to the Committee on the Judiciary.[80] The Senate committee did not hold hearings on the bill and reported it out to the floor on October 4 as Senate Report 851, "Preserving Evidence Pertaining to the Assassination of President Kennedy."[81] The bill was passed over on October 13,[82] and again on October 15.[83] On October 16, the bill passed the Senate by voice vote.[84] Only a few remarks were made on the floor about the bill that went to assure fairness to the property interests (alleged) of the purchaser of the rifle, the Denver oilman.[85] On October 20, the bill was examined by the

Committee on House Administration, found truly enrolled, and was then signed by the Speaker of the House.[86] On October 21, Congress presented H.R. 9545 to the president,[87] who signed it on November 2.[88] It became the Act of November 2, 1965, "An Act Providing for the Acquisition and Preservation by the United States of Certain Items of Evidence Pertaining to the Assassination of President John F. Kennedy," Public Law 89-318.[89]

The bill to preserve the evidence in the assassination investigation passed into law without any dissent in either house of Congress. Included in the voting delegates were four members of the Warren Commission, Senators Richard Russell and John Cooper and Congressmen Hale Boggs and Gerald Ford. The attorney general of the United States supported and indeed provided a model bill to the appropriate committees of Congress. A federal judge had decried the absence of such statute authority.

The Act of November 2, 1965, declared that the national interest requires that the United States acquire and preserve items of evidence considered by the President's Commission on the Assassination of President Kennedy; that the attorney general determine which items should be included; that controversy over compensation would be heard in the court of claims or district courts; that the General Services Administration would preserve such items; that all items would become the personal property of the United States; and that sufficient funds would be appropriated to carry out the purposes of the act.[90]

Attorney General Katzenbach resigned, having not withstood Hoover's sustained opposition to him. President Johnson moved him to the State Department and replaced him with Ramsey Clark. Almost one year after the act was passed, October 31, 1966, Clark identified the evidence to be preserved.[91] The list was published in the *Federal Register* of November 1, 1966.

The determination contained an appendix listing the items to be preserved. The several pages are divided into six parts. Part 1 includes the weapons used by Oswald, a rifle and pistol. (This is, of course, the federal position; no credible evidence connects either the rifle to the murder of JFK or the pistol to the murder of Dallas police officer J. D. Tippit.) Part 2 secures "all items of evidence assigned exhibit numbers by the Warren Commission." Part 3 lists all items of evidence collected by the FBI and assigned FBI exhibit numbers. Part 4 discusses items in the archives not assigned exhibit numbers, which are secured, including tape recordings, films of the motorcade, and TV tapes. Part 5, which covers everything not previously specified, states, "All other items of evidence considered by the Commission . . . which are subject to this notice and not otherwise described" in the preceding paragraphs are included. This would include the Zapruder and Altgens films that were considered by the Commission, were of importance to its deliberations, and figured prominently in its Report. Part 6 asserts United States title to all of the items, which includes the films.[92]

The items secured for national preservation included the bizarre as well as the irrelevant, all mentioned without comment: Marina Oswald's sewing kit and nail file, a bottle cap found on Dealey Plaza, Ruth Paine's camera, Oswald's niece's 1958 camera, Marina's dental appointment slip, Jack Ruby's mother's dental records, and Algerian dock-loading statistics. It is hard to see how these items could conceivably be related to the assassination of President Kennedy. Why did the Department of Justice consider them to be of primary importance to the history of the United States?

The lists in parts 2 and 3 do not include Zapruder's and Altgens's pictures, but part 5 certainly appears to embrace them. The Department of Justice, however, did not acquire the films from their owners, a decision that has fueled much speculation and suspicion among researchers who have studied the assassination and its investigation.

By 1969, after *Life* had escaped the imposition of the federal acquisition law upon its ownership of the Zapruder film, defeated critics' efforts, been itself defeated in a major lawsuit (discussed in a later chapter), and avoided meeting public demands, the magazine's control of the film, unbeknownst to it, was in the hands of a young film technician in an obscure laboratory in New Jersey. In 1969 Robert Groden, a young optical technician working in a New Jersey film laboratory, had obtained a clear copy of the Zapruder film.[93] He had acquired the copy from someone in the laboratory where *Life* had had copies made.[94] Over the next four years he enhanced the film by slowing the speed, isolated the head of JFK on frames depicting the head shots, enlarged some parts of frames, stabilized the frames that had tended to jerk a little, and produced a film version with devastating visual impact.[95] By the close of 1973 he was ready to show the world the enhanced Zapruder film.

Some commentators on the assassination controversy have asked what would have occurred in America if the critics had had possession of clear copies of the film at the beginning of 1964. Would they have been able to overturn the Warren Commission's conclusions and initiate a federal reinvestigation of the murder? It would not have been easy. Given the intensity of the issue in 1965 and 1966, perhaps it was possible they could have forced a clear second look at the assassination. If the emerging antiwar and raging civil rights groups had joined them, they would have stood a better chance of success. Seen from another perspective, the federal government's decision to permit the film to remain in private hands was an excellent move to dampen criticism of the lack of a true investigation into President Kennedy's assassination.

Control and Profits, 1975–1997

By late 1973, Robert Groden had completed his improved version of the Zapruder film. Before it shocked the nation on March 6, 1975, Groden's film would pass through a number of phases, first private showings to friends, then two screenings before assassination conferences, and finally a screening before the staff of the Rockefeller Commission investigating illegal domestic activities by the Central Intelligence Agency.

Initially Groden vacillated over whether to show the film with its improved optics, stabilized frames, and clear color. Finally, late in the autumn of 1973, he hesitatingly screened it for his friend Jerry Policoff; next he showed it to critic Harold Weisberg. He also presented it to a handful of other acquaintances, who strongly encouraged him.[1] It took finished form just at the time the Committee to Investigate Assassinations (CTIA), based in Washington, D.C., had planned a national conference on the ten-year anniversary of President John F. Kennedy's murder. Under the general leadership of attorney Bernard "Bud" Fensterwald, on Thanksgiving Day weekend in 1973, numerous dissenters and critics gathered at the Georgetown University campus. Groden and his friends working with the CTIA planned to give the film its first public showing.

Fensterwald had employed a husband-and-wife team to run the conference for the CTIA. He had found the couple by what he thought was a logical method, by placing an advertisement in the Washington, D.C., underground newspaper the *Quicksilver Times*. Just a week before the opening of the conference, however, the two absconded with the $5,000 treasury, leaving the conference in organizational and financial confusion. By hard work, the CTIA salvaged the affair and ran a successful conference. Only years later, through records produced from a Freedom of Information Act (FOIA) lawsuit, did Fensterwald and the CTIA discover the *Quicksilver Times* had been a controlled organ of the CIA, as part of its secret "war at home" against American activists opposed to the Vietnam War.[2]

At the conference in the great hall of the university, a number of papers were read and speeches delivered. Then seminars were held. On November 22, Groden and Policoff arrived very late.[3] In a rather small side room a floor down, Groden screened the film, throwing the images over the heads of scores of viewers onto a large silver screen. The color, enhancement, and clarity of the improved movie stunned the audience, which produced an audible gasp at the head shot at frame 313. Groden repeated the film several times. As he stepped out to speak, a group from Chicago grabbed Policoff's attaché case, thinking it held the film, which it did not. They attempted to flee, only to be stopped and the case wrenched from their grasp.[4] At the close of the conference Groden screened the film again. No press conference was held, nor did the screening receive any press coverage. FOIA-produced records obtained later revealed that the CIA had covertly covered the conference. The FBI also had extensive secret records on it.[5]

For the next year and two months, Groden showed the film to friends and individuals. The next major showing occurred at the Assassination Information Bureau's Politics of Conspiracy Conference held in Boston on January 31, 1975, when its organizers who had heard of the enhanced film brought in Groden. The AIB was largely a collection of theorists, some of whom embraced the most extreme concoctions about the murder of JFK. The night before the conference opened, Groden appeared at a press conference with Penn Jones Jr.; he then showed the film, and the two answered questions. The press gave the event extensive and prominent coverage. As a result, although only three hundred participants had registered and were expected to attend the conference, the next evening, five thousand people appeared, jamming the hall. Repeated showings of the film had to be made to meet the demand. Its stunning impact pushed many doubters into the conspiracy camp. In this case, press coverage had made the difference.

Among those in attendance were Dick Gregory, a noted civil rights activist and political reformer, and his wife, Lil, who lived in Plymouth and had read the news accounts. Gregory and his wife, along with Groden and his wife, Chris, Policoff, and Robert Salzman of the AIB met in a hotel room later and discussed the film and what step should be taken next. Gregory was slated to speak in Washington to a federal commission inquiring into the illegal roles of the CIA in domestic affairs, including wild charges of possible participation in the assassination of JFK. This body was known as the Rockefeller Commission after its chairman, Vice President Nelson Rockefeller; former Warren Commission assistant counsel David

Belin served as its executive director. Gregory arranged for Groden to show the film in Washington.[6]

On February 4, 1975, Groden screened his enhanced Zapruder film in the office of Commission Senior Counsel Robert B. Olson. The Zapruder film caused a fierce clash with Belin, who in an emotional tirade stood and shouted at Groden. Later, in the commission report, Belin easily refuted some of the grossest claims of the assassination theorists but also attempted to refute the stunning visual impact of JFK's head snapping to the rear after a shot seen beginning at frame 313 with curious and later proven specious medical information.[7]

In the meantime, the host of a popular ABC television program, Geraldo Rivera, who had seen the news account of the Boston press conference, invited Groden and Gregory to appear on his show. On the evening of March 6, 1975, one of the major episodes in the convoluted and tainted history of the Zapruder film splashed across the screens of America's television sets. Rivera screened Groden's copy of the Zapruder film, the first time it had been seen by a nationwide television audience. The movie conveyed shocking and convincing visual evidence that a conspiracy had indeed murdered President John F. Kennedy.

The ABC show affected the continuing assassination controversy in two key ways. The film aroused the public to the film's graphic importance, leading to many additional public appearances for Groden, as well as a body of critics already displaying poor-quality bootleg copies as part of their lectures and conferences. In this way, public viewing of the film materially contributed to already growing pressures from a disturbed American populace, leading to the formation of the House of Representatives Select Committee in 1976 to investigate the assassination. On April 15, 1975, Groden showed the film in the office of Congressman Thomas N. Downing. "It convinced me that there was more than one assassin," wrote Downing in a memorandum explaining why he introduced a resolution to create the committee. Groden also showed the film to "other members of Congress."[8]

In addition to informing the public by making available the information contained in the hitherto suppressed film, the television show also ruptured the relations between the Zapruder family and Time Inc. ABC had not received permission from Time Inc. to show the film or paid for the rights to show it. This violated Time's contract with Abraham Zapruder, which explicitly required it to defend the copyright and make certain permissions were secured, with the two dividing up the money they made. With the growing national unrest over the assassination investigation and the news magazine smarting under the open violation of the copyright agreement, not the first but by far the most serious, Time blustered but chose not to sue the powerful ABC organization and turned the film back to the Zapruder family, Abraham Zapruder having died in 1970.

An indication of Time's view comes from a recent interview with an editor of *Life*. In the summer of 1998, a Los Angeles newspaper columnist met Richard Stolley, the former editor of *Life* and the purchaser of the film, at a journalism seminar, where Stolley explained what happened after the Rivera program. "Time," remarked Stolley, "then decided they didn't want to be responsible for its use any longer and tried to give it to the U.S. government. But Zapruder had died; his family had taken over, so we returned it to them for the sum of $1."[9]

Actually, the issue at stake was broader than Stolley had time to explain. Time had become disillusioned with its holding of the original Zapruder film. A growing vocal public identification of Time controlling a film that apparently proved a conspiracy killed JFK had made private suzerainty increasingly uncomfortable for the large corporation. As far as we can know without access to Time archives, almost a year before the March 6 show, the corporation had sought to rid itself of the film. As early as June 1974, Lawrence Laybourne, vice president of Time, had telephoned Meyer H. Fishbein of the National Archives and Records Service in Washington to propose transfer of the film to the Archives.[10] On October 15, 1974, Laybourne phoned again to propose a transfer. In his notes on the conversation Fishbein noted: "Lawrence Laybourne, Vice President of *Time*, phoned to let me know that he is still proposing transfer of the Zaprudo [sic] film of the assassination to us. (He phoned last June to ask about our interest. It is the copy sold to *Life*.) Lawyers are questioning whether the film has any monetary value for the media. He will continue to propose an offer to us."[11] In February of the next year, Paul Welch of Time followed up this inquiry with a phone call to James W. Moore, director of the Audiovisual Archives Division of the National Archives, to state Time was considering "donating the original Zapruder film to NARS" and would transfer its rights to NARS or some other institution.[12]

Then came the March 6 Rivera show and its aftermath, which sent Time scrambling to resolve the question and free itself from deserved obloquy as well as "legal obligations" to the Zapruder heirs. It returned the film to the Zapruder family. On April 7, prior to signing the papers of transfer, the Zapruders' lawyer, Robert Trien of the New York City law firm of Philip Handelman, telephoned James Moore to ask if the National Archives would provide storage for the original film.[13] Moore said yes, whereupon Trien replied that Henry Zapruder, son of Abraham Zapruder, would deliver the film to the archives later in the week.[14] The deposit did not take place, however, until three years later.

Time's transfer of the film to the Zapruder heirs took place in the corporation's office in Rockefeller Center, New York City, on April 9. The assignment of copyright contract stated that "in consideration of One Dollar ($1.00) and other good and valuable considerations paid to it," Time Inc. assigned the copyright "to the Film taken by Abraham Zapruder of the assassination of President John F. Kennedy" to Lillian Zapruder, Henry Zapruder, and Myrna Faith Hauser, the widow, son, and daughter, respectively, of the deceased Abraham (see document 8 in the appendix).

In a press release of April 10, Time Inc. announced it had "tried for several months to donate the film to the Archives," meaning the original out-of-camera film, but " 'legal obligations' " to the Zapruder heirs had made this impossible.[15] Since it was a "historical document," said Time, "We wanted it in the hands of responsible people." A reporter interviewed the Zapruder heirs, whose spokesman stated the family planned " 'a liberal policy in making it available to the public.' " He further commented, " 'Any eventual monetary gains for the family will be "not at odds" with the film's historical significance.' "[16]

The same day that Time Inc. sold the original film back to the Zapruder heirs, it donated to the National Archives and Records Service, "exclusively for public purposes," a first-generation copy of the 8mm Zapruder film and a collection of color transparency still pictures, comprising one transparency of each frame of the film.[17] "Each of the above items," said Time, "are to be retained in perpetuity for the benefit, enlightenment and scholarship of the people of the United States." The deed of gift protected the rights of the copyright proprietor and provided for viewing of "the Film or copies thereof and the still pictures or copies" only on the premises of the National Archives (see document 9 in the appendix).

Within two days those proprietors, Lillian Zapruder, Henry Zapruder, and Myrna Faith Hauser, formed a Texas corporation, the LMH Company, the name derived from the first initial of each of their names, to which they assigned the copyright of the film for a fee of one dollar (see document 10 in the appendix).[18]

After April 9, then, there were two sets of private Zapruder matters that concern us. The primary film, the original, remained in the hands of Zapruder's heirs and does not reappear until June 29, 1978. Robert Trien's April 7 telephone call, noted earlier, in which he requested and received permission to store the film in the National Archives, seems from the records available not to have been followed up by the LMH Company. At this point a break in our knowledge of the chain of possession occurs. No documentary or oral record covers the whereabouts of the original film for more than three years, from April 9, 1975, to June 29, 1978, when Henry Zapruder delivered it to the National Archives. One can infer he kept it safely in his possession until then.

The record is complete, however, on Time's donation of first- and second-generation copies of the film and transparencies made of most of the frames (the second copy of the film being added to the original discussion). James W. Moore of the National Archives, in a memorandum dated April 16, 1975, notes the acquisition and requests an accession number to "the gift offer."[19] The next day, the National Archives assigned number NN 375-222 to the Time gift. On April 24, James E. O'Neill, acting archivist, "on behalf of the American people," expressed his appreciation for the gift to James R. Shepley, president of Time Incorporated, "for your important and generous contribution to our archival heritage."[20] On April 29, Moore made his "Final Report on the Transfer," noting first- and second-generation copies of the film and color transparencies of the frames had been received.[21] His change of holdings report of May 12 noted accession of "2" films and "323" color transparencies of frames 164–486. They were stored in building 6W3.[22]

The National Archives had requested from Time Inc. a copy of the copyright assignment of Time Inc. to the Zapruder family. On May 13, Robert Trien, attorney for LMH, responded with copies of the assignments of April 9 and April 11, asking that the following copyright notice be attached: "Copyright © 1967 LMH Company. All rights reserved."[23] In his June 3 reply to Trien, Moore remarked he had noted the copyright information and would look forward to hearing from him "about storage of the original 8mm film."[24]

On June 29, 1978, Henry Zapruder finally delivered to the Audiovisual

Division of the National Archives the original out-of-camera Zapruder film. Director James W. Moore was not present that day, and Richard Myers accepted the film and signed the receipt (see document 11 in the appendix). Certain aspects of the acknowledgment are notable. The National Archives agreed to store the film, "free of charge, under secure and proper temperature and humidity conditions. Neither Mr. Myers nor Mr. Moore have any authority with regard to the Film other than storage until such time as an agreement letter from LMH Company (the owner of the Film) is received and signed by Mr. Moore."[25] Myers delivered the film that day to Clarence F. Lyons Jr., chief of the Judicial and Fiscal Branch of the Civil Archives Division (see document 12 in the appendix).

On July 10, Henry Zapruder sent an important letter to Moore concerning the terms of the film's storage, in which he set forth the following conditions:

1. The National Archives would agree to safeguard the film free of charge, under secure and proper temperature and humidity conditions.
2. LMH partners or their duly authorized personal representatives could "permanently or temporarily remove the Film from the Archives at any time."
3. The film would be kept in a secure place in the main archives building at Eighth Street and Pennsylvania Avenue in Washington.
4. No one except LMH partners or a designate in writing by a partner would have access to the film. An exact record of who examined or used the film shall be kept.
5. The film would not be screened or used in any way or copies made or inspected without the written permission of the LMH partners.

With the original film held by the National Archives in courtesy storage and copyright protection seemingly secured, LMH Company from time to time sold the rights to reproduce the film. The typical use would begin with a researcher inquiring at the National Archives about the film. In a letter, the Archives would explain the unique relationship with LMH and provide the address of the company's representative, Henry G. Zapruder. The researcher or would-be user would correspond with Henry Zapruder, who would agree or not agree to its use, set the price, and then provide the researcher with a letter of agreement. Restrictions and time limits for the film's use and return would be spelled out by Zapruder. The client would concur in writing and then be given written permission to take the letter to the Archives and obtain a copy of the film. The Zapruder heirs received and kept all the money.

Despite this seeming formality and concern over copyright protection, bootleg copies of the film continued to be shown throughout the nation. The film's public screening had been continuous since 1969, often well advertised, and sometimes for fees. In fact, several individuals made a good living showing the film. No known comment from the copyright owners about such use of the film appears to have been made, although this observation is limited by the nonavailability of Time and LMH files.

The Film
and the
Struggle
for Access

Profits First
Time Inc. Sues Bernard Geis Associates for Theft and Misuse of Its Zapruder Frames

Five years after its purchase of the Zapruder film, Time Inc. confronted a major challenge to its corporate policy of absolute control of the essential evidence, with the concomitant denial of study, use, and print rights. In defense of its rights, in 1967 Time Inc. sued for damages when author Josiah Thompson's publisher, Bernard Geis Associates, deliberately printed charcoal sketches made of second-generation Zapruder frames. The court held for Geis Associates on the grounds of fair use and dismissed the Time Inc. complaint as having no cause of action.

This unseemly tale begins in the winter of 1965–1966 and spring of 1966, when discontent and travail increasingly marked American life. It was a period in which opposition to the official conclusions on JFK's murder was rapidly forming, when civil rights issues had become a key factor in public life, when ecological concerns had become manifest in a number of reform initiatives, and when a gathering antiwar effort had started its long march to shake the nation.

Consternation over the results of the official investigation of JFK's assassination nourished public discontent in a variety of forms. A spate of books depicting flaws in the official findings of the investigation had appeared by 1966, including Harold Weisberg's *Whitewash* and *Whitewash II*, Edward J. Epstein's *Inquest*, and Mark Lane's *Rush to Judgment*.[1] Joining these authors in criticism were a number of articles of dissent in small-circulation magazines and numerous speakers who appeared on college campuses. A particularly effective format for expressing disagreement with the official findings was popular radio talk shows, which brought the ideas and factual criticism down to the level of the common person. An old American critical spirit came into play over the disturbing nature of JFK's murder and influenced many Americans, including a previously unknown college professor, Josiah Thompson.

In the summer of 1966, Thompson, an associate professor of philosophy at Haverford College in Pennsylvania, forsook his study of the Danish existentialist philosopher Kierkegaard, a man who saw life's meaning in a mystic removal from the world, and plunged into the practical to study the murder of President John F. Kennedy. His inquiry soon led him to propose to write a book on the assassination, a logical step for a young college professor; it would be the first book on the assassination by any college faculty member. Thompson found a publisher in New York City. In September, executives of Bernard Geis Associates met with Thompson, discussed his proposal for a book based on new evidence that he claimed showed the Warren Commission had failed, and decided to publish his proposed book.[2]

Thompson encountered immediate problems. The poor quality and woefully incomplete nature of Warren Commission records that had been deposited in the National Archives stymied his research. For example, he remarked in the introduction to his book that the Zapruder transparencies and 35mm slides in the National Archives were of poor quality and too unclear for his purposes.[3] His efforts to obtain access to *Life's* clearer views of the Zapruder film and frames other than those copies the Warren Commission had deposited in the National Archives led him to approach the magazine for permission to study its copyrighted original or at least obtain better copies. *Life* was a wholly owned division of Time Inc. and not a separate corporation. *Life* refused the professor's request, but Thompson met with Richard Billings, assistant director of photography for *Life* until early 1966, then associate editor in the Department of Newsfronts, to discuss his concerns and needs.[4] This approach would ultimately lead to Thompson acquiring access to *Life's* excellent copies and prints of the film, but not the original.

Just a few days after Geis's decision to publish Thompson's book, exceptional news came from *Life*. On October 7, the magazine printed a one-page editorial by Loudon Wainwright asking for a new investigation into the assassination.[5] Since this call dovetailed with the thesis of Geis Associates' proposed book, its editors arranged for a meeting between themselves, members of *Life's* editorial staff, and Thompson.[6] On October 20 a meeting and luncheon occurred.[7] Present for *Life* were Loudon Wainwright, a writer; Edward Kern, an associate editor in the Department of Special Projects; and Billings. Present for Thompson's side were Geis, his editor Don Preston, and Thompson himself. From the long, lively meeting flowed two points. First, no definitive agreement emerged on the use of the Zapruder frames by Thompson and their appearance in his book. The other outcome of the meeting was significant: *Life* hired Thompson to assist it in investigating the assassination.

On October 31, 1966, Thompson entered into an oral contract with the corporation to serve as a consultant, an agreement that was later put into writing. He was paid a retainer, a monthly salary, and expenses. From his own admittance submitted in papers to the court, he knew before he began work for *Life* that it would not permit him to use frames from the Zapruder film in his book, either copies or originals.

Although Thompson worked mostly at home, he traveled occasionally to New York. He found he still could not examine the primary document, the original Zapruder film, for *Life* blocked access. Instead, he studied an 8mm copy made from the original, a number of 35mm slides made from the original 8mm film, and three-by-four-inch transparencies presumably also made from the original film. Thompson found the *Life* copy of the transparencies to be far superior to the set in the National Archives, although both copies were of the same first generation taken from the master slides on the same day, a fact that puzzled him.[8] The film copy was kept in Kern's office desk in an unlocked drawer, but the slides and transparencies were kept in a locked cabinet in Billings's office. Thompson studied the frames only in Kern's office, usually while Kern was present. A decidedly casual air of control seemed to exist, not what one would expect in a good archive, but perhaps common in a busy magazine office.

At the end of the business day on November 18, 1966, Kern left his office for home, his usual practice. Thompson remained, working by himself on the frames, as was also his usual practice. Kern, however, had forgotten some papers and later that evening returned to his office to fetch them. When he arrived, he caught Thompson with his own camera photographing copies of the *Life* transparencies. This account is undisputed.[9]

Thirty years later, when Thompson testified before the Assassination Records Review Board meeting in the National Archives, he provided his reasoning for taking the illicit photographs. He took them for two reasons that can be considered a type of higher-law doctrine and an attempt to circumvent technical restrictions. On the first reason Thompson remarked, "I had no idea what was going on at LIFE magazine, figured it was a power struggle of some sort," and "thought for posterity, for all of us, it would be very useful to have a copy outside those private hands." His second reason for taking the photographs, he said, was to make certain measurements on the film of JFK's head movements that could only be done in facilities outside the building, and the film could not leave the building.[10]

A curious aftermath resulted from Thompson being caught in the act of stealing an imprint of one of the key artifacts of the assassination.[11] Kern, and later Billings, then George F. Hunt, managing editor, whom Kern informed of the incident, did nothing. They made no statement that Thompson had performed an improper or criminal act, levied no criticism, took no corrective action, did not ask for his exposed film, and permitted him to develop and keep his film and the copies. Moreover, they continued to employ and work with him.

Work continued as normal. Two days later, on November 20, in New York City, Life screened the original film to a group of citizens. Present were Dr. Cyril Wecht, a reputable forensic pathologist and JFK critic; Sylvia Meagher, a renowned JFK critic; Kern; and Thompson.[12] On November 23, Life put Thompson's oral contract into writing. On November 25, the magazine published an issue with the lead article "A Matter of Reasonable Doubt," which featured several of the Zapruder frames and stated that "the case should be reopened."

In January 1967, Life announced it was now going to make public copies of frames 207–212, made from the first-generation copy of the original, long sought by critics who had mounted a nationwide effort to obtain them. (The originals, as previously discussed, had been destroyed during processing.) This was deceptive. No critic ever got to see the frames, and no record exists of anyone receiving copies or viewing them. Then Life's spurt of old-fashioned journalistic inquiry suddenly stopped, and the magazine reverted to supporting the official view of JFK's death, a marked change of direction made more significant by the amount of resources it had already expended and the internal expertise it had developed in laying a factual foundation. There are no historical records to explain the decision.

By mutual consent, Thompson and Life ended their relationship in late February 1967. Life paid Thompson from November 1 to February 28. It, however, retained exclusive control of the central piece of evidence, repulsing all efforts to use the film, and still refused to permit Geis Associates to use Zapruder frames in Thompson's book. This was clear to all concerned. Although Life had profound doubts about the official findings on the murder and disagreed with the factual premises on a number of important points, demonstrating from the evidentiary base that more than one rifleman was required to explain the murder, it denied help to any other effort, however scholarly and responsible.[13]

Until June 22, 1967, Thompson made repeated attempts to secure permission from *Life* to print the frames. For example, either Thompson or members of Geis Associates wrote to the magazine on April 7, April 23, April 27, May 10, June 6, and June 9 with a variety of offers requesting permission to print frames. Finally, on June 22, Bernard Geis made the last attempt. He offered to pay *Life* "a royalty equal to the profits from publication of the Book in return for permission to use specified Zapruder frames in the Book." *Life* refused. With that, Geis Associates abandoned hope and resorted to another approach.[14] For $1,550, Geis Associates engaged an artist to make charcoal sketches of the frames. Presumably their models were the photographs Thompson had filmed surreptitiously in Kern's office.[15]

On November 18, Geis Associates published Thompson's book with the title *Six Seconds in Dallas: A Micro-study of the Kennedy Assassination*.[16] Random House distributed the book; Sylvia Meagher prepared the index and did fact checking. An odd feature of the presentation was that no Zapruder film sketch was reproduced in its entirety (meaning the frame as seen on a viewing screen, not the sprocket and edge matter).

On December 1, 1967, less than two weeks after the publication of *Six Seconds in Dallas*, Time Inc. sued Bernard Geis Associates, Bernard Geis, Josiah Thompson, and Random House, Inc. in the United States District Court for the Southern District of New York over publication of the Zapruder frames, asking for a summary judgment for damages it had suffered. The single-count complaint charged that Thompson had stolen certain frames of the Zapruder film "surreptitiously" from *Life* and that they had appeared in the book as published. Such use, it charged, was an infringement of statutory copyright, an instance of unfair trade practice, and an act of unfair competition.

The frames produced fell into three categories: fifty copyrighted frames contested by *Life*, six frames publicly released in January, and four copyrighted and nonreleased frames *Life* did not complain about. The magazine sought damages for fifty copyrighted frames reproduced in charcoal sketch that had appeared in *Six Seconds in Dallas*.

In the second category of sketches and frames, Geis printed all six of the January release frames, 207–212, on pages xvi, 8, 30, and 217. *Life* concurred in this and made no claim of copyright infringement, although the images in fact contained copyrighted matter and were printed without copyright notice or any explicit or written permission. In the third category, on pages 5, 87, and 130, Geis printed "fair sketches" of copyrighted frames. *Life* also did not protest their use. No copyright notice for the Zapruder frames appeared in the front matter of the book.

On January 15, 1968, the defendants responded, except for Thompson, who lived in Pennsylvania and had not been served with process in New York as required by law. Defendants pleaded nine affirmative defenses: (1) consent given by Billings of *Life*; (2) the Zapruder frames sketched in the book could not be a subject of copyright because they were not original; (3) the film was not creative, for it could only be used in a limited number of ways, and thus enabling it to be copyrighted would actually be appropriating subject matter by a copyright proprietor; (4 through 7) concerned fair use; (8) the First Amendment protects the defendants; and, (9) an injunction would cause the defendants irreparable harm.

On the initial defense, of *Life* consent, the court found against Geis Associates. It held that Billings "had no authority whatever to consent" to give authority from Time Inc. to anyone using the film. Billings, it said, was not an officer in the corporation but down on the twentieth tier of the corporation's structure, a minor functionary. Further, Billings worked in an area without responsibility for rights, the editorial side, not the business side, where would "repose whatever authority the magazine . . . might have to deal with copyright property." Additionally, the court noted that when Billings signed the employment contract for Thompson, he signed as an editor, and the contract did not mention consent or anything regarding use of the film. As a final point in his observations on this defense point, Judge Wyatt noted nothing in the record or in the actions of Thompson and Geis Associates that remotely suggested they were relying on Billings's consent as the reason they went ahead.

The court found that Time Inc. had a legitimate copyright in the film. The Copyright Act provides that "Photographs" may be the subject matter of copyright. The courts and legal commentators have agreed that a photograph is a sound copyright subject. To the argument by Geis Associates that a news event cannot be copyrighted, this, the court said, is true, but in this case what was copyrighted was the "particular form" of the news, not the news itself.

To the Geis Associates' argument that the Zapruder film is not creative and thus not subject to copyright protection, the judge pointed out that, to the contrary, it was. He detailed for the defendants some of the creative aspects of Zapruder's filming that day. Zapruder, he noted, selected the kind of camera, the kind of film, the kind of lens, the area in which the pictures were to be taken, the time they were to be taken, and the spot on which the camera would be operated. If Zapruder had taken his film before the assassination, it would have been copyrightable. "On what principle can it be denied because of the tragic event it records?"

The court found that the case turned on whether Geis Associates had made a fair use of the film. The judge remarked that fair use was difficult to address, with references to congressional and court discussions of its nature and problems. Four essential factors, he believed, went into deciding fair use: (1) the purpose and character of the use; (2) the nature of the copyright work; (3) the amount and substantiality of the portion used in relation to the copyrighted work as a whole; and (4) the effect of the use upon the potential market for or value of the copyrighted work.

His initial reluctance to find for fair use by the defendants turned on the conduct of Thompson in improperly photographing copies of the film and then the "deliberate appropriation" of them in the book. But the judge found "it was not the nighttime activities of Thompson" that enabled Geis Associates to make copies of the film for the book. The same frames could have been seen and studied in the National Archives or in *Life* magazine itself or in the Warren Report.

Further, the court found that the claim of Time Inc. that Geis Associates sought to make a commercial gain by their unfair use of the film was without merit. The offer of Geis Associates to surrender all profits from the book to *Life* "as royalty payment for a license to use the copyrighted Zapruder frames" was a strong point against Time Inc.'s assertion.

The court also found that no competition existed between the plaintiff and defendant as Time Inc. had alleged. It dismissed that point in the complaint, explaining that Geis Associates did not sell Zapruder pictures or prints, and did not publish a magazine. Further, the court stated, from the perspective of profit, "It seems more reasonable to speculate that the Book would, if anything, enhance the value of the copyrighted work."

Finally, the court held that the balance of argument and evidence was in favor of Geis Associates:

There is a public interest in having the fullest information available on the murder of President Kennedy. Thompson did serious work on the subject and has a theory entitled to public consideration. While doubtless the theory would be explained with sketches of the type used at page 87 of the Book and in The Saturday Evening Post, the explanation actually made in the Book with copies is easier to understand. The Book is not bought because it contained the Zapruder pictures; the Book is bought because of the theory of Thompson and its explanation, supported by Zapruder.

Years later, a leading Washington attorney in the field of Freedom of Information Act cases observed that the decision had expanded the fair use doctrine where First Amendment protections are concerned.[17] In the area of citizen rights, Thompson recalled in 1997 for an uninterested review board that the victory was Pyrrhic, for the case had cost him all the earnings from his book.[18]

Beyond the legal implication of the libel suit, Six Seconds in Dallas is significant because it was by far the most important breach in the wall of secrecy erected around the Zapruder film. In an unforeseen and highly dramatic episode, a courageous young author and his publisher unexpectedly wrenched control of the film—and thus debate over the assassination—from a titan of the mass media. It would, however, be another eight years before the public would finally get to see the film as a motion picture. That showing was incredibly more graphic and powerful than the charcoal sketches in Thompson's book and would leave an indelible impression of conspiracy and cover-up on its mass audience.

Neither publication of the charcoal sketches nor the public showing of the motion picture film ensured that it would be correctly interpreted. As we shall see in subsequent chapters, much of the analysis of the film is flawed. But the public access first wrested from the control of Time Inc. has established the centrality of the Zapruder film to understanding of the critical evidence of what transpired in the assassination.

Moreover, while Six Seconds in Dallas made public access to the Zapruder film possible, it did not end the problems posed by private control of the film. As we shall see in the next chapter, still further legal battles remained to be fought before students of the assassination could gain access in a way that permitted them to study the film carefully and convey the results of their studies to the general public effectively.

President John F. Kennedy,
8:45 A.M., November 22, 1963,
speaking to crowd in parking lot
across from the Texas Hotel in
Fort Worth
(John F. Kennedy Library)

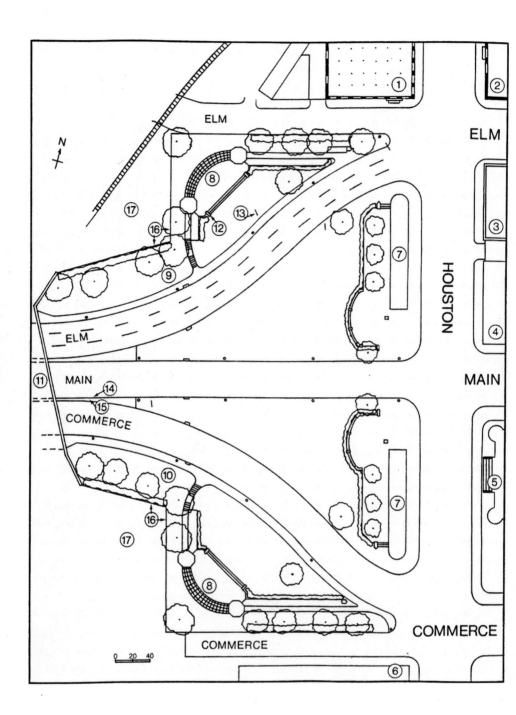

The Texas School Book Depository (AP/Wide World Photos)

opposite:
Map of Dealey Plaza by Katherine Guth, reproduced from *The Assassination of John F. Kennedy: A Comprehensive Historical and Legal Bibliography, 1963–1979,* ed. David R. Wrone and DeLloyd J. Guth (Westport, Conn.: Greenwood, 1980). Key: (1) Texas School Book Depository; alleged assassin's lair on the sixth-floor, easternmost window; (2) Dal-Tex Building; (3) Dallas County Records Building; (4) Dallas County Criminal Courts Building; (5) Old Court House; (6) U.S. Post Office Building; (7) peristyles and reflecting pools; (8) pergolas; (9) grassy knoll north; (10) grassy knoll south; (11) triple underpass; (12) position of Abraham Zapruder; (13) Stemmons Freeway sign; (14) approximate location of curbstone hit; (15) position of James T. Tague; (16) stockade fences; (17) parking lots.

Lyndon Baines Johnson, flanked by his wife, Lady Bird Johnson, and Jacqueline Kennedy, taking the presidential oath on Air Force One. (LBJ Library)

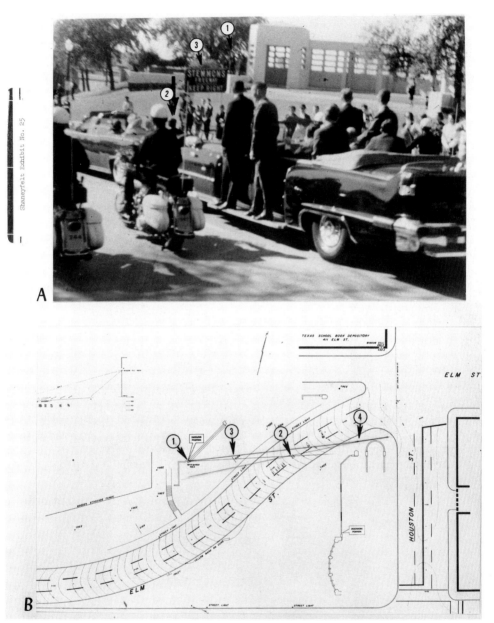

Shaneyfelt Exhibit 25, including Phil Willis's slide number 5 (top) and FBI map (bottom) inaccurately depicting Willis's location at the moment he took the photo. (National Archives)

Enlarged detail of Zapruder frame 202 depicting Phil Willis beginning to lower his camera immediately after taking his slide number 5.

John W. Altgens's photograph of President Kennedy's motorcade showing the wounded president reaching for his throat. (AP/Wide World Photos)

Alleged assassin Lee Harvey Oswald in police custody.
(AP/Wide World Photos)

FBI photograph (by Robert Richter) of
Billy Nolan Lovelady posing before the
Texas School Book Depository.
(Harold Weisberg Archives)

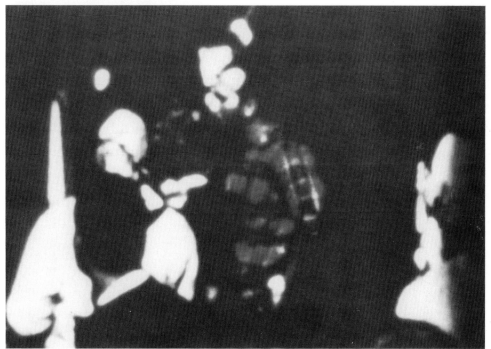

John Martin's photograph of Billy Nolan Lovelady, the alleged "man in the doorway"
of John Altgens's photograph.

Unidentified man hanging curtain rods in Oswald's room at Oswald's boardinghouse, Saturday morning, November 23, 1963.
(Black Star/Harold Weisberg Archives)

Commission Exhibit 399: the magic bullet that allegedly made seven wounds, smashed two bones, left metallic fragments in JFK's neck and Connally's chest, wrist, and thigh, and was subsequently recovered at Parkland Memorial Hospital in nearly pristine condition. (National Archives)

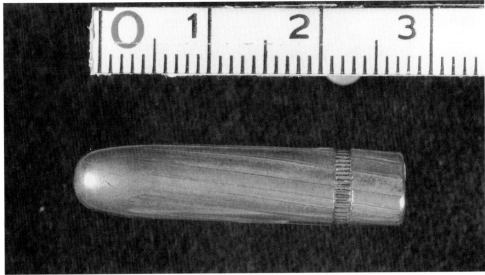

FBI director J. Edgar Hoover. (LBJ Library)

Deputy Attorney General Nicholas Katzenbach.
(LBJ Library)

Warren Commission member Senator Richard Russell.
(LBJ Library)

Warren Commission member Senator John Sherman Cooper and President Lyndon Baines Johnson. (LBJ Library)

FMS Form 197-A
Department of The Treasury

Voucher No. _____
Schedule No. _____
Claim No. _____

VOUCHER FOR PAYMENT
WHERE A SETTLEMENT AGREEMENT HAS BEEN EXECUTED AND ATTACHED OR WHERE A FINAL JUDGEMENT IS ATTACHED

A. PAYMENT DATA: *(PLEASE TYPE OR PRINT CLEARLY)*

(1) Submitting Agency/Office: Department of Justice

(2) Agency/Office Mailing Address: 1100 L St., N.W., Rm. 11034, Washington, D.C. 20530   Attn: Kirk Manhardt   Tel#: 202-514-4325

PAID BY
(For use by Treasury only)

3) Payee(s):   LMH Company, c/o Skadden , Arps, Slate, Meagher &

(4) Taxpayer Identification Number, SSN, or EIN: ████████

(5) Total Amount: Sixteen Million Dollars & 00/100 $16,000,000.00

(6) Electronic Funds Transfer (EFT) Information:

    (a) Payee Account Name: ████████   Bank Name & Address: ████████

    (b) ABA Bank # (9 digits): ████████

    (c) Payee Account #: ████████

    (d) Checking ████████   Savings _____

(7) Briefly Identify Claim: .

B. Agency Approving Official:

This Claim has been fully examined in accordance with Statutory Cite _____ and approved in the amount of

Signed: *[signature]*

Title: Director, Commercial Litigation Branch

Date: August 13, 1999

C. OTHER ACCOUNTING INFORMATION & CERTIFICATION

(For use by Treasury only)

DEPARTMENT OF THE TREASURY
Financial Management Service

FMS Form 197-A

December 1996

Federal payment voucher for the government's purchase of the original Zapruder film. (National Archives)

Jay Watson of WFAA-TV interviewing Abraham Zapruder on the afternoon of November 22, 1963. (Sixth Floor Museum at Dealey Plaza)

A Student, a Scholar, and the Zapruder Film

Gerard A. Selby Jr. and Harold Weisberg versus Henry G. Zapruder et al.

At Gettysburg, Abraham Lincoln spoke of America as a plighted experiment of mankind to see if democracy as the principle of a nation would work in a world of corrupt nations. Not even he could imagine that the decay of his nation's ideal would one day include a critical federal agency turning over to the exclusive control of a wealthy private corporation the basic evidence refuting a presidential commission's official findings on the assassination of the chief executive. Nor would he have been able to imagine that powerful media conglomerates, the nation's intelligentsia, the Congress, the executive branch, and federal and local investigative agencies would not only concur in that decision but also look askance at efforts to rectify the unhappy condition.

Until 1988 a federally defined barrier blocked citizens and scholars who attempted to gain access to the Zapruder film. They met consistent difficulties that thwarted their inquiries, such as having to pay out much money to pursue their interests.

In the early autumn of 1988, two private citizens joined in an attempt to gain access to the film. Gerard "Chip" Selby Jr., a graduate student engaged in completing a documentary video movie on the single-bullet theory, allied with the septuagenarian scholar Harold Weisberg. Together they filed a suit before Judge Thomas Penfield Jackson in the United States District Court for the District of Columbia seeking access to the Zapruder film, Selby to complete his master's thesis, Weisberg to pursue his private studies on the assassination. Attorney James H. Lesar of Washington, D.C., represented them in *Gerard Alexander Selby, Jr., and Harold Weisberg, plaintiffs, v. Henry G. Zapruder and the LMH Company, defendants.*[1] At the time of the filing, an Associated Press story reported Lesar's deep concerns regarding the Zapruder film: "It's a historical event and it's far too important to American history to allow its use to be dictated by a copyright owner who has shown no sensitivity for the uses which scholars and writers want to make of it."[2]

Chip Selby was a graduate student at the University of Maryland, College Park campus, located on the eastern border of the District of Columbia, working toward a master of arts degree in the Department of Communication Arts and Theatre. In April 1985, he elected to pursue the production thesis option for his degree by producing a videotape documentary on President John F. Kennedy's assassination. Through his studies and consultations with authorities, including Harold Weisberg, who lived in nearby Frederick, Maryland, he concluded that the single-bullet theory would be an excellent choice for a documentary. This was proposed by the Warren Commission to explain the fact that a single undamaged bullet without a visible scratch on it had inflicted the two nonfatal wounds on John F. Kennedy and all five nonfatal wounds on John Connally and smashed bones in his chest and wrist. If a single bullet did not inflict all those wounds and damages, then at least one other rifle and rifleman must have caused them. This would prove there was a conspiracy and would collapse the basis upon which the Commission's findings rested. The Zapruder film is an indispensable part of this evidence. Without it, one cannot properly study and fully understand the murder of JFK.

The same month Selby decided to create a documentary, he contacted the law offices of Henry Zapruder, in Washington, D.C., for permission to use the critically important film. A tax attorney, Henry Zapruder was the son of Abraham and acted as the agent for the LMH Company, which now held the copyright to and ownership of the Zapruder film, following Time Inc.'s reversion of both to Lillian Zapruder and her children, Myrna Faith Hauser and Henry.

Zapruder's secretary, Anita Dove, would not answer Selby's request.[3] She advised him to write to Zapruder, setting forth what he intended to do with his documentary. Selby did so at least three times, but Zapruder did not reply.[4]

Selby continued to work actively on his project, doing research, writing scripts, tracking down elusive historical film, arranging interviews, scheduling studio time, and performing the myriad details of putting together his first documentary. He had located a number of experts and reputable authorities whom he interviewed, including Colonel Joseph Dolce, a U.S. Army surgeon and one of the nation's foremost ballistics experts.[5] The Warren Commission staff had discovered in private sessions with him that he vigorously disagreed with the single-bullet theory based on his extensive medical and ballistic knowledge and unique experience in the field. Once he made this clear, the Commission broke off contact with him and did not call him to testify. Selby's interview with Dolce was devastating to the single-bullet speculation of the Commission. In addition, Selby constantly checked his script and findings with researchers for accuracy.

By March 1988, Selby had completed a first draft of his videotape documentary, which he entitled *Reasonable Doubt*. The draft included "substantial" use of the Zapruder film. Unfortunately, he faced both academic and professional imperatives. He had to complete the documentary in order to graduate and afterward to be able to find employment. He had located possible sources for a sale of his movie that would both alleviate his economic difficulties and establish his professional credentials, but these arrangements turned on using the Zapruder film. But after three years of repeatedly requesting permission from Henry Zapruder, Selby still had not been given either a reply or permission. Financial help would come from commercial channels. The Discovery Channel and the Arts and Entertainment Network both expressed a desire to obtain the air rights for a showing of Selby's film in November 1988.

Finally, on June 29, 1988, Zapruder telephoned Selby to inform him that LMH's standard charge for worldwide TV distribution was $30,000.[6] This was approximately the same price LMH would later charge the seasoned director Oliver Stone for use of the film in the motion picture *JFK*. According to some sources, Stone paid between $40,000 and $80,000 for use of the film.[7] Selby replied, stating that the price was an impossible sum for him to raise because he had already gone into debt by $18,000 in making the documentary. He told Zapruder he could sell the documentary to the Discovery Channel for only $10,000 to $15,000. "However," wrote Lesar in explaining the dilemma to the court, "he offered Zapruder several possible payment plans, including giving him all the monies Selby earned from the videotape until the $30,000 was paid off and paying him $5,000 a year for six years, whether or not Selby made any money from the videotape."[8]

Zapruder refused these compromise offers, but he told Selby "that he would 'work something out' because he didn't want to close down Selby's project."[9] In the meantime, he was going on a week's vacation and would contact Selby when he returned. He did not. On July 14, the desperate Selby phoned Zapruder's office only to have his secretary, Dove, tell him Zapruder could not talk to him for two weeks and she had "no idea when

Zapruder would get back in touch with him." She then threatened to sue Selby if he used the film without permission and asked him to send yet another letter. On July 18, Selby sent the letter but got no response.

On September 2, Selby again telephoned Zapruder's office. Dove replied to his inquiry that they would get around to answering his July 18 letter "sometime" and that she and Zapruder had not decided on how much he might have to pay for the film rights. She confirmed the worldwide rights were $30,000 and a national onetime use was $15,000. Zapruder did not call Selby.

The Discovery Channel offered Selby $10,000 for a two-year contract to air the documentary, but it would require the rights to have been secured before airing. After the twenty-fifth anniversary date of November 22, 1988, the value of Selby's documentary would be "substantially reduced."

On October 13, CINE, the Council on International Non-theatrical Events Film and Video Festival, awarded Selby the Golden Eagle Award for *Reasonable Doubt*. The video would represent the United States for the next year in film and video festivals held throughout the world. But none of this would occur without permission from the LMH Company.

In 1988 the National Archives maintained the original Zapruder film, which LMH Company had placed on a type of deposit safekeeping. As described earlier, the original, 486 frames long, contains information not found on the copies. Abraham Zapruder's camera captured an image on all the film, including the area between the sprocket holes. But when the film is projected, this portion of the picture—about 22 percent of the total surface—cannot be seen. On about two-thirds of the frames, the sprocket matter had never been reproduced.

Harold Weisberg wanted to study the sprocket material. He developed a project that would use a professional photographer to photograph the film and make slides. Unfortunately, he could not gain access to the film to carry out his proposed filming for research.

When attorney Lesar discussed Weisberg's project with Henry Zapruder, he interposed no objection to the plans. On November 19, 1987, Lesar wrote the Archives on behalf of Weisberg, requesting slide copies of the frames with the sprocket material:

Mr. Weisberg seeks to have slides made which will capture the missing sprocket hole material. I am advised that this can be done without damaging the original film in any way. All that is required is that a photographer be allowed to bring a camera with a microphotographic lens to the Archives so he can photograph the original film frame by frame onto echtochrome film. This will require one day's time.

I believe this project is very much in the public interest. It will make possible scholarly study of this latent photographic evidence, and it will preserve this "lost" evidence for posterity.[10]

On December 4, Leslie C. Waffen of the National Archives responded to Lesar's request. A set of color slides of the 486 frames containing the images between the sprocket holes could be made for about $1,300. It would require between two and four months to complete the task. Then, he added the critical stricture: "In addition, you will need to obtain written permission from Mr. Henry G. Zapruder before the slide order can proceed."[11]

On January 21, 1988, Lesar wrote Zapruder, enclosing a copy of Waffen's letter and requesting a letter of release.[12] When Zapruder replied almost two months later, he remarked that he had no recollection of whether "you intend to use the requested material for commercial or noncommercial purposes." He requested a letter confirming the type of use it would be put to. If noncommercial, he would provide "a limited license (no license fee) together with authorization for the material."[13] Upon receipt of the letter, Lesar replied that Weisberg intends to use the "requested materials for noncommercial purposes."[14]

Lesar heard nothing more for a month. In April he telephoned Zapruder, asking for the status of the request. Zapruder informed him the letter would be sent "in a couple of days."[15] Two months later, with the letter still not received, Lesar again wrote to Zapruder, asking him to attend to the matter.[16] He received no further communication from Zapruder.

Selby and Weisberg sued for injunctive relief, that is, they asked the court to step in and order the copies of film released to them for their various projects. Their complaint contained four causes of action: the first drove to the heart of the Copyright Act, fair use; the second claim alleged the film's copyright violated the Constitution; the third alleged Zapruder had abandoned the copyright; and the fourth alleged violation of the copyright notice requirement.

On the first claim Lesar argued that Selby and Weisberg sought to use the film in a manner that constitutes "fair use" under the Copyright Act, 17 United Sates Code, paragraph 107. In this he also cited *Geis*, the decision in the Josiah Thompson case discussed in the previous chapter. On the second claim Lesar argued that "the Copyright Act, insofar as it applies to the Zapruder film, violates the First Amendment of the United States Constitution." On the third claim Lesar held that the copyright had been abandoned. His evidence began with Life's seemingly irregular copyrighting procedures. On May 15, 1967, Life registered the film in the Copyright Office as an unpublished "motion picture other than a photo play" under the Copyright Act. In three issues of the magazine prior to that date, it had been registered as "periodicals" under the Copyright Act. In the Life Memorial Edition the copyright had been to "a book" under the Copyright Act.

He argued that in March 1975 the ABC-TV show Goodnight, America, hosted by Geraldo Rivera, showed the Zapruder film without permission, and that Robert Groden and Peter Model's book JFK: The Case for Conspiracy (1976) used twenty-two frames of the Zapruder film.[17] That book remained on the best-seller list for several weeks, but LMH brought no suit for copyright infringement, nor did it make any demand for payment. Further reinforcing his claim, Lesar noted that a number of television stations had shown the film without paying any copyright royalties to LMH. The film was also widely available in unauthorized sales and from bootleg copies; the copies were being sold without notice of copyright. From these facts Lesar concluded that LMH's failure to enforce its copyright constituted abandonment of the copyright, with the consequence that the film was in the public domain.

On the fourth claim Lesar pointed out that LMH Company was required to have affixed to all copies the copyright notice "Copyright © 1967 by LMH Company, All rights reserved." Failure to do so was a violation of the notice provisions of the Copyright Act, Section 19. If the year contained in the notice is more than one year later than the actual year of first publication or year the copyright was obtained, the work is considered to have been published without any notice and to have entered the public domain. Life published it in 1963, but LMH's notice is from 1967.

In addition to the four claims, Lesar put forward the allegation that Selby would suffer irreparable harm in two ways. First, he would be hurt financially and unable to pay off his school debts and the cost of the film. Added to financial damage was his inability to present to the public his views on the Kennedy assassination. On the other hand, Lesar maintained, LMH Company would not be substantially hurt by Selby's use of the film for a very good reason. Since Selby could not pay the fees without the sale of the documentary to the commercial channels, and those sales could occur without the Zapruder film use, there is no possibility of LMH obtaining fees and hence no possibility of harm done to it.

Finally, Lesar argued that there is an overriding public interest in the fullest possible disclosure of information on the JFK assassination that requires the two men he represented to have access to the film in a timely and reasonable manner. He then concluded with a sentence directed at the heart of the question: "At issue in this case is whether one man acting for the alleged copyright owner of perhaps the most vital piece of documentary evidence in the history of the United States is to be allowed to use the Copyright Act to dictate what ideas and information the public may receive concerning the President's assassination and what evidence scholars and researchers may study."[18]

In the end, Selby and Weisberg did not have to go to trial. The case was settled out of court. The terms of the settlement are not known because the conditions of settlement imposed by LMH required silence by all parties, but we do know that Selby's documentary appeared in November and contained portions of the Zapruder film.[19] The documentary, which won a Golden Eagle award, is a solid work that demonstrates the Warren Commission's single-bullet theory is not sustained by objective examination of the official evidence. Weisberg had made arrangements before the trial to have a film expert make slides of the sprocket material in the event he was successful. As of 1998, the sprocket matter had not been photographed.

David Margolick, a *New York Times* reporter whose column, "At the Bar," reported on the case, interviewed Henry Zapruder and his mother, Lillian. "Mr. Zapruder said he charged only commercial interests, not scholars, for the use of the film. Mr. Selby and Mr. Weisberg, he said in an interview, just fell between the cracks. Neither he nor his mother, Lillian, will say how much their family has made from the film, except to insist it could have been far more. 'I think we've been pretty good about it,' Mrs. Zapruder said. 'We could have made copies and peddled it on street corners. Someone else would have made millions on it.' "[20]

The Selby-Weisberg suit was an unprecedented attempt to argue that under certain circumstances the Copyright Act is an unconstitutional infringement of freedom of speech. This exceptional dimension of the suit, in theory, made it a case that had the potential to go all the way to the Supreme Court to find resolution. That theoretical element gave the plaintiffs considerable bargaining power because it raised the stakes and would require

LMH to spend a good deal of money on attorney's fees. Offsetting that considerable leverage, however, was the fact that the financially strapped film producer Selby urgently needed rights to the film.

Considerably strengthening the theoretical considerations of the case came the analysis on the very issue of copyright subservient to critical social issues embraced by the First Amendment from one of the nation's "most powerful lawyers," Melville Nimmer of UCLA Law School. Best known for his multivolume treatise *Nimmer on Copyright*, in the last year of his long and influential legal career he published *Nimmer on Freedom of Speech* (1984).[21] In the words of his student Rodney Smolla, author of a 1992 supplement,

> Professor Nimmer recognized that in some cases—rare though they may be—ideas cannot be separated from their expression, and the importance of disseminating the expression itself may outweigh the copyright owner's interest in controlling the dissemination of that expression. In such cases, Professor Nimmer would have recognized a First Amendment right to disseminate copyrighted works without the authorization of the copyright owner, whether or not such dissemination would be allowed by the fair use doctrine alone. At the time the Treatise was published in 1984, Professor Nimmer had foreseen only one example of such a circumstance—the case of "news photographs." It has since become apparent, however, that there are other possible circumstances where ideas and their expression may be inseparable, and where the importance of disseminating the expression will outweigh the importance of protecting the copyright owner's exclusive right to do so.[22]

In his 1984 treatise Professor Nimmer used the Zapruder film as one of his two illustrations of "news photographs."[23] He wrote, "In the welter of conflicting versions of what happened that tragic day in Dallas, the Zapruder film gave the public authoritative answers that it desperately sought; answers that no other source could supply with equal credibility. Again, it was only the expression, not the ideas alone, that could adequately serve the needs of the enlightened democratic dialogue."[24] He further observed that "in the emerging constitutional limitations on copyright contained in the First Amendment . . . the limitations of the First Amendment are imposed upon Congress itself. . . . The First Amendment privilege, when appropriate, may be invoked despite the fact that the marketability of the copied work is thereby impaired."[25]

Civil Action 88-3043 demonstrates two negative forces at work in American life. Foremost, perhaps, we see the hand of private and commercial control of the primary evidence in the assassination of President John F. Kennedy, an unconscionable factor manipulating our societal travail and critical need for dissemination of the facts it contains. It cost money, time, dedication to higher ends, and much energy for citizens to wage such an effort to obtain access. But the efforts by these two citizens also suggest how private control might dampen the desire of less dedicated scholars to study the Zapruder film and utilize the information it contains in addressing assassination issues.

The other inimical force revealed by the case flows quietly in the background. It is the silent acquiescence to the struggles of Selby and Weisberg by officials in government and federal agencies. These officials are decent men and women with high educational and professional accomplishments, with responsibilities to the nation and to their own integrity, but they were content to permit the key evidence in President Kennedy's murder to be controlled in this rough and arrogant but effective manner. These are men and women who would not lift a finger in defense of citizen-scholar inquiries.

IV

Theorists
and the
Zapruder
Film

Prisoners of Preconception
Conspiracy Theorists, Warren Commission Defenders, and the Zapruder Film

Since November 29, 1963, when *Life* magazine published the first thirty-one black-and-white pictures from the Zapruder film, a number of responsible critics of the official conclusions on the assassination have diligently studied the film and frames, adding to their discoveries of important information as they gained more access to the film. With unflagging energy and a dedication to public ends reminiscent of the idealism found in generations from our formative eras as a nation, they seek to show how the evidentiary matter captured on the suppressed film challenges the official conclusions in the Warren Commission Report. The film's clear and unassailable factual ground, they have demonstrated, refutes the official assertion that Lee Harvey Oswald alone and unaided killed President John F. Kennedy.

The findings of these critics have consistently met fierce rebuffs from an array of institutions, including the media, an often hostile Congress, and academia. Despite such obstacles, they met with some limited success in the field of federal lawsuits. Their most unusual foe in such venues, however, came from neither government nor media nor colleges but from assassination researchers—both conspiracy theorists and Commission defenders—who have consistently misrepresented the Zapruder film. These individuals have sown confusion in the public mind and, as a result of shoddy scholarship and highly speculative accounts, have seriously undermined respect for proper objective dissent from the official findings.

The peculiar nature of the complex Kennedy assassination controversy has forced responsible critics to split their energies and resources into two campaign fronts. One long battle continued against the reluctance of institutional forces upholding the Oswald solution to the murder to inquire into the evidentiary matter captured on the film. The other campaign pitched critics against a dizzying cast of wild speculators in confrontations often as vigorously fought and fiercely conducted as the main engagement.

Viewers of the Zapruder film tend to fall into one of three fundamental types. The first category of viewers includes the scholar-critics who, as just mentioned, objectively study the film. Another group of viewers treat the 486 frames as merely part of the kaleidoscope of events surrounding President Kennedy's death and burial, a riveting and powerful cinematic icon rather than a crucial and incontrovertible piece of evidence in the murder of a head of state.

In addition to the responsible critics and passive viewers of the film there are two sets of theorists—conspiracy advocates and Commission defenders—neither of which adheres to the accepted norms and standards of scholarship nor, for that matter, to the factual records of the case. They are notorious for seeing things in the film that are not there and for not seeing things that are. Ungrounded conjecture flows rapidly and easily from these individuals' pens and computers, and humility often seems to be a stranger to their character. Unfortunately, the press, the public, and officialdom too frequently group all who criticize the official findings into a common category, applying the opprobrious label of conspiracy theorists to all who question government truth, the good, the bad, and the indifferent. Conspiracy advocates run the gamut from the well-meaning to the plausibly paranoid. Commission defenders, on the other hand, include the members and staff of the Warren Commission, the House Select Committee, personnel associated with several other federal inquiries, as well as a number of private authors—all committed to the government's official findings in this case. Since the belief that Lee Harvey Oswald was the assassin is actually only a theory, Commission defenders are—just like conspiracy advocates—theorists.

Beginning in the 1970s, conspiracy theorist Robert Groden vigorously pursued the Zapruder film as the Rosetta stone for solving the assassination mystery. He spoke hundreds of times on the film, usually projecting it once for his audience and then showing it again at reduced speed while commenting on the unfolding scenes. Among his several observations, he claimed to see in frame 413 the head of a man with a rifle in the bushes. Zapruder captured this alleged figure as he swung his camera to his right to film across the corner of the heavily wooded stockade fence area as he traced the receding presidential limousine.[1]

Groden's "bushman" assassin is an excellent instance of a theorist seeing things on the film that are not there and then promoting "his" discovery in lectures and books.[2] But even a quick look at the alleged figure shows Groden's claim to be an illusion based on false initial premises. His assassin possessed an unusual quality for a killer. He chose to stand in plain view in front of the masking trees on the grassy knoll rather than hiding behind them. In any case, a 1977 study by reputable and reliable photographic experts demonstrated that the alleged head was a pattern of foliage, with the rifle barrel actually a twig, and the rifle stock merely an irregular opening in the foliage.[3]

Groden's years of pushing his bushman on the public had given him a high public profile. But the Select Committee's destruction of the bushman explanation had importance beyond the mere fact, for it used the episode to proclaim by inference (an unwarranted inference, to be sure, but one held by much of the public and the media and almost all federal politicians) that all dissenters from the official findings and all students of the Zapruder film share a common bond in irrational proclivities and puerile understanding. Groden thus inadvertently damaged the credibility of all dissenters, especially the scholar-critics who sought to lay a solid base in fact and objectivity for rejecting the federal conclusions on the murder of President John F. Kennedy.

"The man with an umbrella" episode provides another telling example. On the Zapruder film a man with the top of an open umbrella appears in the lower right-hand corner near the Stemmons Freeway sign. He can be seen at about the time the street sign blocked most of JFK's limousine from Zapruder's camera. At frame 213 one begins to see a portion of an open umbrella near the sign, which is seen fully in frame 221 and remains until it slides from view in 230. The figure became known to conspiracy theorist Robert Cutler as The Umbrella Man (TUM) and quickly acquired in the land of theorists a kingdom of its own. Under Cutler's elaboration in two separate books, TUM was part of the assassination plot, a signalman in one version and an actual assassin in another.[4]

In the first version, TUM moved the umbrella as a sign to the waiting assassins behind the grassy knoll and to the president's rear that everything was in order and that they should fire. In the other form, the man actually had a barrel to hold a fléchette built into one of the umbrella staves, with a trigger formed into the handle. According to this far-fetched scenario, TUM inflicted one of the wounds on JFK.[5]

I address the charge first with logic, then with facts. TUM theory is innately irrational, and Mr. Cutler fell into the web spun of his own theory. Let us consider the assertion that TUM was flagman on a hit team. No group of assassins would need a "flag" to signal the time to fire. Assassins could see well enough to shoot accurately. Opportunity and accuracy were needed, but they were not dependent on a designated signal; the latter would conceivably only have been necessary to call off the attack.

There are other problems as well. In addition to an illogical base, factual problems make TUM as a gunman impossible. How does one aim a miniature fléchette hidden in an umbrella and at right angles to the target without a sight? It is hard enough to sight a regular rifle, but this unwieldy, strange mechanism would not have been workable, especially in the gusty wind that blew that day. These mechanical difficulties are not taken into account by the theory.

Also, how does one rule out the several other umbrellas seen on Dealey Plaza that day? It had been raining in Dallas that morning, and several persons still carried them to watch the motorcade. Another one visible on the film, on the south side of Elm Street, was closed and actually pointed toward the limousine. Why is this or another umbrella not considered a potential lethal weapon? On what grounds select one over the others?

Federal officials have rarely had an opportunity to destroy a conspiracy theory down to its last allegedly factual detail. More seldom yet have they had an opportunity to do so on national television. Yet the umbrella man offered them an occasion to do just that. In 1978, on nationwide television, the House Select Committee on Assassinations provided devastating evidence that destroyed the theory.[6] It produced the man who held the umbrella that day, as reported to the committee earlier by the *Dallas Morning News*. He testified and explained why he stood there on the curb of Elm Street with his umbrella on November 22, 1963. He told the committee he had gone to Dealey Plaza with the umbrella to make a political statement. He would open it as JFK passed by, hoping this would embarrass President Kennedy by reminding him of his father's support of pre–World War II policies symbolized by British prime minister Chamberlain's umbrella. He explained, "The umbrella that the Prime Minister of England came back with got to be a symbol in some manner with the British people. By association, it got transferred to the Kennedy family."[7]

Unfortunately, by pointing out the inherent irrationality in this one conspiracy theory, the House committee tarred all critics of the Warren Commission with the same brush. Other explanations were guilty by association. If one conspiracy theory is irrational, then all those who question the official findings are likewise irrational.

As the committee's chairman, Louis Stokes, solemnly commented for the television audience after the committee had thoroughly thrashed TUM, "I would just like to say what is probably equally tragic with the event which occurred on that date has been the rumors and theories which have grown up around such a tragic event in our history. . . . Indeed, over the years many people have profited in continuing to form rumors around one of the most tragic events in our history."[8] Thus The Umbrella Man concoction became an unwitting and very convenient instrument for the forces seeking to repress legitimate criticism of the assassination investigation by diverting attention from the grim facts to the bizarre and equating the bizarre with all criticism of the Commission.

Sometime in the late 1960s, probably 1968, critics obtained bootleg copies of the Zapruder film. They added a sound track taken from contemporary radio coverage of November 25, using a tape of Dallas KRLD's Dan Rather's narration of the images he had just seen.[9] In describing the fatal head shot of JFK at frame 313, Rather says, "you can see" under the impact of the shot the president's head going forward "at considerable speed." His account supports the explanation of a rear shot and affirms a central component of the Warren Commission's conclusion of a sole assassin firing from behind.

In fact, however, the president's head moves slightly forward at frame 312 and then, at frame 313, snaps violently *backward*, not *forward*. The backward snap is in obedience, apparently, to the law of physics, showing the reaction to an impact of a bullet striking the president's head from the front. This overlay of a reporter's voice upon the Zapruder film reinforces the argument in quarters dissenting from the official scenario of the assassination that the nation's media lied to the American people about the facts of the murder.

It is difficult to know how many people saw and heard this voice overlay copy of Zapruder's film; perhaps hundreds of thousands of college students and the general public would be a conservative guess. It appeared in odd places. On the public spaces outside the 1972 Republican National Convention in Florida, foes of the Warren Commission set up a screen and "under all kinds of weird circumstances" showed the film repeatedly to those from the large crowd of civil rights, antiwar, and feminist protesters there to demonstrate to whomever would pass near the canvas.[10]

In his memoirs Rather offers an explanation. He states that early in the morning on November 23, 1963, he and many other reporters viewed the twenty-six-second film in a small room at Zapruder's office. For lack of enough seats, Rather had to stand during the screening, and taking notes was not permitted. An attorney was present, and bids were taken. After viewing the film, Rather ran the several blocks to the KRLD station and narrated over the air what he had just seen. "I described the forward motion of his head," Rather later wrote. "I failed to mention the violent, backward reaction."[11] It was "a major omission. But certainly not deliberate." He then added to his narrative, "I challenge anyone to watch for the first time a twenty-two-second [sic] film of devastating impact, run several blocks, then describe what they had seen in its entirety, without notes."[12]

Most of the factual elements in Rather's account are wrong. The gathering in Zapruder's office was not at all like he described; there was no bidding, and no attorney was present. Stolley, who purchased the film, and Schwartz, Zapruder's partner, said only print folks were present. Rather seems to have linked the actual sale of the film on Monday with the sale of the print rights on Saturday, but obviously with no firsthand knowledge of either event. Other errors of fact, such as the assertion that Rather's KRLD CBS affiliate arranged for the development of the film when it was the ABC affiliate WFAA, leave one puzzled. Neither Stolley nor Zapruder had a copy of the film to show on Monday, for the original and one copy had gone on to Chicago on Saturday, and both of the Secret Service copies were in Washington. More to the point, though, as discussed previously, the KRLD tapes are conclusive proof that Rather actually broadcast the narration of the film he had just seen around 4:00 P.M. on Monday, November 25, not on November 23, and he did not run from the attorney's office to the studio. However, which copy of the film he saw is unclear. Based on the documentary record, it was certainly not the original, and by the chain of possession it could not have been any of the three Jamieson duplicates. Since Rather's book was a collaboration with Mickey Herskowitz, one can infer that perhaps his coauthor hastily drew up that account and Rather, an exceptionally busy man, simply did not have time to verify its accuracy.

When one carefully views the Zapruder film, one notices that it shows camera movement, manifested as a jiggle or a blur, at important points. Federal investigators ignored these jiggles, which seem to correspond to Zapruder's emotional and physical reaction while filming and to his hearing shots and seeing something unusual that caused him to jar his camera slightly. The first discussion of this unusual phenomenon appeared in 1965 in Harold Weisberg's *Whitewash*;[13] the next year he amplified it in *Whitewash II*.[14] "Zapruder," noted Weisberg, "saw something that affected him emotionally and made his camera vibrate intermittently beginning about Frame 190."[15]

When, in July 1964, the Commission called Zapruder to federal offices in Dallas to testify, he remarked on this aspect of his film.[16] The FBI was aware of it, for on the witness stand before the Commission its photographic expert, Special Agent Lyndal Shaneyfelt, grudgingly acknowledged a disturbance of some type was manifested there.[17] In those days of student activism, *Whitewash II* had wide circulation at some colleges. At the University of California at Berkeley, near San Francisco, students who had read Weisberg's account asked the noted physicist on campus, Nobel laureate Luis Alvarez, about the jiggle.[18]

Alvarez thereupon conducted a severely flawed study of the film and published it as if the inspiration was sui generis, for which he received admiring kudos from important people who, like him, possessed no special knowledge of the subject.[19] Unbeknownst to most readers of the article and those who cite it, the government paid Alvarez's costs.[20] Why those who utilized his study and promoted his findings did not also refer to it as a federal project is puzzling, for it violates the standard academic protocol of acknowledging one's intellectual and financial supporters. Indeed, Alvarez's relationship with the federal government was a long-standing one. Years earlier, the physicist had supported federal policies when he testified against J. Robert Oppenheimer during that scientist's censure.[21] The House Select Committee on Assassinations examined portions of Alvarez's JFK study.[22]

Alvarez claims science and physics as his guides in studying the film, yet he accepts without comment or blush nonscientific premises that strongly reduce the merit of his study. For example, he uncritically accepted the findings of the Warren Commission that Oswald alone shot JFK. He claimed to have replicated with a rear shot the backward snap of JFK's head, visible starting with frame 313. He fired shots of the same type of ammunition as Oswald allegedly used, case-hardened jacketed military rounds, at a melon on a post. This "scientific" test supposedly demonstrated that a melon shot from the rear pitches backward—just the way JFK's head reacted starting with frame 313 (according to the Warren Commission). Consequently, no shot from the front was required to force

Kennedy's head backward. And, with no shot from the front, the argument for conspiracy is virtually eliminated. Thus, Alvarez affirms the Warren Commission's findings.

Sadly, Alvarez's "study" is shoddy science, using an analogy that is contrived and silently forced upon the reader. Alvarez's melon rested on a stable fence post. Unlike JFK's head, it lacked vertebrae and a backbone, and in other ways was not linked to any significant characteristics associated with the human body. The human head, of course, also does not have the same density and other features of a melon.

Further complicating his experiment is the fact that he fired a military hardened bullet at the melon. But, contrary to the Commission's findings, the bullet that exploded in JFK's head left numerous tiny fragments of metal that could not have been the result of military hardened ammunition, which is designed not to fragment and whose use was established by the Geneva Convention of 1926. The head shot bullet actually disintegrated upon impact. Thus, Alvarez used the wrong bullets in his experiment, succeeding only in leading the American public further astray in its attempt to better understand (if not definitively solve) the Kennedy assassination.[23]

If the Central Intelligence Agency had not acquired a copy of the Zapruder film and used it to investigate the assassination of President Kennedy, most Americans would probably have considered it to be an unusual dereliction of its dimly perceived duties. This secretive organization, with its private ways, covert political agendas, and lavish funding, leads a life more or less apart from political and public knowledge, leaving many Americans suspicious of its hidden agendas and operations. What we do know about the agency's use of the Zapruder film comes to us largely indirectly, as the result of the fallout either from stumbling onto it in some other agency's records or from some unrelated activity of the CIA. Three instances of the CIA link to the Zapruder film appear in the documentary record and provide fragmentary glimpses of its use.

For example, on December 4, 1964, J. Edgar Hoover, director of the FBI, wrote J. Lee Rankin, general counsel of the Warren Commission, to state that the FBI would make a copy of its Zapruder film copy available to the CIA on a loan basis "solely for training purposes."[24] One of the policemen from Montgomery County, Maryland, who attended the training sessions later remarked on his experiences to critics.[25] One can only speculate what "training" meant, although this revelation did generate a few documents released to critics.[26]

Another CIA link surfaced in the early 1970s during an investigation of the agency headed by Vice President Nelson Rockefeller and directed by former Warren Commission staff attorney David Belin.[27] In the course of its investigation, this Rockefeller Commission acquired a few pages of CIA material relating to the JFK assassination, which Belin buried in the files and did not mention in the published report.[28]

The papers included "briefing boards" made by the CIA's National Photographic Intelligence Center (NPIC) in Washington, which had examined the Zapruder film to ascertain when and how many shots had been fired.[29] This "finest photographic laboratory in the world"[30] concluded in two of the tabulations on the boards that shots were fired at times and points incompatible with the official findings.[31]

Within two days of the assassination, the CIA had made its first study of the film[32] based on an examination of Life's published copies of the Zapruder frames (which also means the agency did not yet have a copy of the movie). One column in the tally sheet cites a shot that occurred at frame 190; other possibilities were frames 213 and 206, with twenty-nine to thirty-six frames between shots. These results glaringly clash with the findings of the official investigation into the assassination of President Kennedy. The President's Commission on Kennedy's assassination concluded that the lone assassin Oswald could not physically have fired a shot before frame 210 and that a minimum of forty-two frames was required between his shots. If a shot occurred earlier or faster, Oswald could not have fired it.

The CIA studies demonstrated Oswald could not have fired all the shots, and that more than one rifleman was involved in the murder. Perhaps this finding explains why Belin, who for years in speeches and writings vigorously defended the Warren Commission conclusions as perfectly sound and unquestionable by reasonable individuals, buried the releases in the files of the Rockefeller Commission rather than place the results in the final report.[33]

The scanty documentation leaves important questions unanswered. Why would such a significant federal agency have studied this important matter and then not have reported its crucial, indeed imperative, findings to the Commission and the president? Who ordered it to do the tests? Why would not the Warren Commission have independently requested the NPIC to study the film? Did the CIA withhold its information from the Warren Commission?

In 1977 the CIA released "Batch D" of its records relating to the JFK assassination. Included within its six-inch-thick pile of documents on legal-sized paper was one covering the European activities of a Frenchman who gave his name as Herve Lamarre. In the 1960s, Lamarre was lecturing in Western Europe on the assassination of JFK and showing the Zapruder film.

Lamarre had a history connected with the 1967–1968 inquiry into the murder conducted by Jim Garrison, the New Orleans district attorney. He had appeared in New Orleans during the trial and had later mailed Garrison a copy of a book manuscript on the assassination written on yellow legal paper, later published in Europe as *Farewell America*.[34] The book was a conspiracy theorist's dream work that mixed oil barons, rich industrialists, and disaffected rogue CIA men into a conspiracy to murder the liberal JFK, whose oil policies, thrust toward peace, and social improvement programs were anathema to the prejudices and a threat to the purses of the cabal members.

Farewell America not only fails as a serious book but does so in spectacular ways. Only two of its pages dealt with the alleged facts of the assassination, and most of those facts are demonstrably false. Most of the book was perfectly designed to appeal to Garrison's self-destructive predilections and prejudices in an apparent effort to either sidetrack or wreck his investigation. The volume was fake, a type of black book; nothing like what it describes happened. Lamarre worked for French intelligence and may have composed the book as a favor for the CIA, a type of clandestine reciprocity. Lamarre also possessed an excellent copy of the Zapruder film,[35] which he used in his European lectures on the assassination.

Perhaps, like the CIA, he sought to direct the public's mind away from the evidentiary reality of the assassination and hook it onto extravagant and enticing conspiracy theories, which could then be easily discredited and thus bolster the arguments of the Warren Commission's defenders, who seemed ever eager to embrace an erroneously conceived theory.

Consider the Thorburn reaction, for example. As President Kennedy appeared from behind the Stemmons Freeway sign, the Zapruder film depicts his arms akimbo and his hands moving to his throat. To some critics this striking feature suggested a frontal shot to the throat, clashing fiercely with the official findings that Lee Harvey Oswald fired all three alleged shots in the assassination from his perch in the easternmost window of the School Book Depository's sixth floor, to the rear of JFK. Among the defenders of the Warren Commission who rejected this supposition of a frontal shot was Dr. John K. Lattimer.

After a study of the Zapruder film, Lattimer claimed to have discovered in JFK's reactions at frames 225–311 conclusive evidence of a physical reaction to the impact of the first shot hitting the president from the rear. As he wrote in an illustrated volume, when the bullet entered JFK at the back of his neck and transited the throat, it brushed the spinal cord, leaving bone chips and causing the arms' involuntary physical reaction.[36] He classified JFK's distinctive arm movement as a Thorburn reaction, after the alleged description of it in an 1889 article by Dr. William Thorburn, "Cases of Damages to the Cervical Region of the Spinal Cord."[37] As President Kennedy emerges from behind the Stemmons Freeway sign, Lattimer argues, he raises "his arms coming from behind the sign to an involuntary physical response caused by the shock to the spine."[38]

Medical evidence, visual examination of the film, and ballistic facts definitively rebut Lattimer's claim. In the first place, he lacked credentials in forensic pathology, which impeded his study and misled his observations. According to authorities associated with the House Select Committee's inquiry, he had "no training, experience, or expertise whatsoever in forensic pathology."[39] He confined his private medical practice to urology.[40] In addition to his lack of relevant medical expertise, his opinion was compromised by political ideology. His dedicated efforts on behalf of proponents of the Warren Commission's findings appeared to be colored by extreme right-wing political views. To individuals like himself, the Commission's depiction of Oswald as a communist, a Soviet traveler, and a malcontent fit perfectly their clouded vision of Cold War villainy.[41]

Unfortunately, Lattimer, either misreading or ignoring the official evidence, merely accepted the Commission's portrait of Oswald as a Red. In his text and footnotes the doctor gives no indication he was even remotely aware of the material or of a generation of work on the background of the alleged assassin that would have suggested otherwise. In actuality, Oswald was an Orwellian in political philosophy and was both loyal to the United States and anti-Communist. No credible evidence, the Commission's views notwithstanding, connects him to the assassination.[42] Lattimer, however, eagerly embraced the official report because it confirmed his worldview.

Medical specialists with expertise in forensic medicine dismiss the Lattimer assertion as untenable.[43] They point out that, among other things, the illustration Lattimer provides of the Thorburn reaction does not actually match the physical reaction experienced by JFK. In the Zapruder film JFK's arms are at the level of his throat, not flopped to his side with forearms raised up at shoulder level as in Thorburn's 1889 description. The hands that clasp JFK's throat are fisted and tight, not loose and to the side, as in the sketch of Thorburn. JFK's elbows are high at chin level and forward of the hunched upper body, not at shoulder level and relaxed as in the illustration. Moreover, in death, JFK's body did not assume the position depicted of the typical Thorburn reaction.

Lattimer's embarrassing effort as a purported forensic specialist suffers from the failure to apply simple common sense. Anyone who grew up in the rough-and-tumble of sports and games and play would fully recognize JFK's reaction is a normal response to a bad injury to the throat. Lattimer also commits a fundamental misreading of the evidence concerning the matter found in Kennedy's throat. It does not consist of bone chips. What he refers to, report prominent physicians and X-ray specialists William Carnes, Russell Fisher, Russell Morgan, and Alan Moritz in the "1968 Panel Review," are "metallic fragments."[44] That fact destroys the Commission's conclusions of a lone assassin. Oswald's only ammunition was a hardened copper-jacketed bullet recovered without damage or proven loss of lead— and this intact jacket did not bear upon its bright copper surface even a visible scratch. It left no metal in JFK's throat, which means that another bullet must have done so, and that another rifle and another person were involved. Such is the jerry-rigged argument of fierce government non-conspiracy theorist Dr. John K. Lattimer.

Equally important, the doctor's assertion that the shot came from the rear is without foundation in the evidentiary base. Every doctor and nurse in Parkland Hospital who saw the president's throat wound before it was allegedly destroyed by a tracheotomy—the only witnesses, and moreover, excellent, experienced doctors and nurses—said it was a frontal shot.[45] This is the only evidence, which Lattimer spurns for his sui generis and political accommodating conjecture.

Among the problematic facts confronting advocates of the Commission's single-bullet theory is that the hole in the back of JFK's jacket is too low for the official bullet to have made it and still transit the neck. That bullet continued on through the body, according to the official account, without striking bone or other hard matter, to exit at the level of the president's Adam's apple, and then in radically altered flight continued on to hit Governor Connally. But the hole in JFK's jacket is so low it makes such a highly convoluted path highly improbable and thus renders the single-bullet hypothesis untenable and the official investigation a failure.

To get around this evidence, Commission defenders explain the low hole as having been inflicted when JFK's jacket was bunched at the top, thus drawing the cloth up high. The bullet, then, while hitting high on the back at the neck region to accommodate the single-bullet requirements, penetrated at the bunch and could appear to leave a low hole when the jacket again lays flat. "Evidence" for this explanation is extremely weak, based largely on conjecture and promoted by Commission defenders like the "forensic specialist" John Lattimer and assassination researcher Edward Jay Epstein. In his book *Inquest* (1966), Epstein tried to explain the low hole by saying the cloth "must have" been bunched while the president was behind the sign, but he offers no proof, only conjecture designed to support the Commission's Report.[46]

Lattimer, for his part, wrote, "It was easier to see that the bullet hole in the coat or shirt might well be at a lower point on either garment when the garment was laid out flat, in comparison to its position at the actual moment of impact, when President Kennedy was indeed waving to the crowds, with his right elbow elevated, as seen in the Zapruder movie."[47] He then includes a *Dallas Time Herald* photograph taken when the limousine apparently was on Main Street, in which the jacket appears to be bunched.[48] The picture shows JFK's arm resting on the side of the car, with his hand raised in a wave. Lattimer concludes that since a single photograph shows JFK's jacket apparently bunched, it was also bunched two blocks later when he was behind the sign at frame 210. He ignores the many other photographs taken along the route that depict the jacket in a normal position, although they have equal validity for consideration.

But as JFK approached Elm Street, his arm in fact did not rest on the side of the limousine. The Polaroid photograph snapped by Jack Weaver just seconds before the Lincoln limousine turned onto Elm Street shows JFK with his arm raised and the jacket in a normal flat position.[49] Further, at frame 202, just after the first shot was actually fired, Phil Willis took a 35mm color slide of JFK. On the slide, less than half a second from the official first shot at frame 210, the coat is not bunched.[50] This is definitive; it is also ignored.

In addition, JFK wore a belt that tightly held his tailored shirt to keep it from bunching, and he was sitting on the tails. The hole in the shirt lies low and corresponds to the position of the hole in the jacket. Equally crucial, Secret Service agent Glenn Bennett, who rode on the running board of the follow-up car, refutes the "bunched coat" claim. He swore that he "saw that shot hit the President about four inches down from the right shoulder."[51] Official observers of the autopsy, Secret Service agents Roy Kellerman, William Greer, and Clint Hill, who were with the president in Dallas, all support Bennett's testimony, as do the official autopsy body chart, the disclosed autopsy pictures, and the president's death certificate.[52] Strangely, although the Weaver and Willis photographs, Bennett's affidavit, and JFK's shirt and belt are in the evidentiary base and are mentioned in various contexts in the extensive literature, Lattimer simply omits them from his stack of evidence.

Authors supporting the Warren Commission and its conclusions who used or substantially referred to the Zapruder film have deliberately or inadvertently corrupted, distorted, and misled readers on its meaning. Few have ever treated it objectively and properly. While this may seem a severe judgment, it is entirely merited, based on a close reading of their works in comparison with the film and the actual evidentiary base. A few prime examples, drawn from the works of writer William Manchester, attorney John Kaplan, historian Robin Winks, and journalist Charles Roberts, will illustrate.

In 1967 Harper and Row published and heavily promoted William Manchester's book The Death of a President.[53] Public interest in the book was extraordinarily high, in part because Manchester had had an earlier relationship with the Kennedy family and because the family disagreed with some of Manchester's statements.[54] The book especially appealed to the eastern liberal establishment, who viewed it as a bona fide inquiry into the murder that would resolve all the disputes that had arisen over the investigation since 1963. It had phenomenal sales.[55] A publisher's delight, it was nevertheless a historian's disgrace. The flaws and factual errors strewn throughout the thick volume conveyed much misinformation to the popular reader, even as the book confirmed the Commission's official findings.[56]

Manchester possessed unique advantages for access to federal records and individuals that will never be repeated.[57] The National Archives provided Manchester, a private citizen, with an office in which to work. He enjoyed full and open access to any and all records he chose to examine, including transcripts of testimony, closed files, and medical records. Officials, witnesses, key participants, and many scientific and investigative authorities opened their doors to this celebrated author. Unfortunately, he chose not to pursue the critical issues such as the hidden autopsy notes, the certificate of death, and the original version of the Zapruder film. He also elected not to meet with evidentiary experts from the dissenting community for guidance, fact checking, and reflective discussions. Given an unparalleled opportunity, Manchester appears to have discarded it for fortune, fame, and a fool's gold reputation.

Manchester's use of the Zapruder film distorts its evidentiary value and is rife with errors. For example, he inaccurately states when Zapruder thought a first shot occurred. In describing the assassination scene, he states the limousine went behind the Stemmons Freeway sign, which occurred around frame 210 and during the official first time Oswald, allegedly lurking in the depository, could see JFK for a shot. According to Manchester:

> The Lincoln moved ahead at 11.2 miles an hour. It passed the tree. Zapruder, slowly swinging his camera to the right, found himself photographing the back of a freeway sign. Momentarily the entire car was obscured. But it was no longer hidden from the sixth-floor corner window. . . . As the Lincoln emerged from behind the freeway sign, it reappeared in Abe Zapruder's line of vision. Abe saw the stifled look on the President's face and was stunned.[58]

But this is not what Zapruder saw, or what he believed, or what the records report. During Zapruder's July 1964 testimony before the Commission, the staffer Wesley Liebeler showed Zapruder several black-and-white frames made from the film.[59] When shown frame 186, Zapruder said, "The shot wasn't fired" yet.[60] For unexplained reasons Liebeler then jumped to frame 207, and Zapruder interrupted the hasty questioning by remarking, "I think this was after that happened—something had happened."[61] He had selected a frame after a first shot and before frame 210. Zapruder had testified to a shot prior to frame 207. He repeated his observation: "I heard the first shot and I saw the President lean over and grab himself like this (holding his left chest area)."[62]

Zapruder could not have seen and described the impact of a shot if JFK was behind the sign and shielded from his view. Yet JFK had to be behind the sign for the official findings to be valid.

In 1967, John Kaplan, a professor at Stanford Law School, published an article on the Warren Report and its critics in the prestigious quarterly journal the *American Scholar*, where he searched out weaknesses of the dissenters and sought to defend the official findings.[63] Within a few weeks he published the article in the equally prestigious *Stanford Law Review*, where he expanded his comments and added footnotes.[64] Kaplan's article was a great solace for many in the academic and liberal community who were disturbed over the terrible charges of failure and corruption levied against the Commission.

In the course of his narrative, Kaplan utilized evidence provided by the Zapruder film to establish the foundation upon which he argued in scholarly support of the official findings:

> The Commission was aided enormously by moving picture photographs taken by a clothing manufacturer named Abraham Zapruder. . . . The photographs not only fixed the President's first wound at somewhere between Frames 210 and 225 (because Zapruder's view was blocked briefly by a sign, the President disappeared from the film at Frame 205 and did not reappear until Frame 225—at which time he seemed to have been hit).[65]

As previously mentioned, though, this is not an accurate reflection of the evidentiary base. JFK does not disappear at frame 205; his head is still visible at frame 207. Zapruder's view of the president was not blocked at the time of the first shot, as Kaplan states, and Zapruder testified to quite the opposite. In addition, Zapruder's testimony, Willis number 5, Willis's testimony, the tremors on the film at frame 190, and similar evidence establish that a shot occurred around frame 190 or 189. Kaplan misstated key facts and seemed determined to accept the methods and findings of the Warren Report. In fact, the overall thrust of his article seems to constitute a counterattack on critics more than a proper inquiry.

A year later, Robin Winks, a professor of history at Yale University, included Kaplan's article in a collection of essays, *The Historian as Detective: Essays on Evidence*.[66] Winks retitled the article "The Case of the Grassy Knoll: The Romance of Conspiracy" and referred to it as "the best analysis that I have seen of the several books on the assassination."[67] In an afternote Winks also philosophized that "in all probability the majority of historians, were they to be polled, would agree that the Commission arrived at the only creditable answers. The information was full and the evaluation accurate but the transmission was bungled."[68] But the investigation was not full, nor was the evaluation accurate. The transmission was not bungled but did precisely what the authors of the Report wished it to do: portray a non-investigation as an investigation. After a book club adopted *The Historian as Detective*, these misguided views received an even wider readership. That was especially unfortunate in light of Winks's valuable contributions elsewhere, with *Cloak and Gown: Scholars in the Secret War, 1939–1961*, providing a prominent example.

Charles Roberts, who served as *Newsweek*'s White House correspondent in the 1960s, was with the press in Dallas on November 22. In 1967 he wrote *The Truth about the Assassination*, a 128-page book, wherein he provided answers to the "innuendoes, suspicions and charges" of critics "that have caused confusion and doubt around the world."[69] He had nothing positive to say about any of the dissenters, the peculiar hallmark of the defenders of the Warren Commission, who have managed to ignore a multitude of genuine contributions made by the Commission's numerous critics. Roberts used ridicule rather than rational argument to refute charges by critics that frames 207 through 211 were missing from the Zapruder film. *Life* had released the frames in question, he said, replaced from their first-generation copy. "The so-called 'missing' frames," he wrote, "showed nothing but a smiling Kennedy, waving at the crowd, before he was shot. Another conspiracy theory, rooted in human error rather than evil design, hit the cutting room floor."[70] It is not clear whether Roberts himself actually saw the missing frames. Either way, his explanation is a mishmash of misstatements and errors. For example, the actual evidence establishes that JFK was shot prior to the missing frames. Further, two of these frames (210 and 211) do not show President Kennedy but instead show the back of the Stemmons Freeway sign.

Over the years, serious defenders of the Warren Commission findings have consistently come up against an immovable object. On the Zapruder film they see when President Kennedy's limousine emerges from behind the Stemmons Freeway sign at frame 224 (and JFK is fully visible at frame 225); one can see that he is obviously wounded and is reacting by putting his hands to his throat, his arms akimbo, elbows out. Twelve frames later, at frame 237, Governor Connally appears to get hit. That, however, presents a problem for the Commission, which argued that the first shot could not have come before frame 210—because a live oak tree obscured the limousine from the depository's sixth-floor window. As previously discussed, at least forty-two frames must pass between shots, but only twenty-seven frames (at most) passed between JFK's and Connally's *separate* woundings.

Thus the governor's wounding occurs too soon to have been inflicted by a second shot from the rifle allegedly fired by Oswald.[71]

The Warren Commission resolves this dilemma by asserting that the same bullet that wounded Kennedy transited his body and then wounded Connally. Yet such a scenario is impossible to reconcile with the evidence as presented by the Commission, leading some of the Commission's defenders to seek alternative ways to explain the nonfatal wounds. Some, for example, have tried to find evidence that the first shot was fired before frame 210. The Commission asserted that it had discovered during the reenactment in May 1964 that Oswald may have had a view through the tree and could have fired at frame 186.[72] "For a fleeting instant," concludes the Report, "the President came back into view in the telescopic lens at frame 186 as he appeared in an opening among the leaves." It cites FBI special agent Lyndal L. Shaneyfelt's testimony before the Commission as support.[73] Page 101 of the Report reproduces three photographs associated with the reenactment: one from the Zapruder film, another of the limousine on the street during the reenactment, and a view from the telescopic sight at Zapruder frame 186.[74] The reenactment photographs do indeed show that an assassin probably had a clear view of JFK at a time corresponding to that frame.

Eminent Yale law professor Alexander Bickel, among others, used this theory concerning frame 186 to defend the Commission's findings.[75] But perhaps the theory's foremost defender in terms of resources expended and influential access to the public was CBS-TV. The four-part special *CBS News Inquiry: "The Warren Report"* aired on June 25, 26, 27, and 28, 1967, with Walter Cronkite of CBS, the nation's leading media personality and its most respected figure, narrating.[76] He informed his audience, "Our analysis of the Zapruder film suggests strongly that the first shot was fired at frame 186."[77] The network had utilized the studies of Luis Alvarez, a Nobel laureate physicist, who had studied the film and decided the jiggle he had discovered at around frame 190 indicated a reaction by Zapruder to the sound of a shot that had been fired at frame 186.[78] CBS acknowledged that Alvarez's study had a major influence on the documentary's conclusions[79]—that is, that Oswald alone fired all three shots. During the last minutes of the fourth show, Eric Sevareid, CBS commentator, even went so far as to suggest that all who disagreed with the Warren Report were "idiotic."[80] That caustic view and, indeed, all of CBS's conclusions, especially pertaining to frame 186, merit closer scrutiny.

First, it should be noted that CBS did not make public the evidence on which its investigation rested—contrary to the standard practice in scientific investigations. Without access to that alleged evidence, it is impossible for scholars to gauge the validity and objectivity of CBS's conclusions. Just as troubling is the fact that CBS apparently decided to ignore *any* serious research—by Sylvia Meagher or Ray Marcus or Harold Weisberg, for example—that contradicted the official findings. Second, it appears that CBS mainly utilized the federal film of the *reenactment* rather than a close analysis of the Zapruder film itself. The reenactment itself was significantly flawed. By no proper standard of evaluation could the May reenactment be considered valid for the conditions in November.

Two critical physical differences existed between the actual November assassination scene and the May simulation. First, the trees had been trimmed, including the oak before the sixth-floor easternmost window of the depository, eliminating or significantly altering leaves, twigs, and branches that had been in place six months earlier. In addition, in May the wind did not blow as it had in November, falsely suggesting a calmer environment and a less shifting target than had existed earlier.

Further, major irregularities in the federal reenactment occurred that render CBS's reliance on it unacceptable. Neither the original limousine nor the original positions of President Kennedy and Governor Connally were faithfully reproduced—and this in a case where inches count. To reenact the scene of the murder, the FBI and staff, in violation of the facts of the evidentiary base, placed the limousine too close to the south curb of Elm Street, away from the tree that exposed the occupants more to view in frame 186, skewing any accurate information one might have derived from the simulated activity.[81]

In addition, inside the School Book Depository the FBI disregarded the actual size of the opening of the window allegedly used by Oswald on November 22. The Warren Commission's own evidence suggests, strangely, that Oswald had positioned himself so that he had to fire through the glass of the only slightly opened doubled window in order to hit the president.[82] But, in the May 1964 reenactment the FBI raised the window wide open and jimmied the rifle to enable its rifleman to get a clear bead on the limousine.[83] Such discrepancies further undermine the theory that Oswald could have sighted JFK clearly at frame 186 and fired the first shot at that moment.

One must also recall that each frame is only 1/18.3 of a second in duration. To say that the single frame 186 permitted an opportunity to fire places a burden on the human eye far beyond its physical capacity to receive and respond to stimuli. In that incredibly brief time frame, it is impossible to record images, sight a target, and fire a rifle. Interestingly, soon after the program was aired, Alvarez published a paper stating that he now believed frame 177, not 186, corresponded to the actual time Oswald had fired his shot.[84]

In 1966, conspiracy theorist George C. Thomson, a southern California soil engineer who in 1964 had published a brief study on the assassination, purchased airtime and gave thirteen radio talk shows on the subject.[85] On the evening of April 10, 1966, over KFOX-FM in Long Beach, California, he broadcast a show entitled "The Third Man in the Car!"[86] He proclaimed that he had proof of a conspiracy that had killed the president. From his study of the Zapruder film he claimed that right after the death shot he saw in the limousine's rear seat a single foot sticking up in the air. This foot, he asserted, came from a Secret Service agent who had lurked, hidden under the jump seats, until then and had rolled out, jumped up, and machine-gunned JFK. In the tangle afterward his foot protruded over the backseat.

Such irresponsible inferences would seem to demonstrate that an un-governed imagination fueled by a fierce belief in conspiracy can lead one to make highly improbable conclusions. Even Thomson's count of men is off. The special assassin would have been the sixth man in the car, counting the driver Bill Greer, Roy Kellerman, Connally, JFK, and Clint Hill. We know that the foot belonged to Secret Service agent Clinton Hill, who ran forward from the follow-up car and pushed Jacqueline Kennedy, who was scrambling over the trunk lid, back into the rear seat.

On September 30, 1996, Lindsey K. Springer of Tulsa, Oklahoma, filed suit in the United States District Court for the Northern District of Oklahoma asking the court to find Secret Service agents William Greer and Roy Kellerman and the Warren Commission guilty of assassinating President Kennedy. No attorney of record is listed.[87] From his analysis of the Zapruder film, Springer claimed to have discovered that the driver of the limousine, William Greer, while sitting in the driver's seat, with his left hand placed his handgun on his right shoulder, aimed the weapon at President Kennedy, and shot him in "the right front temple." According to Springer, Kellerman held the steering wheel and guided the automobile while Greer shot. This allegation collapses at the slightest tug on the factual impossibilities it omits. The Zapruder film does not depict Greer killing JFK. Nor do other films of the assassination (by Nix, Muchmore, and others), which convincingly show Greer did not shoot JFK. If Greer had fired over his right shoulder, the bullet would not have been able to hit JFK in the right temple because it could only enter from the head's *left* front, which in fact is not damaged. JFK's head is not turned to the left, exposing his right temple to the Greer bullet. No other witnesses in the limousine or on the street heard or saw the deed; no police radio picked up the sound of the bullet's report.

In 1993 the reputable firm of Random House published Gerald Posner's heavily promoted *Case Closed*, which supported the Warren Commission conclusions.[88] One of the most error-ridden works ever published on the assassination, Posner's book embraces the theory that a single bullet inflicted two nonfatal wounds on JFK and five on Connally as well as breaking Connally's fifth rib and wrist.[89] To support that position, Posner ignores or misinterprets key facts in the evidentiary base by positing a shot at frame 224.

Recall that the Commission had concluded that a bullet hit JFK at frame 210,[90] and that the Zapruder film clearly shows Connally was not hit until frame 237. Since Oswald's alleged rifle could only load, cock, aim, and fire a shot in a minimum time of 2.3 seconds, or forty-two frames, the next shot could only be fired by frame 252 at the earliest if the first shot came at frame 210. That meant Governor Connally's reaction to his wounds, seen on frame 237, occurred before Oswald could have fired a second time, which in turn requires a single bullet if one is to accept the Commission's lone gunman theory.

If the governor did not react until frame 237 to a bullet smashing into him, how does one account for what happened between frames 210 and 237 to the bullet that left the muzzle of the rifle at two thousand feet per second? That approximately 160 grains of metal must somehow have frozen in space for a second or so, which is a physical impossibility. Since that explanation cannot be accepted as part of reality, the only viable alternative is for a second rifle and another rifleman to have shot that bullet into Connally. The Warren Report, however, proposed another explanation; it theorized that Connally suffered a delayed reaction.[91] But that assertion was refuted by the Commission's own medical testimony, which claimed that a bullet, in crushing about four inches of a fifth rib and cracking the radius into many pieces, should produce a reaction that is "quite prompt."[92]

Posner, however, devised a clever way to make the single-bullet theory work. He asserted that the first shot to hit JFK came later than the Warren

Commission had suggested, at frame 224 of the Zapruder film, and that Governor Connally reacted earlier to the shot than either the Commission or Connally had thought. At frame 224 the bullet passed "immediately" through JFK and Governor Connally at two thousand feet per second. According to Posner,

> At 224, the right front of the Governor's suit lapel flips up from his chest. Discovered in a 1992 computer enhancement by Jeff Lotz of Failure Analysis Associates, this jacket movement may be one of the most important timing confirmations in the case, as it established the moment the bullet hit him. The movement of the jacket took place at the exact area where the Governor's suit and shirt have a bullet hole, as the missile passed through his right shoulder blade and out under his right nipple.[93]

To achieve this "most important timing confirmation," Posner asserts the two bodies reacted in different ways to the same bullet. For his history to function, JFK must react immediately to the shot at frame 224 (for he is seen grasping at his throat in frame 225, or one-eighteenth of a second after the posited hit), and Governor Connally (while hit, according to Posner, at frame 224) must undergo a delayed reaction, until frame 237, to match the visual reaction of Connally on the film. Why did these two men, with human bodies that physiologically were the same, exhibit different reactions to the bullet strike? Unfortunately, Posner never explains.

Posner also holds that a bullet caused the flapping of the governor's lapel. This occurs on just one frame, 224, which shows a slight disturbance in the cloth of the lapel only 1/18.3 seconds in duration. But he does not tell the reader that gusts of wind swept the plaza that day, fitfully blowing throughout the motorcade. Thus, he completely ignores a possible, even probable, cause for the flapping lapel. He further states that the lapel has a bullet hole at the place the bullet caused the flap. But *there is no bullet hole in the lapel of Connally's jacket.* The actual hole in the jacket is about twelve inches from the lapel and two inches below the right nipple, and its passing through the cloth almost a foot away from the lapel could simply not have caused the lapel to flap. In sum, a close and informed reading of Posner's text uncovers numerous errors of this magnitude or greater, which in the end undermine his arguments and his intent to keep the JFK assassination case closed.

By contrast, noted filmmaker Oliver Stone very much wanted to keep the

case open; in fact, he became a catalyst for compelling the federal government to release hundreds of thousands of previously classified documents
relating to the case. His film JFK, an intense and powerful retelling of this
tragic story, attracted sensational and controversial coverage in the national
media and was both lavishly praised and heavily criticized for its treatment
of the assassination, investigation, and alleged cover-up.[94] The film generated much debate within the academic establishment, particularly among
historians, who charged Stone with distorting for dramatic effect matters
relating to the assassination, rather than adhering scrupulously to the historical record.

Many historians, myself among them, were especially disturbed by
Stone's reliance on such error-ridden sources as Jim Marr's *Crossfire* and Jim
Garrison's *On the Trail of the Assassins*.[95] In fact, Garrison himself and his
investigations provide the primary focus for Stone's storytelling, a narrative
that willy-nilly seems to mix fact (including actual footage from the Zapruder film) and fiction, with more regard for entertainment than accurate
documentation.[96] So, although he refused to accept the Warren Commission's failure, in other ways he only further confused our understanding of
the historical record and gave new life to a host of highly irrational conspiracy theories.

In the early summer of 1998, as the Assassination Records Review Board
negotiated with the heirs of Abraham Zapruder for federal purchase of the
film, the *Washington Post* ran two articles on the 486 frames and their merits
by its crack reporter George Lardner Jr.[97] As is normal in such accounts,
Lardner interviewed a number of JFK assassination authorities on the importance of the film for our nation's history. In the story he touched on one
of its evidentiary aspects, Willis number 5.

Critic Harold Weisberg explained to Lardner the significance of Willis
number 5 and how one locates the figure of Willis and understands his
actions on the film. When placed in the context of the Commission's
findings, it is evidence of a conspiracy forever caught on the Dallas dress
manufacturer's 8mm color frames. Willis appears at Zapruder frame 183 on
the south side of Elm Street, where one sees him with a camera to his eye; the
camera remains there through frames 199, 200, 201; at 202, the sound of a
shot made him snap his fifth 35mm slide in reflex. Then comes a blurred
frame 203. At frames 204 and 205 the camera clearly descends from his eye.
Willis number 5 shows JFK in the limousine; beyond him, on the abutment
on the knoll, stands Zapruder and his receptionist, Marilyn Sitzman.

Zapruder also catches Willis on his film. The Zapruder frame can be linked to Willis at frame 202 by a line drawn from Zapruder to Willis following the left shoulder of Secret Service agent Clint Hill riding on the running board of the follow-up car. This establishes a shot at just before frame 190, a time incompatible with the Commission findings. A shot at just before frame 190 also would not line up the bodies of JFK and the governor for a single bullet to transit as dictated by the requirements of the single-bullet theory, also an indispensable component of the official conclusions.

In dispelling the merits of Willis number 5, Lardner skirted the issue while seeming to address it: he changed the problem to one of whether on frame 202 itself, that single frame, the camera is going up or down from Willis's eye. He writes, "It isn't easy to tell . . . whether Willis is lifting his camera or lowering it at Frame 202. Frame 203 is blurred."[98]

But one draws the conclusion that Willis lowered the camera from his eye by examining the whole of Willis's presence in the film; it is decidedly unfair to an understanding of the evidentiary base to center on a single frame. From frames 183 to 201, we see the camera at Willis's eye; at 202 it starts to come down as he steps into the street. Frames 204 and 205 are not blurred, and the camera is down. Lardner's distortion of the meaning of Willis number 5 is merely another of the contradictions and mistakes major newspapers consistently have made when they become tangled with defending the Warren Report.

Altered Evidence, Altered States
An Introduction to Those Who Claim the Film Was Altered

In the last two decades a belief has arisen among many theorists that federal officials covertly altered Abraham Zapruder's movie to assist in and perfect their cover-up of a conspiracy to assassinate President Kennedy. This belief permeates their preconceptions of the assassination and dominates their thinking. The literature asserting alteration of the Zapruder film is extensive, appearing in several books, in many articles and conference papers, and on a score of Internet sites. Since these theorists adhere to many of the same fallacies, a few examples will be sufficient to demonstrate that their assertions lack either facts or plausibility.

Philip H. Melanson's article, "Hidden Exposure: Cover-Up and Intrigue in the CIA: Secret Possession of the Zapruder Film" (1984), appeared in the dissenting journal the *Third Decade* (later called the *Fourth Decade* and now defunct).[1] Melanson's claim for alteration of the Zapruder film fails on the basis of the same evidence used for a similar assertion by David Lifton in *Best Evidence*, which will be discussed at greater length later in the chapter.

More recently, a group of alterationists' essays have been collected in *Assassination Science: Experts Speak Out on the Death of JFK* (1997), edited by James H. Fetzer,[2] a work roundly (and appropriately) criticized in Harold Weisberg's unpublished but insightful study *Badly Reasoned*.[3] The relevant essays on Zapruder film alteration in *Assassination Science* are presented by an odd assortment of theorists: the photographic specialist Jack White's "Evidence . . . or Not? The Zapruder Film: Can It Be Trusted?";[4] attorney Mike Pincher and film student Roy Schaeffer's "The Case for Zapruder Film Tampering: The Blink Pattern";[5] labor relations specialist Chuck Marler's "The JFK Assassination Reenactment: Questioning the Warren Commission's Evidence";[6] medical doctor David W. Mantik's "Special Effect in the Zapruder Film: How the Film of the Century Was Edited";[7] and professor James H. Fetzer's "Epilogue."[8] As Weisberg has shown, these efforts are riddled with countless errors of fact, the failure to credit prior comparable claims, unwitting omissions that destroy the point under consideration, and a host of similar flaws.

Yet, as voluminous as the expression of the alteration charge is, it lends itself to easy examination and to complete and final refutation, for common threads stitch the assertions in common fatal errors. Fundamental flaws mark the scholarship of most of these "alterationists." First and foremost, the exhaustive *Analysis of Selected Motion Picture Photographic Evidence*, prepared for the Assassination Records Review Board by Roland J. Zavada of Kodak, convincingly argues for the authenticity of the film, in direct refutation of those claims.[9] Second, why would the government steal and alter the Zapruder film to hide a conspiracy only to have that alteration contain evidence that a conspiracy killed JFK? Weisberg's *Whitewash* and *Never Again*[10] and the careful study by Ray Marcus in his book *The Bastard Bullet, a Search for Legitimacy for Commission Exhibit 399* (1966) carefully show this.[11]

The role of scholars in a social crisis such as that presented by President John F. Kennedy's assassination does not differ from their role at any other time.[12] The urgent need for facts and the press of crisis do not modify the scholarly approach, mitigate the standard principles of inquiry, or call for new and different methods of examining the subject. If there is a principle of careful, objective inquiry that has been the hallmark of scholarship in the modern world, it is the reasonable attention given to responsible criticism of one's work. By considering the weaknesses, errors, omissions, and similar faults pointed out by others, an author can correct and improve his or her efforts in the common search for the truth. Yet the "alterationists" almost invariably refuse to address the criticisms levied against their views.

Take, for example, Roger Bruce Feinman's Internet critique of David Lifton's *Best Evidence*. Lifton claimed the Zapruder film was faked. In 1993, Feinman published a devastating, profusely documented analysis of Lifton and his book on the Internet titled *Between the Signal and the Noise: The "Best Evidence" Hoax and David Lifton's War against the Critics of the Warren Commission* (slightly expanded in 1999).[13] Yet most alterationists find Lifton's book to be scholarly and a pioneer work in assassination dissent. The authors of the essays in *Assassination Science* cite Lifton fifty times yet do not include Feinman's fine study in their text, notes, or bibliography. It is as if Feinman, a scholar of the assassination with over twenty-five years of experience in the subject, had never written.

In some cases the issue became highly personalized—to no one's benefit. For example, Walt Brown, the editor of *JFK/Deep Politics Quarterly*, published an editor's note to an article by Josiah Thompson in which he lamented Fetzer's personal reaction to responsible criticism of his arguments on the film.[14] Thompson's article contained several references to the same reactions of alterationists to criticisms of their lack of scholarship.[15] The critic Hal Verb, active for thirty-nine years, relates in an article in *Fourth Decade* the intense response to his scholarly review of Fetzer's *Assassination Science*, where he had pointed out significant errors and the factual absurdity of its claim of the Zapruder film's alteration.[16] Verb appropriately remarked, "Should researchers and what they have stated not also be subjected to critical examination as the Warren Commission has? The answer should be obvious."[17]

Contrary to the explanations offered by the alterationists, there was no opportunity to steal the film; there was neither enough time available nor the technical or mechanical means to do so. In addition, federal officials lacked interest in the film, could not know what had to be corrupted, were also confronted with hundreds of other potentially equally telltale photographs, and left a clear trail of evidence depicting their actual handling of the film.

Those who proclaim conspirators altered the film must come to terms with the Zapruder film's sequence of possession, which is thoroughly described in chapter 1. No opportunity existed in the solid chain of custody to enable conspirators to snatch the film. As previously discussed, Abraham Zapruder and his partner, Erwin Schwartz, controlled the original film from the time Zapruder recorded it on Dealey Plaza until he sold it in their office the morning of November 23. The number of individuals who participated in some measure in the processing and then the sale of the film must reach at least three score solid American citizens, from office secretaries to processing specialists to police officers to Schwartz to Jamieson Company employees. The affidavits, memorandums, contracts, and other documents related to these individuals clearly indicate the location of the film until its purchase by Time Inc. and make the case for alteration highly unlikely. Time Inc. absolutely controlled the original thereafter.

When the Kodak and Jamieson companies processed the film, Zapruder, Schwartz, and Secret Service agent Forest Sorrels watched the technicians as they did their work.[18] After development was completed at Kodak, Zapruder, who had much practical experience in the dress business protecting designs from competitors, had the responsible individuals affirm their work with notarized statements.[19] The master film, in its 16mm double form, had to go with Zapruder to Jamieson for copies to be made; Zapruder went into the developing booth to make certain there were no "bootleg" copies. Afterward the master and copies had to be returned to Kodak with Zapruder for developing the copies and slitting at least the original and two copies from 16mm to 8mm film. It was not until after nine o'clock in the evening that Zapruder and Schwartz finally had the completely processed film plus copies.

Zapruder then turned two copies over to the Secret Service at its office on Ervay Street.[20] Agent Max Phillips's note accompanying the shipment of one copy to Washington stated, "Mr. Zapruder is in custody of the 'master' film."[21] (The arch-alterationists Pincher and Schaeffer simply omitted this phrase in discussing the original's alleged afternoon theft.)[22] Phillips was explicit: the time was 9:55 P.M.[23] Since by then Zapruder had already locked up his office, he took the film home with him, as his partner Schwartz and his daughter Myrna so stated.[24] After 11:00, Richard Stolley of *Life* magazine telephoned Zapruder at his home.[25] At that time Zapruder held the master and one copy in his possession.[26] At 8:00 the next morning he had them in his office, having risen an hour or so before.[27] Thus, only when Zapruder was asleep at his home from midnight until six o'clock would any possibility have existed for the alleged conspirators to seize the film for the purpose of alteration.

Such conspirators would have had to enter Zapruder's home, locate the film, steal it, whisk it to the airport, and fly it to Washington in an almost three-hour flight. Then another team would have had to meet the plane, take the film, and speed it to a laboratory, where yet another team altered the frames, no easy task to say the least. In fact, it was an impossible task. Nevertheless, the alterationists claim the film was doctored. To alter the film, hundreds of frames had to be minutely examined and the appropriate ones modified and touched up, a time-consuming process requiring quality work to avoid future detection.

In that painstaking process, a frame one-fourth of an inch in width had to be expanded by projection, then altered by adding or subtracting data, then reduced again, photographed, and processed to produce a new "original." Processing of the film in Dallas took about one hour, which would also be a reasonable time for Washington's alleged covert plant to use. Three copies would take another hour to duplicate from the original. Then a flight home of almost three hours would be required to deliver the faked film to Dallas, rush to Zapruder's home, break in again, and replace the film. Altogether, at least ten hours would be consumed—that is, the film could not have been returned until at least three hours after it had been shown and sold in Zapruder's office, an impossibility that renders the allegation false.

Alterationists also fail to establish that the FBI and CIA or any site in Washington or Dallas actually possessed the technical machines to process and alter Kodachrome II film and offer no verifiable evidence to support such claims. Further, the Dallas film has a unique processing feature that left the letter "D" printed along the entire edge of the finished film that would have to be duplicated by means never alluded to by those who claim the film had been faked.

Contrary to the beliefs of the alterationists, federal officials displayed little interest in the Zapruder film, including the investigative agencies of the Secret Service, the FBI, and the CIA. Secret Service agent Forrest Sorrels, who had accompanied Zapruder and Erwin Schwartz to the Kodak developing plant, actually walked out before processing was finished.[28] In fact, Zapruder and Schwartz later had to hunt him down at the police station.[29] Instead of taking charge of the film at that point, Sorrels asked them to drive it out on their own to the Secret Service office on Ervay Street and give it to agent Max Phillips.[30]

The FBI, for its part, seemed even less interested in the film.[31] Only later in the morning of November 23 did local FBI agents view the film; they had not contacted Zapruder, and they had actually dismissed his film as having no evidentiary value. But, under pressure from FBI headquarters, alarmed at the media's growing interest in the film, the Dallas office borrowed a copy from the Secret Service.[32] But the Dallas office initially possessed no projector and was forced to examine the frames by holding them up to a lightbulb.[33] FBI headquarters did not obtain a copy until Monday, November 25, and then only after bungling its handling of the Secret Service copy.

Regarding the CIA, no scrap of paper, legitimate witness, or indirect source of any merit places the agency or any of its surrogates indirectly or directly in connection with the film on November 22 or the following two days. The documents that came out of the Belin-Rockefeller investigation of the CIA show that the agency did not begin its study of the movie until after photographs had appeared in Life magazine. This thoroughly documented lack of official interest in the Zapruder film drives a stake into the claims of alterationists that federal agencies immediately after the assassination stole or borrowed the film to whisk it away to Washington or any other city or country for alteration.

In any case, it would have been impossible for federal officials to have known in advance that they would have to alter the Zapruder film, when only film technicians at Kodak and Zapruder and his partner had seen it. They could not know because police and federal agents were still investigating the crime in Dallas and the information was in an incomplete, fluid, dynamic state. And, we recall, not even Abraham Zapruder at the Kodak plant or Secret Service agent Forrest Sorrels, who accompanied him, knew for sure what the film contained or even if it had in fact recorded the assassination. How, then, could the conspirators have known to grab it? When we examine the articles by Phil Melanson, Jack White, Mike Pincher, Roy Schaeffer, Chuck Helper, David Mantik, and James Fetzer and the books by David Lifton and Noel Twyman—our representative alterationists—no information is provided on this quintessential issue.

Alterationists offer no explanation for why conspirators plucked Zapruder's film out of the morass of other films, photographs, slides, and videos that were taken on the day of the assassination. Many of those photographs and films remained untouched by investigators, and officials rejected others, including the autopsy films and X rays, the Charles Bronson films taken on November 22 by a citizen that contain critical data (discussed later), and the Phil Willis slides.[34] In fact, the official policy of the FBI was not to look for and not to acquire photographic evidence unless it was pushed into their hands by news stories.[35]

Those who claim film tinkering do not address how conspirators with such unusual gifts for planning the covert operation and pulling off a clandestine feat could at the same time clumsily litter their trail with records and memorandums and indications of fraud so obvious that they would be found out. For these conspirators, the discovery of an altered Zapruder film would have been disastrous, offering powerfully suggestive evidence of an official cover-up.

In the first place, the markings or alterations or jimmying on the film must be free of errors; if the work was imperfectly, grossly, or sloppily done, exposure was certain, and the conspirators would be trapped. Second, all other evidence in the assassination investigation must be cleared of data that would compromise an alteration. Every other film, for example, must be tinkered with to conform to the altered Zapruder film; otherwise contradictions would creep into the official record and raise questions, which would lead to new investigations that might put the conspirators at risk.

Consider, too, that Zapruder was a savvy businessman who from the first knew he had a property of potentially great value. He told Secret Service agent Sorrels within thirty minutes of the assassination that he was going to sell the film for all he could get. His every act supported that end. In the course of Zapruder's processing and duplication of the film, the dress manufacturer carefully supervised the technicians and secured affidavits assuring the integrity of the work, all to maintain commercial worth. He did not let the film out of his secured possession at any time for any reason until he sold it. When he negotiated and obtained a lucrative contract for the film's sale to Time Inc., Zapruder attached his affidavits and swore to the integrity of the processing, duplication, and exclusiveness of the film and copies. Such vigilance also makes it highly unlikely that the film was tampered with during this period.

Similarly spurious is Douglas Ome's charge that Time Inc. allowed the film to be altered. In *Murder in Dealey Plaza*, Horne argues that Time Inc. permitted the film to be taken by federal officials for doctoring.[36] Like Zapruder, however, Time knew it had a treasure in the Zapruder film, and it would do nothing to endanger the flow of revenue it expected from those twenty-six seconds of film.

Those who espoused an altered Zapruder film were excellent subjects for talk shows and reviews. Those who claimed a body theft and those who asserted similar irrational findings were touted as typical of anyone who questioned the validity of the Warren Commission findings, and they quickly drowned the scholars of the assassination in a sea of the palpably false.

Two of the theorists who charge the assassins of President John F. Kennedy altered the Zapruder film are Noel Twyman in *Bloody Treason* and David Lifton in *Best Evidence*. An examination of their claims and scholarship will serve to illustrate the weaknesses found in the claims of alterationists in general.

In 1997, Noel Twyman, a California engineer, published *Bloody Treason: On Solving History's Greatest Murder Mystery: The Assassination of John F. Kennedy,* a 909-page heavily illustrated but very flawed tome[37]—so much so that critic Harold Weisberg devoted most of a book, *Badly Reasoned,* to examining just a small portion of the factual errors he found in *Bloody Treason*.[38] Twyman devotes two chapters to the Zapruder film: his chapter 11, "The Zapruder

Film,"[39] is a general discussion of the film; chapter 12, "The Forgery of the Zapruder Film,"[40] is devoted to the film's alleged alteration. By "forgery" Twyman means alteration of the original, not a completely new counterfeit film.

To alter the film, the conspirators had to possess it. In Twyman's account the original came into their possession through H. L. Hunt, a Dallas billionaire. Twyman asserts that on "the late afternoon"[41] or "evening"[42] or "night"[43] of November 22 or "the next day"[44]—all four times are used by him—Hunt dispatched from his office Paul Rothermel, his head of security, with a substantial amount of money to purchase the developed Zapruder film.[45] The source he uses states Rothermel said "late afternoon," which was hours before development of the film had been completed, but that chronological impossibility poses for Twyman neither a logical problem nor a question of his conspiracy's authenticity.

How the aged Hunt would have known so quickly about the existence of this momentous reel of film and its precise contents is not explained. Twyman bases his claim of Hunt's purchase on the statement of a single person, a criminal who had been captured robbing a bank. After his bungled robbery attempt, this man claimed he had deliberately botched the heist in order to be captured and thus provide himself an alibi during the JFK assassination, of which he alleged he had foreknowledge.[46] The robber, according to Twyman, had embroidered his story by saying he had received information on the Hunt purchase from Rothermel.[47]

After Hunt obtained the film, Twyman argues, a federal agency rushed to alter it and then substituted the new master for the original in Life's possession and exchanged altered copies for the copies held by authorities. The mechanics and logistics of this arrangement, the details of corruption and the coordination entailed, along with the complete lack of any documentation, are simply not addressed.

But Twyman could not be more mistaken. Hunt and Rothermel were in Washington, D.C., that afternoon and for the next thirty days.[48] Immediately after the assassination, Rothermel became concerned for the safety of Hunt. A former FBI agent, he contacted the FBI, who advised him to take Hunt to Washington. So, far from being diabolically concerned with unknown evidence on an undeveloped film, Hunt and Rothermel had fled Dallas entirely as fast as they could.

But in addition to these alleged malefactors being absent from the scene of their purported crime against the nation, Twyman faced an equally effective cinematic barrier to his conjectures. He fails to establish if any Washington institution possessed the capabilities to develop Kodachrome II film. Without that specialty machine, his faked new original would be in black and white, which the conspirator *Life* somehow printed in color in its later editions.

Twyman provides five primary conclusions concerning the Zapruder film.[49] First, he says, it was altered, or forged in his terminology, by having frames spliced out. He fails to explain precisely which frames were removed and how removal would have been detected. The reader is left to accept his assertion as fact. Nor does he explain exactly what evidence the conspirators removed, which is also left to the reader to surmise.

Second, he contradicts himself. At one point, he states he could not decide whether "JFK was first hit either just before or after he passed behind the freeway sign." But he also states, "When he emerged from behind the sign, he had already been hit."[50]

Third, he draws upon the "sworn testimony" of allegedly credible eyewitnesses to back up his claim that the Zapruder film shows JFK's limousine came to a "virtually complete stop." Those witnesses, however, are never identified, and the film does not support his claim.

Fourth, he charges that the allegedly altered film hides the blowout at the rear of JFK's head described by doctors and nurses. In fact, there was no rear-side blowout, as I note elsewhere. Medical authorities mistook for a gunshot hole a flap of skin with bone and bloody matter attached that was thrown back over the head on a hinge of skin.

Fifth, Twyman claims that Governor Connally shifted position after he was struck, but he does not provide clear evidence for this assertion, which rests on his claim that a frame of the Zapruder film differs from a photograph taken by Mary Moorman from the south side of Elm Street toward the rear of the limousine.

"Beyond a reasonable doubt," Twyman concludes, "frames had been removed by the conspirators to conceal evidence."[51] Yet his claims and assertions inspire a great deal of doubt. In the end, he cannot explain why, if the conspirators sanitized and altered the film to rid it of proof of conspiracy, evidence remained on the film that proves beyond question Oswald could not have fired all the shots.

In addition to presenting implausible and inaccurate charges of an alteration of the Zapruder film, *Bloody Treason* is suffused with errors about the assassination and its investigation. These weaknesses are so pervasive that they render the book an undependable source, as illustrated by the following two examples. The first is Twyman's treatment of the autopsy doctor's notes. He writes:

> On Sunday afternoon, November 24, Dr. Humes burned the original notes he recorded at the autopsy in his fireplace. Why would Humes have burned his notes in such an important, historical autopsy? To me, the answer seemed obvious: Dr. Hume must have burned his notes to eliminate discrepancies with his final report—discrepancies that would have, must have, been revealed had his original notes been retained.[52]

But Hume's notes were retained, not destroyed. Humes testified before the Warren Commission that he burned the first draft of his autopsy report after he knew Oswald had been killed, which meant after he knew there would be no trial. He testified: "In the privacy of my own home, early in the morning of Sunday, November 24th, I made a draft of this report which I later revised, and of which this represents the revision. That draft I personally burned in the fireplace of my recreation room."[53] Asked when he made those changes, he replied, "Someone had a television on and came in and told me that Oswald had been shot."[54] Moreover, as he testified, he held his notes in his hand.[55] In one of the major scandals of the official investigation, those vital notes then disappear from the official records.[56]

A second example is provided by Twyman's depiction of Oswald's character. Twyman refers to Oswald as "an avowed Communist, traitor and 'promoter' of pro-Castro literature, and who had been watched by the FBI, would be employed in Top Secret photographic work for the U.S. government."[57] None of this is a valid reflection of the official records.[58] The Cubans held that Oswald was no friend, but if he had been, what he did was negligible. He had printed only a thousand handbills, and most remained undistributed when he was killed. That was all. His New Orleans Fair Play for Castro chapter did not exist, although he pretended it did; it was simply Oswald's invention.

Oswald never said he was "an avowed Communist." He was, according to the Commission's published documentary record, virulently anti-Communist, anti–U.S. Communist, anti–Soviet Communist, and anti-Socialist.[59] "I hate the U.S.S.R. and the Socialist system," he wrote, as the Commission quoted in its Report.[60] He was never, in any meaning of the word or even in the faintest degree, a traitor. The Soviets suspected him of being an American agent and had him under constant surveillance, including eavesdropping on his marriage bed. If Oswald had been a traitor, upon his return to America he would have been arrested and charged with that offense.[61]

Contrary to Twyman's charge, the printing plant in Dallas where Oswald briefly worked was only a printing plant and nothing else. It did not engage in "Top Secret photographic work" for the government. Nor did the FBI post a watch on Oswald. Only after he wrote to the then Communist newspaper the *Daily Worker*, and on that basis alone, did it open a case file. These examples typify the history found in *Bloody Treason*, leading to the unavoidable conclusion Twyman's scholarship is not dependable.

Another key theorist who has charged that the Zapruder film was altered is David Lifton, whose book *Best Evidence: Disguise and Deception in the Assassination of John F. Kennedy* was published in 1980. This 746-page best-seller claimed that federal officials stole President Kennedy's body while it was on the flight to Washington and altered it.[62] As an integral part of his conspiracy charges, Lifton also claimed the CIA had altered the Zapruder film.[63] With a large following of adherents to doctrines seemingly rooted in extensive research and copious documentation, he continued to promote his claims through several printings of the hard cover and numerous paperback printings. However, when the sources for his charges and the scholarship he employed are critically examined, his most egregious claims simply cannot be sustained or given the slightest credence.

After presenting a brief, inadequate, and misleading account of the film's chain of possession, Lifton asserts, "I suspected it had taken a secret detour, but I could find no direct evidence to prove that."[64] His proof finally came to him, he said, fortuitously from a "group" of CIA documents Paul Hoch obtained in 1976 under the Freedom of Information Act and passed on to him. Based on a study of those agency documents, Lifton believes the film was in CIA possession "possibly" on the night of November 22 and certainly within "a few days." The documents, he further asserts, demonstrate the CIA had the film at its National Photographic Interpretation Center before the FBI laboratory studies assigned numbers to the frames, implying that the FBI film examined by the Commission was therefore altered, with misrepresentation of the evidence.

As demonstrated elsewhere in these pages, no opportunity existed on November 22 for the CIA to acquire either the Zapruder film or a copy of it. The evidence, the timing of the film processing, and the complex nature of the event all preclude a theft. Lifton offers no evidence to the contrary.

He does not provide his readers access to his CIA documents, nor does he cite a source where they can be obtained and studied. Fortunately, in 1976 critic Harold Weisberg also received from Paul Hoch the same set of documents Hoch had provided David Lifton.[65] Weisberg published them in facsimile form in the epilogue of the second edition of his book *Photographic Whitewash*, along with a fine analysis and commentary.[66] They include four pages of what are termed briefing boards, but without date or name of originator attached; they display the figures for several studies of the film.

A close analysis of these documents proves the reverse of Lifton's claim that the CIA had possessed the film before the FBI numbered the frames. The CIA in fact used the frame numbers assigned by the FBI. The FBI's frame numbering begins with the first appearance of the motorcade at the end of Elm Street. Zapruder filmed for a while, stopped, then, as he testified, began again. The numbering of hundreds of frames starts with the first scene. Each of the CIA studies of the film ends at frame 312, at the time JFK is struck in the head. (The shot actually hit, according to the Commission, between frames 312 and 313.) The dramatic frame 313 of the head exploding comes a tiny fraction of a second after the fatal shot.

Lifton claims the CIA influenced *Life* magazine's presentation of Zapruder film frames, citing a CIA study to support his claim. But he fails to note that that very study is clearly based on the CIA's analysis of the *Life* magazine presentation—not the reverse.

He asserts further that the CIA made a new master copy of the Zapruder film with the incorporated alterations and rushed three copies to Dallas as substitutes for the originals. But he fails to offer hard evidence for such conjecture. Furthermore, the CIA, like the FBI, presumably lacked the specialty machines necessary to process Kodachrome II film, whose use would have been required to create "the new master" in color. Lifton does not establish that this unusual processing machinery was even available in Washington, let alone in the CIA laboratory. Without a special machine only a new black-and-white master would have been possible and manifestly is an impossible substitution for a true color master.

Nevertheless, Lifton maintains that there is evidence that the CIA altered the film. For example, he notes that he "discovered splices on the film which had never been mentioned by Time-Life," beyond the now well-known splice at frame 207 that removed frames 208 through 211 and left frame 212 badly damaged and a composite of two others.[67] That splice was first revealed by Harold Weisberg in his 1965 book *Whitewash* and subsequently highlighted in the works of such reputable scholars as Ray Marcus and Sylvia Meagher (none of whom are mentioned by Lifton). Regarding his newly "discovered" splices, Lifton provides no frame numbers, identifies no places on the film where such splices can be detected, and fails to describe their physical appearance or content.

As further evidence of copying, he notes that JFK's "occipital area, where Dallas doctors saw a wound, appears suspiciously dark, whereas a large wound appears on the forward right-hand side of the head, where the doctors saw no wound at all."[68] Lifton tries to argue that this apparent discrepancy—between what the doctors saw in the hospital and what he claims to see in the Zapruder film—is an "artifact of copying," the result of the CIA's having tampered with the film in an effort to comply with the Warren Commission's predetermined identification of Oswald as the assassin. But, again, he provides no frame numbers or any other identifying feature for the reader to examine. More important, a close examination of the Commission's Zapruder film slides of individual frames (when screened to five feet) clearly refutes what Lifton claims to have seen. In fact, there is no "suspicious" spot, much less a blowout wound on the back side of JFK's head, but there is indeed (contrary to Lifton's doctors) a large wound at the right front of his head.

The foregoing, of course, undermines Lifton's claims regarding the CIA's supposed alteration of the film, an effort supposedly designed to help convince the public that Oswald was the assassin. But if Lifton had more thoroughly examined the CIA's own official study of the film, he would note that the agency concluded that the first shot must have been fired at Zapruder frame 190 or just before, which requires a second gunman, for it was physically impossible for Oswald or anyone else from the easternmost window of the School Book Depository's sixth floor to have fired a shot at JFK before frame 210.[69] Why, one must wonder, would the CIA have succeeded in tampering with the Zapruder film to hide evidence of a conspiracy and in the end actually provide evidence that *reveals* a conspiracy? Perhaps one could argue a shoddy effort by the agents in question, conducted under hair-raising circumstances and a horrendously tight schedule. It would not be the first time a CIA effort had faltered. But, in fact, all the available evidence seems to suggest that the agency never attempted, much less accomplished, an alteration of the film.

Such lapses on Lifton's part are far too frequent. Other examples can be found in *Best Evidence*, the most startling of which is Lifton's claim that his unnamed conspirators actually stole JFK's corpse, altered it to fit with evidence implicating Oswald, and then surreptitiously returned it. In this far-fetched and unsubstantiated scenario, the conspirators—while the presidential party in Air Force One prepared to return to Washington in those minutes just prior to and during LBJ's swearing-in ceremony in the front cabin—took the body from the bronze casket at the plane's rear and put it in a body bag they had hidden in an unidentified place on the plane. When the plane reached Washington, they furtively removed the body from an opening on the darkened far side of the plane, while the empty bronze casket was removed on the other side in view of the crowd and in the light of cameras, then placed in an ambulance for the official motorcade. The covert team then supposedly transported the body by helicopter to Walter Reed Army Hospital, where they manipulated it to suggest only shots from the rear (thus making Oswald the sole assassin). Then they rushed the body in a plain gray shipping coffin by a black hearse to Bethesda Naval Hospital, where the empty bronze casket had been taken and where the conspirators entered through a rear gate and then placed the body back in its original casket, without detection by the Secret Service, hospital officials, or the Kennedy family. Unfortunately for Lifton, the actual evidence contradicts his charges at every point.

First, no opportunity to steal the body existed on the plane. Lifton omits from his account that the body was wet, dripping in blood and other fluids that, when lifted from the coffin, would have left telltale signs and alerted aides, crew, and guards.[70] Parkland hospital nurse Doris Nelson testified that when placing the corpse in the casket "extensive bleeding from the head [occurred] and they had wrapped four sheets around it but it was still oozing through."[71] The cloth beneath the president was soaked, and a plastic form was laid on it to prevent seepage through the casket. Further, when the pallbearers placed the coffin on board, steel wrapping cables were placed around it and its lid to prevent shifting during takeoff and landing and in case of air disturbances in flight, as must be done to cargo on airplanes for safety. Removing and replacing such cables would have required time and opportunity that were unavailable to any would-be conspirators.

In addition, the casket was under ample armed guard at all times during the flight, a fact that Lifton neglects to mention.[72] Secret Service agent Richard Johnsen discreetly stood a few feet away in the hallway entrance,[73] while

Brigadier General Godfrey McHugh, JFK's aide, stood at attention beside the casket throughout the trip and during the swearing-in ceremony.[74]

Lifton, however, states that soon after the casket was placed on board, McHugh left it to check on why the plane had not departed, allowing conspirators to steal the body. But immediately upon the publication of *Best Evidence*, McHugh wrote a letter to *Time* magazine in which he denied Lifton's claim that he had left the body unattended.[75]

Finally, most of JFK's aides and clerical staff were in the rear of the plane, with key aides sitting close by the casket from the moment it was secured at the rear of the plane.[76] But Lifton does not mention this.[77] In fact, he asserts the Kennedy people all went forward to the swearing-in ceremony, thus leaving the casket without protection. That assertion, how-ever, runs counter to evidence provided by LBJ's secretary, Marie Fehner,[78] and by the Secret Service,[79] both of whom were ordered to record the names of all attendees at the swearing-in ceremony. Both lists show that the majority of JFK's aides and staff were not present, a fact also confirmed by Cecil Stoughton, White House photographer, who snapped over a dozen photographs of the ceremony.[80] Especially given the tiny size of the forward cabin, how could it have been otherwise?[81]

No army helicopter at Andrews Air Force Base secretly ferried the corpse to Walter Reed Hospital.[82] Aside from the presidential helicopter, the only other one present brought in Lieutenant Sam Bird's casket team,[83] some-thing noted both in William Manchester's *Death of a President* and in the Military District of Washington records for November 22, sources with which Lifton was quite familiar.[84] Nor was the far side of the plane dark-ened to shield the furtive removal of JFK's corpse. Instead, it was bathed in klieg lights, and thousands of persons watched along the fence that bent backward along that side, providing, in effect, a well-lit and very public stage for any would-be body snatchers.

Nor did any vehicle, much less the alleged black hearse, pass through the back gate of Bethesda. As proof to the contrary, Lifton cites some navy men at Bethesda who said they saw an ambulance come up Fourteenth Street from Walter Reed Hospital.[85] But their testimony is somewhat sus-pect because there is no Fourteenth Street leading out from Reed; a section of that street was eliminated when the hospital was constructed.

Also, Colonel Russell Madison was stationed at Bethesda and left each day through that gate as a shortcut home, *except* on the late afternoon of November 22, when he found the gates shut and padlocked with no guard posted who could be countermanded by officers to open it.[86] That, of course, made it fairly difficult for any body-snatching vehicle, already on a very tight schedule, to deliver its goods as described by Lifton.

Officials never lost contact with the casket, so the replacement of the allegedly altered corpse was impossible. General McHugh was always close to the coffin,[87] never losing contact with it from the time it was unloaded from Air Force One until the ambulance parked at the mortuary jetty, where he assisted in its removal. In addition, FBI agents James W. Sibert and Francis X. O'Neill Jr. met the plane, watched the casket being removed and placed in the ambulance, followed it in the third car of the motorcade, kept the casket constantly in sight from the airport to the hospital, and then helped unload the casket and witnessed the autopsy. A key paragraph in their official report states as follows:

> The president's body was removed from the casket in which it had been transported and was placed on the autopsy table, at which time the complete body was wrapped in a sheet and the head area contained an additional wrapping which was saturated with blood. Following the removal of the wrapping, it was ascertained that the president's clothing had been removed and it was also apparent that a tracheotomy had been performed, as well as surgery of the head area, namely, in the top of the skull. All personnel with the exception of medical officers needed in the taking of photographs and x-rays were requested to leave the autopsy room and remain in the adjacent room.[88]

Their comment regarding the body's condition matched the description testified to by the Dallas nurses who placed him in the coffin, information also absent from Lifton's account. Nurse Diana Bowron: "We wrapped some extra sheets around his head so it wouldn't look so bad."[89] Nurse Margaret Henchliffe: "We . . . wrapped him up in sheets [and] he was placed in the coffin."[90]

On "surgery to the head" Sibert and O'Neill were mistaken, as Sibert later testified before the House Select Committee in 1977. "It was thought by the doctors [at the autopsy] that surgery had possibly been performed in the head-area," but "this was determined not to be correct following detailed inspection and when the piece of bone found in the limousine was brought to the autopsy room during the later stages of the autopsy."[91]

Admiral George Burkley, President Kennedy's physician, and two Secret Service men who had been in the Parkland Hospital emergency room with

JFK, as well as others, were in the autopsy room, sitting in the amphi-theater audience. They had seen the corpse at Parkland and would have spotted any alterations immediately. Additionally, the X-ray photographs of the skull show jagged lines, not the clean, sharp lines of an operation.[92]

Nor was there any gray coffin used to spirit away JFK's corpse, although such coffins used for interring deceased military personnel were hardly unusual at Bethesda. The fact remains—based on witness testimony—that JFK's body was indeed transported in a bronze casket, from which it was not removed until its arrival at Bethesda.

Finally, it should go without saying that the complex logistics involved in perpetrating such an incredible feat would have required a large cast of conspirators able to communicate with each other and respond at a mo-ment's notice to shifting events. Among other things, it was not until Air Force One approached Washington that Jacqueline Kennedy made the deci-sion to use Bethesda for the autopsy, which would have required conspira-tors to place duplicate teams at both Walter Reed and Bethesda. Further-more, some conspirators had to have been on board the airplane to steal the body, fly it to Walter Reed, work on it there, transport it to Bethesda, and switch it to the bronze casket. The large but indeterminate number of conspirators would most likely have had to include air traffic controllers, enlisted men, military officers, special technicians, and medical personnel, all working together covertly and able to maintain silence forever. Under the weight of all these improbabilities, Lifton's erroneous claims collapse.

It never happened. The body was not stolen.

Strangely, despite the numerous significant flaws in Lifton's work, a number of authors and students of the assassination avidly promote the book and its arguments. They laud it, either oblivious to its faults or unable to come to grips with the factual details of the assassination in a meaning-ful way. Noel Twyman, for example, in his *Bloody Treason*, offers this ful-some praise of Lifton: "I hold his pioneer work to be the largest single contribution to the solution of the John F. Kennedy murder mystery."[93] James Fetzer, in *Assassination Science*, sees Lifton's *Best Evidence* as a "classic work."[94] And British author Anthony Summers has promoted many of Lifton's mistaken claims in his best-selling *Conspiracy*.[95]

With such uncritical support for their untenable claims, "alterationists" like Lifton and others have made a proper study of the assassination and its investigation much more difficult to pursue than need be. In the process, they have helped discredit other much more reliable researchers who agree that there was indeed a conspiracy but have been much more responsible in documenting their claims.

To politicians and bureaucrats, to federal investigative officials and mainstream intellectuals, to press owners and television commentators who fiercely maintain the official findings of no conspiracy, the alterationists have been a godsend.

V

The Film
and the
Evidentiary
Base

10   Official Federal Policy

Do Not Investigate

At 10:59 A.M. on Monday, November 25, as Richard B. Stolley, *Life*'s agent in Dallas, waited patiently to purchase the remaining rights to Abraham Zapruder's film, the horse-drawn caisson bearing the slain president's body left Capitol Hill for the funeral ceremony. The somber procession pulled the flag-draped casket between thick crowds of silent spectators while a nation watched and grown men wept. Only a few blocks from the muffled drum cadences in Department of Justice offices, federal lawyers and Federal Bureau of Investigation agents frantically engaged in activity of a dramatically different nature. The deputy attorney general of the United States had just had typed and was distributing copies of a secret memorandum he had written the evening before. It set forth the policy he and the director of the FBI had agreed upon and the new president had approved. The murder of President John F. Kennedy would not really be investigated. This political decision would direct the subsequent inquiry and especially affect the study and use of the evidence contained in the Zapruder film.

The assassination crisis had dramatically deepened when at 12:21 P.M. eastern standard time on Sunday, November 24, Jack Ruby, a sleazy Dallas nightclub owner, slipped past scores of guards in the basement of the Dallas Police Station and killed Lee Harvey Oswald. The death stunned the nation and sent official Washington reeling. The news sent Deputy Attorney General Nicolas Katzenbach, already staggering from the murder of JFK, into an emotional reaction. With Attorney General Robert Kennedy incapacitated by his brother's death, Katzenbach was running the Department of Justice.

Katzenbach, a World War II veteran and former college professor, belonged to what can be called the eastern establishment. He came from wealth, had attended private schools, graduated from a prestigious university, and received his law degree from a top school. He served admirably under President Kennedy, earning his spurs during the civil rights struggles. That he had done so made it all the more disturbing that during the crisis following JFK's assassination he displayed a poor grasp of crucial issues and seemingly turned his back on basic constitutional principles in favor of a rush to judgment that secretly presumed Oswald's guilt long before the Warren Commission began its investigation and, for that matter, even before the Commission had been established.

Throughout the tumultuous day on November 24, the distressed Katzenbach received telephone calls from officials, friends, and mentors. Three times Dean Rostow of Yale Law School contacted his "groggy" former student, recommending "a Presidential Commission be appointed of very distinguished citizens" to investigate the murder in order to use their prestige to convince the public that all was right.[1] The rattled Rostow, a professor of law and a scholar of the American judicial system, without question or doubt held that Oswald, "the bastard" in his words, killed President Kennedy, a judgment based on his viewing of television and reading of newspaper accounts and undoubtedly colored by Cold War paranoia. Not certain that the exhausted and emotional Katzenbach had comprehended him, Rostow telephoned the White House and spoke with LBJ's assistant Bill Moyers. Subsequently, it appears that Rostow's suggestion for a presidential commission may have been adopted (with LBJ's agreement) by Katzenbach and articulated in his written memorandum of November 24, typed and distributed the next day (see document 13 in the appendix).[2]

Throughout the afternoon Katzenbach and officials contacted each other, hammering out a plan of action for investigating the assassination. It is important in this context to recall the great fear of Soviet Russia and communism that held much of America in its grip, influenced the mind-set of the intelligentsia, fueled the fanaticism of the Far Right, permeated the thinking of the media,[3] and drove the Joint Chiefs of Staff.[4] Katzenbach's motivation appears to have centered on fear of loss of government mastery, which might lead the roused public to insist on retaliation against the Soviets.

During this time of crisis, Katzenbach was in contact with Hoover[5] and Johnson.[6] In the throes of the assassination crisis, these three men devised a policy toward the murder investigation that took advantage of this national hysteria about the Soviets. They worked behind its ideological shield to create a predetermined solution to JFK's murder that would reassure the American public, even if it necessarily precluded a free and open inquiry. In fact, at 4:15 P.M., Katzenbach even wanted to issue an immediate public statement: "We are now persuaded that Oswald killed the President; however, the investigation by the Department of Justice and the Bureau is continuing!"[7] The FBI refused to put out such a statement and opposed Katzenbach's efforts, which died stillborn.[8]

On November 25, while Katzenbach was having the memorandum distributed, he explained to the FBI liaison to his office that "this memorandum was prepared by him after his discussion with the Director."[9] From the bureau's side Hoover's conversation with his staff on November 25 established that LBJ, Katzenbach, and the director had worked out the doctrines. He told the staff that Katzenbach had spoken with the White House, requesting a definitive FBI report on the "Oswald case." No suggestion appears in the records that either Katzenbach or Hoover doubted Oswald's guilt.[10] Secret Service logs confirm the White House telephone calls to Katzenbach.[11]

Hoover's main motivation, however, appears to have been to protect the institution of the FBI, not to investigate the murder. In the vast amount of the FBI documents relating to the assassination investigation examined over the course of decades—numbering in the hundreds of thousands—there appears to be no concern over a possible foreign origin to the assassination or concern that the American public would become unhinged and push for a war with the Soviets (and thus nuclear war). Hoover had immediately proclaimed Oswald's sole guilt. On November 22 at 4:01 eastern standard time, he telephoned Robert Kennedy to tell him "we had the man who killed the President," and "his name is Lee Harvey Oswald."[12] Hoover excitedly told everyone he met and all who telephoned that Oswald was the sole perpetrator of JFK's murder, and neither he nor anyone in the FBI's headquarters or in its field offices ever considered anyone else.[13] Quite conceivably, Hoover hoped to keep the nation focused on Oswald's quick capture rather than the FBI's failure to prevent the assassination.

In Dallas the bureau reaction was precisely the same and just as immediate. For example, within a couple of hours of the assassination, Sergeant H. C. Sherrill of the nearby Richardson, Texas, Police Department, notified the Dallas FBI it had a strong suspect in the murder. An agent annotated the report before filing, "Not necessary to cover as true subject located."[14] And, this before Oswald had been identified, let alone booked, or the crime investigated. Even the morning of the next day the special agent in charge of the Dallas Field Office denied the Zapruder film had any evidentiary value, although he had never seen it.[15] In Washington, too, the same non-investigative approach was followed. At Bethesda Naval Hospital, where the JFK autopsy was conducted, the FBI refused to acquire the photographs and X rays or autopsy report, although these were absolutely necessary to locate the wounds on JFK's body. As Alex Rosen, head of the General Investigative Division, expressed it in a memorandum to FBI official Alan Belmont: "It is not recommended that we request these photographs and X-rays through the Secret Service at this time as it does not appear that we shall have need of this material."

In any case, Katzenbach's memorandum reflects Hoover's and LBJ's mutual desires on the issue:[16] "The public must be satisfied that Oswald was the assassin: that he did not have confederates who were still at large; and that the evidence was such that he would have been convicted at trial."

Trailing after that dictum, as something more than an afterthought but certainly no more than a pro forma priority, was this statement: "The only other step would be the appointment of a Presidential Commission of unimpeachable personnel to review and examine the evidence and to announce its conclusions. This has both advantages and disadvantages. I think it can await publication of the FBI report and public reaction to it here and abroad."

In effect, the memorandum concluded, prior to the government's formal investigation, that Oswald must ultimately be declared the assassin and that a blue-ribbon commission of reputable officials must publicly confirm that conclusion once their deliberations were finished.

Although the policy was kept secret, officials followed its principles throughout the inquiry. This can be profusely illustrated, but I shall consider only five major examples: Hoover's distribution of the memo, the selection of Earl Warren to head the Commission, the FBI report, Warren's guidelines to the Commission and staff, and communication of the document to the Commission staff. The first illustration of the policy's employment is found in Hoover's communicating the memorandum to the top six officials of the FBI and no lower in the echelon.[17]

President Johnson had a difficult time convincing the highly esteemed chief justice to serve on the President's Commission to Investigate the Assassination, but he finally did so. In the Oval Office, by appealing to Warren's patriotism and invoking Cold War paranoia, the president solemnly warned Warren that 40 million people could die if he did not accept the chairmanship and quickly bring closure to the Commission's investigation. Warren wept, but he took the job.

Clearly, LBJ was implying that if the public perceived Oswald to be part of a much larger plot—that is, a communist conspiracy—there would be calls for retaliation, which could quickly escalate into nuclear war. For that reason and in keeping with the Katzenbach memo, the crime had to be shown to be the work of Oswald alone and a deed committed for purely personal reasons. With that realization, a reluctant Warren accepted the chairmanship of a commission, seeking to shut down the communist conspiracy rumor mill and confirm Oswald as the lone assassin.

In his first meeting with the Commission staff on January 20, 1964, Warren restated Johnson's appeal when he explained the reasons he accepted the task. As recorded in a memorandum for the record by staff member Melvin Eisenberg (see document 14 in the appendix), he reported:

> The President stated that rumors of the most exagerrated [sic] kind were circulating in this country and overseas. Some rumors went as far as attributing the assassination to a faction within the Government wishing to see the Presidency assumed by President Johnson. Others, if not quenched, could conceivably lead the country into a war which could cost 40 million lives. No one would refuse to do something which might help to prevent such a possibility. The President convinced him that this was an occasion on which actual conditions had to override general principles.[18]

What truth was there to the possibility of demands by the American public to retaliate against the perpetrators of JFK's murder, assumed to be Soviet, that would escalate to nuclear war and could only be blocked by making Oswald the sole unaffiliated assassin? The evidentiary base reveals none. In Johnson's published public papers, telephone logs, oral histories of key aides, and documents relating to the assassination, there is no mention of and no worry expressed over such a potential disaster. The only incident came on November 26, when in Mexico City one Gilberto Alvarado-Ugarte walked into the American embassy claiming he had seen Oswald in the Cuban Mexican embassy taking money to kill JFK. After a tumultuous scare, Hoover's agents, in a splendid performance, busted the background to the story, broke the agent in interrogation, and learned he was a Nicaraguan spy attempting to use the assassination to foment rumors to lead the United States into war with Russia.[19] On November 29, top officials knew beyond question that there was no Soviet war threat. All rumors had proved to be groundless, no alert of our armed forces anywhere had been ordered, nor did any occur, certainly a sine qua non for a war threat. Nor has serious contemplation of the possibility of war ever been discovered in the documentary record. Johnson's primary motivation appears to have been to establish command over the executive branch and govern. The policies set forth in the memorandum would achieve that end.

A third expression of the Katzenbach doctrines appeared in the FBI's report of December 9, 1963, on the assassination.[20] This important document, known also as Commission Document 1, served as the blueprint for the Commission's investigation, with the Warren Report really being an expression of the December 9 report. Its five volumes fully expressed and impressively affirmed the Katzenbach principles: only Oswald was considered as an assassin; he had no confederates. And the evidence it set forth established "that he would have been convicted at trial."

But the December 9 *Investigation of Assassination* was, like its parent Katzenbach memorandum, political in nature. Although a report of a criminal investigation, its five volumes contained just two hundred *words* on the assassination itself (see document 15 in the appendix). It omitted one of the shots fired, overlooked one of the wounds on the body of JFK, and omitted similar critical facts.[21] The volumes primarily contained a diatribe against Lee Harvey Oswald, painting him as a communist when in fact the evidence shows he was an Orwellian in philosophy and anticommunist, antisocialist, and anti-Soviet in practice.

The evidence for Oswald's anticommunism is extensive and definitive. For example, his favorite books were George Orwell's anticommunist classics *1984* and *Animal Farm*.[22] Moreover, the FBI and the Commission could not find a single witness or provide any fact to support the charge he was a communist or pro-communist. No personal contact with a Communist Party official is known. Additionally, Oswald did not have a clear understanding of communist or socialist ideology as attested by those who knew him, for instance, by the statement of Ruth Paine, a friend of his wife in Irving, Texas, among others. An informed and knowledgeable student of Soviet Russia, she amusedly remarked Oswald was so ignorant of Soviet beliefs that he did not know the difference between its two basic clashing ideologies of Trotsky and Stalin.[23]

When we turn to his speeches and writings, the same anticommunist fervor is apparent. In 1963 he delivered anticommunist and antisocialist speeches at a Jesuit college in Battles Wharf, Alabama.[24] Furthermore, in his writings Oswald consistently expressed hatred of the communist and Soviet systems.[25] "I hate the U.S.S.R. and Socialist system" and "I hate and mistrust Communism" are typical phrases sprinkled through his journals and letters.[26] When he was in Russia the Soviets thought he was an American agent,[27] and his Russian friends asked him to stop damning and cursing Communism.[28] The Commission's oft-cited left-wing Fair Play for Cuba Committee run by Oswald in New Orleans as inferred proof of his leftist leanings[29] was "entirely fictitious," devised by him just for private reasons.[30]

Scores of federal officials and politicians read the FBI's five-volume report of December 9, 1963, yet in the vast surviving records of the official investigation only a single criticism can be found. Federal agents, presidential assistants, attorneys and officials from the Departments of Justice, State, and Defense, the secretary of the navy, congressmen, senators, Justice Warren, and others with extensive experience in the principles of evidence and in law enforcement, men with common sense and a lifetime's experience in analyzing documents, mutely accepted this patent absurdity as a definitive statement on the assassination of President Kennedy. Seen from the perspective of history, this refusal to comment negatively or to leave even a note in their papers, or to mention it in their memoirs, or otherwise to have recorded their views of the report is an incredible fact perhaps explainable only by their fear of the bureau's reaction to any dissent, so great was its power and so certain would be its retaliatory crushing response. The exception was the general counsel of the Department of Defense, John T. McNaughton. McNaughton was an esteemed authority on evidence, had written textbooks for law courses on evidence, had edited a new edition of the legal classic *Wigmore on Evidence,* taught in many American law schools, and was as candid in his comments as he was ignored by his fellow attorneys, officials, and politicians.

"My principal suggestion relates to what is *not* in the report," he replied to Katzenbach's request for an evaluation of the report. "It does not include evidence relating either to the number of shots which were fired or to the injuries sustained (with the exception of the one found in the President's back)." After discussion of these points, he remarked "that the authors had made up their minds as to the implications of the evidence before the evidence was stated." One bullet, he continued, was not accounted for. In addition, "there was no reference to a paraffin test on Oswald's face." The handwriting exhibits, he says, are "humorous," meaning incompetently selected, for their subject content raises questions about the conclusions best not raised: Why did the State Department grant Oswald a passport so quickly, and why suggest Oswald was trying to shoot Connally instead of Kennedy? This memorandum from such an esteemed expert implies that officials and top individuals involved with the investigation were perfectly aware of the political cover-up engineered by the bogus FBI report.

The Department of Defense suppressed McNaughton's dissent. Four years later it refused to permit his critique to be included in the Warren Commission holdings in the archives on the incredible grounds that "no purpose can be served by" such a move. Ten years later it required a threat of a lawsuit against the Department of Justice by the indomitable critic Harold Weisberg to force Katzenbach's file copy into the public domain.[31]

Another example of the Katzenbach memorandum's guiding influence can be seen in Warren's first memorandum to Commission members. He issued it on January 11, 1964, a month after the first executive session of the Commission and *before* the newly assembled staff had begun its investigation. In that memo, "Tentative Outline of the Work of the President's Commission," he declared that Oswald was the sole assassin, that only three shots had been fired, and that the motive was personal, not conspiratorial. Fifty percent was on "Lee Harvey Oswald as the Assassin of President Kennedy," 30 percent covered "Lee Harvey Oswald Background and Possible Motive," and 20 percent was a description of the assassination, "Assassination of President Kennedy on November 22, 1963, in Dallas."[32]

A last example of the memorandum's circulation is found in its appearance in staff files. Department of Justice attorney Howard Willens was the department's liaison to the Commission and its staff director, the second in command of the staff after J. Lee Rankin, chief counsel. As a result of a lawsuit, critics found a copy of the memorandum in Willens's Commission files at the department, bearing his initials.[33]

As these key elements illustrate, the Katzenbach doctrines influenced the simulated investigation from top administrators to staff and agents. They imposed upon the official investigation the absolute need to control, and associated with that need came its Siamese twin of corruption. This includes the treatment of the Zapruder film.

When on December 5, 1963, the seven members of the President's Commission on the Assassination of President John F. Kennedy gathered for their first meeting—an executive session the stenographic transcripts for which the Commission classified and treated as top secret—they took upon themselves heavy duties laden with grave responsibilities for the nation. Although not immediately apparent to the average citizen caught up in the trauma of President Kennedy's death, at stake from the start of the commissioners' inquiry was the integrity of that America's distinctive and celebrated political system.

But such integrity is certainly called into question, in light of the Commission's use (or misuse) of the Zapruder film. Instead these distinguished members—Earl Warren, Gerald Ford, Hale Boggs, Richard Russell, John Sherman Cooper, Allen Dulles, and John McCloy and their eighty-four-member staff, with the aid of the FBI and CIA—behind a veil of needless secrecy over the next nine months carefully manipulated the evidence found on those uncommonly vital motion picture frames in order to maintain control over their predetermined solution of a lone, single assassin.

The Commission had neither the right nor the need to classify anything. Had the police not made it possible for Jack Ruby to kill Oswald, Oswald would have been tried in public, with all that was alleged made public. Nothing would have been classified—nothing kept secret.

In the history of the Republic there has never been a peacetime federal commission or committee with as much power and funds as a grieving America lavished on the Warren Commission. The official documents establishing the Commission set it on its grim course with explicit instructions.[34] By the terms of an executive order the Commission's seven members had "to ascertain, evaluate and report upon the facts relating to the assassination and the subsequent violent death of the man charged with the assassination."[35] The purpose of the Commission was "to examine the evidence" already developed and all other evidence "that may hereafter come to light" and "to make such further investigation" as "it finds desirable."[36] It received full powers of subpoena, to compel appearance and testimony as well as to compel the production of records.[37] Further, the Commission could utilize any resources the executive departments of the federal government possessed in order to achieve its ends,[38] an extraordinary component of its inquiry. Congress did not stint; it provided for any funding that it might need. Thus, the Commission had no constraints placed upon its acquisition, analysis, and use of the Zapruder film and any other film.

It is a valid supposition that without the Zapruder film the Warren Commission's conclusions about Lee Harvey Oswald would have been more difficult to refute. The evidence in the film stood as a major barrier to the federal authorities' efforts to impose their preconceived solution of Oswald as the lone assassin. This may also explain why, in light of the Katzenbach memo, the Commission used few of the other films and photographs available to it. Moreover, strange as it may seem, in the mass of records one finds no census or definitive list of all the other films taken in Dealey Plaza on November 22. The Commission, its staff, and the FBI seem to have treated the entire photographic base with a studied disdain, perhaps because the official investigators did not want to address evidence that might jeopardize their "solution" of the crime—that Oswald alone killed Kennedy.

In 1964, however, the establishment and influential media largely refused to address the photographic base of the federal inquiry. In the words of critic Sylvia Meagher, it bore "a large responsibility for the tranquilization of the American public and its complacent acceptance of the Warren Report."[39]

With no official system to identify, record, and make available for study the films and photographs of the assassination, the public had to rely on the critics, private citizens, to perform this essential task. Unfortunately, they possessed neither access mechanisms to most records nor sufficient resources; they further lacked a safe central depository or other professionally managed facility to receive what film and information they had found. The citizen scholars and critics further learned in bruising, sometimes losing, battles that federal judges, officials, and bureaucrats were determined opponents to their efforts. As a consequence, the cinematic and photographic record is inadequate, incomplete, and imperfect, with many films and photos now lost for good.

Nevertheless, over five hundred films and photographs of all types have been identified, including Polaroid, motion picture, television, slides, black-and-white, and color, associated with that day in Dallas.[40] And yet, strangely, the Commission examined only about sixty photographs and films and brought into evidence only about thirty.

The Commission's and FBI's treatment of the Charles Bronson and Robert J. E. Hughes films vividly illustrates the federal dereliction of responsibility while enabling us to understand the Zapruder film milieu. The Bronson film was evidentiary dynamite. At nine o'clock in the morning of November 25, 1963, three days after the murder of President Kennedy—but early the first working day after that murder—Walter Bent, sales service manager of the Eastman Kodak Company, the same firm that had developed

Zapruder's film, telephoned the Dallas FBI office and spoke to FBI special agent Milton L. Newsom.[41] His company had just received film from Charles Bronson to be developed. In his package Bronson had included a note advising Kodak that the film may be of the assassin as he fired the shots. Would the FBI, said Bent, be interested in viewing the film?[42]

Newsom's memorandum of the conversation reads as follows:

Mr. WALTER BENT, Sales Service Manager, Eastman Kodak Company, Processing Division, 3131 Manor Way, telephone FL 7-4654, Dallas, telephonically advised his company had received two rolls of 8 milimeter [sic] Kodachrome and one roll of 35 milimeter [sic] film in a package from Mr. CHARLES BRONSON, Chief Engineer, Zarel Mfg. Company, 9230 Denton Drive, Dallas, Texas.

Mr. BRONSON enclosed a letter with his film, stating that the film had been taken at the instant President KENNEDY was assassinated. BRONSON also advised in the letter that from the position he was stationed when he took the film, he feels quite certain the Texas School Book Depository Building was clearly photographed and he feels that the window from which the shots were fired will be depicted on the film. He stated for this reason he believes he may have a picture of the assassin, as he fired the shots.

Mr. BENT stated Mr. BRONSON's letter indicated he desired to be cooperative regarding the film with proper authorities and BENT is of the opinion that BRONSON will have no objection to turning the film over to proper authorities in the event it is of value to the investigation.

Mr. BENT stated that he would make arrangements with Mr. BRONSON to view the film at the Kodak Processing Center and would arrange this so that FBI Agents could be present and at the same time interview BRONSON concerning his film of the scene.

Mr. BENT assured his full cooperation regarding all film received of a like nature that may possibly be connected with this matter and arrangements were made with him to immediately notify SA NEWSOM of any film of possible value.

The Eastman Kodak Processing Service Division receives all color film made by 8 milimeter [sic] Kodachrome in this area and also most other film for the area is processed by this division. Mr. BENT explained that his employees have not worked since Saturday and they are due back to work at 11:30 PM, 11/25/63. When processing of recent film orders begins, he expects other films taken at the approximate time of President's assassination.

He said that BRONSON's film should be processed and ready for viewing by 3:00 PM. He was told that SA NEWSOM would meet with him at that time.[43]

Bent then phoned Bronson and set up a meeting at the Kodak plant for 3:00 P.M.

At 3:00 Special Agents Milton Newsom and Emory Norton appeared at the plant and together with Bronson watched the films.[44] Afterward they did not ask for copies. When they returned to their office, they wrote up a memorandum on the films that in part said:

Films taken by Mr. BRONSON at the time of the President's assassination including 35 mm. color slides which were taken with a Leica camera, and 8 mm Kodachrome film were reviewed. These films failed to show the building from which the shots were fired. Film did depict the President's car at the precise time shots were fired; however, the pictures were not sufficiently clear for identification purposes.

One of the 35 mm. color slides depicted a female wearing a brown coat taking pictures from an angle, which would have, undoubtedly included the Texas School Book depository Building in the background of her pictures. Her pictures were evidently taken just as the President was shot. Approximately five other individuals in the photo were taking pictures at the time.[45]

Despite this potentially valuable information, the Dallas FBI refused to obtain copies of the films; it also suppressed any knowledge that those films even existed. Either through neglect or far worse, the FBI buried both memorandums in the Dallas office with not a word going to Washington. No one would ever know the films existed.

The films lay in Bronson's storage files until fifteen years later, when critic Harold Weisberg's successful FOIA lawsuit (CA 78-0322) pried loose the FBI Dallas field office files. In the released files he discovered the Newsom memos. He alerted Earl Golz of the *Dallas Morning News* and Gary Mack, a Dallas critic, who tracked down Bronson in Ada, Oklahoma.[46]

On November 22, Bronson had stationed himself near the corner of Houston and Main Streets on the plaza's south peristyle atop a four-foot-square, four-foot-high abutment. Right before and during the assassination, he took slides with his Leica Model III, a 35mm camera, and also used his 8mm Keystone Olympic K-35 movie camera.

About six minutes before the motorcade appeared, Bronson shot a few 8mm frames facing north up Houston Street, using a wide-angle lens, then stopped. As the motorcade appeared down the street, he took another brief sequence, then changed cameras. With the 35mm he snapped two pictures of JFK as the limousine turned onto Houston. He then switched back to his movie camera and filmed a few seconds of the president moving toward Elm Street. When the limousine turned onto Elm behind foliage, Bronson changed once more to his Leica, trying to be ready to take a photograph when the car would emerge from behind the trees and shrubs.

As Bronson was still preparing to take a picture of JFK, a shot rang out, and its sound made him instinctively jump and snap the shutter. The slide appears to have been taken at about frame 229 of the Zapruder film. From Bronson's distant position atop the peristyle abutment, the limousine appears quite small on the slide. Bronson then quickly changed to his movie camera and filmed the limousine, capturing President Kennedy just as the death shot struck his head.

What do Bronson's pictures show? The FBI agents reported after a close viewing of them that "the films failed to show the building from which the shots were fired." On the contrary, the films actually do show the building—that very "assassin's" window—in ninety-two frames. What they *do not show* is Oswald in the window shooting President Kennedy. The FBI missed or had no interest in that crucial detail. Or, more ominously, as some have suggested, they may have deliberately suppressed this evidence because it undermined the Commission's Oswald-did-it theory. Perhaps that is why Newsom declined copies of Bronson's film, stating that the death shot sequence was not clear enough for identification purposes.

But to identify what? The sharp 35mm film shows the limousine and all its occupants, the surrounding area, the grassy knoll, along with dozens of identifiable witnesses, and much more. Yet the FBI seemed curiously unimpressed by the film's potential value. This is strange, if not duplicitous, behavior.

For example, to have seen five persons in the Bronson films photographing the assassination and not to have moved quickly to identify them with the bureau's vaunted detective abilities, gather their films, and study them could easily strike one as criminal dereliction of duty. To this day, the FBI has yet to offer a credible explanation for this malfeasant behavior.

The Bronson film's shameful treatment typifies the fate of much of the assassination's photographic evidence. Other films, such as Altgens's and Willis's pictures, got into the Commission's hands only because it could not avoid them. Ike Altgens's photograph of the front of the depository building snapped from south of Elm Street, at Zapruder frame 255, became part of the Commission's record when it appeared on the front page of newspapers. It posed a difficult problem for authorities because it shows what almost certainly is Oswald standing with other spectators on the steps of the depository watching the motorcade pass when, of course, he was supposed to have been on the sixth floor shooting JFK. Some of Phil Willis's slides became part of the official case only when he started to sell them commercially.

When the FBI did obtain film it could not ignore, it sometimes altered its meaning. The Robert J. E. Hughes film provides an instructive example. Hughes, who worked as a customs examiner for the U.S. Treasury in the Terminal Annex Post Office just south of Dealey Plaza, owned a Bell & Howell 8mm motion picture camera. Over his lunch hour on November 22 he walked to the plaza and positioned himself on the southwest corner of Houston and Main Streets to film the presidential motorcade.[47]

At about 12:20 Hughes began the first of a series of short filming sequences with his camera directed east up Main Street. He then filmed the presidential limousine coming up Main to turn onto Houston, paused, and then resumed filming as the limousine turned onto Elm Street. As the JFK vehicle moved before the depository, Hughes turned his camera to other parts of the motorcade and then stopped filming. He heard shots. He looked toward the presidential limousine, with Jacqueline Kennedy in distress, as it moved under the triple underpass and disappeared. He began to film again, for several seconds scanning the tumultuous scene.[48]

On Monday, November 25, Hughes had his film developed at Sears, Roebuck and then took it to the FBI office, where he turned it in for examination for possible evidence.[49] The bureau made copies of the film and returned it to its owner. In its December 9, 1963, report on the assassination, the bureau discussed the Hughes film and in Exhibit 29 printed a blowup of one of its frames, which accidentally captured part of the Texas School Book Depository.

The reproduced portion shows the two easternmost windows, but there is no indication that it is a tiny part of a frame or that the frame came from a motion picture. The caption reads in part, "Film shows an object in the window of the sixth-floor room from which the shots were fired as the President's car passed the Depository Building. The object is not susceptible to identification because of the quality of the pictures."[50] This ambiguous language hides a grim fact. Actually, the FBI laboratory studies of the film had reached an unequivocal conclusion that there was no person in the window: "There are no images . . . in the form of an individual. The forms recorded in this window can be interpreted as in the same general shapes as boxes."[51] The FBI excluded this information from its exhibit. In addition, the bureau was also inexact regarding the time Hughes took the photograph, stating that the "picture was taken moments before assassination."[52] It should have been much more precise, for clearly one can see the limousine directly beneath the depository.

Apparently the results of the study would have safely lain in FBI files and not been brought into the Commission investigation but for the appearance of one of the early books on the assassination. Early in 1964, before the Commission had completed its inquiry into the assassination, Thomas G. Buchanan published *Who Killed Kennedy,* in which he claims that the Hughes film shows *two* silhouettes in the alleged assassin's window at 12:30.[53] Once this notion was exposed to public knowledge, it had to be formally addressed by the Commission.

In its Report's "Speculations and Rumors" section the Commission contradicts Buchanan's allegations by asserting the film was "taken at 12:20 P.M., 10 minutes before the assassination," and calls the silhouettes "shadows from the cartons near the window."[54] But its official evidence—the film itself—shows the limousine passing directly beneath the window at the same time, so it must have been taken within seconds of the assassination. Equally crucial *and* unacknowledged, the Hughes photo does not show Oswald in the window.

In the Hughes photograph, with the shooting just a few seconds away, the assassin had to have been in the window—unless, of course, the shots had come from somewhere else. And that is precisely what the Hughes image seems to suggest. But the Hughes film was not unique in that regard.

In retrospect, it now seems quite conceivable that, if Abraham Zapruder's film had not come to public notice in such dramatic fashion, the

Commission might have been able to avoid it, too. But his motion picture came to reporters' attention almost immediately.[55] Within the hour following the assassination, Dallas Secret Service agent Forrest Sorrels visited Zapruder's office.[56] At 2:00 P.M., Zapruder appeared on television describing the murder scene and mentioning his motion picture.[57] The next morning Zapruder showed it in his office and sold it to *Life* magazine.[58] The national radio networks broadcast that fact, and CBS ran a dramatic verbal description of what Dan Rather said the film showed—and did not show.[59]

Subsequently, *Life* vigorously publicized the film. In its November 29 edition the magazine ran a series of stunning prints enlarged from the film.[60] This added to the nation's shock. Everyone knew about the Zapruder film then. In such public circumstances, of course, federal investigators and the Commission could hardly avoid the film. So they devised ways to define and frame its content.

In an ordinary murder investigation when evidence like the Zapruder film has been determined to be vital to understanding the crime, it is typically acquired or seized by authorities to prevent its misuse and to assure that it is not tainted and will remain usable as evidence. But neither the Warren Commission nor the federal investigative agencies adhered to this standard or obeyed the dictates of common sense. In fact, the Commission never acquired the original film or even a full set of slides of each frame made from it.

Refusal to acquire the best evidence in a complete and pristine condition had a double impact on the murder inquiry. First, it enabled the Commission to avoid evidence it wanted to—and had to—avoid. Second, as long as the original film remained in the hands of its owner, Time Inc., anyone seeking to investigate the assassination in the future would face barriers in attempting to examine the information-laden original.

Further, the Commission refused to depose Zapruder until July 22, 1964, the month after the scheduled release of the Report, eight months after the assassination, and two months before the Report of more than nine hundred pages was actually printed. But for an odd coincidence, one of those that appear often in the history of the investigation, Zapruder might not have been called at all.

In early June, the FBI leaked to the press a story about its conclusions that stated three bullets had been fired, with two hitting JFK and one Governor Connally.[61] It neither mentioned nor accounted for the shot that had damaged a curbstone or the spraying residue that had slightly wounded citizen James Tague. Soon after the story appeared, Tom Dillard, a *Dallas Morning News* photographer, was assigned to cover a Dallas function where he encountered Barefoot Sanders, United States attorney in Dallas. Dillard told him the recent press account was incorrect or at least incomplete, for on the day of the assassination he had covered a shot that had struck a concrete curb and had published a picture of it.[62]

Sanders, following up on Dillard's statement, directed one of his staff, Assistant United States Attorney Mary Jo Stroud, to convey the information to the Commission. Stroud sent a letter to the Commission's chief counsel, J. Lee Rankin, and enclosed a photograph of the damaged curb taken by Dillard.[63] This sent Rankin scurrying. The Commission now had no alternative. Public knowledge of the Tague shot with a published photograph meant the Commission had to scrap its original scenario of three shots striking the occupants of the limousine, two hitting JFK and one hitting Connally, and fall back on Arlen Specter's single-bullet invention in order to accommodate its declaration that only three shots had been fired.

But, to make its three-bullet theory persuasive, the Commission was forced into contorted reasoning compelled by the difficulties encountered in trying to duplicate the shooting by Oswald. First, the Mannlicher-Carcano rifle allegedly used by Oswald was physically incapable of performing the shooting feat calmly assigned to it by the Commission. The official evidence demonstrates the rifle was literally a piece of junk, apparently converted by sheer force of official rhetoric into a killing machine of supernatural capacities. It was in such poor shape that the weapon had to be overhauled before it could be tested.[64] Its scope was structurally defective and could not be focused to an aiming point.[65] It also "fired high and to the right," forcing the bureau to add shims to stabilize the sight.[66]

The army also tested the rifle. Ronald Simmons Jr., chief of the Infantry Weapons Evaluation Branch of the Ballistics Research Laboratory at Aberdeen Proving Grounds, Maryland, testified to having provided additional repairs because his shooters "could not sight the weapon in using the telescopic sight." They had to add two more shims, one to adjust it vertically, and the other to the side.[67] The "trigger pull" operated in "a two-stage operation where the first—in the first stage the trigger is relatively free, and it suddenly required a greater pull to actually fire the weapon."[68] This tended to move the rifle off target. Additionally, the amount of effort required to open the bolt after firing to eject the spent cartridge and insert a new bullet was so great that it threw off the rifle, and the shooter had to re-aim.

The army assembled three of the finest marksmen in America, all rated as "masters," to duplicate Oswald's alleged feat. Not one of them could do so, not even after the rifle and firing conditions were altered to favor them. Yet the alleged perpetrator Oswald himself was rated officially by the marines as only a poor shot. The marksmen had even used a more convenient height: the test firing position was thirty feet high, whereas Oswald's alleged position had been sixty-one feet high. Further, their test targets were stationary, unlike JFK's moving limousine, and they were not forced to fire through two panes of glass. They also fired scores of practice shots to acquaint themselves with the rifle and conditions and set the sight when they should have fired the weapon cold, since Oswald by the official evidence never fired the Mannlicher-Carcano or any weapon in the year leading up to 12:30 P.M. on November 22.[69]

Yet, with all these advantages, deceptively passed off to the public as an identical duplication of the shooting, the best riflemen in America could not duplicate Oswald's alleged feat. But the Commission still relied on the tests as partial proof of Oswald's guilt. If the tests had been performed in public, with full exposure of conditions and issues, it could not have attempted such a charade.

The Marine Corps evaluated Oswald as only a "poor shot" at best, according to Lieutenant Colonel A. G. Folsom Jr., who evaluated Oswald's Marine Corps marksmanship.[70] On May 6, 1959, at El Toro Marine Corps base in California, using the standard Marine Corps M-1 rifle, Oswald scored a 191, a bare point above the minimum qualifying score. It also appears unlikely that between May 1959 and November 1963 his ability could have improved.

Accurate shooting is a physical skill that requires constant practice.[71] Since his move to Russia and his subsequent return, Oswald had fired weapons only twice. He hunted once with a .22 caliber rifle[72] and once with a shotgun.[73] In the former instance he "could not hit the side of a barn," and in the latter he missed a close rabbit.[74] Based on this knowledge alone, it must seem highly unlikely that Oswald could have, according to the Commission's findings, slain the president with only three shots in six seconds.

The Commission members now also—thanks to Dillard and Sanders—

had to account for the shot that damaged the curb and caused Tague's wound. (Even the Dallas policeman L. L. Hill had recorded this shot on his police tapes: "I have one guy that was possibly hit by a ricochet from the bullet of the concrete."[75] Tague also had reported it to Deputy Sheriff Eddy Buddy Walthers.)[76] But they had to do so in a way that kept the total number of shots at three. Thus the Commission decreed that the first shot inflicted all seven nonfatal wounds on JFK and Connally, the second shot hit the curbstone, causing spraying concrete to slightly wound Tague, and the final shot killed JFK.

To prop up this newly adopted conclusion, the Commission moved to secure the curbstone, to depose several witnesses associated with the Tague shot, to depose Zapruder, and to rewrite the heart of the Report around the single-bullet theory.

On July 7, 1964, Rankin wrote Hoover requesting additional investigation of the curb shot. On July 15 two agents of the FBI Dallas office examined the area and reported they could find no damaged curbstone. When Rankin persisted, Hoover dispatched agent Lyndal Shaneyfelt to Dallas. He contacted Dillard and James Underwood, a Dallas television photographer, who had also photographed the curb, and easily found the precise portion of curbstone. The curb showed no damage, for it had obviously been patched, although this is never referred to in any official documents. A scientific examination made for Henry Hurt, the author of *Reasonable Doubt*, later established it was a patch of cement paste, a substance radically different from the concrete of the curbing.[77] Shaneyfelt had city workers cut out the curbing, a piece about eighteen inches long, and brought it back to Washington.[78]

In Washington the FBI laboratory examined the piece by spectrographic analysis, ostensibly looking for evidence of a bullet's impact but apparently ignoring the obvious fact that the curb had been patched. Indeed, in no official document, study, report, or discussion of the curb shot and the wounding of Tague, whether by the FBI, the Warren Commission, the House Select Committee on Assassination, or any federal agency, would the patch ever be admitted or discussed. In its study of the patch, the FBI found only two elements—lead and antimony—out of a possible eleven elements contained in the alleged assassination bullets.

When the Commission asked the FBI to define the path of the Tague bullet from the sixth-floor easternmost window of the depository, it reported the shot would have corresponded to frame 410 of the Zapruder film. The bullet would have passed high in the air above JFK, to strike the curb 260 feet from his location in frame 313.[79]

In order to make its theory work, the Commission had to call a number of witnesses central to the single-bullet theory and also associated with the Tague shot, including Zapruder himself. Zapruder, however, never actually appeared before the Commission. A single lawyer, Wesley Liebeler, questioned him in secret on July 22, 1964, behind the closed doors of the office of the United States attorney in Dallas.[80] Liebeler was a thirty-three-year-old wunderkind six years out of the prestigious University of Chicago Law School and a member of a major New York City law firm. By contrast, Zapruder was almost twice his age, had been born in Russia, and had suffered from the ravages of pogroms and hunger before immigrating to a better life in America.

Zapruder possessed a keen memory. Thanks to his location and telephoto lens, he also had one of the best views of the assassination of anyone in Dealey Plaza. He had been standing on the four-foot-square, four-foot-high concrete abutment of the pergola on the slope of the north grassy knoll when he filmed the presidential motorcade from its appearance at the plaza at Houston and Elm Streets until the limousine disappeared under the triple underpass as it sped to Parkland Hospital. His telephoto lens, of course, greatly magnified everything he filmed.

The Commission, however, viewed Zapruder's deposition primarily as a loose end that had to be tied up for the sake of appearances. In fact, it waited until the last minute to call Zapruder to testify, and then only when circumstances beyond its control eliminated any alternative. For Liebeler, Zapruder was one of a large number of loose ends that had become his responsibility. He had had an exceptionally busy day on July 22, grinding out six important witnesses, including Zapruder. (On July 23 he turned out five more, and the next day, joined by another assistant counsel, he banged out another two.) On July 22, with only a court reporter present, Liebeler questioned the critical witnesses. At 10:40 P.M., he deposed Emmett Hudson, the Dealey Plaza groundskeeper who described the grounds and testified to seeing a shot hit JFK from the front.[81] Hudson noted, "They have moved that R. L. Thornton Freeway sign and put up a Stemmons sign," which with other alterations in the grounds meant the FBI and Commission reenactments of the assassination sequence were not true to the conditions of November 22, a fact Liebeler simply ignored.[82] At 11:50 he interviewed Mrs. Donald Baker, née Virgie Rachley, who testified to standing near the street curb and seeing a shot hit the pavement of Elm Street behind the limousine.[83] She recalled, "Well, after he passed us, then we heard a noise. . . . I saw a shot or something hit the pavement."[84] Liebeler gave her a photograph upon which he asked her to locate the place she saw the strike. She could not. But the photograph he presented her had been taken from the opposite direction from her position on the plaza and did not show the Elm Street pavement at all.[85] Thus her testimony was skewed.

Liebeler devoted the afternoon to photographers—each of whose pictures destroy the official conclusions. At 12:45 P.M., he interviewed James "Ike" Altgens, a Dallas Associated Press photographer.[86] From the south side of Elm Street Altgens had taken a photograph of JFK and the limousine as it passed the depository. Behind the limousine, in the doorway of the building, stands a man who from other and officially ignored evidence appears to be Oswald.[87] At 1:00 Liebeler deposed Zapruder,[88] and then at 2:30 Phil Willis, who had snapped critical slides of the assassination (discussed elsewhere) in fewer than five pages of transcripts. Liebeler's questions appeared to be carefully structured to avoid matters of substance.[89] At 3:15 he deposed Willis's daughter Linda Kay.[90]

On July 23, Liebeler continued his assembly-line interrogations. At 10:00 A.M. he deposed waitress Helen Markham, who was a Commission witness to Oswald's alleged shooting of Tippit.[91] During a telephone interview with a critic, however, Markham had provided a description of the man she had seen that did not fit the description of Oswald she had given officials. Liebeler played her a tape of the telephone call, but, under oath, Markham swore she had never spoken with him. "And I never heard this lady's voice before"—a comment she made about her own voice.[92] Liebeler, surprisingly, seemed unconcerned by this apparent perjury. At 1:00 P.M. he took the testimony of Joe Marshal Smith, a Dallas police officer who right after the shots had rushed to the grassy knoll, where he had encountered a man who identified himself as a Secret Service agent, even though the official record states that no Secret Service agent was at the plaza.

At 2:00 Liebeler deposed Harry Holmes, United States postal inspector, to testify about Oswald's postal boxes.[93] At 3:15 he deposed James Tague, who had stood near the triple underpass and had been slightly wounded,[94] whose clearly pro forma questioning consumed only six pages of transcript, twenty-two pages less than that of Oswald's befuddled former landlady. At 8:16 that evening, he deposed Deputy Sheriff Eddy Buddy Walthers, to whom Tague had reported the shot and who saw the blood on Tague's face.[95]

At 10:00 A.M. on July 24, Liebeler deposed Buell Wesley Frazier once again to ask if he had ever before seen Oswald carry a package into the depository.[96] The answer was no. Five minutes later he deposed Dallas policeman Edgar Leon Smith Jr., who upon hearing the shots had drawn his pistol and run up the grassy knoll and behind the fence to search for the shooter.[97] That night at 9:15, Liebeler's cocounsel Burt Griffin deposed Dallas police captain Perdue William Lawrence, who had been in charge of traffic control on the day of the assassination, which included assigning officers to protect the motorcade route.[98]

Zapruder's testimony was essentially squeezed in among this flurry of last-minute Dallas depositions rather than given appropriately special attention before the Commission in Washington, D.C. Only Liebeler, the court reporter, and Zapruder were present. Here was a witness who should have been intensely grilled by the commissioners themselves rather than by their errand-boy lawyer. And, given the vagaries of memory with the passage of time, one must also wonder why the Commission waited a full eight months to call Zapruder. In that interim, his recollections could have been influenced or contaminated by 240 days of relentless press and television coverage. During that same period, the commissioners had built their Oswald lone-gunman theory around the Zapruder film in a way that shielded the public from apparent contradictions and without ever calling upon the filmmaker himself to testify.

Yet, amazingly, when Zapruder finally was deposed, his recorded testimony took only seven and one-half pages of the seventh volume of hearings. About one page is devoted to housekeeping matters (his name, addresses, legal notices, and the like), leaving only six and one-half pages for actual testimony, and much of that was volunteered by Zapruder rather than coaxed by a largely disinterested Liebeler.

By contrast, the testimony of Mary Bledsoe, one of Oswald's Dallas landladies for less than a week, consumed twenty-eight pages of the printed transcripts and shed little light on the case.[99] Still, the three assistant counsels who deposed her eagerly embraced her obvious dislike of Oswald. Cab driver William Whaley's rambling and confused testimony took eighteen pages.[100] Cecil McWatters, the bus driver whose bus Oswald allegedly rode briefly right after the assassination, was granted a full thirty pages and a trip to Washington with Whaley.[101] Among other things, he confused Oswald with a regular rider, a teenage troublemaker.

That these peripheral figures received a royal reception while Zapruder got a quick run-through suggests that the purpose of his deposition was not to elicit information on the crime but simply to tie up a potentially problematic loose end. It was apparent that continuing to ignore him could have been disastrous.

Nowhere in Zapruder's deposition does Liebeler elicit from him basic, defining facts about his film and his camera that would have been central in a court of law or any genuine investigation. The transcript does not include the type of camera and film that was used, the type and magnifying qualities of the telephoto lens, how and where the film was processed, the terms of sale to Time Inc., and many other questions relating to the handling of the film that day and to the chain of possession of the original and the copies made from it.

In deposing Zapruder, Liebeler used as an aid not his color pictures but the FBI's black-and-white prints, in which some clarity is lost. Zapruder volunteered testimony on their poor quality: "You take an 8 millimeter and you enlarge it in color or in black and white, you lose a lot of detail. I wish I had an enlarger here for you."[102] This is in striking contrast to the excellent exhibits that were prepared for other aspects of the Commission's investigation. For example, the FBI constructed a full-scale model of Dealey Plaza. It also made a detailed and illustrated laboratory study of the hairs it vacuumed from Oswald's blanket, as though anyone—other than his wife—had any interest in them.[103]

Whenever Zapruder volunteered answers that included important information for which Liebeler had not asked, Liebeler cut him off and changed the subject. One instance was particularly important. Critic Harold Weisberg described the background to it and the responses:

> The middle of three large signs on the north side of Elm Street was between Zapruder and the President for about 20 frames, from about 205 to 225. Because of the downward grade to the underpass, at the beginning of the sequence, only part of the President's head is still visible over the top of this sign. The Commission's entire case is predicated upon the assumption that the first shot could not have been fired prior to frame 210, for that is the portion of the film in which, even on a still day, the President first became a clear shot from the sixth-floor window.

Zapruder was explaining how he took his pictures. "I was shooting through a telephoto lens . . . and as it (the Presidential car) reached about—I imagine it was around here—I heard the first shot and I saw the President lean over and grab himself" (7H571).[104]

"Here" refers to a frame of the FBI's black-and-white pictures, but, incredibly, Liebeler does not ask Zapruder to identify the frame he referred to, nor does he himself insert it. This oversight made it easier for the Report to ignore Zapruder's testimony that he saw the first shot hit JFK earlier than the time in the official account. With the sign obscuring his view of the president's body and hands from frames 205 to 225, this means Zapruder saw a shot strike prior to frame 210.

A few minutes later Zapruder called Liebeler's attention once again to that spot on the film. Liebeler turned over to "picture 207" and remarked, "It appears that a sign starts to come in the picture . . . [and] was in the way."[105] Zapruder replied, "Yes; but I must have neglected one part—I know what has happened—I think this was after that happened—something had happened."[106] Zapruder was trying to explain that JFK had been shot already by frame 207, which would have been before frame 210 of course, and thus by a bullet that Oswald could not have fired. Liebeler, however, ignored Zapruder's implication and quickly changed the subject.

Another chapter discusses "Willis number 5," the fifth slide taken by Phil Willis, that corresponds to frame 202, snapped as an involuntary reaction to hearing a shot. This shot may have occurred just before frame 190, less than a second before frame 202, and very likely corroborates Zapruder's testimony. At frame 190 the film suddenly becomes fuzzy, a condition that could have been caused by Zapruder's reaction to the horror he had just seen—in magnification.[107] Liebeler, however, seems to deliberately avoid this line of evidence. Zapruder dolefully concludes: "I know very few people who had seen it like that—it was an awful thing and I loved the President, and to see that happen before my eyes—his head just opened up and shot down like a dog—it leaves a very, very deep sentimental impression with you; it's terrible."[108]

George Orwell put it well: control the past to control the future. By restricting and regulating public knowledge of the evidentiary worth of the Zapruder film, the Warren Commission, in effect, did just that.

About two months after the September 1964 issuance of the Warren Report, the Commission published its twenty-six volumes of hearings and exhibits, totaling ten thousand pages. Copies of 160 Zapruder film frames appeared in volume 18 as Commission Exhibit 885 (CE 885).[109] The printing did not include color, and the black-and-white copies used in the Report are less clear than the color copies made for the Commission by Time Inc. The printing process reduced clarity even more.

The copies printed as CE 885 contain errors. Frame 283 is printed twice, once labeled as 284 (the actual frame 284 is not printed).[110] Frames 314 and 315 are reversed. These frames are crucial ones, coming right after the terrible head shot at frame 313. Recall that the alleged fatal bullet should have struck JFK in the back of the head, propelling his head forward. Witnesses, however, described JFK's head snapping violently backward and then to the left. This orients the death shot to the grassy knoll, meaning to JFK's front and right, an impossible shot for Oswald. Even the FBI, in its commentary for the Commission, described the head reaction on the film as "the President's head snaps to the left."[111] James Altgens, the AP photographer standing on the south curb of Elm Street, recalled, "Pieces of flesh and blood and bones appeared to fly from the right side of the President's head and pass in front of Mrs. Kennedy to the left of the presidential limousine."[112] Because of the printing error involving frames 314 and 315, the head's violent reaction to the shot was reversed, making it appear that the shot came from the rear.

In addition, the unprinted black-and-white copies are five generations removed from the original and thus are significantly less clear.[113] The difference is most striking when they are compared with first-generation color frames. The frames should have been reproduced in color, even at greater cost, and with each frame given a full page. The Government Printing Office that year printed color volumes on trees in national parks, historic airplanes, and cooking recipes, suggesting that the decision to print in black-and-white was not dictated by budgetary concerns.

On one page the Report derives the speed of the limousine from the Zapruder film.[114] On another page, using the same base of the Zapruder film, it establishes that foliage blocked a view of the limousine from the sixth-floor window from frames 166 through 209 and that a sign blocked the camera's view of JFK from frames 210 to 225.[115] The single-bullet scheme, likewise pegged to the movie, appears on three pages, with a discussion of the last shot on two pages.[116] Another page links the Altgens picture to frame 255 and also asserts that the sound of the first shot caused Phil Willis to take his fifth slide, which is claimed to be from the same time as Zapruder's frame 210. This baldly misstates the official evidence on Willis.[117]

On page 63, Howard Brennan, the steamfitter who sat on a small ledge across from the depository and claimed to have seen Oswald in the window, "identified himself in the Zapruder movie."[118] But what the federal authors omit is that Brennan is in fact visible with his head turned toward his left shoulder watching the limousine go down Elm Street until frame 206, and at frame 207 his head whips to the right shoulder, looking to the east, not at the depository's sixth-floor window. On page 453, it uses the film as its basis for its description of Secret Service agent Clinton Hill's run to the limousine to climb aboard.[119]

On six pages it reproduces six frames (166, 186, 210, 225, 313, and 255),[120] coupled with photographs taken of the same frames during the reenactment in May. On another full page a photograph depicts an FBI agent taking the reenactment photographs with the rifle, a camera attached, standing on a tripod.[121] The reenactment procedures inaccurately reproduced the situation of November 22. The lower window is open to the sash, enabling the simulation weapon to aim, and achieving the proper angle of deflection to see the limousine on the street below. On November 22, the sash was closer to the sill. Additionally, the shrubs and trees had been trimmed, the street markings repainted, and the signs moved, rendering the claim that it was a reenactment not true and its portrayal as accurate a misstatement of reality.

In addition to overcoming physical impossibilities by simply ignoring them, the Commission included frame 186 (discussed in an earlier chapter), which is alleged to have been taken at the only break in the foliage before frame 210 where a shot could have been taken. But this is based not on the conditions of November 22 but on the May reenactment, after the trees have been trimmed and on a day without a strong wind. While frame 313—the "death shot"—appears, it does so without frames 314 and 315 showing the direction of the head, which would conceivably have raised doubts about the Commission's conclusion that Oswald had shot and killed Kennedy from the rear.

As these key elements illustrate, the Katzenbach doctrines influenced the simulated investigation from top administrators to investigators. They imposed upon the official investigation the absolute need to control, and associated with that need came its Siamese twin of corruption. This includes the treatment of the Zapruder film.

11 The Man in the Doorway

In the midst of the assassination, Associated Press photographer James "Ike" Altgens, standing on the grass on the south side of Elm Street, snapped a picture of the presidential limousine. Through the windshield President Kennedy can be seen slumped in his seat, hands reaching toward his throat. The Texas School Book Depository is in the background, with a crowd of spectators clustered near its entrance, watching the motorcade. In the doorway stands someone who looks very much like Lee Harvey Oswald. After taking another picture of the limousine speeding away, Altgens made a "mad rush" for his office, and by 12:57 his photograph moved over the AP wires to newspapers across the nation, the first of the assassination photographs that was widely printed.[1]

The Warren Commission Report claimed the figure in the doorway was actually Oswald's twenty-six-year-old look-alike coworker, Billy Nolan Lovelady. "The man on the front steps," the Commission stated, "thought or alleged by some to be Lee Harvey Oswald, was actually Billy Lovelady, an employee of the Texas School Book Depository, who somewhat resembles Oswald."[2]

Using the Zapruder film as a timing device, the FBI and the Commission determined Altgens's shutter snapped at the time of Zapruder's frame 255.[3] This, however, created something of a public relations problem, for quite by accident the black-and-white photograph seems to show Lee Harvey Oswald standing against the west side of the Texas School Book Depository's main doorway. If that is true, then Oswald could not have been the assassin, for by frame 255, the assassination was *already* in progress. Altgens's photo prompted many media photographic experts to ask, "Isn't that Oswald in the doorway looking at the assassination?" The FBI said no, that was actually Billie Lovelady, who worked in the depository with Oswald. Particularly in greatly enlarged photos, the two men do look alike. However, critic Harold Weisberg's investigation makes the persuasive case that the man in Altgens's photo was Oswald, not Lovelady.[4]

First, it is helpful to examine the Commission's allegations regarding Oswald's whereabouts in the early afternoon of November 22. Commission officials alleged Oswald was on the sixth floor of the depository at the time of the assassination, even though the evidentiary record suggests otherwise. They claim immediately after the assassination, police officer Marrion Baker and building manager Roy Truly had rushed up the stairs toward the top floor, but on the second floor Baker spied movement in a lunchroom through a small window in the closed stairwell door.[5] Baker burst into that room to confront Lee Harvey Oswald at the Coke machine.[6] Truly identified Oswald as an employee, and so Baker let him go.[7] Later the Commission concluded Oswald, lurking on the sixth floor, had shot JFK, hidden his rifle, rushed to a door leading to the stairs, rapidly descended the stairs, the only available way down, and calmly met the two men at the pop machine, even though no witnesses had seen Oswald do these things. In fact, the Commission ignored its own evidence that proved he could not have been there at that time.

The Commission's claim broke into two parts. The first part "reconstructed" Oswald's alleged flight down to the second floor; the second part "reconstructed" Officer Baker's movement up to the second floor. For the claims to hold, the Commission had to get Oswald down the stairs to the Coke machine on the second floor in time for Baker to rush in and meet him without Oswald being seen by Truly, who was well ahead of Baker as they ran up the stairs. If Baker arrived before Oswald could get there, Oswald was innocent. The Report says, "The time actually required for Baker and Truly to reach the second floor on November 22 was probably longer than in the test runs."[8] Their evidence indicates the opposite.

The bogus reconstruction using a stand-in and timed by a stopwatch was unblushingly corrupt.[9] To begin with, the assertion that there was an assassin's lair on the sixth floor is false.[10] The boxes near the window on the sixth floor, alleged to have been moved by Oswald to make a sniper's lair, had been moved and stacked there from the western half of the sixth floor by workers in the normal process of laying a new floor.[11]

Timed by a stopwatch, the stand-in started at the window with the rifle in his hand, then walked across the floor to the stairway door.[12] As he entered the doorway and took off down the stairs, he handed the rifle to Secret Service agent John Joe Howlett, who walked over to the stack of boxes where the rifle had been found and leaned over as if to deposit it.[13] In the first effort the Oswald stand-in got to the second floor in one minute and fourteen seconds. In the second effort he took one minute and eighteen seconds.[14]

Officials, however, omitted essential components of the alleged assassin's flight to the second floor: time spent lingering at the window,[15] wiping the rifle clean of fingerprints,[16] squeezing through the shielding wall of boxes around the window,[17] all of which added seconds. They also omitted the necessarily slow walk around the edge of the loosely slatted board floor to avoid detection, for three earwitnesses on the fifth floor testified that they had heard no one moving around on the sixth.[18]

Even more troubling in the timing formula were the Commission's claims regarding the disposition of the rifle.[19] When Deputy Constable Seymour Weitzman and Deputy Sheriff Eugene Boone discovered the rifle on November 22, it was well hidden. Weitzman, one of the few Dallas officers with a college degree, in engineering, was articulate and careful in his testimony. He also had clear recollections. Strangely, he was deposed in Dallas by assistant counsel Joe Ball[20] with only the stenographer present, whereas Boone, who was less articulate, went to Washington to testify before, confuse, and provide incomplete information to the Commission members.[21]

Weitzman related that the rifle was found inside a square of chest-high boxes. The assassin would have had to scale that shielding wall twice, once to get in and again to get out. Inside the wall of cartons, squeezed between other boxes, the rifle was standing on the tip of its upper butt, with the upper tip of its muzzle leaning on a box. It was covered with paper and had been placed under two overlapping boxes, piled one on the other. It "was covered with [other] boxes. It was very well protected as far as the naked eye," the constable told Ball.[22]

They had to search hard to find it; according to Weitzman, "eight or nine of us stumbled over that gun a couple of times."[23] When shown a photograph of the boxes on the sixth floor, he said that the rifle was "more hidden" than depicted there.[24] In 1967 Weitzman explained to CBS News that "Bone [sic] was climbing on top and I was down on my knees looking, and I moved a box, and he moved a carton, and there it was."[25]

Much time and effort would have been required to hide the rifle so well, climb over the wall of boxes twice, place the rifle carefully, cover it with paper, place two boxes over it, and then climb back over the boxes again. This is the official evidence known and avoided by those conducting the "reconstruction." To have the stand-in just lean over the boxes to simulate the hiding is a studied insult to the evidence but also the only method that would allow reenactors to get Oswald's stand-in to the second floor before Baker—which they still could not do.

But in addition to skewing the timing, the authorities also failed to fingerprint any of the boxes in question, although they fingerprinted many other boxes and packages on the sixth floor. Why not? Perhaps because there *were* no prints—at least *not* Oswald's—that would have cast doubt on Oswald's guilt. On the other hand, if the gloveless Oswald was indeed the sixth-floor sniper, his prints should have been all over those boxes.[26]

To make their scenario seem to work officials also had to render invisible the testimony of three witnesses. They omitted from the evidence the testimony of Jack Dougherty, who was working on the fifth floor near the stairway and heard no one come down the stairs.[27] They also eliminated from their consideration the testimony of two secretaries, Sandra Styles and Victoria Adams, who had been on the fourth floor. After the last shot they had fled to the stairway and were in fact on the stairs at the time Oswald had to have been there—and, according to Adams, he was not.[28]

As officials speeded up Oswald's flight, they also slowed down Baker's movements, for Oswald had to be inside the lunchroom *before* Baker and Truly arrived at the second floor.[29] They timed Baker's movements during the first run-through at one minute and thirty seconds, and during the second run-through at one minute and fifteen seconds.[30] But these calculations misrepresent what actually happened. First, the reenactors placed the starting point farther from the depository, when photographs show Baker closer,[31] and they started the officer's movements after the last shot, although the evidence shows the motorcycle cop actually began his dash to the depository after the first.[32] These silent reconfigurations of the scene added seconds to Baker's movements. The reenactors had Baker walk the first time and "trot" the second, whereas the evidence shows Baker "madly ran."[33] Again, the slower pace added critical seconds to the officer's time. Truly was ahead of Baker on the stairs, the door was closed, and he saw no one go into the lunchroom; that time was eliminated.[34] Neither Baker nor Truly saw the mechanical door close, meaning more time would have been necessary.[35] A careful examination of the official evidence by critic Howard Roffman shows that Baker actually got to the second-floor lunchroom in no more than a minute and ten seconds, perhaps much sooner.[36] This is long before Oswald could have arrived from the sixth floor in the timing of the artificial reconstruction.

Baker, as a key witness for the Commission, was in many ways untrustworthy, confused, ignorant, and a fabricator. Each time officials deposed or interviewed him, he gave conflicting stories on whom he saw and on which floor, with "each and every relevant detail contrary to the Commission" testimony.[37] In particular, the Commission members ignored what he volunteered and was true: that Oswald could have gotten to that second-floor lunchroom before him if Oswald had come up from the first floor.[38] On the other hand, they completely embraced Baker's testimony that Oswald could not have come into the lunchroom any other way except through the door to the stairs leading to the sixth floor.[39] Baker's official testimony on this point, in fact, contradicted hard evidence to the contrary, for workers (including Oswald) had access to another short stairway in the southwest corner of the building that led from the first floor to the lunchroom.[40] Many workers used it to go to the second floor. Oswald in fact had just told police he had come up from the first floor.[41] After the confrontation with Baker at the Coke machine, Oswald left the lunchroom by the same way he had entered and descended to the first floor, where he had been minutes earlier watching the motorcade.[42]

Not only could the federal reconstructions not place Oswald on the sixth floor without corrupting the evidence, but also authorities had scientific tests and other evidence that excluded him from being on the sixth floor shooting the president, which they either ignored or hid. One key piece of evidence was provided by tests made on paraffin casts of Oswald's face, which established he had not in fact fired a rifle that day. Paraffin tests rest on a well-known fact that when a rifle is fired, gases blow back on the shooter's face and hands, depositing detectable residues. At midnight on November 22, the Dallas police performed the normal tests on Oswald to detect any deposits, using warm liquid paraffin on his right cheek and both hands to make casts. As it hardened, the paraffin would remove and capture any deposits from his skin and pores. Police sent the casts to Dr. Martin F. Mason, director of the Dallas City-County Criminal Investigative Laboratory at Parkland Memorial Hospital, who at 10:45 A.M. on November 23 tested them with the reagent diphenylbenzidine.[43] The results showed "no traces of nitrates" on the right cheek, which meant Oswald had not fired a rifle, but they were positive for traces on the hands.[44]

In its Report the Commission dismisses paraffin tests by asserting that "a positive reaction is . . . valueless" in showing a suspect fired a weapon and thus "unreliable."[45] This is disingenuous. To be sure, ink, paper, and many other common objects that Oswald's hands touched that day during the normal course of his work could have caused a positive reaction, but as the Commission's own official evidence proved, the *absence* of traces is exculpatory. Oswald's cheek had none; he had not fired a rifle.

Not satisfied with the Dallas testing, the FBI in its laboratory also performed a more refined spectrographic test of the samples, a scientific test used by law enforcement for sixty years in similar cases.[46] The FBI lab drew the same conclusion about residues on the cheek. Then, under pressure from the Commission, the FBI submitted the paraffin casts to a third, even more sophisticated test. They took the samples to the Atomic Energy Commission facilities in Oak Ridge, Tennessee, where Dr. Frank Dyer and Joel F. Emory tested them using neutron activation analysis (NAA), a procedure that utilizes an atomic reactor. The atomic scientists reported that the cheek casting "could not be specifically associated with rifle"; in addition, the hand samples could not be connected with the chemical traces of the revolver cartridges.[47]

Upon receiving word of the findings, FBI headquarters immediately ordered its agents not to release or make known the results to anyone in order "to protect the Bureau."[48] The results were neither released nor utilized by the Commission. Nevertheless, after a bitterly contested lawsuit that lasted ten years, critic Harold Weisberg and his attorney James Lesar obtained the NAA raw data and the results from the bureau and the Oak Ridge authorities.[49] Weisberg discovered an additional element to the tests that was devastating for the official findings. The FBI had used a control in making the tests. Seven different men had fired the Mannlicher-Carcano rifle, and NAA officials had made paraffin casts of their cheeks, which were then tested for residues by the reactor. The control firings had deposited heavy residues on the control cheeks.[50] Oswald's cheek cast had no such residues or any traces whatsoever. He had not fired a rifle. This further supports Oswald being in the depository doorway at the time of the assassination.

Six witnesses and a photograph place Oswald on the first floor during or about the time of the crime: Junior Jarman, Harold Norman, Carolyn Arnold, Robert MacNeil, Pierce Allman, and Terry Ford, and, of course, the photograph by Ike Altgens. In custody Oswald referred to eating his lunch on the first floor and seeing two employees, Junior Jarman and Harold Norman.[51] Oswald could not have known this unless he had actually seen them there. From a careful examination of Jarman's and Norman's testimony, critic Howard Roffman has determined they were on the first floor from sometime a little after noon until approximately 12:20 or 12:25.[52]

Also significant is the statement of Carolyn Arnold, who saw Oswald on the first floor at 12:25.[53] Originally, the FBI interviewed Arnold four days after the assassination and incorrectly quoted her as saying "a few minutes before 12:15 PM."[54] Aware of the problem, in March two FBI agents reinterviewed her for the Commission.[55] When they wrote her answers out in longhand on yellow pads for her to sign, the agents misstated the time at 12:25 A.M. and asked her to sign.[56] She corrected the time to "about 12:25 P.M."[57] The FBI typed it as 12:25 P.M.[58] The Warren Report does not mention Carolyn Arnold, nor do the Commission's twenty-six published volumes of hearings and exhibits include her testimony.

While Arnold's formal statement exonerates Oswald, the information provided by three newsmen who rushed into the depository—Robert MacNeil, Pierce Allman, and Terry Ford—also attests to the presence of Oswald on the first floor right after the Altgens photograph was taken. Robert MacNeil, then a journalist for NBC, rode in the press bus of the motorcade. Upon hearing the shots, he ordered the driver to stop the bus and ran first to the hill, to find only confusion, then back to the depository to seek a telephone.[59] "As I ran up the steps and through the door," he wrote, "a young man in shirt sleeves was coming out. In great haste I asked him where there was a phone. He pointed inside to an open space where another man was talking on a phone situated near a pillar and said, 'Better ask him.' "[60] It seemed to have been Oswald, but MacNeil was not absolutely positive.

Pierce Allman, program director of WFAA-TV in Dallas, and Terry Ford, radio promotion director of WFAA, gave statements similar to MacNeil's (some weeks *after* the assassination). They watched the motorcade from the corner of Elm and Houston Streets. After the shots rang out, Allman stated in a January 31, 1964, interview with Secret Service agent Robert Warner, they ran "full speed into the Texas School Depository Building with the intention of locating a phone and calling his television station."[61] Just inside the building he "met a white male" whom he asked the location of a telephone. The man pointed to a phone. Allman said he could not identify the man "positively" as Oswald.[62] Ford related a similar story and stated he could not "remember if Oswald was the man."[63]

The statements by Allman and Ford are especially important when seen in context. During his interrogation Oswald had related to Captain Will Fritz of the Dallas police that on his way out of the building two Secret Service men had stopped him, but all agents were at Parkland Hospital. Wearing suits and with press credential tags hanging on their clothes, Allman and Ford easily fit a layperson's description of an agent. The Secret Service believed Allman and Ford to be the men Oswald saw.[64]

The official evidence shows Oswald ate his lunch on the first floor. He then walked to the depository doorway and watched President Kennedy's limousine pass. Afterward he walked up to the second floor by the southwest corner stairs, crossed the work space, entered the lunchroom to approach the Coke machine, where Baker abruptly rushed in upon him. He left the same way he had entered, down the hallway, across the work area, to the stairs, down to the first floor, and out of the building. He took time on the way out to stop and direct three men to telephones. But time, definitely, was what Oswald was running out of.

The answer to the question of whether Altgens's photo captured Oswald standing in the doorway of the depository turns on at least three basic ways the Commission and the FBI had to establish it. First, they could have printed good photos of Oswald and Billy Lovelady side by side and judged them, which they never did. Second, they could have had the several score employees of the depository examine Altgens's photo. Although they did take statements from almost a hundred people, only three were asked generally about it—Billy Lovelady, Buell Frazier, and Bill Shelley—and, as we shall soon see, their testimony was delayed, confused, and tainted. Third, in addition to photo comparisons and seeking witnesses, investigators could have utilized Oswald's shirt to prove identification.

This shirt would worry the FBI and the Commission staff and lead to extraordinary official deception. But instead of using it, they diverted attention to the physical characteristics of the figure in the doorway, whether he looked like Oswald or Lovelady, where reasonable persons can find ambiguity. In the publications of the Commission, no good, clear photo of Oswald's shirt appears and certainly none of the doorway figure.[65] The copy of the Altgens photo used is actually a fourth-generation, badly cropped print from the *Saturday Evening Post*, which loses detail and makes the doorway figure less distinct.[66] Only by visiting the National Archives could one see the actual shirt worn by Oswald that day, examine its color, and understand its features. It is long-sleeved, has a grass leaf pattern, and is rust brown with gold flecks scattered through it.

No picture of the shirt Lovelady wore that day and claimed to have identified for the Commission appears in its publications. But careful researchers found tucked away in the twenty-six volumes of the Commission hearings and exhibits a May 1964 newspaper clipping and interview with Lovelady in which he describes the shirt he wore as "a red-and-white striped sport shirt buttoned near the neck."[67] Puzzled by this discrepancy with the actual Oswald shirt, critics discovered in Commission records in the National Archives FBI photos taken of Billy Lovelady in the shirt he claimed to have worn that day. It does not come close to looking like the shirt worn by the figure in the doorway or the Oswald shirt. It is short-sleeved, with vertical two-inch-wide blue and white stripes.

Thus, critics began to wonder whether the glaring shirt differences might mean the figure in the doorway was not Lovelady but possibly Oswald. They began to search for more photographic evidence to bolster their suspicions. They first sought to examine the largely ignored films of the assassination for a picture showing the shirt Billy Lovelady wore that day. After hard work they found it in the John Martin film. When the presidential motorcade moved through Dallas, a number of amateur motion picture enthusiasts scattered along the route took 8mm motion pictures of the momentous event. One of these amateurs, John Martin, shot twenty-five feet of 8mm color film.

At about 12:10 Martin left his office in the Post Office Terminal Annex, located on the southwest corner of Dealey Plaza, to station himself on the west side of Houston Street near the Commerce Street corner. The depository was one block to his left, or north. He filmed as the president's limousine appeared out of the east on Commerce and turned right onto Houston, then he ran north almost to Elm Street to a position on the far end of the park's northern reflection pool, where he took more pictures. He did not film the assassination but immediately afterward captured the milling crowd in front of the depository, among whom Harold Weisberg would ultimately determine stood Billy Nolan Lovelady. Martin lingered on the plaza, continuing to take pictures.

Before Martin returned home that evening, *Life* magazine had contacted his family; soon it acquired his film, taking it to its New York City headquarters for study and possible use. More than two weeks later, on December 11, the Dallas FBI office notified Washington about the film and what had become of it. On December 17, New York City FBI agents visited *Life's* offices and borrowed the film, sending it to Washington, where the bureau made a copy and then returned the original. The records do not indicate that the bureau then (or ever) studied the film as evidence in the crime. *Life*, though, decided the film had no commercial value and soon returned it to Martin.

In a few weeks a Dallas amateur venture incorporated part of Martin's film into a local documentary. Following the assassination, housewife Anita Gewertz, an amateur motion picture buff, worked to find other area residents who had filmed that day, eventually locating eighteen films. It is somewhat startling to realize that Gewertz, in her spare time, managed to locate eighteen films taken during the motorcade and murder of the president of the United States, whereas the massive resources of the federal government and its premier investigative agency never located one of them. What they did recover—the work of Zapruder, Altgens, Willis, and so forth—had been foisted upon them by external circumstance or when it became known in the press or otherwise had entered into public knowledge. The later words of a secret FBI internal examination of its handling of the president's murder properly expressed the view of a top official that the FBI's investigation was similar to "standing with pockets open waiting for evidence to drop in."[68]

Gewertz and her friends founded Dallas Cinema Associates, edited portions from the eighteen films, including John Martin's, into *President Kennedy's Last Hour*, and sold copies. Eventually Wolper Productions marketed a 16mm commercial version. Copies of both versions wound up in the Commission records, but they were never examined or studied.

Only in March did the bureau interview Martin, but even this was forced. The federal attorney in Dallas, Barefoot Sanders, learned from Postal Inspector Harry Holmes, an associate of Martin, that Martin had not been interviewed. Sanders wrote to the FBI about this omission, more than three months after the bureau had acquired a copy of his film. The film remained unexamined during 1965 and 1966. Then, from Dallas and New York City came two developments that would ultimately compel a close look. In early 1967, Mrs. Billy Lovelady telephoned Harold Weisberg. She complained that the FBI photographs he had reproduced in *Whitewash II* depicting her husband in a short-sleeved, vertical-striped shirt were in error. As Weisberg related in his memorandum to himself on the incident:

She insists it is "my Billy" in the doorway, that the FBI never asked him what shirt he had worn that day, and that he had worn a red-and-black check with a white fleck. The checks, she says, are about two inches. When I said the Altgens picture shows no check, she replied that it is not as clear as the enlargement "as big as a desk," about 30 X 40 inches, the FBI showed them the night of Nov. 25, 1963. Demanding money in return, she promised me a picture of Lovelady in the check shirt she says he wore that day and not since and an affidavit affirming the above. She alleges testimony was edited, FBI reporting was inaccurate and not all in the evidence.[69]

Apart from the account of FBI tactics, she introduced yet another element in the search for a picture of or the actual shirt Lovelady wore on November 22. If the shirt did not match Oswald's shirt, it was not Lovelady in the doorway but Oswald. Heretofore, on the basis of FBI and Commission records, critics thought they had been looking for confirmation of a short-sleeved vertical-striped shirt; it turned out Lovelady was wearing a checked shirt. Notably, neither a striped nor a check shirt resembled the shirt on the figure in the doorway. Mrs. Lovelady's comments also seemed to mean Billy was not wearing the Oswald shirt.

Then, early in 1967, an opportunity arose that eventually led to the discovery in the Martin film of Lovelady. "Long John Neble," host of a popular five-hour evening New York City talk show featuring Neble's reactionary politics, invited Harold Weisberg to appear and discuss the president's murder. Weisberg quickly discovered Neble had sprung a trap on him by inviting Victor Lasky and Kirin O'Dougherty to join the discussion. Lasky, a longtime critic of JFK, adamantly supported the Warren Commission findings. O'Dougherty was a key associate of the conservative William F. Buckley.

Weisberg ripped them apart, refuting their points, attacking their facts, and revealing that their support of the findings was based on blind ignorance and a truth-vitiating political premise rather than knowledge and fact. After two and one-half hours of contentious questioning and heated battle, the program took its normal thirty-minute break for the news and to allow the participants to have refreshments. At this point Neble, Lasky, and O'Dougherty abruptly canceled the rest of the show.

Soon thereafter Weisberg received a letter from Dick Sprague, a businessman then living at the University Club in New York, who had listened to the Neble show and wanted to know if there was some way that he could help. Weisberg inquired if he traveled much. When Sprague said yes, Weisberg sent him the addresses of the eighteen persons who had contributed to *The President's Last Hour* with the suggestion he contact Mrs. Gewertz and examine complete copies of the individual films, especially the Martin film, and report back. Sprague did precisely that. Some years later, in 1975, as he revisited the problem of the Altgens photo, Weisberg surmised that it was possible no one had looked into an overexposed area of the Martin film for evidence of Lovelady. He asked Robert Groden, a film expert he knew, to do so. In July 1976, Groden sent him a blowup of the overexposed Martin frame taken right after the assassination. It shows Lovelady milling in the crowd outside the depository in a long-sleeved black-and-red plaid shirt buttoned at the collar with no buttons unbuttoned.

The Martin frame gives us an authentic look at the shirt Lovelady wore. At this time we have established Oswald was on the second floor of the building or moving down the stairs to the first floor. Moreover, since this image was filmed after the murder, Lovelady could have arisen from the steps or walked in from some other location or, in the Commission's theory, moved out of the doorway into the crowd. Only by comparing the shirts can we eliminate Lovelady as the man in the doorway.

The Warren Commission, however, ignored the shirts entirely to insist that the Oswald look-alike in Altgens's photo was Lovelady by focusing exclusively on witness testimony, taken months later and after the witnesses had seen photos and knew of the controversy. It relied on the testimony of three witnesses: Billy Lovelady, "who identified himself in the picture," and depository employees Wesley Frazier and Bill Shelley, "who also identified Lovelady."[70] But the facial features of Lovelady and Oswald were similar enough to confuse even those who knew Lovelady. When Lovelady's own children saw Oswald's image on television on November 22, they exclaimed, "There's daddy!"[71]

The Commission, however, actually misrepresents Frazier's and Shelley's alleged identification of Lovelady standing in the doorway. With respect to Shelley, the Commission's Report misrepresents his April 7, 1964, testimony. Contrary to the Report, he never *explicitly* said Lovelady stood outside on the steps near him. In fact, his earlier statements to officials state the opposite.[72] On March 18, he had told FBI agents E. J. Robertson and Alfred Neeley, in a statement used by the Commission staff counsel Joe Ball to prepare for the April 7 testimony, "Billy N. Lovelady, who works under my supervision for the Texas School Book Depository, was seated on the entrance steps just in front of me."[73] *Seated*, not standing. In Frazier's

case a falsely marked exhibit taints his testimony and renders his identification of Oswald as invalid and its use as improper.[74] As critic Sylvia
Meagher has reported, the Commission asked both Frazier and Lovelady
when they testified to mark with an arrow on the same print of the Altgens
photograph the person thought to be Lovelady. Both supposedly did so, but
the photo contains only one arrow.

Supporters of the official findings also focused on the ambiguous facial
characteristics rather than the critical evidentiary item of Lovelady's shirt to
link Lovelady to the doorway. Commission member Gerald Ford's view in
Portrait of the Assassin is typical of this mistake. He uses only Junior Jarman
to support his contention it was Lovelady standing in the doorway when he
writes that Jarman said, "Lovelady [was] on the stairway as you go out the
front door." But how could Jarman know that? What the future president
omitted was that, at the time of the attack and when the Altgens picture was
taken, Jarman, according to Commission evidence, had left with Harold
Norman at about 12:20 or 12:25 for the fifth floor of the depository—that is,
he was not on the first floor at 12:30.[75] Thus, he could not have known the
disposition of spectators on the depository steps, who had been milling
and jostling for good positions just minutes before the motorcade appeared. Yet, four pages later Ford contradicts Jarman and himself by citing
Harold Norman, Jarman's coworker. Norman states that he saw Lovelady
"sitting on the steps there."[76]   So ?

The identification of Oswald in Altgens's photo, however, is also based
on the shirt he was wearing. Using a high-power magnifying glass, the
picture and Martin's frame can be examined. First and most startling, the
shirt's color and pattern identify it as Oswald's. Oswald's shirt was expensive but old. As noted earlier, it had a pattern like a grass leaf, essentially
brown with gold flecks through it. But, as we have seen, Lovelady's shirt
had two-inch dark blue (almost black) and red squares or checks, separated by thin white lines.

Second, using a magnifying glass, certain defects in Oswald's shirt can
also be detected in the Altgens photo. For example, on the right edge of the
open Oswald shirt is a small tear that is also present on the shirt of the
figure in Altgens's photo. Also, on Oswald's shirt the top three button-
holes are stretched, meaning the shirt could not be buttoned at the collar or
for the next two buttons. In the several photographs of Oswald in custody,
his shirt displays the same open throat and neck as does the shirt on the
man in the doorway and the shirt in the archives. By contrast, Martin's

Lovelady shirt is buttoned at the top as well as at the next two buttons, none of which Oswald's could do.

Third, the collars of the two shirts furl differently. In addition, the cuffs are of a different type in size and construction. Finally, Oswald's shirt is loose and baggy, whereas Lovelady's has a more tailored fit.

Such persuasive evidence supports Oswald's location in the doorway of the Texas School Book Depository viewing the motorcade at the moment the president was shot. Conceivably, Oswald himself tried to explain this and urged his captors to confirm his story by locating witnesses who would verify his location in the doorway and lunchroom. Just as likely, amid the chaos of his capture and initial incarceration, and in the face of official pressure to pin the assassin's badge on him, such protests of provable innocence were brushed aside as the rush to judgment gained momentum.

Zapruder frame 189

Zapruder frame 190

Zapruder frame 191

Zapruder frame 192

Zapruder frame 193

Zapruder frame 194

Zapruder frame 195

Zapruder frame 196

Zapruder frame 197

Zapruder frame 198

Zapruder frame 199

Zapruder frame 200

Zapruder frame 201

Zapruder frame 202

Zapruder frame 203

Zapruder frame 204

Zapruder frame 225

Zapruder frame 237

Zapruder frame 260

Zapruder frame 313

Zapruder frame 337

Zapruder frame 338

Earl Warren, Chief Justice of the Supreme Court and presiding member of the Warren Commission, delivers the Commission's official report to Lyndon Johnson at the White House. From left to right are Commission members John J. McCloy, J. Lee Rankin (general counsel), Senator Richard Russell, Representative Gerald Ford, Earl Warren, President Johnson, Allen Dulles, Senator John Sherman Cooper, and Representative Hale Boggs. (LBJ Library).

The Head Shot and Zapruder Frames 337 and 338

The evidence on frames 337 and 338 of the Zapruder film could alter the course of American history. From his perch atop the concrete abutment, Abraham Zapruder had recorded these frames almost one and one-third seconds after the death shot, fired according to the Commission between his frames 312 and 313. In fine color detail these two frames clearly show the back of President Kennedy's head undamaged, with his clothing intact and unbloodied.[1] It proves that the shot that caused the president's massive head wound came from the front and that there was no shot in the back of his head, thus affirming that two or more assassins conspired to kill him.

Like so many of the key pieces of evidence associated with the investigation of the assassination these frames have a tortured, manipulated history, not to mention decades of neglect by defenders of the Warren Report. On February 25, 1964, Herbert Orth, assistant chief of *Life* magazine's photographic laboratory, carried the original film from New York to Washington to screen it for the Commission staff members and representatives of the FBI and Secret Service. This central piece of evidence in the assassination of President Kennedy was *Life*'s property, and the magazine would not permit the federal government to use it, only view it under supervision. This was a flawed arrangement, to say the least, for a central piece of evidence in a criminal investigation.

Afterward Orth agreed to provide the FBI 35mm color slides of frames 171 through 334 so that the detail they contained might be studied more thoroughly, which he promptly did, but for unexplained reasons he added nine more frames, numbers 335 through 343.[2] In testimony before the Commission the bureau's photographic expert, Lyndal Shaneyfelt, stated that a complete set was not requested because the investigation required only the "pertinent" ones.[3] An April 21, 1964, letter from J. Edgar Hoover to the Commission covers the bureau's receipt of "three sets of these slides . . . [with] 169 slides in each set."[4]

For unknown reasons the FBI made a series of black-and-white copies of only frames 171 through 334 from the *Life* set, leaving aside frames 335 through 343. The bureau then bound the 160 frames into a portfolio volume, squeezed two per page,[5] that is, frames 171 through 207 and 212 through 334, because, as noted elsewhere, frames 208 through 211 were destroyed and frame 212 badly damaged during *Life*'s processing. The Commission printed the images as Exhibit 885 (CE885) in volume 18 of its *Hearings*, where the poor copies served for many years as the only source of information on many parts of the film that was available to citizens who could not visit the National Archives.[6]

Through his research critic, Harold Weisberg recovered the nine slides omitted from CE885. As discussed in his book *Photographic Whitewash*, published in 1967 and reissued in 1976, Weisberg knew the Commission had requested the missing nine frames from *Life* and believed they had to exist.[7] Soon after the book's appearance, the archivist in charge of the Commission records at the National Archives telephoned him to apologize and said there had been a mistake. They had now, he informed Weisberg, put the nine slides in a tray for viewing and would permit him to see them. Weisberg did so immediately, examining the frames in a room where he sat near a wide doorway and looked at the projected frames on a screen that was about five feet wide. He operated the projector very slowly. After two frames, 335 and 336, he was startled to see on 337 and 338 what the bureau's mistake had obscured.

On these frames one sees that the president has been propelled violently backward, then is falling over to his left twisting toward his wife. As he falls over, it is possible to see, for one-ninth of a second, what is not seen in motion on the film. The back of President Kennedy's head, neck, shirt collar, and suit coat are seen in surprisingly sharp detail. There is no blowout of the back of the head. No hair is out of place on the back of his head; there is no blood on the back of the head, nor on his collar, neck, or jacket. These two frames were recorded more than a second after the fatal shot at frames 312 and 313.

The time consumed by two frames is one-ninth of a second, which is why what they show is so hard to pick up when watching the Zapruder film. But that information is extraordinarily crucial, for it disproves the official explanation of Lee Harvey Oswald as the lone assassin, a theory that absolutely requires the fatal shot to strike JFK in the back of the head. Thus, within the iron parameters of the official findings, an exit shot had to have caused the gaping head wound. But to exit, the transiting bullet had to have an entrance in the rear of the head, which the Commission asserted existed: "The smaller hole in the rear of the President's skull was the point of entry and the larger opening on the front right side of his head was the wound of exit," reads the Report.[8] But there was no hole in the rear of the skull. The Commission misstated that fact, despite the availability of other corroborating evidence: the autopsy protocol, the autopsy photographs, the nine slides themselves, and the testimony of witnesses.

On Sunday morning, November 24, Dr. James J. Humes, the head of the autopsy team and a lieutenant commander in the United States Navy, drafted the holographic autopsy protocol in his home.[9] Immediately after Jack Ruby killed Oswald at 12:21 P.M. eastern standard time, Humes burned the autopsy in his recreation room fireplace and drafted another.[10] With Oswald dead, there would be no trial, and the autopsy would not be submitted to cross-examination in court. (He did not burn his notes, for weeks later the Commission counsel held them in his hand during Humes's testimony.) Humes then took the draft protocol to Admiral C. B. Galloway at Bethesda Naval Hospital, where the admiral made substantive changes in it, adding and eliminating phrases and words, before having it typed.[11]

The draft protocol (i.e., the surviving holograph) is on ordinary tablet paper marked with faint blue lines, much like the tablets used by schoolchildren. On page 7 Humes wrote that in the rear of the president's head there was a "puncture wound tangential to the surface of the scalp." The admiral crossed out this phrase and replaced it with "lacerated wound."[12] The difference in meaning is enormous. Thus we see that in this original report by the person performing the autopsy, there was no mention of a hole in the back of the head. "Tangential to the surface of the scalp" cannot and does not mean a hole in the back of JFK's head.

Black-and-white prints of the autopsy photographs themselves offer evidence that further and definitively argues against a rear-entry head wound. They include two photographs of the back of JFK's head, neither of which as much as hints at a rear entry for the fatal shot. In addition, the nine frames, 335 through 343, depict President Kennedy moving violently backward and to the left. According to the incontrovertible laws of physics, this is necessarily the reaction to the impact from a frontal shot. That violent movement is visible, patent, and irrefutably present.

Several eyewitnesses reinforce this view. Among the best were motorcycle policemen Jim Chaney and Douglas Jackson, who rode on the right flank of the motorcade, about six feet from JFK, with Chaney almost touching the limousine. Full access to the information they could provide was blocked by the decision of the FBI and the Commission not to interview them or any of the other fourteen motorcycle policemen of the escort, leaving citizens and critics to sort through the chaff for a missed kernel. What they had to say might have complicated or destroyed the official efforts to pin the assassination on Lee Harvey Oswald.

Late in the afternoon of November 22, Dallas's KRLD-TV, a CBS affiliate, from a position at the end of the third-floor corridor of the Dallas police station, filmed through the crowd. Halfway down the corridor, leaning with his back to the wall with his helmet still on, Chaney told reporter Bill Mercer that he had seen a shot "hit him in the face."[13]

On November 28 the FBI briefly interviewed Chaney but only to ask him a single question: Had he seen Jack Ruby the day after the assassination? The answer was no. The information possessed by this closest eyewitness external to the limousine who was a trained law enforcement officer assigned to protect the president proved to be of no interest to federal officials. He was never again interviewed, nor did the Commission staff take his testimony.[14]

Eleven years later, the FBI, in a face-saving move, finally interviewed Jackson, who saw "President Kennedy struck in the head above his right ear, and the impact of the bullet exploded the top portion of his head, toward the left side of the presidential vehicle,"[15] confirming both a frontal shot and the direction of its force from right to left, not back to front. This perfectly fits with the frames' evidence.

Right after the assassination, police and deputy sheriffs brought a number of individuals into the sheriff's office on Houston Street to be interviewed. One of these individuals, Faye Chism, had been standing with her husband, John Chism, to the right of the Stemmons Freeway sign on the north side of Elm Street as the motorcade passed by. About the head shot she said, "It came from what I thought was behind us."[16] Her husband told the deputy, "I looked behind me."[17] A. J. Millican, who stood on the north side of Elm, said the "shots came from the arcade between the bookstore and the underpass," which would appear to be the pergola area behind Zapruder.[18] Jean Newman, who had also stood near the Stemmons sign, said the president fell to his left—that is, in reaction to the impact of a shot from his front.[19] William Newman was standing on the north curb just a few feet from JFK when he saw the death shot hit. "By this time he was directly in front of us," he swore, "and I was looking directly at him when he was hit in the side of the head."[20] A side hit could not have come from the rear.[21]

Emmett Hudson, the groundskeeper, had been sitting on the steps leading down from the grassy knoll to the street and to the right of Zapruder. Hudson had seen the president fall to his left under the impact of the last shot.[22] Marilyn Sitzman, from atop the abutment with Zapruder, had a clear view of the head shot. She was neither called as a witness nor interviewed by officials. Just after the assassination a reporter for the *Dallas Times Herald* had rushed to the scene and spoken with her. His notes on what Sitzman saw are clear: "Shot hit pres. Right in the temple."[23] In 1967 she related to an interviewer that "the shot that hit directly in front of us . . . hit him on the side of his face. . . . Between the eye and the ear. And we could see his brains come out. . . . it exploded his head more or less."[24] Charles Brehm stood ten feet from the limousine. Immediately after the shooting he said to a newsman who had rushed up to the plaza, "The shots came from in front of or beside of the President." He explained that the president did not slump forward as he would have after being shot from the rear.[25]

Ken O'Donnell and Dave Powers, JFK aides who rode in jump seats of the Secret Service follow-up convertible about fifty feet behind the president, were in an excellent position to see the murder and hear the sound of gunshots. Years later, over a dinner with a fellow Bostonian, Speaker of the House Tip O'Neill, they related they had heard two shots from the hill or grassy knoll. Before publishing his account of the conversation in his memoirs, O'Neill confirmed it with Powers. Independently, Powers also had informed a critic that he had so told the FBI but the bureau was not interested.[26]

On the right running board next to Powers and O'Donnell stood Secret Service agent Paul E. Landis Jr., who saw "the President's head split open with a muffled exploding sound." Although he was uncertain of the precise source of the shot, his reaction "was that the shot came from somewhere towards the front . . . the right-hand side of the road," where he looked in vain for signs of a shooter at the hill and at the overpass. After he returned to Washington, Landis set down his recollections for the Secret Service, which communicated them to the President's Commission, but no one took his testimony.[27]

Also witnessing the assassination from a vantage point to the rear of the presidential limousine, but several score more feet back on the southeast corner of Elm and Houston Streets, was Hank Farmer. At 5:36 P.M. on

November 22, he telephoned the Dallas FBI office to report he had seen President Kennedy hit in the face by a bullet from the front and Governor Connally hit in the back by a bullet fired from "the opposite direction." Although Farmer was later interviewed by the FBI, no record of an interview has yet been turned up, and the Commission staff did not take his testimony.[28]

As related in a previous chapter, Abraham Zapruder's testimony and statements on November 22 placed the source of the head shot to the front of JFK. To two newspaper reporters on the scene right after filming the assassination, he said the shot hit the president in the face. To the plant manager at Kodak he explained he thought the shots came from behind him. That night he told a Secret Service agent that the shot "came from behind." And before a Warren Commission's assistant counsel eight months later he stumbled under rough, quick questioning and said he did not know.

Some ask whether JFK's severe front head wound, as seen most vividly in the Zapruder frames, was one of exit or entrance. If the wound was one of entrance, then there also must have been an exit. Contrarily, if it were suggested that the wound was one of of exit, then there must have been an entrance wound. In both interpretations of the wound it would seem there must be a corresponding rear wound to accommodate the physical fact of a bullet transiting President Kennedy's head.

The concern partially rests on a faulty presupposition. It improperly assumes the killing bullet had to be of the same caliber, type, and character as the bullet found in Parkland Memorial Hospital and tagged as Commission Exhibit 399. That bullet, with a lead core and a copper sheath, is of hardened metal, designed under the terms of the Geneva Convention for military bullets so it would not disintegrate or split up upon impact.[29] The bullet that caused the awful head wound was a different kind that broke into tiny pieces, many of them "dust-like."[30] This distinction alone strongly suggests that two different rifles were engaged in the killing of JFK.

The bullet left scores of tiny fragments in the head; the fragments did not have enough power to penetrate even the soft tissue of the brain. On the X rays the pattern of dispersal can be reasonably interpreted as a pattern laid down from a frontal shot.[31]

Another important consideration is the character of the wound, which was both an entrance and an exit wound. The bullet exploded when it struck JFK's head, blasting out bone, brain tissue, blood, and other matter in all directions. Some flew to the president's rear. One piece of the skull flew across the trunk lid behind JFK. In the Zapruder film at frames 345 through 406, one sees Mrs. Kennedy scrambling to catch it as Secret Service agent Clint Hill jumps on the back bumper and reaches up to shove her back in the seat. Matter flew to the right, lightly spraying the two motorcycle policemen riding on JFK's right flank. Matter flew to the president's left, drenching the two cyclists on that side. Matter exploded upward, visible on the Zapruder film spraying up into the air at rapid speed. In addition to behind, left, right, and up, matter and fragments of bullet were thrown ahead. Fragments struck and dented the interior chrome trim along the top edge of the windshield and also hit the windshield. Tissue, blood, and matter also flew downward, covering the seats and floor. At Parkland Hospital the Secret Service agents hosed out the limousine, and in Washington agents cleaned it further, finding small fragments of bullet. Thus, the wound is one of both entrance and exit.

In addition, when the bullet struck the right side of the skull, the explosive force cracked the skull in several places, with much of the skull remaining in place but rent by fissures. The force, though, sent several skull fragments flying from the limousine, to be found later on the plaza. Yet other fragments pulled loose from the skull but adhered to the scalp skin. On a hinge of scalp a loosened piece flapped back, exposing the blasted inner head, as well as showing adhering matter exposed on the underside. Some who saw this flapped skin caused by the damage from the front head wound mistakenly believed they saw a wound in the rear of the head. Later doctors fitted the pieces of skull back into place like a grisly puzzle. They found no hole in the back of the president's head.

Over the last decades a large number of theorists have claimed the photographs of the assassination and the autopsy materials were faked by federal authorities to hide the patent, clear, and solid evidence they contain of a conspiracy. Chief among the alleged doctored images are the Zapruder frames. These charges, however, are without logical or factual foundation. A closer examination reveals that they are not actually based on an analysis of the official evidence and are marred by gross errors or misunderstandings that undermine or refute their own arguments.

A conspicuous example of such erroneous views can be found in the work of Dr. Gary L. Aquilar, who has an essay in James Fetzer's recent book

Murder in Dealey Plaza.[32] Relying on an impressive list of qualified doctors and witnesses, he argues that there was a blowout in the back of JFK's head. But Zapruder frames 337 and 338 convincingly contradict that contention. In fact, they establish beyond question that the official findings on the assassination are wrong and that two or more gunmen killed President John F. Kennedy.

Photographic Proof of Conspiracy
Zapruder Frame 202

A detail in a photograph's background depicts Abraham Zapruder atop the pergola's concrete abutment, his eye to his camera's lens as he films the assassination. His receptionist, Marilyn Sitzman, stands next to him, straining to hold on to his coat to keep him from falling. Printed in the Warren Commission's twenty-six volumes of hearings and exhibits, the photograph is a blowup of a 35mm slide snapped from the south side of Elm Street by Phil Willis. It shows JFK in his limousine moving down Elm Street with the hill or grassy knoll and pergola in the background, a street sign slightly above and to the immediate left of the limousine and the Secret Service backup car in the foreground. The fifth of the slides he took that day, Willis number 5 corresponds to Zapruder frame 202. The evidence in both plus the evidence in frames just before and after Zapruder's frames 181 through 206 prove a shot was fired immediately before frame 190. This means at least one other gunman was involved, if one accepts the Commission's view that Oswald could not have fired a shot before frame 210. Nor does this conclusion demand arcane skills, abstruse arguments, or special training to understand and master. The facts are simple and clear, the judgment sure and unalloyed by doubt.

Yet authorities completely ignored this startling evidence, an analysis of which cannot be found anywhere in the 912 pages of the Warren Report or the twenty-six volumes of testimony and exhibits on which that report is based. This omission should not be all that surprising if one recalls how early the Commission committed itself to the conclusion that Oswald alone assassinated JFK. That, in turn, does not allow a shot before frame 210. Anything that established that a shot came before frame 210 directly contradicts the Commission's lone assassin theory.

Before proceeding, it is necessary to recall certain basic points in the official conclusions in order to understand the uncommon importance of

Abraham Zapruder's frames 181 through 206 and its affirmation by Willis number 5.

In its September 1964 Report, the Warren Commission held that from the easternmost window of the School Book Depository, Lee Harvey Oswald,[1] alone and unaided and for purely personal reasons,[2] fired three shots: "The preponderance of the evidence, in particular the three spent cartridges, led the Commission to conclude that there were three shots fired."[3] Oswald killed President John F. Kennedy, severely wounded Governor John B. Connally, and very slightly wounded James Tague, who was standing near the triple underpass.[4] One shot missed.[5] The Commission claimed it did not know which one: "The evidence is inconclusive as to whether it was the first, second, or third shot which missed."[6] But its conclusions and evidence are constructed precisely and unequivocally on the first shot striking the president no sooner than frame 210.

According to the Commission, two shots hit JFK.[7] The first struck him "near the base of the back of the neck,"[8] then "passed through the President's neck,"[9] exited the throat,[10] and continued on into the body of Governor Connally to inflict five wounds and break two large bones.[11] The second of the two shots to strike Kennedy "entered the back of his [the president's] head and exited through the upper right portion of his skull"[12] at a time corresponding to between frames 312 and 313 of the Zapruder film and killed him.[13] The missed shot hit the curbstone near Tague's feet, spraying him with concrete and slightly wounding him.[14]

Oswald, according to the official conclusions, stood ("he was standing up")[15] and sat ("the boxes in the window . . . serve[d] as a gun rest")[16] in the depository window.[17] But constraints external to the building made it impossible for Oswald to fire the first shot before frame 210. "The foliage of an oak tree . . . came between the gunman and his target,"[18] blocking his view of JFK from frame 166 until frame 210.[19] The Commission stated that "the President was not shot before frame 210,"[20] which was the first time Oswald could possibly have fired a shot.[21]

The Warren Commission's allegations are so tightly constructed and facts so interlocked that if a shot occurred prior to frame 210—no matter how little before frame 210—Oswald could not have fired it.[22] The majority of defenders of the official findings who have examined the Warren Commission Report have concurred but only by ignoring Willis number 5 and Zapruder frames 181 through 206.[23]

On the morning of November 22, 1963, Phillip L. Willis, an "independent real estate broker" and retired air force major disabled in World War II, took his daughters Linda Kay, aged fourteen, and Rosemary, aged ten, out of school. Together with his wife, Marilyn, they went to Dealey Plaza to view the president and vice president's motorcade. He brought his Argus 35mm camera. As he testified before a staff member of the Warren Commission, Willis positioned himself on the northwest corner of Houston and Main on the edge of the plaza across from the county jail and a block south of Elm Street.[24]

From the corner he shot three pictures. One captured the president approaching to turn north onto Houston Street. Another depicted the motorcade turning onto Houston. He took the third picture "from the rear after he [JFK] proceeded down Houston." Then Willis ran across the plaza to station himself "on the south curb of Elm Street" before the limousine approached to take another picture. From ten feet away he snapped his fourth "of the President directly in front of the Texas School Book Depository." Then he quickly moved "down the street slightly to try to get another view" with his camera to his eye, "looking through the viewfinder to try to get another picture of him before he went out of range." "Three seconds" later, before he was ready to take a picture, "a shot caused" him "to squeeze the camera shutter," and in reaction to the sound he "took picture No. 5."[25] Then Willis lowered his camera.[26] He and his family remained on Dealey Plaza for another hour. He continued to take pictures, more than the twelve he sold commercially.

Some who have read Willis's Commission testimony have raised concerns about the reliability of his memory because he also testified to seeing the JFK limousine stop, which suggests possible faulty recollection. Willis, however, was not alone in holding to a belief that the limousine halted. Scores of other bystanders thought that it had. Through a careful review of the films, primarily Zapruder's, though, the Commission and the FBI determined that the limousine in fact did not stop but only slowed down momentarily.[27] Greer, the Secret Service agent driving the limousine at 11.2 miles per hour, heard the sounds of shooting and/or the disturbance in the rear seats and spontaneously turned to glance at the rear seat; in so doing, he momentarily slowed down, but he did not completely stop the limousine. This created the illusion among many that Greer had halted the car, when in fact he had not.

Moreover, every official or private person who had contact with Willis believed then and believes today that he was fully credible. This includes

FBI agents, Dallas policemen, Warren Commission staff, CBS and *Life* reporters, investigative journalists, and critics of every stripe and shade. He was an impressive, solid person who appears to have been quite rational and responsible in every aspect of his life. Besides, the slide, independent of Willis's oral testimony, establishes that, by definition, a conspiracy killed JFK and that Lee Harvey Oswald did not fire the first shot at frame 210 or after.

On Willis's fifth slide President John F. Kennedy is seen in his limousine. In the foreground is the Secret Service backup limousine with agents on the running boards.[28] In the far background, beyond the limousines of the motorcade and to the right of the Stemmons Freeway sign, one sees Abraham Zapruder standing on one of the pergola's decorative concrete abutments filming the motorcade.[29]

On Zapruder's film, particularly the portion between the sprocket holes, Phil Willis appears on frames 181 through 206. By frame 199 he is visible with his camera raised to his eye. At frame 202 the camera is still raised, and he has begun to step into the street. Frame 203 is blurred. At frame 204 the camera has come down, and frame 206 is the last frame in which Willis appears. Willis testified that he took that slide when he was startled by hearing the shot: "The shot caused me to squeeze the camera shutter. . . . That picture was made at the very instant that the first shot was fired."[30] Calculating from the instant of the shot being fired, to its being heard, to Willis's physiological reaction and snapping of the shutter, it is likely that his slide was taken earlier than Zapruder's frame 202, probably just prior to frame 190.[31] Because the camera turned at 18.3 frames per second,[32] the time from frame 190 to frame 202 was less than a second.

In addition, Willis number 5 is slightly out of focus, reflecting that Willis snapped the shutter before he was completely focused. Zapruder's frame 202 captures this moment just as Willis was finishing taking his fifth slide and beginning to step onto the curb, indicating that the first shot must have occurred before frame 210 and thus demolishing the official conclusions on the assassination. The Commission, however, thought otherwise, despite both Willis number 5 and Willis's deposed testimony.

On July 22, 1964, Phil Willis appeared before Assistant Counsel Wesley Liebeler and a court reporter in the offices of the United States attorney, at the Post Office Building in Dallas, Texas, at 2:30 in the afternoon.[33] Afterwards Willis was disgusted with Liebeler. "He just asked what he wanted to know and that's all," Willis told an interviewer years later. "He told me not to elaborate, he didn't want too much information, just what he asked me."[34] Indeed, the forty-five-minute session of July 22 seems to reflect a highly uninquisitive Liebeler. Had Liebeler been more curious, Willis might have told him (1) that he was "sure all three shots fired found their mark";[35] (2) that the last shot came from the front;[36] and (3) that Willis's wife, Marilyn, who was never called to testify, also claimed she had heard the last shot come from the front.[37] Further, the Commission failed to pinpoint for the record Willis's precise location at the time he snapped his fifth slide, even though the Zapruder film *does* locate Willis with precision.

At his deposition, Willis nevertheless tried to provide information on where he stood, but Liebeler gave him short shrift, asking, "So, you are not able to tell us exactly where you were when you took the picture?"[38] Willis attempted to answer by referring to a shadow cast by a tree near his position and mentioning other visual landmarks. He referred to the John F. Kennedy Memorial Edition of *Life* magazine. "This picture No. 2 on page 4 . . . there is a tree in the background. The only tree in that immediate vicinity on that side of the street. And the shadow of that tree is shown in slide No. 5 that I took, which would show my position. . . . if you look in my picture here, you can see the shadow in that picture."[39] But Liebeler cut him off before he completed his explanation with an "all right" that seemed to suggest Willis's view on the matter was of little moment. Even so, the Zapruder film itself easily pinpoints Willis's precise location. He stands on the bare spot at the extreme eastern edge (the viewer's left) of the shadow cast by the only tree. Yet Commission officials then used a map of Dealey Plaza furnished by the FBI that was itself highly flawed.

This map, ostensibly used to analyze the relationship between Zapruder frame 202 and Willis number 5, was drawn on May 24, 1964, by Dallas County surveyor Robert H. West. This was the same West who had drawn a map of Dealey Plaza for the Secret Service back on December 5, 1963. Why he had to draw a second map is unclear. In any case, an undated exact tracing of the May 24 map subsequently became Commission Exhibit 882. On June 4, 1964, in Washington before five commissioners, two other members of the staff, Waggoner Carr of the Texas Court of Inquiry, and an observer from the bar association, staff counsel Arlen Specter deposed Leo J. Gauthier, an inspector for the FBI and the person in charge of the bureau's exhibit section.[40] Gauthier testified that on May 24, 1964, West had made the survey map of Dealey Plaza for the bureau to use in the reenactment and then described the map and commented on its authenticity.[41]

The map from May, however, reflected crucial and misleading changes on Dealey Plaza that were important to the Commission's mislocation of frame 202 and Willis in snapping his fifth slide. One in particular is important. By May, highway crews had moved the Stemmons Street sign several feet north from Elm Street toward Zapruder's position, although it is impossible to determine whether the height of the sign had also been changed or whether the maintenance crew had modified its angle in relation to the street. The groundskeeper Emmett Hudson had testified to this and other changes that had occurred in Dealey Plaza since the assassination.[42]

Using a tracing of the May 24 surveyor's map reflecting the altered features of the plaza, FBI agent Lyndal L. Shaneyfelt prepared a study that affirmed the official findings of no conspiracy by "demonstrating" that Willis number 5 was taken at Zapruder's frame 210. This marked map became Shaneyfelt Exhibit 25, which the Commission's assistant counsel Norman Redlich introduced when he deposed Shaneyfelt on September 1 in Washington.[43]

This map could not have been more poorly designed. It was small, only about a foot square, and the original in the archives is so faintly labeled that much of it is illegible; the printed version is practically unreadable.[44] Harold Weisberg accurately described it in his *Whitewash*: "This exhibit is the prize winner. It includes the entire area from Houston Street to the triple underpass, five hundred feet, in three and a half inches. It is indistinct, unclear and incomplete. The lettering is so fine that it cannot be read with a magnifying glass under strong light."[45]

On this minuscule map, the FBI photographic expert drew three lines, the first one leading from Zapruder to Willis. He then drew a second line from Willis's position to JFK and ending at the Stemmons Freeway sign (all of which are marked on the chart). The third line passed from Zapruder to the Stemmons sign, then through the sign to JFK. Shaneyfelt asserted that these three lines prove that the first shot could not have come before frame 210.

Unfortunately for the historical record, this conclusion was based on four falsehoods:

1. The FBI's photographic expert appears to have pushed JFK farther west than he was at the time of frame 210.
2. The Stemmons Freeway sign was positioned in its *new* location, not where it had been at the time of the assassination.

3. Shaneyfelt also mislocated Willis. Shaneyfelt explained to Redlich how he fixed Willis's location: "I first determined from correspondence, that Mr. Willis was standing along the south curb of Elm Street, approximately opposite the Texas School Book Depository building."[46] He wrote Willis a letter and asked him to describe the location, adding, under prompting from Redlich, "I feel that the exact establishing of the position of Mr. Willis would not add a great deal of additional accuracy to my present conclusions."[47] Using the same basic information he had attempted to give the Commission, Willis responded to the FBI agent. We know that he did from an offhand remark he made years later to an interviewer, but we have no way of knowing what Shaneyfelt did with the information except that his map sets an ambiguous position.

But the exact location of Willis was crucial for establishing distances and times and relationships. According to Shaneyfelt's vague reference "to the south side," Willis could have been placed anywhere along several score feet of curbing from frames 166 to 210 of the Zapruder film. The Zapruder film, however, *does* fix Willis's location exactly.

4. The FBI photographic expert's inaccurately drawn lines from Willis to JFK to the sign and from Zapruder to the sign to JFK completely obscured the truly key linear linkage at frame 202, running from Zapruder to Secret Service agent Clint Hill's left shoulder as he stood on the running board of the follow-up vehicle to Willis. Obviously, such inaccuracy made it easier for the Commission to cling to its foregone conclusion regarding Oswald's guilt.[48] But leaving Willis number 5 aside for the moment, a close examination of Zapruder frames 190 through 200 suggests otherwise.

The Commission printed black-and-white slides of the Zapruder film, two to the page, in volume 18 of its hearings and exhibits volumes.[49] From the time of their appearance, critics had noted the frames are fuzzy starting at frame 190. Even an untrained eye can readily discern the abrupt change in clarity. When one views the excellent copy of the film and slides in the National Archives the fuzziness stands out. This view was echoed subsequently in the late 1970s by the House Select Committee's photographic expert, who reported two significant blurs or jiggles on the Zapruder film, the second coming at about frames 313 to 319, corresponding to Zapruder's physical reaction at the time of the head shot, and the first due to a similar reaction at frames 190 to 200, conceived as the time of a shot.[50] As Dr. William Hartmann related before the committee:

> HARTMANN. About frames 190 to 200 there is a strong blur reaction initiated. So having concluded that this is in fact, that the blur sequence around 313 to 319 is in fact a response to the gunshots, I would think that the logical inference would be that the blur sequence, the blur episode running typically from 190 to 200 is also a response to a possible gunshot. And we know that the President emerged from behind the sign somewhat later, some frames later, showing in fact a reaction to such a wound. So this could very well be the blur or startle reaction to the gunshot that caused the back wound to the President.[51]

Other pieces of evidence seem to support this reading of the Zapruder film. For example, Hugh Betzner Jr. stood on the south curb of Elm Street a few feet east of Phil Willis and took three photographs. The third corresponds to Zapruder frame 186.[52] Immediately after taking it, as Betzner related later that afternoon to the Dallas County Sheriff, "I heard a noise. I thought the noise was either a firecracker or a car had backfired."[53] This corresponds to about frame 190.

In addition, President Kennedy's and his wife's reactions starting around frame 190 are indicative of a significant change. In frames 180 through 190, JFK is seen waving to the crowd on the north side of Elm; then, about frame 193, his arms become wooden, and his wife begins to turn from the crowd on the south side of Elm to look at him. Their movements indicate that something is amiss.

Affirming the reactions of the president and his wife is the statement of motorcycle policeman Jim Chaney, who rode on the right rear flank of the limousine. In the late afternoon of November 22, a local KRLD television reporter taped Chaney in the third-floor corridor of the Dallas Police Department. The first shot came, Chaney said, when "Jackie was looking to the left." This precisely dovetails with the disturbances captured on the Zapruder film and corresponds to about frame 190, for at about frame 202 she starts to turn to the president. Chaney was not deposed, and no statement about the assassination was even taken from him.[54] Mrs. Kennedy's recollections sustain Chaney's account. "No, I was looking this way, to the left, and I heard these terrible noises. You know. And my husband never made a sound. So I turned to my right."[55] Willis told the Commission that at the time of the first shot Mrs. Kennedy "was looking to the left."[56] Ken O'Donnell, JFK's aide riding in the follow-up car, said, "She appeared to be immediately aware something happened. She turned toward him."[57] From S. M. Holland, who viewed the motorcade from atop the triple underpass, comes further corroboration. At the time of the first shot, he saw Mrs. Kennedy was looking to her left, but upon realizing something was wrong, she "turned around facing the President."[58]

Further support for a shot at about frame 190 comes from the report of Secret Service agent George Hickey, who rode in the backseat of the follow-up car. On November 30, 1963, he submitted a report of his activities on the twenty-second to Gerald Behn, agent in charge of the White House detail.[59] He wrote that, as the limousine moved down Elm Street, "After a very short distance I heard a loud report which sounded like a firecracker. . . . I stood up and looked to my right and rear." But nothing caught his attention, so he turned to look at the president.[60] On the Zapruder film no agents react to anything until Hickey suddenly rears and turns to his right beginning at frame 195, sustaining his account.

The testimony of a number of witnesses who were on the north side of Elm Street suggests a shot at around frame 190. Victoria Elizabeth Adams worked in the Texas School Book Depository, a twenty-three-year-old employee of Scott, Foresman Company. On April 7, 1964, she testified to Commission counsel David Belin that at the time of the assassination she was standing with three other women, Sandra Styles, Elsie Dorman, and Dorothy May Garner, looking at the motorcade through a fourth-floor window, the sixth and westernmost window on the floor.[61] The women watched the presidential limousine turn onto Elm Street, then "a tree" obstructed their view. "And we heard a shot." This would place a shot prior to frame 210, the first time the limousine cleared the tree and the line of sight made it possible for a shot allegedly to be fired by Oswald. Dillard Exhibit D, a photograph of the front of the building taken after the second shot and before the third, shows many of the fourth-floor windows, with the window Miss Adams said she was looking out of open.[62] Belin ignored her testimony on the shot and did not depose her three coworkers.

On July 22, 1964, Abraham Zapruder himself testified before staff counsel Wesley Liebeler. He explained that through his telephoto lens and before the Stemmons Freeway sign blocked his view at frame 207, he "saw the President lean over and grab himself like this (holding his left chest area)."[63] But this means a shot definitely occurred before frame 210 and most probably at or just prior to frame 190. That, of course, contradicts one of the Commission's crucial findings, which in turn raises significant doubts about Oswald's guilt, "reasonable doubts" that might have acquitted him in a court of law.

A Command Appearance
Jim Garrison, Zapruder, and Zapruder's Film

Only once in thirty-five years of the assassination controversy did Abraham Zapruder and his twenty-six-second film appear in a legal forum. It occurred in a New Orleans courtroom in the teeth of concerted official federal opposition. During the first days of February 1967, the startling news broke that the district attorney of New Orleans, Jim Garrison, was investigating the assassination of President John F. Kennedy and had suspects in mind. Soon he arrested a local businessman, Clay Shaw, claiming that he had participated as a local organizer and director of the assassination. Among other threads alleged to lead from Shaw to Dallas was Lee Harvey Oswald.[1]

A tall and physically imposing presence, Garrison was also brilliant and widely read, invariably well dressed, and possessed of good manners and an intense gaze. Unfortunately, in his obsessive zeal to unmask the real murders of JFK, he made major mistakes and miscalculations.

That is truly sad, for he was gifted, indeed courageous, beyond the ordinary meaning of the word, in attacking the federal whitewash of the assassination. Both before and after the trial of Shaw, he functioned properly and with considerable merit. Only in the JFK inquiry did he drift far off course, damaging his own reputation and undermining efforts to get at the truth behind the assassination. With public support, generous funding, and the incredible power of the state courts as his ally, he wasted an enormous amount of time, talent, and funds in the irrational pursuit of a criminal charge without the slightest legal, factual, or even theoretical foundation.

To fully discuss the flaws in Garrison's investigation, its many controversial episodes and twists and turns, would take us far afield and require a much longer book than is practical here.[2] Suffice it to say that Garrison had been deeply influenced by the first generation of critical books on the assassination, chief among them Harold Weisberg's *Whitewash*.[3] Inspired by these challenges to the Warren Commission Report, he began a strange and ill-fated quest.

For example, in November 1968, Garrison tried to observe the anniversary of JFK's assassination by issuing arrest warrants for Robert Lee Perrin and Edgar Eugene Bradley, who were, he proclaimed, the actual assassins on the grassy knoll. In the absence of any documentary evidence, Garrison nevertheless linked Perrin with the religious right-winger Carl McIntyre of New Jersey and Bradley, who worked for him. His horrified staff, having failed to talk him out of making such bold but unprovable allegations, sought Weisberg's help. Louis Ivon, Garrison's chief investigator, promised Weisberg the help of his investigators for whatever evidence he needed. In two weeks Weisberg put together a report that made it impossible for Garrison to proceed with his questionable project. Weisberg established beyond a shadow of doubt that Perrin had killed himself in 1962, the year before the assassination, and that Bradley's alleged involvement had no basis in fact.

In another instance, Garrison suddenly was seized with the erroneous belief that one of three men photographed as they were escorted out of Dealey Plaza by police officers was directly involved in the assassination. Weisberg again came to Garrison's rescue by confirming that the three men were winos, common drunks, who drank cheap wine whenever and wherever they could. On the day of the assassination, they had been hiding out in an unattached boxcar parked more than two blocks south and a block to the west of the plaza, a fact verified by nearby postal workers. They had simply been swept up into a belated dragnet conducted by the Dallas police. But twenty-three years later, in Garrison's *On the Trail of the Assassins*, a book filled with a myriad of factual errors, misrepresentations, and outright fabrications, he remained convinced of their conspiratorial involvement.[4]

The centerpiece of Garrison's investigation and allegations was the trial of Clay Shaw, which opened in late January 1969. In conjunction with that trial, he sued in the local District of Columbia court of Judge Charles W. Halleck Jr. to determine if the autopsy and X rays, rifle, and other associated materials should be released as evidence linked to Shaw. The federal government fiercely fought that release. Bernard "Bud" Fensterwald, a Washington attorney, represented Garrison, with Harold Weisberg recruited as an expert authority on the assassination and Cyril Wecht, a noted forensic pathologist, brought in to address the medical aspects.

Halleck ruled in Garrison's favor, thanks to the thorough preparations and persuasiveness of Garrison's "team." But, strangely, before Garrison in New Orleans even heard the decision he telephoned Assistant District Attorney Numa Bertel and ordered that the suit he had just won be dropped. Garrison had become convinced that the whole hearing was a CIA plot. The result of this delusion was a lost opportunity of monumental proportions.

For the first time—and as it has turned out the only time—the rifle, the X rays, and other autopsy materials could have been brought into a courtroom not controlled by the federal government and would have been subjected to examination by objective experts. But Garrison turned his back on this opportunity and walked away. Nevertheless, the Clay Shaw trial proceeded, with Garrison initially alleging direct links between Shaw and Oswald.

Indeed, Oswald's short life had a long association with New Orleans, where he was born in 1939. He had spent several years of his youth in the city and then returned there during the summer of 1963 seeking work. During that strange summer he became involved in a number of radical activities associated with the "Cuban question." But, oddly, during the trial of Shaw, Garrison argued that Oswald did not have any relation to JFK's murder. Ultimately, the jury deliberated and delivered both a major defeat and a partial and indirect victory for Garrison. On the one hand, it found Shaw innocent of all the charges. On the other hand, in a postdecision poll the jury members indicated that they believed that President Kennedy had died as a result of a conspiracy but that Garrison had not proved Shaw's involvement in it.

In the midst of these tumultuous proceedings, the Zapruder film came back into focus. Garrison had subpoenaed the film from the reluctant owner, Time Inc., which fought the subpoena and lost. In April 1967, he showed the film to the grand jury, followed by commentary by several critics knowledgeable about the film. These were primarily Harold Weisberg and Raymond Marcus, although others, such as Mark Lane, also testified.

On May 11, 1967, Ray Marcus appeared before the New Orleans grand jury for several hours. Present were members of the Orleans Parish grand jury; Jim Garrison, district attorney; Alvin Oser, James Alcock, Richard Burnes, Andrew Sciambra, and William Martin, assistant district attorneys; and the secretary Maureen Thiel. A native of Los Angeles, Marcus was one of the early dozen or so critics of the official findings. The previous year he had published a small, convincing book entitled *The Bastard Bullet* that critiqued the Commission Exhibit 399 (CE399), the single bullet that had allegedly produced all seven nonfatal wounds, a theory Marcus considered deeply flawed.[5] In reserved, careful language he described the Zapruder film for the jurists. His testimony fills 137 pages.[6]

Before he began, Marcus related the difficulties he and other researchers had had in obtaining access to the frames, evidence crucial for any serious investigation of the assassination. Marcus then thoroughly recapped the single-bullet theory and CE399, relating both directly to the Zapruder film, which he contended provided evidence that contradicted the Warren Commission's findings.

The following year, as the Shaw inquiry continued, James L. Alcock, executive assistant district attorney for the Parish of Orleans, requested a subpoena duces tecum for Time Inc. He wanted the "foreign corporation doing business in the State of Louisiana" to "diligently and carefully search for, examine and inquire after and produce" the film of Abraham Zapruder and cause it "to be brought before the Grand Jury" on April 4, 1968.[7] The film, Alcock stated, had never been publicly shown. He requested the original film be produced "because several of the copies which have been made available to select federal employees do not correspond with and are not true and accurate reproductions of the original film." *Life* eventually produced a poor copy of the film, which was repeatedly shown in the courtroom, but marked the copy so it would be possible to spot any bootleg versions that might be made by Garrison and associates.

On February 13, 1969, when Zapruder testified regarding the film's authenticity, the courtroom was set up with easels and a model of Dealey Plaza created by Garrison's team.[8] Zapruder described the circumstances of his filming the assassination and marked his location on the model. He recalled: "I saw the approaching motorcade of the President coming from Houston Street, turning left on Elm Street and coming down towards the underpass. As they were approaching where I was standing I heard a shot and noticed where . . . he grabbed himself with his hand towards his chest or throat and leaned towards Jackie."[9]

When the assistant district attorney who conducted the examination moved to introduce and show the Zapruder film, Shaw's defense attorneys objected. Judge Edward A. Haggerty Jr. removed the jury from the room and had the film screened for the court to see if it could be admitted. He ruled it could be shown and would later rule it could be shown as often as the state liked. The members of the jury were brought back in, and the film was screened for them four times, twice in slow motion. Then, when it appeared Zapruder's testimony was completed, jurors twice asked to have the film screened yet again.

Garrison utilized every opportunity to screen the film, apparently seeking to fix the images in the jurors' minds. The next day the prosecution showed it three more times in association with FBI agent Lyndal Shaneyfelt's testimony. Then Herbert Orth, chief of *Life*'s laboratory, testified and introduced a number of black-and-white pictures made from the film plus 120 slides of frames, all of which were shown to the jury. Dr. John Nichols, a professor of pathology at the University of Kansas, came next. He testified that the medical evidence supported a conclusion of two or more conspirators, and the Zapruder film was shown yet again along with slides. Nichols related the wounds on the two occupants of the limousine to various points revealed on the film. During the summation of the prosecution's case to the jury, slides of the head shot were again shown.

Almost as soon as Garrison launched his investigation, a number of writers and producers of television shows popped up to report and write on the phenomenon. There are so many of these that they alone would require a thick book to present and discuss. Edward Jay Epstein, however, provides a good example from this group.

In 1968 Viking Press published Epstein's *Counterplot*, his second book concerned with the assassination and its investigation.[10] It was based on his essays about the Garrison case that had appeared in the *New Yorker*.[11] His previous book, the very brief and seriously flawed *Inquest: The Warren Commission and the Establishment of Truth*, had been a best-seller in both the United States and Europe.[12]

In *Counterplot*, Epstein attacked Garrison for being theory ridden, incompetent, and a promoter of the bizarre, charges that were valid and indeed in some instances even muted. But even as he attacked Garrison's mistakes and wild speculations, he was reinforcing the equally flawed Warren Commission conclusions. For example, in rightfully dismissing Garrison's bizarre suggestion that the missing Zapruder frames 208 through 211 may have been destroyed to hide ballistic evidence, Epstein inaccurately noted that those frames, while missing from the Warren volumes, are not missing from a copy of the film that *Life* holds.[13] In fact, Epstein says, they have been published in Josiah Thompson's *Six Seconds in Dallas* and revealed no ballistic evidence.[14] Epstein, however, seems to be unaware that the originals had in fact been accidentally destroyed by *Life* when it processed the film. He also appears to be extraordinarily uncurious about the Warren Commission's own apparent lack of interest in those missing frames.

In any case, the Zapruder film continued to attract national attention, becoming in the process a kind of cause célèbre. Penn Jones Jr., an editor of a weekly Texas newspaper and a fierce critic of the official findings, received a copy from Garrison and immediately moved to make it freely available to other critics. "Why, God damn it!" the short, wiry, boot-clad Jones told me in 1975, "you can't keep the crucifixion of Christ for yourself and you can't keep the Zapruder film for yourself either." On November 21, 1969, Greg Olds, editor of the Austin-based *Texas Observer*, told his readers he would sell them copies of the Zapruder film at his cost. "Whatever you believe, you owe it to your country to see the Zapruder film. If you do see it, you won't believe the Warren Report." His was an "eighth or tenth generation copy," but a friend had promised to get additional copies from an unnamed source for "$2.50 or $5 each." But Time Inc. moved to stop him. "That would be a major lawsuit," said Dick Pollard, *Life*'s director of photography. "I can assure you it is illegal. You can argue public interest, but not the copyright law. You know, there are a lot of nuts running around trying to prove something. The Library of Congress has a dupe they show to any qualified researcher."[15] He actually meant the National Archives instead of the Library of Congress. Regardless, his implication was clear—Time Inc. would not allow American citizens easy access to the film.

For the next few years, across the nation, ordinary citizens as well as critics showed mostly poor copies of the Zapruder film thousands of times on college campuses, at public lectures, to legislators in the state capital of Wisconsin, in the homes of the wealthy, at book club meetings, in the back rooms of bars, and in numerous other places, many of them advertised in newspapers and on radio—thanks in part to Garrison's efforts in a misguided cause.

Unfortunately, Garrison's debacle killed public interest in reopening an inquiry into the assassination of President Kennedy and disillusioned many critics. The institutional order that had embraced the official findings of the Commission and had blindly stood with them now breathed a sigh of relief with Garrison's self-destruction. For many citizens the "innocent" Shaw verdict confirmed in their minds that there were no valid grounds for questioning the official findings on the assassination.

Twenty years later, Garrison would publish his last book on the assassination, *On the Trail of the Assassins*, which displayed a penchant for bizarre plots involving rogue CIA, errant military officers, and right-wingers—all conspiring to kill a president opposed to their aims. The book caught the eye of Oliver Stone, who used it as a source for his film JFK, which, despite its laudable impetus for reopening the investigation, perpetuated numerous misconceptions and factual errors about the assassination. By inflating the person, performance, and contributions of Garrison beyond any semblance to historical reality and by concocting a bizarre mulligan stew of conspirators, JFK further confused an already thoroughly confused public, even as it provoked renewed attention for the case. As provocative and influential as Stone's film was, its effectiveness pales in comparison to the visceral impact and paramount importance of the less than half a minute's worth of 8mm celluloid recorded by an amateur filmmaker in Dealey Plaza on the afternoon of November 22, 1963.

The Film
and the
Single-Bullet
Theory

Official Allegation
A Single Bullet Explains All
Seven Nonfatal Wounds

Like many others, I believe that in the first days after the assassination public awareness of the Zapruder film likely blocked federal efforts to define Lee Harvey Oswald immediately as the lone assassin and forced officials to develop allegations that could be fit into the film's incontrovertible facts. Among other things, without the film's conspicuous and sudden appearance, Commission officials and the FBI could have easily hedged and manipulated the analysis of the timing of the first and subsequent shots. But confronted with *Life*'s Zapruder frame reproductions, seen by fifty million citizens and widely discussed, their options became far more limited.

To recap, according to the official allegations, from the easternmost window of the sixth floor of the Texas School Book Depository, sixty-one feet above Elm Street, Lee Harvey Oswald fired three shots[1] at the president from a Mannlicher-Carcano 6.5-mm rifle.[2] The third shot, which corresponded to frame 313 of the Zapruder film, struck the president in the head and caused his death.[3] One shot missed the occupants of the limousine and inflicted the slight wound on James Tague, standing several hundred feet away near the triple underpass.[4] This left one bullet, the first one fired, according to the Commission's own reconstruction, to inflict the seven nonfatal wounds on President Kennedy and Governor Connally riding 176 feet from the window. That recovered bullet the Commission assigned the identification number CE399.[5]

Official dicta claimed that CE399 entered the back of President Kennedy's neck, transited his body, and emerged from his throat, passing through his shirt collar and necktie knot; it then struck Connally from the rear in his right armpit, smashed four inches of his fifth rib, emerged from his body under his right nipple to smash his right wrist and burrowed three inches inside his left thigh.[6] It then lurked until just the right moment and sneaked back three inches to emerge from that single hole. The bullet was virtually pristine when, in the official account, it was discovered on the ground floor of the hospital after falling out from under the mattress of Governor Connally's stretcher.[7] All but CE399's emergence occurred in the maximum time of twenty-seven frames of the Zapruder film (frames 210–237), about a second and one-half for the bullet that left the rifle traveling about two thousand feet per second.

By mid-June 1964, the Warren Commission Report was completed and ready to be printed. As part of its prepublication publicity campaign, federal officials had begun to leak its findings to the press. Among the points that these press accounts featured was the finding that only three shots had been fired, one inflicting two wounds on JFK, one inflicting five wounds and busting two bones on Governor Connally, and one killing JFK. That finding held until Tom Dillard, a Dallas newspaper reporter, read one of the "three-bullet" news stories. Dillard told the United States attorney for Dallas, Barefoot Sanders, that the story he had just read was impossible. He knew from his reporting on November 22 that yet another bullet had also struck the curb near the triple underpass and that the spray of concrete from its impact had slightly wounded citizen James T. Tague, who stood on the curb.

Sanders immediately contacted the Commission staff about this revelation, which the Commission already knew about but had fully intended to ignore. Now its omission was not only public but also well known by both a newspaper reporter and the United States attorney, which posed a major dilemma for the Commission. It could not allow a fourth bullet and still keep Oswald as the sole triggerman. The time between the first and last shots would not allow for Oswald to get off all four.

So, to make Oswald-the-assassin conform to the newly revealed evidence of Tague's wounding, the Commission decided that the shot that had wounded President Kennedy had also wounded Governor Connally, and the second shot had actually missed both men and gone on to wound Tague. This became known as the single-bullet theory.

Examination of the Commission staff's papers in the National Archives discloses that assistant counsel Arlen Specter, now a senator from Pennsylvania, was in charge of the preliminary work devising the theory. Those papers also suggest that Specter and other assistant counsels simply ignored or rejected any opinions at variance with the single-bullet theory. Among those so shunned were the opinions of Dr. Joseph Dolce, the army's top authority on bullets and bullet wounds, who by official military policy was to be called in as consultant in all gunshot cases involving VIPs. After his initial meeting with the Commission staff, including Specter, he was not, however, called in to consult with the Commission again, nor did it ever formally call him as a witness.

Few of the Commission's conclusions have aroused more skepticism and opposition from critics and the general public than the claim that one bullet, CE399, inflicted all *seven* nonfatal wounds on President Kennedy and Governor Connally.[8] What is most often not understood, though, is how foundational that single-bullet explanation is to the entire edifice of the official findings.[9] Without that explanation a conspiracy is required to explain the wounds inflicted on President Kennedy, Governor Connally, and James T. Tague. And any critical examination of that explanation must necessarily focus on the Zapruder film.

The Warren Report states: "Examination of the Zapruder motion picture camera by the FBI established that 18.3 pictures or frames were taken each second, and therefore, the time of certain events could be calculated by allowing 1/18.3 seconds for the action depicted from one frame to the next."[10] The bolt-action Mannlicher-Carcano rifle could be worked at a minimum of 2.3 seconds, or forty-two frames, between shots.[11]

According to the Commission, Oswald fired the first shot at frame 210, the first time the limousine was beyond the tree line and he could sight and pull the trigger.[12] Kennedy is seen reacting to that first shot as he fully emerges from behind the sign at frame 225, his fists raised to his throat. If one accepts that finding, the next possible time Oswald could have fired a second shot was frame 252 (210 plus 42). But the Zapruder film shows Governor Connally hit sometime "between frames 235 and 240."[13] That forced the Commission to adopt the single-bullet theory because Oswald could not have ejected an empty cartridge, rammed a bullet into the chamber, aimed, and fired in time to have shot Connally. Without that theory, the Commission would have had to acknowledge the existence of at least one other rifleman, which by definition means a conspiracy.

The Commission, however, alleged that a single bullet that wounded JFK at Zapruder frame 210 transited his body and continued in flight to wound Connally, then fell off his stretcher in the hospital, where it was found in nearly pristine condition. That bullet was recovered in Parkland Memorial Hospital and numbered as CE399. Its origin, weight, and condition are essential, if contested, components in the Commission's allegations. Its Report states unequivocally that CE399 "was found on Governor

Connally's stretcher at Parkland Hospital" by Darrell C. Tomlinson, the hospital's senior engineer.[14] Although he "was not certain whether the bullet came from the Connally stretcher or the adjacent one," the Commission nevertheless baldly asserted "that the bullet came from the Governor's stretcher."[15]

CE399 weighed 158.6 grains, was "slightly flattened" on one end, and was "unmutilated."[16] The Report does not say it was the base rather than the impact end that was slightly flattened, nor that copper sheathed the lead alloy core of the bullet, with the lead alloy visible only on its crimped and rimmed base.[17] The latter fact is important for understanding the various metal fragments deposited by CE399 in its remarkable journey. Strangely, the Report contains no photograph of this critical bullet. On the other hand and even stranger, it does print a full-page diagram of the component parts of one of Oswald's pubic hairs, which has no conceivable relationship to the crime.[18] In any case, the Commission claims the bullet inflicted two wounds on President Kennedy and five on Governor Connally, breaking two of his bones. But a close examination of the wounds and their locations makes the Commission's claims highly suspect.

The Commission asserts there was an entrance wound on JFK's back, located at the level of the neck, and an exit wound on his throat. The Report locates JFK's rear wound on the neck, "near the base of the back of President Kennedy's neck slightly to the right of his spine."[19] More specifically: "It was 5½ inches from the tip of the right shoulder joint and approximately the same distance below the tip of the right mastoid process [the bump behind the ear]."[20] This location, repeated several times throughout the Report,[21] is of great importance to the Commission's claim. If, for example, the wound was on the president's back rather than the neck, then the bullet transiting at a downward angle could not exit the throat and could not continue on to hit Connally's armpit. The Commission also asserted that the "neck wound" was an entrance wound, based on what the autopsy doctors claimed to have found: a small hole and a clean wound: "The wound was approximately one-fourth by one-seventh of an inch (7 by 4 millimeters), had clean edges, was sharply delineated and had margins similar in all respects to those of the entry wound in the skull."[22]

But the holes in the back of JFK's suit coat and shirt (he wore no undershirt) suggest the Commission's calculations were inaccurate. On the suit jacket a hole ¼ inch in diameter appeared that was 5⅜ inches below the top of the collar and 1¾ inches to the right of the center back seam.[23] The damage to the shirt's back was similar to that inflicted on the jacket's back.[24]

The Report says that this bullet came from behind, high, and to the right of JFK, passed through his body without hitting bone or any other hard substance, and then exited from the president's throat.[25] "The bullet had exited from the front part of the neck" and "below the Adam's apple."[26] How the bullet, coming at a steep angle down from the depository, changed its direction to pass through the body without striking anything to deflect it and exit below the Adam's apple is, to say the least, hard to comprehend.

The Commission, however, did not waver. The bullet, it claimed, emerged at the level of the necktie knot: "A missile entered the back of his clothing in the vicinity of his lower neck and exited through the front of this shirt immediately behind his tie, nicking the knot of his tie in its forward flight."[27] The Report alleged each flap of the shirt collar had a tear made by the passing bullet: "A hole seven-eighths of an inch below the collar button and similar opening seven-eighths of an inch below the button hole. These two holes fell into alignment on overlapping positions when the shirt was buttoned."[28] And, somehow, the nick on the tie's left side made by the transiting bullet allegedly lined up with the collar holes.[29]

Since the tracheotomy performed by the Parkland doctors destroyed the wound's actual character ("obliterated" it)[30] but certainly not its approximate location (which federal autopsy surgeons could have defined by measuring the distance from the lips of the incision to a fixed point), the wound's description rested on the doctors' recollections before the Commission. The doctors concurred the wound, which was one-fifth inch in diameter, could not be called an exit wound based exclusively on its appearance: "It could have been either [entry or exit]."[31] But it was found to be an exit wound based on "other known facts," such as the "autopsy, distance the bullet traveled, and tested muzzle velocity of the rifle," authorities merely asserted and did not explain further.[32]

Governor Connally received wounds on his right back, right chest, right wrist, and left thigh. His fifth rib was smashed, as was his wrist bone. The bullet, traveling on "a downward angle," entered the governor's chest through the back at his right armpit, although the precise measurements and descriptions are not included in the Report. Why was it considered a wound of entry? "Because of the small size and clean-cut edges of the wound."[33] How the bullet changed its direction, going up from the wound in the back of Kennedy's "neck" to his Adam's apple and then "downward" toward Connally is explained in tortuous text, based on the commissioners highly flawed reenactment of the assassination, not on careful study of the Zapruder film.

The bullet shattered Connally's lateral and anterior right fifth rib and exited below the right nipple.[34] "It left a ragged 2-inch (5 centimeters) opening on the front of the chest."[35] Although the Report does not tell us how badly the bullet was damaged, in fact about five inches of Connally's fourth rib were also crushed by the impact, a telling detail in light of the near-"pristine" bullet found on the stretcher at Parkland Hospital.[36]

On the back of Governor Connally's right arm, about two inches above the wrist joint on the thumb side, the alleged CE399 bullet inflicted a wound one-fifth of an inch wide and one inch long.[37] Because cloth and thread entered the injury, the doctors concluded it was an entrance wound. Here again, the Report's language becomes vague on the nature of the damage to the bone, which in fact was broken into many pieces. The bullet subsequently emerged on the palm side, where three-fourths of an inch above the crease of the right wrist a one-fifth-inch-long hole was made.[38]

The last of the five wounds the Commission claimed was inflicted on Governor Connally by CE399 was a puncture wound in his left thigh. According to its Report, "The Governor suffered a puncture wound in the left thigh that was approximately two-fifths of an inch" in diameter and "located approximately 5 or 6 inches above the Governor's left knee."[39] Apparently, CE399 itself, rather than a "small fragment," caused "a tangential wound, penetrating at low velocity and stopping after entering the skin."[40] How far it entered the flesh is not stated, although this information is central to an understanding of the bullet's path. It later exited the wound at Parkland Hospital, through the same hole it had entered, but the Report does not explain how this physically occurred, saying simply that it "had fallen out of the thigh wound"[41] and leaving the reader with yet another puzzle unsolved by this investigation.

The Commission alleged that metal fragments were found in only two of the wounds, the governor's wrist and left thigh. In the wrist "as revealed by X-ray . . . small fragments of metal" were found.[42] In addition, "X-ray examination disclosed a tiny metallic fragment embedded in the Governor's leg." Typically imprecise, the Report provides no information on the number, size, or weight of these fragments.

Why are the metal fragments so important? First, the recovered bullet CE399 weighed 158.6 grains, which was well within the weight variations of unfired bullets. "The weight of the whole bullet prior to firing was approximately 160–161 grains and that of the recovered bullet was 158.6 grains."[43] This statement doesn't take into account the metallic loss in the barrel's rifling—0.5 grains, never mentioned—as well as misrepresenting the weight variations of Carcano bullets testified to by Commission expert witnesses that put 159.1 grains within the variable weights of the bullets. If the metal deposited in the body weighed more than was missing from CE399, it would require another bullet to have left it. The Report states, "All these fragments were sufficiently small and light so that the nearly whole bullet found on the stretcher could have deposited those pieces of metal as it tumbled through this wrist."[44] (All the doctors, however, said the opposite.) Second, the Report does not explain how CE399 could have left metal in the wounds. It was copper sheathed and was in pristine condition. The only place for the lead to exude was the base. Since the lead fragments in Connally's wrist and thigh could only have come from the base of the copper-clad CE399, the bullet must have yawed—and remained yawed—in order to put its butt end first. (And there are fragments not mentioned in the Report.) The butt badly smashed the wrist bone and punctured the thigh and in the contact deposited lead. The Report does not present a photograph of the bullet and its butt end to show how it looked after breaking two tough bones and depositing lead in two wounds (more details will be discussed in a later chapter).

To repeat, the Commission concluded that "the same bullet traversed the President's neck and inflicted all the wounds on Governor Connally."[45] Since the third of the three bullets alleged to have been fired that day killed JFK and the second was used to account for the wounding of Jim Tague, that left only the first bullet to inflict the nonfatal wounds. The Report claims President Kennedy and Governor Connally were lined up in the limousine so that the transiting bullet could have hit JFK's "neck," gone through his throat, and then struck Connally's right armpit. As the Report describes it, "The relative positions of President Kennedy and Governor Connally at the time when the President was struck in the neck confirm that the same bullet probably passed through both men."[46] But since JFK's Adam's apple was to the left of Connally's armpit, a bullet in straight flight from JFK's necktie knot must have hit Connally smack in the back of the neck. Why did this not occur? The president, the Report says, "sat on the extreme right," and the governor sat "6 inches from the right door,"[47] thus accommodating the putative flight of CE399. Commission Exhibit

697, a half-page photograph of the limousine *taken much earlier* during the motorcade, is printed next to the text to provide visual support for this key fact.[48] Connally appears not snug to the right but with his hands in his lap, and JFK does have his arm on the door. Of course, CE697 is highly convenient for the Commission's single-bullet theory, unlike a full-page photograph of an appropriate Zapruder film frame depicting the relative positions of the two men near the moment of the actual shooting, when both were far to the side, with their right arms resting along the right side of the car.

The Commission ineffectively utilized three sets of experts in questions related to CE399: the autopsy doctors and Parkland Hospital medical personnel; three FBI experts and a State of Illinois authority on bullet identification; and three wound ballistic experts from the Wound Ballistic Branch of the U.S. Army Chemical Research and Development Laboratories at Edgewood Arsenal, Maryland.[49] In the third group, Dr. Alfred G. Olivier performed the ballistic tests under the supervision of Dr. Arthur J. Dziemian, with assistance from Dr. Frederick W. Light Jr.[50] Olivier and Dziemian "concluded that it was probable that the same bullet passed the President's neck and then inflicted all the wounds on the Governor."[51] Dr. Light emphatically concurred: "The same bullet traversed the President's neck and inflicted all the wounds on Governor Connally."[52]

As part of their ballistic tests, the doctors simulated the wrist wound by firing bullets with the Carcano rifle 210 feet into "bone structures."[53] The tests, the Report alleges, proved the "wrist was not struck by a pristine bullet, which is a missile that strikes an object before hitting anything else."[54] CE399 could not have struck Connally's wrist first and remained pristine, for it would have been going too fast, with too much power, and upon impact would have smashed its nose. Since CE399 did not have a smashed nose (although no photograph of it or the test bullets is printed), this is additional proof for the Commission that it had passed through JFK and the governor's chest before hitting the wrist with reduced force caused by the friction of transit. If the bullet struck the wrist first, "the nose would have been considerably flattened, as was the bullet which struck the bone structure."[55] The logical fallacy is so apparent it should not require comment, given the contradictions between the "pristine" theories and the actual "pristine" evidence.

The Commission's reenactments relating to CE399 were deeply flawed, especially the simulated firing on Dealey Plaza in May 1964. Officials claimed a faithful reenactment of scenes, where limousine and stand-ins supposedly mimicked the positions of JFK and Governor Connally as seen on frames of the Zapruder film, leading to the Report's conclusion that a single bullet inflicted all nonfatal wounds.[56] But was the Commission's reenactment faithful to the facts?

The factors to be considered for a faithful test included the proper location of the limousine on the road, the correct placement of the bodies in the limousine, the sitting posture of the stand-ins, and the precise lineup of the stand-ins' bodies in the limousine as of November 22. If any one of these factors varied from the original as much as a fraction of an inch, it would have rendered the tests false. If, for example, the simulated bullet path laid down in the reenactment missed the nick in the necktie by a quarter of an inch to the left, then CE399 would have flown into the shoulder, not the armpit, of Governor Connally and missed the rib.

Curiously, in the same paragraphs lauding the reenactment's scientific measurements and faithful replication, officials also noted the guesswork and approximations underlying the alleged scientific tests. For example, another car was utilized for the test that was merely "similar in design" to the original, although absolute precision was imperative.[57] Or, as noted in the Report, "Two Bureau agents with approximately the same physical characteristics sat in the car in the same relative positions as President Kennedy and Governor Connally had occupied."[58] Why "approximately," when the slightest variation would render the replication false? Again, "The foliage of an oak tree . . . was approximately the same as on the day of the assassination."[59] Why "approximately," when one of the most unusual shots in the world was about to be simulated after the foliage ceased to block the line of sight? "The position of President Kennedy's car when he was struck in the neck was determined with substantial precision."[60] What is "substantial" precision? Precision is an exact term, and a difference from the original of a tiny fraction of an inch would skew all simulated hits and exits and flight paths. Were the jump seats the same distance from each other and the backseat, and were they elevated to the same height as they were at the time of the assassination?

The Report contains numerous other examples of qualifications and apologies for the reenactment test: "The angle [of Connally's wounds] could not be fixed with absolute precision, since the large wound on the front of his chest precluded an exact determination of the point of exit";[61] "the probable angle . . . assuming that he was sitting in a vertical position;"[62] "The exact positions of the men could not be re-created; thus, the angle could only be approximated";[63] "If the Governor had not turned in exactly the way calculated, the alinement would have been destroyed."[64] That the reenactment seems to have been based on far too much guess-work is a grim mockery of what a proper criminal investigation should have been.

As an important side note, further undermining one's faith in this part of the official investigation, several standard scientific tests were not conducted, and the results of others were not discussed in the Report. For example, the copper traces left by the bullet on the clothes of Governor Connally could have been analyzed and scientifically proven to be from CE399. Officials waited six months until the clothing was contaminated and tests could not be performed. The metallic fragments taken from Connally's body could have been submitted to tests that would have either scientifically linked them to CE399 or declared they were not connected, in which case they would have supported the notion of a conspiracy.

Even more disturbing to one's trust in the inquiry's fidelity are the results of scientific tests left out of the Report and its construction of the single-bullet theory. Bureau spectrographic examinations of the damage to the tie and collar revealed, in the words of Director J. Edgar Hoover, that "no copper was found which could be attributed to projectile fragments." If copper-clad CE399 had passed through the cloth, it would have had to leave copper tracings. Their absence means the bullet did not pass through and requires the alleged exiting hole to be higher on JFK's body, making it impossible on its alleged forward flight to have a sufficiently sharp angle to have struck Connally in the back. No bullet passed through JFK's collar and tie, and this fact alone wrecks the invented single-bullet thesis and requires another rifle and another shooter to account for the several wounds on Connally.[65]

A simple, clear, and sound way to show that the single-bullet theory was valid was to submit bullet CE399, the fragments taken from Connally's chest and wrist, and smears or residues—all asserted to be the ballistic signature of CE399—to neutron activation analysis (NAA), which could scientifically prove or disprove a common origin. A striking bullet leaves identifiable and retrievable deposits and fragments roughly similar to a fingerprint but not as unique.[66] With even a tiny specimen the procedure indicates the composition of what is tested and the concentration of each component element. A scientist can then determine if fragments, bullet, and deposits came from the same bullet or the same manufacturer's batch of bullets.

At Oak Ridge, Tennessee, scientists performed NAA on selected fragments and deposits for the FBI, but the bureau did not release the results even to the Commission. After a fiercely contested ten-year court battle for the NAA metallic testing (and the NAA paraffin testing discussed previously), critic Harold Weisberg and his attorney James Lesar were finally provided not with the report on the metallic tests but with hundreds of jumbled pages of scattered raw data, a fraction of the known whole, which could not be used to draw any conclusions about the results of the nuclear reactor tests.[67]

On remand Weisberg obtained numerous documents and took some four hundred pages of deposition testimony from four FBI agents who had evaluated and tested key items of evidence. Some of the evidence directly contradicted the affidavit of Special Agent John W. Kilty, who swore under oath that he had not done NAA on the limousine windshield damage. Weisberg also learned that agents who investigated the ballistics were often ignorant of basic facts. For example, Special Agent Cortland Cunningham, who performed the initial ballistic testing of CE399, testified he was not aware it had been wiped clean before being sent to the FBI laboratory; Special Agent John F. Gallagher, when presented with a photograph of JFK's shirt collar, did not know the difference between a buttonhole and a bullet hole. If the FBI agents' testimony can be given credence, and some is suspect, a picture emerges "of an FBI Laboratory as bungling, uncoordinated, amateurish, inept, and anything but thorough, precise, and reliable."[68]

Many factual weaknesses and critical omissions of key evidentiary components of a criminal inquiry suffuse the claim that a single bullet, CE399, inflicted all seven nonfatal wounds on President Kennedy and Governor Connally. They are enough to raise serious doubts about the bullet as a legitimate explanation for the wounds. Contrary to the official allegations, the official *evidence* proves CE399 does *not* relate to the wounds or to the crime in any way. Those allegations, the evidence demonstrates, actually rest on baseless conjecture by Commission officials who knew when they made it up it was impossible.[69]

When we turn from those allegations to the actual official evidence, a much different story emerges. As demonstrated, Oswald could not have been on the sixth floor at that fateful moment, let alone at the window, and therefore he fired no weapon. The magic "single" bullet did not enter JFK's back, leave by his throat, puncture his collar and tie, smash Connally's chest and wrist, or punch into and pull out of his thigh. Nor was the serendipitously discovered pristine bullet related to the official account of the woundings in any way. Moreover, the Commission, its staff, and the agents of the Federal Bureau of Investigation were fully aware of the reality provided by the unimpeachable official evidentiary base, so much of which they themselves, over a course of many months, had assiduously assembled and carefully studied.

According to the official allegations, Lee Harvey Oswald, a book handler in the Texas School Book Depository, sneaked a Mannlicher-Carcano 6.5-mm rifle to work that morning.[70] A paper bag found on the sixth floor, officials claimed, was used to disguise the disassembled rifle as a package of curtain rods.[71] He then carried the disguised rifle to the sixth floor of the depository, at a time never stipulated, where at some unspecified time before the motorcade appeared, he reassembled it.

Allegedly Oswald at an unspecified time piled boxes of books in stacks to shield the southeasternmost window from the rest of the floor, a labor incompatible and directly clashing with all witness testimony. He next stacked either two boxes of books on the floor by the window with one behind it as rifle rest,[72] or else one box on the sill and two on the floor,[73] or else three boxes on the floor;[74] all three configurations, however mutually exclusive, are official allegations. But he then used none of these arrangements, for the officials baldly contradict themselves and assert that he stood during the shooting.[75] The Commission further alleges that Oswald fired three shots when JFK's limousine passed by the depository. He next chambered a live bullet that he would not fire,[76] lingered briefly,[77] and then quickly fled across the floor to the northwest corner to the stairway, the only exit, in order to descend to the second floor, the only way down from the sixth floor.[78]

On the flight across the floor to the stairway, Oswald allegedly hid the rifle between some book boxes near the stairs. On the second floor he exited the stairs into a lunchroom area.[79] At that point, the Commission tells us, police officer Marrion Baker and building manager Roy Truly, ascending the stairs from the first floor, rushed in from the stairwell and confronted Oswald standing at the Coke machine.[80] Baker shoved his pistol into Oswald's stomach.[81] The time when they met was never accurately specified, but it occurred soon after the shooting, approximately one minute and a few seconds. Truly told Baker that Oswald worked in the building.[82] Then Truly and Baker left via the stairs to continue a hurried search of the upper floors of the building.

The official evidence, as discussed in a previous chapter, shows without the slightest doubt that none of this is true, except a single point: that Baker and Truly met Oswald at the Coke machine on the second floor. The rest is allegation unalloyed by evidence, devised for the political purpose of convicting Oswald of the murder, not for defining the facts of the murder.

According to the Commission's Report, expert examinations concluded that the Mannlicher-Carcano rifle found by a police search of the sixth floor of the School Book Depository had fired CE399. On this the Report is unequivocal: "The nearly whole bullet from the stretcher" was "fired in the C2766 Mannlicher-Carcano rifle."[83] That bullet, according to the Report, inflicted all seven nonfatal wounds on President Kennedy and Governor Connally, as well as breaking two of Connally's bones.

But the actual official evidence establishes with absolute certainty that this is false. Among other things, the Commission omitted a central fact in stating the Mannlicher-Carcano rifle uncovered on the sixth floor fired the bullet CE399. It does not say *when* the rifle fired CE399, which could have been easily determined by one basic, simple, and inexpensive test. It is typical for investigators of a gunshot crime to use a rod to push a cotton swab down a gun's barrel to detect traces of any residue from a fired bullet. The FBI, however, failed to swab the Mannlicher-Carcano barrel on November 22 to see if it had been fired that day.

Interestingly (some might say ominously), the FBI also failed to conduct an appropriate swab test during the investigation of Dr. Martin Luther King's assassination, or, rather, it failed to conduct one on the right weapon. Days before going to Memphis, James Earl Ray had purchased a new .243 rifle in a Birmingham gun store and then within a few hours had returned to the shop to exchange it for a Gamemaster .30-06 rifle. That returned rifle had no relationship whatsoever to the crime; moreover, it was heavily coated with Cosmoline, making it impossible to fire. Nonetheless, the FBI swabbed its barrel while neglecting to swab the barrel of the rifle it alleged fired the fatal shot.[84]

As there is no physical evidence that the Mannlicher-Carcano 6.5-mm rifle fired CE399, or any other bullet, on November 22 in Dallas, neither are there any credible eyewitnesses. The Commission's sole alleged eyewitness, Howard Brennan, sitting on a wall across from the depository, did not testify to the rifle actually being fired, only aimed, and his testimony is so flawed that his statements lack any credence whatsoever.[85] In fact, no evidence links Oswald directly to that rifle.

Officials claimed Oswald sneaked the rifle into the depository disguised as a package of curtain rods. He lived in a small rented room in Dallas, but his wife, Marina, and two small daughters lived thirty miles away in Irving with Ruth Paine, a charitable woman then temporarily separated from her husband. After work on Thursday, November 21, Oswald hitched a ride to Irving with a fellow employee, Buell Frazier, who lived a few doors from Paine.[86] The next morning, November 22, he returned carrying a paper-wrapped package, explaining to Frazier that it held curtain rods for his apartment.[87] The Commission bluntly said Oswald "gave a false reason" because his Dallas rental "had curtains and curtain rods."[88] The package actually carried the 40.2-inch-long Mannlicher-Carcano dismantled into pieces, the longest part being 34.8 inches, that Oswald had retrieved from the Paine garage, where he had kept it hidden in an old blanket. Upon reaching the parking lot near the depository, Oswald, carrying the package with one end tucked under his armpit and the other cupped in his hand, walked ahead of Frazier, who remained behind to tinker with his old car, and entered the building.[89] In some way that is not specified he allegedly carried the package to the sixth floor and assembled the rifle, discarding the sack on the floor near the easternmost window. The sack had been con-structed with wrapping tape and paper taken from the depository, which Oswald had to have fabricated in Irving.[90]

Despite the confident tone of the Commission's allegations, however, 100 percent of its evidence proved Oswald did not take a rifle into the Texas School Book Depository. The only two individuals who saw Oswald's pack-age, Frazier and his sister Linnie Mae, under repeated questioning never wavered in stating it was about 28 inches long, too short to have held the rifle.[91] Jack Dougherty, the Report's only witness cited for Oswald carrying the package into the depository building, testified to the exact opposite: that Oswald had entered empty-handed.[92] The discarded sack found on the sixth floor did not appear on the initial crime scene photographs; the Commission resorted to drawing an outline on a crime scene photograph to indicate where it supposedly had been, which casts strong doubt on the sack's integrity as evidence.[93] At midnight on November 22, Dallas police questioned Frazier, who had seen the package most closely. Then they gave him a polygraph test, which he passed. Oswald, the coworker attested, "definitely" carried "a thin, flimsy sack like one purchased in a dime store."[94] Police then showed Frazier the sack found on the sixth floor and asked him if it was the one Oswald had carried. Frazier said he never had seen it before. Frazier said that the sack the police presented to him was made of paper, "the type a grocery store received the five-pound bags of sugar in . . . very thick and stiff."[95] His statement excludes the sack as valid evidence.

Scientific testing of the bag proved beyond any question that it had not held the rifle pieces. A highly impressionable paper, it bore no appropriate folds;[96] nor did it bear the inevitable scratches, markings, or abrasions that necessarily would have been imposed by use.[97] "I couldn't find any such markings," swore the FBI expert.[98] Nor did the bag show any oil stains.[99] The absence of oil residues when the rifle itself was well oiled is conclusive evidence that the bag never held the weapon.[100]

The Commission also stated that Oswald's fingerprint and palm print were found on the bag, but it failed to observe that the bag was actually from Oswald's work area and the fact that his print was found should have been expected; its absence would be significant.[101] But with all the handling of the easily imprintable bag attributed to Oswald—taking the paper from the depository, transporting it home, making the sack, packing it with the rifle, taking it back to work, carrying it into the building, and removing the rifle—how it could bear only those two prints was never addressed. More damning, the official test of the bag for prints lacked integrity and renders any statement concerning the prints unacceptable. For example, the bag did not carry the fingerprints of the discovering officer, who had held it up by his naked hand for a camera to snap a picture, meaning the police either forged the bag used as evidence or corrupted the testing or both.[102]

The Commission's own evidence also proves Oswald could not have taken either the paper or the tape that fastened it into a bag from the depository supplies; without paper and tape, there could be no bag.[103] The paper and the tape came exclusively from the depository,[104] and they were obtained only in the last two days before November 22.[105] Oswald did not carry them along when he went to Irving to visit his estranged wife the evening of November 21. He could not have secreted the bulky materials on his person without being easily detected.[106] The tape came from a dispensing machine at the depository and could only be obtained wet, an impossible condition for transporting it.[107] The machine was never left unattended, and no employees ever asked for tape or paper or came into the area where they were held, including Oswald.[108]

At NIGHT

But the evidence indicates that the curtain rod story is valid. Oswald's brief comment to Frazier the morning of November 22 that the sack he carried held curtain rods is supported by spurned official evidence.[109] The rods came from extras stored in the cluttered Irving garage and were intended for his rented room in Dallas.[110] Contrary to the Commission's falsely derived statement, Oswald's rented room needed curtains.[111] A series of photographs taken of the room "the next morning," November 23, by Black Star newsman Gene Daniels shows the landlady and a workman busy hanging curtains on the large window running almost the length of the sun-drenched first-floor room to tidy the place for the coming viewing by reporters.[112]

The official *evidence* of the discovery of CE399 is radically different from the account provided in the official *allegations*. The President's Commission in fact could not link the bullet discovered in the Parkland Memorial Hospital corridor by Darrell Tomlinson, the hospital engineer, to Governor Connally's stretcher. When the Commission unequivocally stated in its Report that CE399 was "found on Governor Connally's stretcher," it was merely asserting.[113] The official evidence, however, suggests a distinctly different scenario, one that does not even tell us which stretcher the bullet came from, how it got into the corridor, or even if Connally's stretcher was then in the corridor, or whether CE399 is the "single" bullet in question.

On March 20, 1964, Tomlinson testified to the Commission that on the ground floor he had found an unidentified stretcher on the elevator of a hospital type, high and with wheels, not an ambulance type.[114] It was the standard procedure in the hospital for the operating room on the second floor to shove stretchers into the elevator descending to the emergency room on the ground floor,[115] where someone could find and remove them.[116] Tomlinson wheeled it off into the hall.[117] This could not have been Connally's, which was an emergency room or ambulance type with a different physical configuration.[118]

Also, contrary to the allegations of the Commission, Tomlinson was not alone that afternoon in the corridor.[119] He testified that where the stretchers were parked, "many people went through" during the time he was there.[120] "I don't know how many people hit them," he added, referring to the stretchers, opening the sinister but perfectly reasonable implication that someone could have planted the bullet.[121] Moreover, he was not there constantly. He "made several trips" in the course of his operating the elevator before discovering the bullet, meaning opportunities existed for someone passing through to plant the bullet.[122] In any case, Tomlinson's account is straightforward. After working for about an hour around the elevator that he converted from automatic to manual, he saw a doctor entering the men's room push aside the stretcher blocking the door.[123] When the doctor came out of the rest room, he did not return the stretcher to its original position.[124] Tomlinson walked over and "pushed it out of the way where we would have clear area in front of the elevator . . . up against the wall."[125] As he told the Commission: "I bumped the wall, and the spent cartridge bullet rolled out that had apparently been lodged under the edge of the mat."[126]

We further learn from the official evidence that contrary to the official allegations,[127] Tomlinson knew nothing about the origin of the stretcher in the elevator. When asked which stretcher he took off the elevator, he answered, "I am not sure."[128] His other comments about the stretchers in the elevator or corridor include "I really don't remember"[129] and "I don't know."[130]

Strangely, when Commission counsel Arlen Specter deposed Tomlinson, he pressured him to testify that CE399 came from Connally's stretcher.[131] But Tomlinson stood firm against Commission pressure. Finally, in exasperation, Tomlinson testified that he would not be able to sleep at night if he said what Specter was pressing him to say: "I am going to tell you all I can, and I'm not going to tell you something I can't lay down and sleep at night with either."[132] In the face of Tomlinson's resolute testimony, Specter and his fellow staff members and the commissioners still embraced the improbable.

The bullet had not been seen in the emergency room where the clothing was removed, nor when the governor was wheeled to and into the operating room. It had not fallen out when his body had been lifted to an operating room table or when his stretcher had routinely been pushed into the elevator. It had not been seen on the elevator, nor had it rolled out from under the mattress when the stretcher was shoved out of the elevator. It had remained completely invisible until it had emerged from *under* that unidentified mattress on an unidentified stretcher. The *official* evidence provides ample time and much opportunity for the planting of that most magical of bullets, which could have taken place when a doctor had to urinate.

Critic Harold Weisberg's comment on the official evidence is succinct and valid: "This bullet, taken from the floor after having been jarred out presumably from underneath a mattress of an unidentified stretcher, is the one the Report describes as 'found on Governor Connally's stretcher.' "[133] There are additional troubling aspects connected with CE399 that challenge its authenticity. For example, is CE399 the bullet Tomlinson actually found in the corridor of Parkland? The Report merely asserts that to be true, but the official evidence suggests otherwise. From the official allegations, one would conclude that Tomlinson picked up the bullet when he discovered it; instead, he left it where it had fallen and contacted O. P. Wright, chief of hospital security. What happened next only came to light during the airing of CBS's four-part series on the Warren Report in 1967. Reporter Eddie Barker of KRLD-TV questioned Wright:

WRIGHT: I told him to withhold and not let anyone remove the bullet, and I would get a hold of either the Secret Service or the F.B.I. and turn it over to them. Thereby, it wouldn't have come through my hands at all. I contacted the F.B.I. and they said they were not interested because it wasn't their responsibility to make investigations. So, I got a hold of a Secret Serviceman and they didn't seem to be interested in coming and looking at the bullet in the position it was in then.

So I went back to the area where Mr. Tomlinson was and picked up the bullet and put it in my pocket, and I carried it some 30 or 40 minutes. And I gave it to a Secret Serviceman that was guarding the main door into the emergency room.

BARKER: Mr. Wright, when you gave this bullet to the Secret Service agent, did he mark it in any way?

WRIGHT: No, sir.

BARKER: What did he do with it?

WRIGHT: Put it in his lefthand coat pocket.

BARKER: Well now, did he ask your name or who you were or any question at all about the bullet?

WRIGHT: No, sir.

BARKER: How did the conversation go? Do you remember?

WRIGHT: I just told him this was a bullet that was picked up on a stretcher that had come off the emergency elevator that might be involved in the moving of Governor Connally. And I handed him the bullet, and he took it and looked at it and said, "O.K.," and put it in his pocket.[134]

Wright had not been called as a Commission witness, but Richard Johnsen, the Secret Service agent, did leave a covering document that accompanied the bullet he turned over to his superiors and which appears in one of the Report's twenty-six supplementary volumes. Typed at 7:30 P.M. the day of the assassination on an ordinary sheet of paper and without an addressee, Johnsen's document stated: "The attached expended bullet was received by me about 5 min., prior to Mrs. Kennedy's departure from the hospital. It was found on one of the stretchers located in the emergency ward of the hospital." He received it from "Mr. O. P. Wright, Personnel Director of Security, Dallas County Hospital District."[135] Eight days later, on November 30, Johnsen sent a letterhead memorandum to the chief of the Secret Service, James J. Rowley, approved and signed by Secret Service agent Gerald Behn, head of the White House detail, in which he recounted the same information.[136]

The night of November 22, Johnsen turned the bullet over to Gerald A. Behn. An FBI interview of Behn from November 27, 1963, describes one part of the movement of the "bullet" from the Secret Service to the FBI. FBI agents James W. Sibert and Francis X. O'Neill interviewed Behn and reported: "[Behn] . . . stated that on learning of such a bullet being found at the Dallas Hospital he inquired of a group of his Agents who had returned from the Dallas trip on the night of November 22, 1963, and Secret Service Agent Richard Johnsen produced this bullet which had been handed to him by someone at the hospital who had stated that it was not known whether or not the President had been placed on the stretcher where the bullet was found."[137] Note that Behn did not say he handled the bullet, nor was he called as a witness by the Commission.

James Rowley, chief of the Secret Service and the next recorded holder of the bullet, gave it to Elmer Lee Todd of the FBI. Information regarding this transfer to Todd is tucked into a July 7, 1964, memorandum from the FBI Dallas Field Office discussing its showing CE399 to witnesses. It reports that Rowley gave the bullet to Special Agent Todd of the FBI's Washington Field Office.[138] Yet when Rowley later testified before the Commission, he was not questioned at all about the bullet or its origin.[139] Behn apparently had given the bullet to Rowley, but no known memorandum proves that.

Subsequently, Todd carried the bullet to the FBI laboratory and delivered it to FBI agent Robert A. Frazier.[140] Both agents initialed it. Yet neither man was ever questioned about the bullet by the Commission.

Confirmation of the lab's receipt of the bullet comes indirectly from another Sibert and O'Neill document, this one a report on President Kennedy's autopsy, which they witnessed at Bethesda Naval Hospital. The autopsy surgeons there were "at a loss to explain" the action of a purported "military" bullet that performed far differently than any other military bullet. A bullet with a significantly different composition and impact signature had left the minute fragments in JFK's head. The bullet had shattered into about forty dustlike particles that looked on an X ray like stars at night, as per the testimony of navy commander James J. Humes, who supervised the autopsy on JFK.[141]

Sibert telephoned the "the Firearms Section of the FBI Laboratory" seeking some explanation for the odd action of this alleged military bullet. Instead of an answer to his query, however, he was told about the discovery of a bullet in Dallas:

> SA Charles S. [H?]illion advised that the Laboratory had received through Secret Service Agent RICHARD JOHNSON [sic] a bullet which had reportedly been found on a stretcher in the emergency room of Parkland Hospital, Dallas, Texas. This stretcher had also contained a stethoscope and pair of rubber gloves. Agent JOHNSON had advised the Laboratory that it had not been ascertained whether or not this was the stretcher that had been used to transport the body of President KENNEDY.[142]

Note that neither Johnsen nor any law enforcement office had any firsthand knowledge of where the bullet was actually found, apparently a matter of little consequence to the Commission.

After the telephone call, Sibert informed the chief autopsy surgeon, Dr. Humes, of the discovery of a bullet at Parkland. Humes initially assumed that the bullet had not penetrated deeply into the president's back and had worked its way out by the doctors during cardiac massage. Two days later, he changed this hasty preliminary assumption and said in his autopsy report that the bullet transited the body of JFK, entering the back and exiting the throat, something subsequently contested by the official evidence.

Neither Tomlinson, Wright, Rowley, nor Johnsen could confirm CE399 as the bullet they had seen or held, leaving unchallenged the Commission's unsupported and thus highly problematic assertion regarding the bullet's identity.

In late May the Warren Commission requested that the FBI "trace" certain pieces of the evidence, including CE399, "by exhibiting the original or photographs" to the witnesses. On June 2, 1964, FBI headquarters forwarded several pieces of evidence to the Dallas field office by registered airmail.[143] One of these was CE399.

On June 12, 1964, in Dallas, FBI special agent Bardwell D. Odum interviewed Darrell C. Tomlinson at Parkland Memorial Hospital and showed him CE399. Tomlinson stated that "he cannot positively identify the bullet as the one he found and showed to Mr. O. P. Wright."[144] That same day Odum interviewed Wright and also showed him CE399. Wright "advised he could not positively identify C1 [CE399] as being the same bullet which was found on November 22, 1963."[145] Back in Washington on June 24, FBI special agent Elmer Lee Todd interviewed Secret Service Agent Richard E. Johnsen and showed him CE399. "Johnsen advised he could not identify this bullet as the one he obtained from O. P. Wright, and gave to James Rowley."[146] The same day Todd interviewed Chief Rowley of the Secret Service and asked him to identify CE399: "Rowley advised he could not identify this bullet as the one he received from Special Agent Richard E. Johnsen."[147] As it turned out, only Todd, who of course was at a much later point in the chain of possession, was able to confirm CE399 as the bullet he had received from Rowley, identifying it by his initials on an attached tag.[148] Thus, the official evidence is mute on CE399's precise connection to the bullet discovered by Tomlinson.

The FBI performed several scientific tests on CE399 to determine, among other things, the bullet weight and the nature of markings other than rifling marks found on it. Yet it failed to perform the obvious test for blood and other human matter that would have been left on the bullet if it had struck a human.

As noted previously, the Commission, drawing upon the FBI tests, asserted a whole bullet before firing would weigh 160 to 161 grains.[149] The "stretcher bullet" weighed 158.6 grains.[150] According to the Commission, the bullet shed fragments in Connally's body as it passed through. An official examination of the JFK X rays made in 1968 found it also left "several small metallic fragments" in Kennedy's "neck region."[151]

Consequently, if the weight of the lead lost in the firing exceeded what could have come from CE399, then CE399 could not have been the source of the fragments. The fragments would then require at least one additional bullet and that, in turn, would have required at least one other rifle and at least one other assassin. That means there had to have been a conspiracy.

Moreover, each of the three doctors who performed the autopsy testified that CE399 could not have left the fragments in JFK's body. Commander Humes held the bullet in his hands when he replied that he did "not understand how it could have left fragments in either of these locations." On the bullet fragment in Connally's thigh: "I can't conceive of where they [fragments] came from this missile."[152] Commander J. Thornton Boswell and Lieutenant Colonel Pierre J. Finck, who assisted Humes at the autopsy, confirmed Humes's testimony. When Finck was asked if he wanted to modify anything that Humes had said about CE399, he answered, "No."[153] Boswell agreed.[154] Dr. Robert Shaw, a Dallas surgeon who worked on Governor Connally's wounds, testified before the Commission. When he was shown CE399, he declared that "more than three grains of metal" were "in the wrist."[155]

On the afternoon of March 31, 1964, FBI ballistics expert Robert A. Frazier testified in Washington before the Commission on the weight of CE399. "Exhibit 399," he told counsel Eisenberg, "weighs 158.6 grains." The weights of standard 6.5-mm bullets varied, he said, which was normal. They could vary "a portion of a grain, or two grains, from 161 grains," which was the normal weight. In his expert opinion, "There did not necessarily have to be any weight loss to the bullet . . . because 158.6 is only a grain and a half less than the normal weight."

The FBI weighed CE399, according to the official account, but the evidence demonstrates it did so only after two weight-reducing functions had occurred. First, the bullet had been fired. A bullet propelled through the rifling of a gun at two thousand feet per second is stripped of about 0.5 grain of metal, which the FBI and Commission did not mention. That means CE399 weighed approximately 159.3 grains (158.6 plus 0.5 equals 159.3) before it left the barrel and fell within Frazier's normal weight category.

Second, the Bureau weighed the bullet only after removing two metal samples to use for scientific testing.[156] The Commission nonetheless acknowledged only the removal of a single tiny sample from the nose of the copper jacket, with no mention of another sample visibly cut from the base.

Not until five years after the close of the investigation were critics able to obtain evidence to verify that the FBI had indeed removed other metal from the base.

This proof came from New Orleans. In the 1969 trial of Clay Shaw for conspiracy to kill President Kennedy, Special Agent Frazier testified he also took metal from the lead core base.[157] Later critic Harold Weisberg published his photograph of CE399's base, which clearly shows Frazier's tool mark in the metal made during removal and the unnecessarily large quantity of lead it included.[158] These two FBI samples and the half grain lost in firing alone account for all the missing lead in CE399, if they do not exceed it.

This necessarily means that any lead that appears in the bodies of President Kennedy and Governor Connally could not have come from CE399 and requires a different bullet—meaning another assassin—to account for it. The physical presence of lead in both bodies alone proves that a conspiracy killed the president of the United States.

The Commission's Report also failed to address the meaning of certain characteristic markings found on the bullet. Special Agent Frazier, a firearms expert, in reply to a question from assistant counsel Eisenberg, testified that the fine microscopic marks on CE399 "could be the result of the bullet striking some object after it was fired . . . even a piece of coarse cloth, leather or some other object."[159] In this testimony Frazier did not connect that bullet with the crime. Further, as stored in the National Archives, CE399 had dangling from its lead core tiny hairlike strands and balls of lead compound. Critic Howard Roffman discovered CE399 had shed these pieces onto the bottom of the storage canister.[160] This means, among other things, that a testing sample did not have to be cut from the base for spectrographic analysis. This cutting Frazier did do, as he admitted in Weisberg's FOIA lawsuit (CA75-226).[161]

The unreported small removals, the hairlike pieces, the absence of a clearly defined chain of possession, the failure of every witness to the finding and delivery of the bullet to identify the bullet, and the failure to even try to establish that the rifle had been fired that day certainly encourage the belief that evidence was doctored, ignored, or even fabricated to support allegations of Oswald's guilt.

Finally, the Commission and FBI failed to test for any foreign matter residue on the bullet and relate it to the victims. This bullet allegedly went through two bodies, inflicting serious wounds, breaking two large bones, and allegedly leaving behind fragments. Yet it was clean, a physical impossibility. "The bullet was clean," testified Frazier.[162] When asked, "There was no blood or similar material on the bullet when you received it?" Frazier replied, "Not that would interfere with the examination, no, sir."[163] Tests could have identified traces of blood and matter and perhaps link them to JFK or Connally, thus supporting the single-bullet theory or showing that those traces were not from them. The Commission's counsel returned to the subject again in the course of deposing Frazier, who reaffirmed: "No, there was no test made of the materials."[164] By contrast, Frazier also testified that other bullet fragments found in the limousine—CE567 and CE569—had "a very slight residue of blood or some other material adhering."[165] Neither that suggestive and troubling contrast nor the FBI's failure to test those deposits on CE399 was mentioned in the Report.

Thus, in summation, the official evidence establishes that CE399, the magic bullet of the Commission's single-bullet invention, should not be considered an authentic piece of evidence. It also seems to suggest that officials knew this. Since CE399 lies at the heart of the Commission's allegations denying conspiracy while framing Lee Harvey Oswald for the murder of President Kennedy, its removal by the official evidence damages the official findings beyond repair.

16 Official Evidence
The Seven Nonfatal Wounds

The official allegations of the Warren Commission Report state that a single bullet, Commission Exhibit 399, passed through the neck of President Kennedy, causing two nonfatal wounds.[1] In the official scenario a bullet came from high behind him and to his right at a speed of two thousand feet per second to hit him on the neck; "he was struck in the neck,"[2] creating " 'a wound of entrance.' "[3] After entering JFK's body, the bullet did not encounter bone or other hard matter. "No bone was struck by the bullet which passed through the President's body,"[4] on a downward angle, to emerge from his throat at the level of his necktie knot, where it damaged the knot and his shirt collar.[5] "It traveled downward and exited from the front of the neck, causing a nick in the left lower portion of the knot in the President's necktie."[6] While these claims are presented as confident, solid statements reflective presumably of solid fact, sound research, and keen professional judgments, the official evidence reveals them to be incorrect. Not one of these allegations is true. Moreover, federal officials knew their evidence proved this.

While some of the nation's finest forensic pathologists, men with outstanding abilities and reputations who had worked with the government on cases, lived close to Washington, and were available, the federal authorities unaccountably selected three military doctors who had never done a forensic autopsy to perform President Kennedy's postmortem examination. (From the government's perspective, the basic problem was not a medical problem but one of control.) These were James J. Humes and J. Thornton Boswell, of the United States Navy, and Pierre Finck, of the United States Army.[7] Dr. Cyril Wecht, former head of the American Academy of Forensic Sciences, a doctor, a lawyer, a professor of medical law at Duquesne University, and one of the nation's top forensic pathologists, said of Humes and Boswell, "You must remember, Humes and Boswell had never done medical-legal autopsies in their careers. It [the autopsy] was really inept."[8]

Michael Baden, New York City's chief medical examiner and chair of the House Select Committee's medical panel, concurred with Wecht's assessment in a biting critique of the three prosecutors' abilities. In his book *Unnatural Death: Confessions of a Medical Examiner*, he stated Humes "had never autopsied anyone with a gunshot wound."[9] The three doctors "didn't know the difference" between "an entrance and an exit wound."[10]

Bizarrely, officials ultimately placed JFK's posterior nonlethal wound at the level of the neck—in spite of a slew of hard facts defined by medical, ballistic, eyewitness, and clothing evidence that clearly argued otherwise.[11] By corruption of the evidence, they inaccurately located the hole on JFK's neckline higher than its actual site several inches down on his back. The Report states that a "bullet wound was observed near the base of the back of President Kennedy's neck slightly to the right of his spine."[12] Moreover, it fixes the point with precise measurements when it alleges: "The hole was located approximately 5½ inches (14 centimeters) from the tip of the right shoulder joint and approximately the same distance below the tip of the right mastoid process, the bony point immediately behind the ear."[13]

The Commission further alleges that the bullet proceeded through the body "at a slightly downward angle,"[14] to exit "in the area of the knot of his tie."[15] Commission Exhibits 385 and 386—an artist's representation of the official location of the wound—graphically reinforce this allegation, although the artist never saw the actual wounds. They were "drawn to a certain extent from memory," testified Humes.[16] They do not reflect the official evidence. Instead of providing the navy illustrator with the photographs and other essential materials from the autopsy that a medical illustrator would normally employ in making sketches, which even the most hardened supporter of the official allegations would assume transpired, Dr. Humes supplied only oral recollections. In their executive session meeting of January 1, 1964, the commissioners revealed they were fully aware of the problem of the illustrations' fidelity and agreed with their chief counsel, J. Lee Rankin, that "we don't know whether those . . . conform to the autopsy or not."[17]

CE385 depicts the head and upper torso of the president.[18] An arrow points to where the bullet allegedly entered at the neckline and, traveling at a slight angle downward, exited at the shirt collar level. CE386 depicts the back of JFK's head and shoulders, illustrating, among other things, a bullet hole in the neckline muscles to the right of the spine, directly below the earlobe, and above the line of his shoulders.[19] The downward angle, as stressed earlier, is critical to the career of the single bullet in the official explanation. CE399 had to strike JFK's back high enough to continue through the body at an angle of declination sufficient to exit low on the throat. It then, according to the Commission, continued on in flight to hit Connally in the right armpit, which is below the level of the throat.[20]

The official evidentiary record, however, clearly shows that the artist's rendering inaccurately located the nonlethal wound. JFK's jacket and shirt both locate the hole on the back, not the neck.[21] Kennedy was wearing an expensive suit jacket and a handmade shirt tailored for him by Charles Dillon of 444 Park Avenue. (He wore no undershirt.) A bullet hole appears in the back of each.

In fact, the Report itself states that a hole appears on the jacket about 5⅜ inches below the top of the collar and 1¾ inches to the right of the mid-seam, as well as 5¾ inches below the top of the collar and 1⅛ inches to the right of the middle of the shirt.[22] By the Report's own declaration and in contradiction to its formal finding, the holes in the jacket and shirt are in the back, not at the level of the neck, and thus would have been too low for a bullet fired from the depository's sixth floor to have inflicted JFK's nonlethal wound and still exit at the level of the necktie knot. Yet the Report places the hole in the back, following the assertion the hole was in the neck.[23]

The Commission further concluded that "the fibers pressed inward" at the hole in JFK's clothing, establishing it "as a bullet entrance hole."[24] But its official evidence does not say this. FBI agent Robert Frazier implied that the fibers could be bent the other way by artificial means just as easily, and without a chain of possession or knowledge of the coat's original status, the bent fibers provided dubious supporting evidence for the Commission's claim.[25] But the FBI itself also did its part to muddy these waters. For example, its Exhibit 60 consists of photographs of JFK's shirt, collar, and necktie, with an inset enlargement of the hole in the shirt's back set in the left margin.[26] The enlargement has printed the hole upside down, which places the sharp edge of the hole at the top and leaves the impression the bullet came from a high position, the alleged location of the assassin.[27]

Most important, every federal agent who saw the president's body on November 22 stated the bullet hole was on the back, not the neck. Three Secret Service agents who officially observed the body during autopsy placed the rear nonfatal wound on the back. During his testimony before the Commission, Roy Kellerman, the agent in charge, repeatedly described the wound for counsel Specter as a "shoulder" wound, "just below" the "large muscle between the shoulder and the neck."[28] Kellerman also reported that he called Secret Service agent Clint Hill into the autopsy room to view Kennedy's wounds. In a statement for authorities Hill related, "I observed a wound about six inches down from the neckline on the back just to the right of the spinal column."[29] The third Secret Service agent to view the body was William Greer. During his testimony he affirmed that the hole was in the "upper right shoulder area."[30]

In addition to the three Secret Service agents who saw the wound on the corpse's back, another agent in the motorcade had seen a bullet hit JFK's back. Glenn Bennett rode on the running board of the backup limousine and was looking at President Kennedy when he saw the bullet "hit the President about four inches down from the right shoulder."[31] Joining the three Secret Service agents in the autopsy room as official observers were two FBI agents, who also reported the wound was in JFK's back, not neck. Agents James W. Sibert and Francis X. O'Neill Jr., in their report on their observations entitled "Results of Autopsy on John F. Kennedy," said they saw on the corpse "a bullet hole . . . below the shoulders and two inches to the right of the middle line of the spinal column."[32]

In addition, the medical personnel attending to the Bethesda postmortem said the president's wound was on the back, not the neck. For example, Commission counsel Specter deposed James J. Humes, the navy pathologist in charge of the autopsy. Specter showed him the coat and shirt and asked him to describe the location of the bullet holes. Humes placed them "approximately 6 inches below the top of the collar, and 2 inches to the right of the middle seam."[33] He added that the location "corresponds essentially with the point of entrance."

Fervent apologists for the Commission have argued that the coat and shirt "humped" or "rode up" on Kennedy, enabling the bullet to hit the jacket and shirt at the invented fold and then pass into his neck at the location that would affirm the single-bullet explanation. Aside from the numerous irrationalities of this particular device to skirt the evidence,[34] the fifth slide taken by Phil Willis, discussed in an earlier chapter, proves this is not true. Taken just a fraction of a second after the first shot, the slide shows the well-tailored jacket in its proper position.

The official "Autopsy Descriptive Sheet" of JFK, which consists of a single mimeographed page, with a body outline and items to be filled in, also places the bullet hole on the back, but Commission members tried to mask its evidence.[35] Dr. J. Thornton Boswell of the autopsy team made notes on this standard autopsy sheet, locating the wound *on the back* at the level of the third thoracic vertebrae, to the right of the back wound. Admiral George Burkley, the president's physician, wrote on the margins, "verified," and signed his name, thus providing the attestation of a second physician to the low location.[36] As critic Harold Weisberg has conclusively shown, when the Commission printed the "Descriptive Sheet" as part of CE397, Dr. Burkley's signature and verification were missing. The erasure of the verification had the effect of stripping away support for the authenticity of the wound descriptions provided by the president's physician.[37]

The official death certificate of President Kennedy located the rear non-fatal wound on the back, yet it appears to have been misplaced or hidden in the printing files of the Commission, where few would ever think of searching for documents.[38] Dr. Burkley reported on the certificate that a "wound occurred in the posterior back at about the level of the third thoracic vertebra."[39] Burkley was never called as a witness. The death certificate was never referred to in testimony, not printed in the Report, not included in the ten thousand pages of supporting evidentiary volumes. Yet the Commission must have been aware of such a crucial oversight; it even possessed receipts of the document's transmittal from the Secret Service.

We know, however, that the Commission members were aware that the autopsy photographs placed the hole on the back, not the neck. During the January 27, 1964, executive session meeting of the Warren Commission, J. Lee Rankin, chief counsel, informed the members that "we" had one of the autopsy pictures showing the wound on the back: "We have the picture of where the bullet entered in the back, that the bullet entered below the shoulder blade to the right of the backbone, which is below the place where the picture shows the bullet came out in the neckband of the shirt in front, and that bullet, according to the autopsy didn't strike any bone at all, that particular bullet, and go through."[40] Thus the commissioners and their staff had full and definitive knowledge of the true location of the president's back wound and surely also knew the implication (for any future findings of Oswald's sole guilt) of an entrance hole located below the exit hole.

Commission officials have consistently asserted the back wound was one of entrance, but the official evidence says otherwise. In the first place, the judgment of the military doctors was so undermined by their lack of experience in forensic medicine that nothing they report in forensic terms can be presumed to be accurate. In the second place, the autopsy materials and medical testimony are so riddled with falsehoods, corruption of documents, and distortions that little credence can be placed in any statement of the medical doctors without some type of corroboration, which does not exist here. Consequently, their description of the back wound as one of entrance must be viewed with caution.

The Report, quoting Dr. Finck, said of the back wound: " 'The basis for that conclusion [that it is a back wound] is that this wound was relatively small with clean edges . . . and that is what we see in wound of entrance at a long range.' "[41] Their reasons make no logical medical sense. Small in relation to what? The throat wound? But that was actually smaller.

Dr. Finck does not mention the absence of a bruise ring which can be characteristic of wounds of entrance and typically not wounds of exit. The contradiction is notable: the Parkland doctors described the throat wound as small with clean edges; does that mean it also was an entrance wound? Not according to the Commission and its Report. In fact, an exiting bullet punched out that back wound, a bullet that continued over the trunk of the limousine to strike the pavement. One witness testified to seeing it hit on Elm Street.[42]

The bullet path through JFK's body was not dissected, apparently, as the autopsy doctors stated, because they could not feel a pathway with a probe that went in only three or four inches and stopped. But the medical doctors improperly probed the body. As the autopsy photographs show, they had placed the corpse on the table with its arms pulled over the head, a distortion of the original position when the body was struck by the bullet. The extended over-the-head arms moved the muscles beneath the skin of the back so that the scapula blocked the passage.

There were metal fragments in the bullet's pathway, as revealed in a report by the autopsy doctors, the 1968 Clark panel review, the Parkland doctors, and federal agents. In 1966 the three autopsy doctors, Humes, Boswell, and Finck, inspected the photographs and X rays being transferred to the National Archives to "authenticate" them, although they had never seen the photographs, which raises a question of what they authenticated. In a secret report without a decipherable date, they related that "no evidence of a bullet or of a major portion of a bullet" appeared in the body of JFK. But as Harold Weisberg has shown, that ignored the minor fragments that were present.[43]

The doctors' 1966 report of fragments is also confirmed in Attorney

General Ramsey Clark's 1968 Panel Review of the autopsy records and X rays as part of the federal government's effort to block Garrison's New Orleans trial. The 1968 panel doctors—William Carnes, Russell Fisher, Russell Morgan, and Alan Moritz—reported the presence of metal fragments in the neck. In the lower neck, "just to the right of the cervical spine immediately above the apex of the right lung, . . . several small metallic fragments are present in this region."[44]

Additional support for the presence of metal fragments in JFK's neck comes from the Parkland surgeon who performed the tracheotomy and also from the FBI. Malcolm Perry, who performed surgery on JFK's throat during the emergency, observed to Weisberg that he noted bruising of the president's pleura that could only have been from bullet fragments.[45] Supporting the surgeon's observations was the testimony under court order of an FBI agent. In 1977, Weisberg and his attorney, Jim Lesar, as part of an FOIA suit deposed FBI special agent Robert Frazier, who had performed tests on Oswald's rifle and had testified on ballistics to the Commission. In response to Lesar's question about whether he knew of metal fragments in JFK's neck, Frazier responded, "I knew there were small fragments."[46]

The presence of fragments requires collision with a hard object, which in this case could have only come from striking bone, something officials have always denied. Among other things, that means that the metal could not have come from CE399, and this for two basic reasons. First, the single bullet of the theory is copper clad with only a copper crimped base available to leave fragments. A headfirst bullet could not leave fragments, and CE399 did not do so. Second, CE399 was almost its original weight, if not within the limits of standard variations. Metal had been washed out of Connally's chest, his wrist contained several fragments, and there was a fragment in his thigh. The presence of all these fragments essentially wrecked the magical single-bullet explanation for the nonfatal wounds, creating a domino effect by arguing for another bullet from another gunman, which means a conspiracy, which contradicts and destroys the Commission's findings.

The single-bullet explanation requires both no fragments and a low throat wound. Without an exit wound at the shirt collar level, the Commission's theory cannot work. In fact, evidence shows that a bullet coming from the front made the anterior neck wound. Two emergency room nurses and all six Parkland doctors who treated the president said the bullet wound in his throat was an entrance wound. The Commission asserted the tracheotomy performed through the wound destroyed its character. This forced all description of the wound upon the expertise of Dallas doctors and nurses, who were highly qualified professionals and who, despite the Commission staff's efforts to intimidate them, managed to record their views eventually.

Dr. Charles Carrico, for example, reported a "small penetrating wound" or wound of entrance.[47] Nurse Margaret Henchliffe testified that "we take care of a lot of bullet wounds down there," and the wound was "an entrance bullet hole."[48] Dr. Malcolm Perry, a surgeon with much experience with bullet wounds and knowledge about bullets, in a press conference at 3:16 P.M. on November 22, 1963, three times referred to the wound as an entrance wound: "A bullet hole almost in midline";[49] "there was an entrance wound in the neck";[50] and "the wound appeared to be an entrance wound in the front of the neck."[51] In an interview with Weisberg eight years later, Perry repeated his statement, adding that he saw "a ring of bruising around it . . . as they always are."[52]

The wound was above the shirt collar; no bullet damaged the shirt collar and necktie. Only one person in all the world saw the president's throat wound before his shirt and tie were removed: Dallas surgeon Charles Carrico. He testified before the Commission that the wound was above the shirt collar and demonstrated with his hands where it was.[53] "I see," said Commission member Allen Dulles. "And you put your hand right above where your tie is?" Answer, "Yes sir."[54] Yet the Report ignores Carrico's testimony.

In fact, the damage to the shirt and tie came from other sources than a bullet. The nurses, following standard emergency procedure, cut the front of the shirt and tie, inflicting all the damage suffered by the cloth.[55] Damage to the buttonhole side is a vertical slit running to the neckband seam from just below the hole through the band. Damage to the button side is horizontal, running only on the seam of the band. The slits do not overlap when the shirt collar is buttoned and do not coincide with the damage to the necktie knot, which alone proves the bullet could not have made them. The rips are too long to have been made by short-shanked CE399. Federal officials not only failed to print a photograph of the shirt damage but also later refused to let anyone see the president's shirt until forced to by Weisberg's lawsuit, which yielded not a visual inspection of the shirt but only a photograph of it.

Zapruder frame 190 clearly shows that JFK was directly behind Governor Connally in the automobile. CE399 allegedly passed through JFK's neck to exit at his throat and continued on to hit Connally's right armpit. But since the midline of the president's throat was to the left of Connally's armpit, a bullet in straight flight could not strike it but would veer slightly to the left, toward Connally's left shoulder, or over it and off into the blue. The only way for the bullet to hit the governor where his wounds occurred was for the bullet, in midair, to somehow veer to its right to line up with the governor's right armpit, then change directions once again to go forward and also to change its angle and go downward to hit the ribs. It also must have yawed and turned its butt end permanently forward for the rest of its careening course, for it left metal in the chest wound, wrist, and thigh that could only have come from the copper jacket bullet's butt end. This bizarre official allegation of the flight of the bullet never occurred in fact. It could not, for following such a path would violate the fundamental laws of physics.

A bullet entered at Governor Connally's right armpit, shattered his fifth rib, and exited beneath his right nipple. A bullet shattered his right wrist, entering at the back and leaving at the base of the palm. The Commission claims the wounds were made by the same bullet, CE399, which also caused JFK's nonlethal wounds.

The Commission, however, omits from its discussion of the wounds the fact that a bullet fragment was found in the governor's chest and remained there,[56] or that other fragments were washed out (the number is not known, nor is the chain of possession or location of these fragments known with any certainty). The broken bones in Connally's wrist contained many fragments—more, according to the medical testimony, than were missing from CE399.

On October 17, 1986, Chip Selby, a graduate student in film at the University of Maryland, interviewed Dr. Joseph Dolce, an army colonel. Selby was completing his master's thesis with a documentary on the single-bullet theory, *Reasonable Doubt*, and Dolce was vital to the story. In ballistics Dolce's reputation and expertise were unsurpassed. Chairman of the Wound Ballistics Board, he had been a battlefield surgeon for three years during World War II and had conducted "a tremendous amount of research" on ballistics for the army for many years.[57] He was also to have been consulted on all gunshot wounds to VIPs, but in JFK's case he was not.

Belatedly, in March 1964, the Commission staff brought him in to join several other experts in a conference on the wounds of Connally, which he argued could not have been inflicted by CE399. He then performed tests with the Mannlicher-Carcano rifle, firing 6.5-mm bullets at the wrist bone of ten cadavers. Every one of these bullets was severely deformed, even without having first destroyed four inches of the rib. Connally, Dolce later told Selby, was hit by two bullets. A separate bullet hit his rib at the frame of Zapruder's film "where Connally's cheeks puff out," which would be frame 237. Then another shot, probably fired from the grassy knoll, hit the wrist. The Commission never called Dolce to testify. The Report ignored his conclusions and in its appendix misrepresented the tests.[58]

Connally's thigh wound also creates problems for the single-bullet theory. The arterial surgeon Malcolm Perry examined Connally's thigh wound and its X rays. Weisberg's study of the wound and his early interview with Perry further refute the single-bullet theory.

Perry related that the thigh wound was tiny, "much too small to have been caused by a [an entire] bullet."[59] In fact, he explained, the wound was "caused by a flat and small fragment" that penetrated about ½ inch deep into the flesh and then moved parallel with the skin for about 3 to 3½ inches before stopping. But there is no place on the pristine bullet where the fragment could have originated. Further, the fragment weight alone exceeds the lead lost from CE399. By this evidence CE399 could not have caused the governor's thigh wound.

The single-bullet theory to explain the nonfatal wounds suffered by President Kennedy and Governor Connally is without merit. The official evidence disproves it—ironically, the very evidence the Commission generated in its nine-month investigation and was fully cognizant of.

Most likely, CE399 did not inflict any wounds at all and was planted in the hospital by an unknown person or persons. But a bullet coming from the front struck JFK in the throat above the shirt collar and necktie at about frame 189 or 190 of Zapruder's film and transited through his back. It exited his back at the level of the third thoracic vertebra, to fly over the trunk lid and hit the street. Another bullet fired from somewhere behind him hit Governor Connally in the chest at about frame 237. A different bullet hit the back of Connally's wrist several frames later. The origin of the sliver in Connally's right thigh is not accounted for and comes from a fragment of another bullet.

Between frames 312 and 313, a bullet from the front hit JFK in the right front of the head and killed him. One bullet missed the car and its occupants to strike the curb near the triple underpass, spraying concrete that slightly wounded an onlooker, Jim Tague. Several reports exist of other shots striking outside the two bodies and the car, but it is difficult to obtain sufficient solid evidence to be confident about them.

The single-bullet theory falsely imposed upon the evidence represents a political solution to President Kennedy's assassination devised before the inquiry even began. It served to circumvent uncomfortable facts that gunfire came from the front as well as the back, none of it initiated by Oswald.

In the afternoon of September 18, 1964, Commission member Senator Richard Russell spoke by phone with President Lyndon B. Johnson.[60] It was just six days before the seven members of the President's Commission on the Assassination of President John F. Kennedy would assemble in the White House and solemnly hand Johnson a copy of its 912-page Report, which found Lee Harvey Oswald alone and unaided killed President Kennedy. That morning the conservative Democrat from Georgia had completed the last executive meeting of the Commission, one that he had adamantly insisted upon. He then slipped quietly away to Georgia.[61] LBJ had tried to telephone him all afternoon. Russell, at home in Georgia, finally returned the call.[62] The conversation was remarkable. Neither Russell nor Johnson believed a single bullet could account for all seven of the nonfatal wounds of President Kennedy and Governor Connally—the crucial conclusion at the heart of the Commission's Report: "Well, I don't believe it," said Russell.

"I don't either," Johnson replied.[63]

Neither of the men acknowledged then or later that their rejection of the single-bullet invention meant, and could only mean beyond the slightest doubt, that a conspiracy had killed JFK. If the single bullet did not inflict every one of the seven nonfatal wounds inflicted upon President Kennedy and Governor Connally in the time span unimpeachably defined by the Zapruder film, then the foundation of the Report was destroyed.

The tape of the conversation, with its startling admissions, comes from the Lyndon B. Johnson Library in Austin, Texas. It was released thirty years after the fact, when both men had been dead for a generation and with most of those who had criticized their Report scattered and their waning effectiveness largely wrecked by Commission apologists and paranoid conspiracy theorists.[64]

The practical President Johnson realized that the firing feat claimed for Lee Harvey Oswald was impossible. It was absurd to think that a single bullet in that time span and under those circumstances could have hit two men, made seven wounds, busted two tough bones, and come out virtually without a scratch. LBJ had been born and reared in rural central Texas, where weapons were common and their mechanics understood. He had been around rifles all his life and had shot them many times, just as he had associated with men who had used rifles and well knew what one could and could not do with them. Taken together with an astute political judgment, practical insights, and keen intelligence, LBJ's disbelief in the single-bullet concoction was to be expected.

Although President Johnson did not make public his disbelief in Oswald as a lone assassin, there are glimmers of it in the historical record now available, thanks to the Freedom of Information Act. For example, Cartha DeLoach, the number four man in the FBI, recorded his late-night conversation with President Johnson's special assistant Marvin Watson on April 3, 1967. According to Watson, "The President had told him in an off moment that he was convinced that there was a plot in connection with the assassination. Watson stated the President felt the CIA had something to do with this plot."[65] And, whereas this "quiet" but troubling behind-the-scenes dissent from the highest level of American government never impinged upon the public's awareness, the voices of other, more vocal, dissenters did. By the third anniversary of JFK's death, a number of dissenting books had appeared that vigorously argued that the official allegations against Oswald were severely flawed. President Johnson himself, through Marvin Watson, asked the FBI to get information for him on "the authors of books dealing with the assassination of President Kennedy." On November 8, 1966, the bureau responded—not with sound and informative data on the seven authors so that he could form a judgment but with what can only be classified as deliberate disinformation. Years later, when FOIA suits forced the documents out of FBI control, one of the defamed authors aptly summed up the secret report made about him as "outright lies, complete fabrications, distortions, and misrepresentations"[66]—all designed to discredit the dissenting authors and, in effect, deflect LBJ away from such concern.

The public brouhaha created by District Attorney Jim Garrison's effort to try a New Orleans businessman for the murder of JFK further reinforced LBJ's anxieties over the Commission's official findings. In early April 1967, a skeptical Washington columnist, Jack Anderson, flew to New Orleans to interview Garrison and returned convinced that Garrison was on the right track. Anderson then spoke with George Christian, President Johnson's press secretary, who also suspected there had been a conspiracy and said so. He suggested Anderson speak with the FBI, which he did on April 4.[67] FBI records regarding Anderson's conference with the bureau reflect LBJ's ongoing distrust of the Commission's Report.[68]

Only after leaving office did LBJ go on record with his concerns, in an interview conducted by Walter Cronkite of CBS news. However, CBS waited until after Johnson's death in 1973 before making public his comments on the Kennedy assassination, which had been excised from the original broadcast.

He had discovered, LBJ said to Cronkite, that after he became president the United States "had been operating a damned Murder, Inc. in the Caribbean." He believed JFK might have died in retaliation for those acts. This is known as the "blowback" or "kickback" theory—a deadly boomerang effect caused by American efforts to assassinate Castro.[69] It is an interesting theory but one that has never been substantiated by convincing evidence. Nevertheless, the main point here is that LBJ clearly did not believe his own investigative Commission. Bizarrely, neither did the man whose name is most closely associated with the authorship of the Commission's final Report. From the day he assumed chairmanship of the Commission until the day of his death, Earl Warren firmly believed that a Soviet conspiracy had assassinated President John F. Kennedy.

As discussed more thoroughly elsewhere, President Johnson, through aides, had had a difficult time getting Earl Warren to accept the chairmanship of the Commission. In desperation, Johnson finally asked for a private meeting with the chief justice in the White House. There he convinced him to take the chair because, if he did not, "forty million people" could die in a nuclear war, words recorded in Warren's *Memoirs* and later conveyed to his staff at the outset of the investigation as the reason he finally consented to accept the Commission's chair. Nearly a decade later and in retirement, he reiterated in a 1972 television interview that if he had not taken the chair, the world would have been "incinerated."[70] In retrospect, the unspoken subtext of this consistent declaration seems to be that, by fingering Oswald as the lone assassin, the Commission, under Warren's leadership, made it impossible for anyone to use the assassination as a pretext for war with the Soviet Union, which inevitably would have gone nuclear, with disastrous results for the world. Wise or not, that decision, that commitment to Oswald as the lone assassin, created a lie of historic proportions, one that has been perpetuated by the Warren Report's defenders ever since.

LBJ and Warren, however, were not alone in their belief in a conspiracy.

At 10:00 A.M. on the morning of September 18, in a rented fourth-floor hearing room of the Veterans of Foreign Wars building in Washington, D.C., the President's Commission on the Assassination held its final executive meeting. Every member, including Richard Russell, was present. The meeting was tense. The Commission's Report was set in type; on the evening of September 22, the presses would roll. Two days later the members would present a copy to LBJ, and on September 27 the Report would be generally available to the public. It was at this point that Russell, reading from typed notes, formally declared his dissent from the Commission's findings. (While his comments are in neither the Commission files nor the minutes of this meeting, a copy of his notes survives, which Harold Weisberg confirmed.) Russell believed (1) that there had been a conspiracy to kill President Kennedy; (2) that Oswald had not done all the shooting; and (3) that the Commission had not been told the truth about Oswald's background. He based some of his dissent on viewing the Zapruder film:

> I do not share the finding of the Commission as to the probability that both President Kennedy and Governor Connally were struck by the same bullet. The expert testimony, based on measurements and surveys, including reenactment of the motortrip of the Presidential party on that fateful November 22nd presents a persuasive case. However, the movement of one of the victims by either leaning forward or to either side or rising a few inches from his seat would have made a considerable difference in the mathematical computations. . . . Reviewing the Zapruder film several times adds to my conviction that the bullet that passed through Governor Connally's body was not the same bullet as that which passed through the President's back and neck.[71]

He insisted to Warren that he "just put a little footnote in there at the bottom of the page saying 'Senator Russell dissents.' "[72] But Warren, who demanded unanimity, refused. Finally Warren agreed to specific changes in the wording proposed by John J. McCloy to gain Russell's signature: that some members did not believe Oswald acted alone, that a conspiracy had existed, and that Russell's dissent would be recorded.[73] Unfortunately, the inserted second, third, and fourth conclusions of the Report masked Russell's firm doubts and, in fact, reiterated that Oswald was the sole source of all bullets fired that day:

2. The weight of the evidence indicates that there were three shots fired.

3. Although it is not necessary to any essential findings of the Commission to determine just which shot hit Governor Connally, there is very persuasive evidence from the experts to indicate that the same bullet which pierced the President's throat also caused Governor Connally's wounds. However, Governor Connally's testimony and certain other factors have given rise to some difference of opinion as to this probability but there is no question in the mind of any member of the Commission that all the shots which caused the President's and Governor Connally's wounds were fired from the sixth floor window of the Texas School Book Depository.[74]

4. The shots which killed President Kennedy and wounded Governor Connally were fired by Lee Harvey Oswald.

While the minutes of the Commission meetings, numbering over seven thousand pages by September 18, were verbatim, transcribed by the court reporters furnished by the firm of Ward and Paul, no stenographer was asked to record Russell's formal dissent. Thus no official transcript or record of Russell's dissent exists. Yet, at the time, Russell had been assured that his words had been officially recorded for posterity. Some years later, he learned otherwise.[75]

In 1968 Harold Weisberg brought Russell, then terminally ill with emphysema, documented proof that Commission counsel J. Lee Rankin and Warren had simply erased the record of his dissent. Stricken and outraged, Russell urged Weisberg to disprove the Report "he had been tricked into signing."[76] Had he lived longer, he would have been the key supporter for a reexamination of the assassination and its investigation.

Two other Commission members shared Russell's doubts to some degree. John Sherman Cooper, Republican senator from Kentucky, also doubted the single-bullet explanation of the final Report and, as early as August 1964, recorded his objection. In the papers of J. Lee Rankin, chief counsel of the Commission, are found Cooper's August 20 comments on the draft of the Report. On chapter 3, page 1 of the draft, Cooper asked, "On what basis is it claimed that two shots caused all wounds? . . . It seemed to me that Governor Connally's statement negates such a conclusion. I could not agree with this statement."[77] Russell's arguments during the last meeting of the Commission also helped persuade Cooper that the theory was wrong.

In an April 1971 interview with Hugh Cates for the Russell Library at the University of Georgia, Cooper recalled the September 18 meeting and agreed with Russell's statements in opposition to the single-bullet theory. Cooper commented that Russell told his fellow members he would "never sign that report" if the Commission said categorically that the shot passed through both men. The evidence, according to Russell, was not conclusive. "I think," continued Cooper, "he's correct."[78] Many years later, in a letter to Edmund Johnston dated February 9, 1978, Cooper stated that he thought there was "a misunderstanding about what you may consider my opinion to have been on the 'one bullet' theory when I was serving as a member of the Warren Commission. Senator Russell opposed the 'one bullet' theory and I also opposed it."[79]

Commissioner Hale Boggs, a Democrat from Louisiana, also had reservations, although less vigorous ones, about the single-bullet theory. For example, on Christmas Eve 1966, Russell wrote to Alfredda Scobey, a law assistant on the Court of Appeals, State of Georgia, who had worked with him on the Warren Commission inquiry: "As I recall, Congressman Boggs had mild doubts."[80] And Boggs himself, as recorded in a 1966 interview with critic Edward Jay Epstein, said, "I had strong doubts about it."[81]

In addition to such eminent individuals, several federal agencies, including the FBI, CIA, and Secret Service, held views that clashed with the single-bullet theory of the Warren Commission. They simply did not believe CE399 wounded both men, although it required FOIA lawsuits to reveal much of this many years after the fact.

In its December 9, 1963, five-volume report on the assassination, designated Commission Document 1, the FBI stated three bullets were fired.[82] The first wounded John Kennedy, the second wounded John Connally, and the third killed President Kennedy. The impossibility of the second shot being fired in the time frame imposed by the Zapruder film is ignored, as are the wounding of Tague and the existence of a possible fourth bullet. While at odds with the Commission's single-bullet theory, the FBI conclusion still posited Oswald as the sole assassin, reinforcing the Commission view.

Like the FBI, the Secret Service in a December 5, 1963, surveyor's chart on the assassination area depicted three shots fired, with each separately hitting an occupant of the car.[83] Tague again was ignored. In its December 18 report, however, the agency avoided any comment on the shots, except to say "shots" were fired, an extraordinarily vague comment for the agency in charge of JFK's protection.[84]

As mentioned in an earlier chapter, the Central Intelligence Agency's photographic laboratory analyzed the Zapruder film and concluded the first shot came about twenty frames before frame 210, an impossibility for Oswald firing from the Texas School Book Depository. But even when FOIA suits made this information available in 1975, it was largely ignored.

On March 31, 1964, in its rooms at 200 Maryland Avenue, N.E., Washington, D.C., the President's Commission took the testimony of Ronald Simmons, chief of the Infantry Weapons Evaluation Branch of the Ballistics Research Laboratory of the Department of the Army.[85] Present were Commissioners Earl Warren, John J. McCloy, and Hale Boggs, as well as staff members J. Lee Rankin, the general counsel, and Melvin Eisenberg and Norman Redlich, assistant counsels. Two observers from the American Bar Association, Charles Murray and a future justice, Lewis Powell, listened to the testimony. Leon Jaworski represented the Texas Court of Inquiry.[86]

Simmons testified to the results of shooting tests that established Oswald could not have fired the three shots in less than six seconds. The tests were a travesty of the scientific method, with grossly distorted results that favored the Commission's theories. First, the shooters were not true to the known qualifications of Oswald. The Marine Corps, it is recalled, officially rated Oswald as "a rather poor shot" who achieved only the minimum score required by the military—and this required his buddies working the test range to cheat for him. Moreover, there is no evidence of Oswald firing any weapon in the four years prior to the assassination. The army, on the other hand, used three riflemen "rated as Master by the National Rifle Association," the finest marksmen in America.[87]

In addition, the army falsified the height from which Oswald had allegedly fired. It built a thirty-foot tower at Aberdeen Proving Grounds, Maryland, as the firing stand rather than replicate the sixty-foot-high window perch Oswald allegedly used. It also used stationary targets rather than the moving and descending one Oswald allegedly shot at.

The army marksman also used a repaired and improved rifle. Although the FBI had earlier had to overhaul the rifle to test it, the army masters nevertheless found it "could not be sighted in using the telescopic sight." Subsequently, the army added two shims, "one to adjust it vertically, the other side to the side,"[88] and permitted the marksmen to practice prior to test firing although there is no evidence of Oswald ever practicing. On November 22 he had not fired a rifle for four years.

Even with the skewing of tests, the master shots still could not come close to the required accuracy. They missed the last target or the fatal head shot six times out of ten and the second shot the first four times. In addition, none of them, not one of this nation's best shots, could duplicate the required time frame.[89]

Key officials at the state and local level also disputed the Commission conclusions of a lone assassin. Both Governor and Mrs. Connally, for example, testified that JFK was hit by the first shot and Connally by a second shot. Mrs. Connally told the Commission, "I heard a noise . . . and it came from the right. I turned over my right shoulder and looked back, and saw the President as he had both hands to his neck . . . and he just sort of slumped down. Then very soon there was the second shot that hit John."[90] Governor Connally testified, "I heard this noise which I immediately took to be a rifle shot. I instinctively turned to my right because the sound appeared to come from over my right shoulder . . . failing to see him. . . . I was turning to look back over my left shoulder into the back seat, but I never got that far in my turn. I got about in the position I am in now facing you, looking a little bit to the left of center, and then I felt like someone had hit me in the back."[91]

In Dallas the officials who would have prosecuted and investigated the crime, District Attorney Henry Wade and Chief of Police Jesse Curry, did not believe the Warren Report's findings. Wade believed Oswald was an assassin but that he had an accomplice. "I have always felt," he wrote Weisberg on October 10, 1968, "that there was an accomplice of someone else involved in this matter."[92] Knowledge of Chief Curry's dissent comes from an FBI record. Agent Charles T. Brown Jr. reported a conversation with Lieutenant Jack Revill of the Dallas Police Department: "Revill told [Brown] that Curry had told Revill 'that two men were involved in the shooting.' "[93] As Weisberg reports the memorandum, "One of Curry's reasons was something he had been told by his police" in JFK's motorcycle escort.[94] What that was has not survived in the historical record.

For a generation and a half, the dominant American view of the Warren Commission and its allegations that a single bullet wounded two men has been that no known dissent existed among officials. According to the promulgators of this myth, the evidence of CE399's legitimacy was so overwhelming, the investigation so thorough, and the individuals conducting the inquiry of such sterling reputation that the bullet's extraordinary physical feat was beyond question. But this conception of the investigation was never valid and could only be held in the teeth of facts to the contrary. Yet innumerable members of the media, intellectual establishment, and political, legal, and judicial systems have all embraced and defended the single-bullet fiction, helping to sustain what amounts to a coup d'état.

VII

The Struggle to Free the Film

Federal Purchase
The Government and the Zapruder Film, 1963–2000

Thirty-five years, seven months, and twenty-four days after the assassination of President Kennedy, the federal government paid the heirs of Abraham Zapruder a lucrative sum for possession of his famous film but failed to purchase the film's copyright at the same time. On August 1, 1998, the United States had seized the film under the aegis of the Act of 1992. Then had followed a lengthy secret negotiation with the heirs until July 19, 1999, when under the structure of an arbitration agreement they and the United States reached an accord.

With the acquisition of the twenty-six-second filmstrip, the United States of America became the fourth and presumably final owner of the physical film. Abraham Zapruder had originally owned it for twenty-one hours until November 23, 1963, when he had sold the film and copyright to Time Inc., keeping a part interest in future sales. In 1966 the United States, under the terms of federal legislation, had had an opportunity to acquire it but had elected not to. Nor did it choose to do so in 1975 when the then owner, Time Inc., had attempted to give the film to the United States but had been foiled by the Zapruder heirs. On April 9, Time Inc., charging a price of one dollar, had returned the film and copyright to the heirs, who became the third owners and copyright owners.

Copyright itself is a privilege, not a right. Over two hundred years ago the beleaguered states of North America closed fifteen years of revolutionary war, Indian battles on the frontier, economic depression, and civil insurrections to implement the Constitution of the United States of America "in order to form a more perfect union, establish justice . . . [and] promote the general welfare."[1] To that end they vested in a Congress "all legislative powers,"[2] among them the power "to promote the progress of science and useful arts, by securing for limited times to authors and inventors the exclusive right to their respective writings and discoveries"[3]—the Constitution's so-called copyright clause. Upon this sentence rests the legal justification for the laws of copyright enacted at the federal level, which protect all copyright holders, including the Zapruder heirs.

The issue of copyright concerned the Commission staff. Ultimately, several frames of the Zapruder film were printed in the Warren Commission Report, and volume 18 prints frames 171 through 207 and 212 through 334, as well as exhibits that used fourteen frames.[4] On April 29, 1964, the question of whether to use the copyrighted Zapruder film and other material was raised by Commission staff member Richard Mosk in a memorandum to assistant counsel Norman Redlich: "I want to put into a memo the point I raised with you yesterday, re, the question of whether we might infringe copyrights held by LIFE magazine if we publish their photographs. . . . I do not think the government can be enjoined, although I recall seeing law review articles on the point. We might consider asking for permission to publish this material."[5] Subsequently, J. Lee Rankin, chief counsel of the Commission, raised this copyright issue via telephone with Time Inc. attorneys. On July 9, 1964, an attorney from the Manhattan offices of Cravath, Swaine & Moore, representing Time Inc., wrote as follows to Rankin, requesting the Commission to provide suitable copyright notice:

> Confirming our telephone conversations, I understand that the Warren Commission, in its Report, presently intends to use certain photographs of President Kennedy's assassination which are owned and copyrighted by my client, Time Inc., publisher of Life Magazine. It is, of course, entirely agreeable with my client that such use be made, without charge, provided that a suitable copyright notice appear in connection with those photographs. That notice should read "Copyright 1963 Time Inc. All rights reserved." Or, if you prefer, a C in a circle can be used in connection with that statement instead of the word "Copyright."
>
> I wish to emphasize that this request is made in order that other news media may not be misled into believing that, because the Warren commission has utilized those photographs those media, also, may use them. If that should happen, it would be necessary for us to institute litigation against such news media and we are anxious to avoid that trouble and expense of any such litigation, while reserving to you the opportunity of utilizing the photographs for the Warren Commission Report. Your cooperation in utilizing the copyright notice will be greatly appreciated.

This, of course, seems to suggest that Time Inc. viewed its copyright as superior to the rights of the nation in investigating the assassination of the chief executive, which is certainly contrary to the established laws and procedures in most state courts where the evidence to try the crime comes under public control during the trial. The Commission had the authority by Executive Order 11130 and Senate Joint Resolution 137 to use and print whatever it wanted.[6]

Indeed, it proceeded to print the Zapruder frames *without* copyright notice. Overall, as well as in relation to the Zapruder film, the Warren Commission's effort to define, assemble, secure, and protect the evidentiary base of the assassination was inadequate, belated, and politically tainted. Much of the evidence the Commission assembled (and much that it published) was irrelevant to the assassination investigation, and not a little odd, such as pregnancy records of Marina Oswald or her nail file, statistics on Morocco dock loadings, and Jack Ruby's mother's dental records. On the other hand, it neglected to collect much of the relevant film and photographic evidence or to interview all Texas School Book Depository employees to trace Oswald's movements in detail that morning, evidence much more directly material to the investigation.

Prior to the completion of its work, the Commission had requested the acting attorney general to take the necessary steps to retain the evidence it had used. He did nothing. In November 1964, a month and a half after the Commission had disbanded, its chief counsel, J. Lee Rankin, wrote to acting attorney general Ramsey Clark reminding him of the Commission's prior request that the Department of Justice retain the evidence, an exceptional situation for a criminal investigation where one would normally expect this issue to have been addressed in the first week of organization.[7] What is even more unusual is that federal commissions have historically worked under systems that preserved their records.

The Department of Justice did not immediately respond to Rankin's request. The problem required work to resolve. Texas law controlled, for at that time the murder of the president was a local, not a federal, crime. No trial had occurred, and no conviction had been obtained. So confiscating evidence under the umbrella of those circumstances was not an available option. Texas, unlike most states, had no confiscation provision for weapons used in criminal cases.

Then news emerged and a public discussion ensued about a rich Colorado oil man, J. J. King, who had proudly purchased for $10,000 from Marina Oswald her husband's 6.5-mm Mannlicher-Carcano rifle and .38 pistol—the most valuable and collectible weapons in the world, he proclaimed. This ballyhooed incident coincided with the first appearance of serious public dissent from the official findings, including Harold Weisberg's *Whitewash*. Talk radio shows, small magazines of opinion, and members of the public had begun to express doubts about the Commission's Report. In response the Department of Justice scrambled to secure all evidence, including the Mannlicher-Carcano rifle.

On June 29, 1965, Attorney General Ramsey Clark wrote to Congressman Byron Rogers, chair of the Committee on the Judiciary, requesting appropriate legislation to assist this effort and appended a suggested bill.[8] On August 19 the judiciary committee reported out the bill as amended.[9] In the committee hearings an attorney for J. J. King argued against the legislation, maintaining the following: (1) the State of Texas had jurisdiction over the case and the evidence, and this bill was a serious challenge to states' rights in all areas and could invite further federal transgression; (2) by moving in the heat of emotion to override normal scrutiny, the bill would establish a most dangerous precedent and a basic threat to the future security of all personal property rights; (3) the bill grants carte blanche to the attorney general to determine what should be identified and retained as evidence, shifting authority from the legislative to the executive branch; and (4) the bill is an attempt to correct past oversights of the executive branch—the Department of Justice—to heed the requests of the Commission to protect the evidence.[10] Despite these protests, the bill had passed the House[11] and Senate by October 18 and was signed into law by President Johnson on November 2, 1965.

Also known as Public Law 318 of the Eighty-ninth Congress, "An Act of November 2, 1965, Providing for the Acquisition and Preservation by the United States of Certain Items of Evidence Pertaining to the Assassination of President John F. Kennedy" contained six sections.[12] Section 1 established the preeminent national interest in all the evidence considered by the Commission: "It is hereby declared that the national interest requires that the United States acquire all right, title, and interest, in and to certain items of evidence, to be designated by the Attorney General pursuant to section 2 of this Act, which were considered by the President's Commission on the Assassination of President Kennedy."

Section 2 placed the responsibility for such acquisition in the Department of Justice: "The Attorney General is authorized to determine, from time to time, which items should" be acquired and preserved by the United States. The determination should be published in the *Federal Register* within one year from the date of enactment of the law.

Section 3 designated the path to be followed for citizens to pursue any claims and set a deadline for them: the "United States Court of Claims or the United States district court for the judicial district wherein the claimant resides shall have jurisdiction" on any claim for just compensation for any item, "*Provided*, That the claim is filed within one year from the date of publication in the Federal Register of the determination by the Attorney General with respect to such items."

Section 4 directed the National Archives to preserve the records. Section 5 stated that all the items acquired are the personal property of the United States. Section 6 was a blank check to carry out the nation's will. Appropriate sums as "may be necessary to carry out the purposes of the Act" were authorized.

The act's unambiguous language certainly included the Zapruder film under its umbrella, for the Commission did in fact examine, consider, and use the film in its investigation. The film was essential to its conclusion. Section 3 would appear to cover both just compensation and copyright interest, meaning, it seems, that Time Inc. had one year after the attorney general published a forthcoming list in the *Federal Register* to file a claim and then prevail in court, or else the film and copyright became the exclusive property of the nation.

One day shy of the legal full-year limit, Attorney General Ramsey Clark published a determination in the *Federal Register*.[13] "I have determined," wrote Clark, "that the national interest requires the entire body of evidence considered by the President's Commission on the Assassination of President Kennedy and now in the possession of the United States to be preserved intact." This includes all the items of evidence not owned by the United States that were considered by the Commission and not returned to their owners, as well as "the items of evidence already owned by the United States." The change in the language from Public Law 89-318 is notable. The act stipulated all items of evidence "which were considered by the President's Commission." Clark's determination adds the phrase "and now in the possession of the United States," which restricts the items eligible to be seized. It omits the Zapruder film and many other items not "now in the possession of the United States" but in private hands.

In Section 1 it listed Oswald's rifle and pistol. Section 2 contained six pages of three columns listing the hundreds of other items retained under the act, including Oswald's letters, books, registration cards, diary, and so forth. Section 3 listed several motion picture films and videos in the National Archives, but not the Zapruder film.

Section 5 was a catch-all paragraph that referred to "all other items of evidence considered by the Commission, if any, which are subject to this notice and not otherwise described in the provisions of paragraphs 1, 2, 3, or 4." Most important, Section 6 stipulated that the acquisition of an item of evidence hereunder does not constitute an acquisition of any copyright or other literary property right associated with such items.

As a group, the items both covered and excluded by Clark's determination represented a supremely odd and inconsistent selection process by the government. For example, Clark's dictum covered Item D80, Michael Paine's "Minox camera," which police seized from the home of Paine's estranged wife, Ruth, Marina Oswald's landlady, although its utility for the investigation was never explained. It also covered Ruth Paine's personal stationery and books, as well as a Baby Brownie camera (given by Oswald in 1958 to his brother Robert's daughter) and Marina Oswald's medical records (including children's birth certificates)—none of which provided information of any consequence or significance to the investigation. At the same time, it excluded such key evidence as the Zapruder film, Ike Altgens's crucial AP photo of Oswald in the depository doorway watching the president pass, and, incredible as it might seem, the revolver Jack Ruby used to kill Oswald.

In response to Public Law 89-318 and, one year later, Clark's formal determination, only one citizen directly affected by the ruling challenged the government. J. J. King, the Colorado oil man, sued the federal government to regain the $10,000 he had paid Marina Oswald on March 29, 1965, for title to her husband's pistol and rifle, to be his when the government released them, which it instead seized.[14] After six court cases King was ultimately refused the weapons but was paid compensation for their confiscation. A special master, appointed by a Texas federal district court, determined the value at $17,729.37, but because the weapons had been used to commit an act of a "depraved mind" the court awarded only $3,000. But the district court was overruled when, on February 26, 1973, the Fifth Circuit Court of Appeals declared that a collector's interest had to be taken into consideration. As a result, King was awarded the full amount of $17,729.37.[15]

Meanwhile, and for decades to follow, the Zapruder film remained in private hands. In March 1975, ABC television showed a copy of the film without having obtained permission from Time Inc. Noting the public's strong response to the show, the heirs of Abraham Zapruder requested that Time Inc. sue ABC, with half of the proceeds going to the heirs under the terms of the original sale contract. Time Inc., however, became disenchanted with the opprobrium and controversy caused by its continual ownership and offered to turn over the original film to the government. The heirs fought this move. Time Inc. resolved the issue by selling the film back to a Zapruder family corporation, LMH, for the sum of one dollar, which then licensed the film's use in the decades that followed.

Among the film's more prominent licensees was the film director Oliver Stone, whose JFK debuted in December 1991 and quickly became one of the most hotly debated films ever made. Based largely on District Attorney Jim Garrison's highly flawed and disappointing book, On the Trail of the Assassins, Stone's JFK offered an equally flawed and kaleidoscopic "counterargument" to the Warren Commission's faulty conclusions. Aswirl with conspiracy theories involving a rogue's gallery of miscreants, including the Mafia, communist and anticommunist sympathizers, pro- and anti-Castro followers, American intelligence agencies, and the "military-industrial complex," Stone's film was designed as a cinematic incitement for the American public to reengage with JFK's assassination and its shoddy official investigation.

So powerful was JFK's impact on the public's conscience that it generated a flood of mail to congressional offices in an election year for many startled congressmen, most of whom had seldom encountered such an emotional outpouring on any other issue. The public was definitely agitated and pushed Congress to reopen the case that too many had considered closed for too long. In response, Congress drafted legislation designed to unearth and consolidate all federal records on the assassination into a single collection or archives. Seven years later, the federal government would also use this law to purchase the original Zapruder film.

On March 26, 1992, forty-one congressmen introduced in the House of Representatives House Joint Resolution 454, the Assassination Materials Disclosure Act of 1992, to provide for the expeditious disclosure of government records in the 1963 assassination of President John F. Kennedy, to establish a President Kennedy Assassination Materials Collection, and to establish the Assassination Materials Review Board as an independent agency. The same day, ten senators introduced Senate Joint Resolution 3006, with stronger content and a more sophisticated structure. Throughout the spring and summer, House and Senate committees held hearings on the pending legislation, followed by further debate and finally passage of Public Law 102-526, 106 Stat. 3443, also known as the President John F. Kennedy Assassination Records Collection Act of 1992.[16]

The act created the President John F. Kennedy Assassination Records Collection at the National Archives and Records Administration, required the expeditious transmission of pertinent documents to the Archivist and public disclosure of such records, and established an Assassination Records Review Board (ARRB) of five members to "ensure and facilitate the review, transmission to the Archivist, and public disclosure of Government records related to the assassination of President John F. Kennedy."

Having lost his bid for reelection, President George H. W. Bush chose not to appoint members to the ARRB, and President-elect Bill Clinton dallied for well over a year, but on April 11, 1994, the five board members selected by the White House and four scholarly societies were sworn in. The American Bar Association had recommended John R. Tunheim, a chief deputy attorney general of the State of Minnesota. The Organization of American Historians had nominated Kermit L. Hall, a professor of history and law at Ohio State University. The Society of American Archivists had recommended William L. Joyce, associate university librarian for rare books and special collections at Princeton University. The American Historical Association had tabbed Anna K. Nelson, distinguished adjunct historian in residence at the American University as a professor of foreign relations. The White House staff was permitted to recommend one member, Henry F. Graff, professor emeritus of history at Columbia University.

Although all five members of the ARRB were reputable individuals, none had ever pursued or acquired any specialized knowledge concerning the assassination or its investigations. Indeed, their apparent "neutrality" on the subject provided one of the underlying rationales for their selection. And, at least publicly, the five members appeared to accept the validity of the Warren Commission Report's conclusions in most regards, if not in all aspects of its investigation. Regardless, their appointment in effect reassured the public that its concerns about the assassination would now be engaged and addressed.

Section 11a of the act deserves special notice. The rules of construction contained in its first paragraph strong language that some researchers surmised could and should have been applied to the Zapruder film and copyright:

> PRECEDENCE OVER OTHER LAW. When this Act requires transmission of a record to the Archivist or public disclosure, it shall take precedence over any other law (except section 6103 of the Internal Revenue Code), judicial decision construing such law, or common law doctrine that would otherwise prohibit such transmission or disclosure, with the exception of deeds governing access to or transfer or release of gifts and donations of records to the United States Government.

In effect, section 11a gave the government the power it needed to assume rightful ownership of the Zapruder film.

Initially the Zapruders (i.e., LMH Company) and their attorney did not see any danger to their ownership and copyright stemming from the passage of the act, but that would soon change. In March 1993 a New York state lawyer and assassination researcher, Mark Zaid, telephoned his friend attorney James Lesar in Washington, D.C. Long active in assassination research and the legal issues surrounding it, Lesar told Zaid that he thought the act of 1992 might have trumped the Zapruder family's copyright and control.[17] Within a few days Zaid and fellow assassination researcher Charles Sanders of New York City, an entertainment attorney with a specialty in copyright, collaborating on a law review article about the act, had a conference call with LMH's attorney in Washington, James Silverberg, who was apprised of the possibility that the Records Act might have stripped the Zapruder film of its copyright. A few days later Silverberg appeared at the National Archives.

At approximately 4:00 P.M. on Monday, March 15, 1993, less than an hour before closing time, Silverberg showed up at the Picket Street Annex of the National Archives, announcing that he had come to pick up the original film.[18] He identified himself to Archivist Alan Lewis as the attorney for LMH and presented three documents as bona fides: a copy of the July 10, 1978, letter of agreement; a copy of a June 29, 1978, receipt from Dick Myers, Archivist from the Audio Visual Division of the National Archives;

and a notarized letter of Friday, March 12, 1993, signed by Henry Zapruder and authorizing Silverberg to remove the original film from the National Archives. He planned to fly the film to Dallas at 8:00 P.M.

Taken aback by the sudden request so late in the day, Lewis sought authorization to comply with Silverberg's request. Unfortunately, neither the branch chief, the division head, the audiovisual specialist, nor the assistant branch chief was available. He did, however, locate Michael Kurtz, the deputy archivist of the United States, and had Kurtz discuss the matter with Silverberg on the phone. Kurtz requested that Silverberg's authorizing documents be faxed to him.[19] In the meantime, Lewis had the original Zapruder film brought out of cold storage and prepared it, along with a duplicate master copy, in case a decision would be made to give a copy to Silverberg.[20]

Around 5:00 P.M., Mary Ronan, an attorney from Kurtz's office, telephoned Silverberg and discussed the matter with him. She informed him that the recent legislation on records held by government agencies relating to the assassination of President Kennedy appeared to clash with the Zapruder family's agreements with the National Archives and other rights. Until the General Counsel of the National Archives had an opportunity to review the issues involved and consult with the Department of Justice, the archives could not and would not surrender the film, for if it did so "the agency would be in violation of federal laws."[21]

Silverberg replied that he had expected the archives to function in terms of the 1978 letter of agreement and that any difficulties could be worked out later. Frustrated, he "implied legal action and/or held out the threat of money damages to be recovered" if he did not get the film.[22] In the end, he realized he would not be able to obtain the film at that time and so departed.

That day Christopher M. Runkel, attorney-advisor on the Legal Services Staff of the National Archives, drafted a memorandum on the subject. According to his reading of the Assassination Records Act, he believed that the Zapruder film is an "assassination record." He recommended that the archives not release it to Silverberg "or to any other private person" until he and the Department of Justice considered it more fully.[23]

On April 2, 1997, in the Archivist's Reception Room at the National Archives and Records Administration building in Washington, the Assassination Records Review Board opened a public hearing to seek "public comment and advice on what should be done with camera original and motion picture film of the assassination that was taken by Abraham Zapruder."[24] Included among its "interesting group of experts" assembled to testify were Robert Brauneis, associate professor of law at George Washington Law School, Washington, D.C., an expert on the legal concept of taking; Josiah Thompson, assassination critic and subject of the Time Inc. lawsuit against Geis Publishing; and, as previously discussed, James Lesar, a Washington attorney and president of the Assassination Archives and Research Center, a private organization, who was involved in scores of Freedom of Information Act cases and a suit over the Zapruder film.

John Tunheim, chair of the ARRB, turned the meeting over to Jeremy Gunn, general counsel of the ARRB, who set forth the reasons for the hearing and defined an assassination record under the Act of 1992 as "any 'record that is related to the assassination of President John F. Kennedy . . . that was made available for use by . . . the Warren Commission.' The record reflects that the Zapruder film was . . . explicitly and specifically requested by the Warren Commission, and the Warren Commission and the staff were shown versions of the original Zapruder film. This would seem to suggest that within the statutory definition the Zapruder film qualifies as an assassination record."[25]

Gunn more precisely defined the parameters for discussion on this subject. The ARRB was not "seeking comment from the public on whether it was one of the most important records of the assassination." That was a "foregone conclusion," he added. It was not deciding whether the film was an assassination record under the act, for it was. It was not questioning, if no costs were involved, whether the United States should possess the Zapruder film. It was not determining whether the film was authentic, as some had charged. It was not questioning whether the LMH Company owned the Zapruder film, for that would be a matter for the courts to determine. It was not determining whether LMH's copyright in the film was valid, for that, too, was a matter for the courts.[26]

Gunn then stated the basic issue:

Rather the core question for the Board today is whether it should undertake an action that would effect a "taking," in constitutional terms, of the original film, or whether the Board should seek a negotiated arrangement with the Zapruder family . . . that would attempt, to (A) make high quality copies of the Zapruder film easily available to the public for the first time, (B) provide for forensic testing of the film, to determine in part any questions relating to authenticity and (C) would ensure that the U.S. Congress has an option, if it so chooses, to purchase the film.[27]

Under the second option, the negotiated settlement, the ARRB's counsel explained that LMH would be encouraged to make a digitalized high-quality copy of the film that would include the material appearing between the sprocket holes.[28] This version would then be made available to researchers for individual use under a copyright license from LMH, which would continue to hold the copyright. The public would not be permitted to use the film for commercial purposes. In addition, Congress would be given an option to purchase the film and have the government take permanent possession of it. Finally, the government would be permitted to make all "appropriate forensics tests of the original film" to evaluate the film's authenticity.[29] Thus, from the beginning of its proceedings, the ARRB considered the "taking" might exclude copyright ownership by the United States.

Following Gunn's opening remarks, Tunheim introduced Professor Robert Brauneis, who argued that, since "Congress has eminent domain powers over both real estate and personal property," the question before them was this: Did Congress's 1992 statute authorize the ARRB to exercise eminent domain?[30] In response, Brauneis said it was "a close call," with arguments to be made on both sides.[31]

In favor of an authorized taking were two major provisions in the Act of 1992, including 5(c)(1), which directs each governmental agency to define, organize, and transmit each "assassination record" to the JFK Collection, and 5(d)(3), which directs the National Archives to place all "assassination records" in the JFK Collection.[32] In addition, the Senate report on the act also emphasized the need to establish public confidence in the government by securing such records as the Zapruder film.[33]

On the other hand, Brauneis continued, section 11a of the Act of 1992 creates an exception on deeds of gifts to the United States. Although the Zapruder film had been deposited in the National Archives under "a storage agreement," the courts might interpret that wording broadly and include the film as an exception.[34] Further, Brauneis testified that the Act of 1992 does not make any reference to eminent domain or just compensation, and that the legislative history explicitly says the act would create no economic hardship on individuals or businesses, which hardship conceivably could be inflicted upon the Zapruder family.[35] Noting that the Supreme

Court has ruled that the exercise of eminent domain over property must be explicit or a necessary implication, he concluded that in a tight case like this the court might not agree that the JFK act actually authorized the taking.[36]

Attorney James H. Lesar followed Brauneis.[37] After complimenting the scholarly exposition of Professor Brauneis, he remarked that he had a "different take" on some matters that "may have some bearing on the ultimate issues." He felt that the "bits and pieces" of a statute were important to consider, but the overarching purpose of the Act of 1992 must be paramount in coming to any decision.[38] Lesar then proceeded to articulate seven points driving to the heart of the issue before the ARRB. He argued that the act intended to gather all records related to the assassination of President Kennedy and preserve them. Under that consideration, the Zapruder film was certainly one of the records and ought to be gathered.[39]

He also observed that he felt "the JFK Act has already effected a taking." Specifically section 11a provides that the act overrides all prior statutes, including the Copyright Act, a point not addressed by Brauneis.[40] That, of course, had significant implications for any determination of the film's intrinsic commercial value. Lesar noted that

> the commercial value of the film is hardly separable from the copyright in the film. And it also has implications in terms of public access because under both the JFK and the Freedom of Information Act, if it is an assassination record, and I think unquestionably it is, then the public has a right to have copies of the film . . . so, that leaves you with the question of the value of the actual physical copy, the camera original, as divorced from the copyright. And it seems to me that that value is greatly diminished.[41]

Lesar then noted that section 4 of the act also supported a taking by the ARRB.[42] Under that clause the Archivist was charged with "ensuring the physical integrity and provenance of all records." If the film remained subject to "the caprice and whim of private ownership," that responsibility could not be fulfilled by the Archivist. Lesar also argued that the film belonged in government possession and ownership in order to guarantee that it would keep pace with advances in technology. The government must assure that "the public may have access to the information provided by any advances in technology that can take place."[43]

In addition, Lesar cited copyright and First Amendment scholar Melville

Nimmer, who held that "in a certain narrow class of cases the first amendment interest in enlightened democratic dialogue overrode the copyright interest." Nimmer provided two examples of such cases, the My Lai massacre and the Zapruder film, arguing that "it would be unconscionable that the copyright interest would supersede the overwhelming public interest that could not be fulfilled in any other way but through access to the photographs."[44]

Lesar concluded his testimony by observing that the case was still theoretically open, and in the slight chance others might be charged with JFK's murder, the film was potential evidence for use at their trial.[45] Overall, Lesar's calm, articulate, and well-grounded testimony made a deep impression on the five board members. Afterward George Lardner Jr., a veteran reporter for the *Washington Post*, told Lesar that Gunn had said that the ARRB had bought his [Lesar's] argument in favor of the taking "hook, line, and sinker."[46]

Subsequently, on April 24, 1997, the board met and decided by unanimous vote that the Zapruder film was an assassination record and directed that it be transferred on August 1, 1998, to the John F. Kennedy Assassination Records Collection at the National Archives and Records Administration (NARA).[47] Inexplicably, however, the board refused to take the copyright with the artifact itself. It formulated its resolve in a "Statement of Policy and Intent with Regard to the Zapruder Film" that declared as follows:

> *Resolved*, that the Zapruder film is an "assassination record" within the meaning of the President John F. Kennedy Assassination Records Collection Act of 1992;
>
> *Resolved*, that the Review Board will do all in its power to ensure that the best available copy of the Zapruder film shall become available to the public at the lowest reasonable price;
>
> *Resolved*, that the Review Board offers to work cooperatively with LMH Company to: (a) make the best possible copy of the Zapruder film to be placed in the National Archives and Records Administration for scholarly and research uses, (b) to establish a base reference for the film through digitization, and (c) to conduct all appropriate tests to evaluate authenticity and to elicit historical and evidentiary evidence; and
>
> *Resolved*[,] that the Review Board intends to exercise its authority, as formulated in its enabling legislation, to direct that the film be

transferred, on August 1, 1998, to the John F. Kennedy Assassination Records Collection at NARA, and that the Review Board will work with Congress to resolve this issue.[48]

In the months before the film officially became government property on August 1, 1998, the Department of Justice negotiated with the Zapruder heirs over the matter of compensation. Assistant Attorney General Frank Hunger was put in charge of government negotiations. On June 4, ARRB members met with Representative Dan Burton, chairman of the House Government Reform and Oversight Committee, to present their case for federal acquisition. Burton, in a June 5 letter to Hunger, offered his committee's full support for the Justice Department's negotiations. As George Lardner Jr. reported, "Burton assured him that his committee 'will not attempt to second-guess your sound judgment in seeking either a negotiated settlement of the cost or in litigating the case before the appropriate court. We need the original film to remain in the National Archives.' "[49]

As of the middle of June the two parties remained far apart.[50] The Zapruders then hired Robert S. Bennett, a Washington attorney, to promote their interests.[51] Bennett asked the government to pay $18.5 million for the film and the copyright, but the Department of Justice rejected that price as too high. It countered with an offer of $750,000 and suggested "it might go as high as $3 million."[52]

While the negotiations continued, two other notable developments occurred. In late July 1998, a commercial video of the Zapruder film appeared in bookstores nationwide, selling for $19.95.[53] MPI Teleproductions of Orlando Park, Illinois, published *Image of an Assassination: A New Look at the Zapruder Film*, which was produced under the auspices of the LMH Company and edited by Scott Rathbun and Chuck Pelini. H. D. Motyl produced and directed the forty-five-minute digital replication of the Zapruder film, which included the sprocket matter.[54] Presumably right after the April 24, 1997, declaration of the taking by the ARRB, LMH began to work with MPI to digitize the original film, a careful and difficult process recounted and illustrated on the video. The effort produced the best copy of the movie available for general researchers, superior in some respects to the original. In addition, the video contains a history of the film, including accounts from persons who worked with Abraham Zapruder, experts in film, and federal archivists.

In addition, on September 25, 1998, the Eastman Kodak Company of

Rochester, New York, submitted to the ARRB its technical report on the authenticity and history of the filming, printing, and duplicating of the original Zapruder film.[55] Authored by the renowned film expert Roland J. Zavada, *Analysis of Selected Motion Picture Photographic Evidence* had its genesis in 1996 when Zavada, retired from Eastman Kodak Company, met with the staff of the ARRB to discuss the authenticity of the Zapruder film, which had become a matter of some concern for a number of misguided assassination theorists.[56] By February 1997, the ARRB had proposed a plan funded by Eastman Kodak for Zavada to authenticate the Zapruder film, and by August 1997, Zavada and his team had begun their final investigation, thoroughly and painstakingly tracing the history of the film, its development, and its copies.[57] In the end, Zavada concluded that the film and its copies in the National Archives were in fact authentic. The thunder and powder spent by the theorists proclaiming a fake and charging a switch were without a foundation.

On October 15, 1998, the United States Department of Justice and the LMH Company entered into an arbitration agreement "to provide a fair, cost-effective, non-judicial method of rendering a binding determination of the amount that Government must pay as just compensation for taking the private property of LMH pursuant to the President John F. Kennedy Assassination Records Collection Act of 1992." The agreement stated that the United States was purchasing only the film itself and not the copyright: "LMH has retained ownership of the Copyright. The Government's right to use the Film is governed by the copyright laws of the United States, including the doctrine of Fair Use."

Both parties agreed to a panel of three neutral arbitrators.[58] LMH was to select one, the Department of Justice was to select another, and the two parties together would select the third. On January 6, 1999, the panel was named.[59] The Department of Justice selected Arlin M. Adams, a Philadelphia lawyer and former federal appeals judge and independent counsel for the prosecution of influence-peddling allegations against officials in the Reagan administration, particularly Sam Pierce. LMH selected Kenneth R. Feinberg, a Washington lawyer. The third member was Walter Dellinger, a former acting solicitor general in the Department of Justice in the Clinton administration.

While the system of arbitration began its process of deciding the sum to be awarded to the Zapruders, the family filed two suits against the United States of America, barely meeting the cutoff date for filing under the statute

of limitations. Since under federal law LMH had six years from the enactment of the act of October 26, 1992, to file a suit for payment, both parties
agreed that notwithstanding the agreement LMH "may file a civil suit
against the Government to challenge the authority of the Government to
take the Film and to seek just compensation if, in the sole judgment of
LMH, the filing of such action may be necessary to preserve such claims
under the applicable statute of limitations." Under the first suit the family
sought just compensation for the taking of the film; under the second suit
they challenged the legality of federal seizure. As under the agreement, they
stayed both suits, pending the outcome of the arbitration process.

In the first suit, the Zapruders alleged that on August 1, 1998, the United
States "took the Zapruder film from LMH" despite operation of the following mitigating factors that entitled them to proper compensation. According to LMH, this action violated LMH's twenty-year-old written agreement with the National Archives to return the film upon LMH's request.
LMH argued further that it had a record of cooperation with and support of
scholars and researchers; that the film had been sold in a manner supporting the dignity of the subject and affirming the honor of the nation; that
LMH had met the demands of the commercial market with "sensitivity and
concern for the subject matter by prohibiting the use in advertising" or
commercial use that "might be considered exploitative or in bad taste";
that a technologically superior copy had been made to support and sustain
scholarly research; that LMH had produced and provided a digitized copy
and royalty-free license that "would have allowed the United States to have
all the information contained on the original and all necessary rights";
and that LMH had suffered economic losses in support of the national
interest by having accepted compensation for the film far below the fair
market value.

In the second suit, LMH challenged the authority of the United States to
take the Zapruder film on August 1, 1998.[60] But it also filed a motion to stay
judicial proceedings pending the settlement of the arbitration process with
the United States as per the arbitration agreement and the following year
would file a notice of dismissal of the case.[61]

On November 23, James Lesar's Assassination Archives and Research
Center of Washington, a private research organization, and Passage Productions, a documentary film producer, filed a suit in the U.S. District
Court for the District of Columbia against LMH, the Department of Justice,
and the National Archives and Records Administration.[62] They sued to

force the government to include the copyright in the negotiations and to challenge the validity of the copyright itself. Passage Productions also sought a fair price for its intended use of the film in a documentary program scheduled for the History Channel in November. That broadcast was in jeopardy because the LMH Company's asking price was prohibitive.[63] In early 1999 the suit was dismissed as per a private agreement in return for Passage Productions receiving a reduced but undisclosed price for the use of the film and the copyright portion of the suit being dropped.

On August 3, 1999, the arbitration panel announced in a two-to-one decision "that the sum of $16 million is a fair and accurate reflection of the true value of the Zapruder film at the time of the taking."[64] The dissenting vote came from Walter Dellinger, who argued that the price was too high, with an award of "$3–5 million" much more reasonable. That hefty price, however, did not include the transfer of copyright. The panel's majority declared that "the United States is required only to pay just compensation for the original of the film, LMH retains commercial control of the images."[65] Further, the film could be used only in the National Archives and only for study purposes: "Any purchaser of the film could not publicly project the film or exhibit copies of its frames without infringing upon the LMH copyright."[66] But such a requirement presents problems to any researcher who both studies the film *and* desires to disseminate his or her views regarding it. The researcher either must describe the film purely in words (an inadequate solution) or must pay whatever price the copyright holders demand for the privilege of reproducing images from the film, whether or not that price is affordable or fair.

All of this is more or less spelled out in the arbitration panel's report, *In the Matter of the Zapruder Film*, despite its confused reasoning, incomplete record, poor writing, and sometimes condescending and imperious tone. In particular, the report's description of what the film depicts and why that is so significant is woefully inadequate, perhaps presuming that by now the film's contents and significance had become common knowledge. But even the awarding of the $16 million is framed oddly: "We are comfortable that the sum of $16 million is fair and an accurate reflection of the true value." Comfortable?

The report also states that Zapruder received $150,000 for license fees "to Time and Life magazines" when in fact Zapruder actually gave up ownership—that is, sold the film to Time Inc., including the copyright, and was paid that sum for it, *plus* also paid one-half of Time Inc.'s future sales of the pictures beyond the original $150,000. Nowhere in the document does one learn how much Time Inc. and the Zapruder family actually earned from the film between 1963 and 1975, which remains a mystery in an arbitration settlement that rests part of its conclusion on the earnings from the film in toto. Nor does one learn anything about the Zapruder heirs' threat to sue for Time Inc.'s failure to obtain and share licensing fees as the impetus for their resumption of the film's ownership and copyright. Nor are any of the other suits (such as those by Harold Weisberg and Chip Selby) well explained.

The arbitration panel provided at best only a rather desultory account of its reasons for awarding Abraham Zapruder's heirs such a large compensatory reward for a piece of evidence so crucial to any investigation of the assassination that it should have been placed in the public domain years ago. In particular and despite much evidence to the contrary, the panel amazingly declared "that the film presently provides no immediate answers to the various questions surrounding the death of President Kennedy."[67] Yet in their hearings they had heard from no witnesses and saw no evidence that would permit them as neutral arbitrators to make a judgment on such an issue, and they resolutely sought none.

On the one hand, the panel agreed the film provided "the most complete recording of President Kennedy's assassination,"[68] which of course made it an exceedingly valuable piece of evidence in a murder case of such importance. On the other hand, the panel defined such "value" primarily in terms of what the heirs had lost rather than what the government had rightfully gained:

> In what appears to be a most unusual act, the Government "took" the film from its private owners, concluding that its historical importance was so significant that it should be secured under Government protection. For the Government to pass special legislation to secure the film—an act that was not duplicated in the case of the Lincoln memorabilia or copies of the Declaration of Independence or the other historical items referred to during the arbitration hearings—is significant in determining a fair valuation of the Zapruder film.[69]

The panel also was far more sympathetic to the estimates of LMH's appraisers than to the government's. Appraisers hired by the government placed the film's value between "$784,000 and 1,000,000."[70] They arrived at the lower figure as the inflation multiple of $150,000, the original earnings, which itself was in error because the earnings from Time Inc. sales were chopped out of the record. Not surprisingly, LMH appraisers determined the firm's value "as an icon" to be much higher—"ranging from $25,000,000 to no less than $40,000,000," with LMH counsel stressing that the federal seizure had cost LMH more than $10,000,000 in lost income. One auction house expert also testified the film could be worth "double or triple that" ($50 to $75 million). This latter testimony and figures greatly impressed the panelists, especially in light of Bill Gates's recent purchase of the Codex of Leonardo da Vinci for $30 million. Ultimately, such testimony convinced the panel's two-member majority to award a much higher amount than recommended by the government's lawyers.

Seven weeks later LMH filed a notice of dismissal of its two lawsuits, indicating that the company was satisfied with the award.

I believe the United States should not have been compelled to purchase the film or its copyright (which, of course, LMH retained). The abysmal federal failure to acquire the essential copyright is not merely regrettable but censurable, especially since no one—the attorneys for LMH or for the Justice Department—addressed the film as evidence in a crime. The film, when objectively examined, contains irrefutable proof that a conspiracy was responsible for the murder of President John F. Kennedy.

Further detracting from the sad performance, the records associated with the purchase of the film, including reports, hearing minutes, memorandums, studies, correspondence, and similar items,[71] were not made available to scholars or the public until after I had filed[72] suit for access to the records pertaining to the negotiations with LMH.[73] Subsequently, the Department of Justice released approximately seventy-five hundred pages associated with its negotiations for the purchase of the film.[74]

On January 27, 2000, the Houston Chronicle reported that the children and grandchildren of Abraham Zapruder had donated the film's copyright, along with almost two thousand other items in the family's collection, to the Sixth Floor Museum of Dallas. The museum read the family's statement: "Since November 22, 1963, our guiding principle has been to strike a balance between respect for the sensitive nature of the film's images and an appropriate response to the public's demand for access to the film. We have selected the Sixth Floor Museum for this gift because we are confident that those responsible for its administration share our values."[75] To its credit, the Sixth Floor Museum at Dealey Plaza in Dallas has thoughtfully and effectively fulfilled its responsibilities in that regard and is to be commended for doing so under such difficult circumstances.

I still maintain, however, that in 1963, after determining the Zapruder film's evidentiary importance, the federal government should have seized both the film and the copyright. Certainly by 1999, it should have taken both without paying anything to the LMH Company. There are good reasons for thinking this, beyond the obvious fact of its evidentiary status. Among other things, the Zapruder family had already made a considerable fortune from the sale and licensing of the film, somewhere in the neighborhood of $1 million—more than sufficient *and just* compensation under the circumstances. More important, because the film establishes that two or more individuals killed President Kennedy, it conclusively refutes the official conclusion of the federal investigation. The film is vital to maintaining the public's strong belief in the essential integrity of government and its public servants. In the face of that importance, treating the Zapruder frames as a species of ordinary private property is baffling. The fact that it had been treated that way would remain merely puzzling if it were not so tragic and thus outrageous.

Rather than damaging constitutional guarantees of private property, as some commentators contended and many bureaucrats have agreed, a taking of the Zapruder film and copyright without payment would have in fact reinforced the principles of a truly democratic society that had in the first place created the very concept of constitutionally protected private property.

Epilogue
The Zapruder Film and
American History

The Zapruder film will remain forever an integral part of the investigation of President John F. Kennedy's assassination. Its history provides undeniable evidence of a conspiracy—in effect, a coup d'état—although it does not give us any clear clues as to the identities of the conspirators. It does, however, provide undeniable proof that members of the Warren Commission, its staff, and the FBI failed miserably in their investigations (see document 16 in the appendix) and, in the process, undermined our faith in federal officials and spawned countless silly and bizarre counterclaims that have only further confused the historical record. They have been periodically countered by Warren Commission apologists and lone-gunman-Oswald theorists—like Jim Bishop, Edward Jay Epstein, Jean Davison, and Gerald Posner—who have only thrown more silt into these already muddied waters.

My sincere hope is that my book will provide at least a modest impetus not simply to revisit the Zapruder film itself but also to confront and, to the extent possible at this late date, correct our collective failure to set the record straight regarding the murder of our president.

APPENDIX: DOCUMENTS

NUMBER 1.
Secret Service agent Forrest Sorrels's history
of film to Inspector Thomas J. Kelley, January 22, 1964

On January 22, 1964, Secret Service agent Forrest Sorrels set forth a memorandum on how the service obtained its copy of the Zapruder film. He errs in recalling he picked up the films at Zapruder's office. On the night of November 22, Zapruder took them to the Secret Service office in Dallas. Sorrels misspells McCormick's name.

United States Government Memorandum
U.S. Secret Service CO-2-34,030
To: Chief Attention Inspector Kelley   Date: January 22, 1964
From: SAIC Sorrels, Dallas
Subject: Zapruder Film of the Assassination of President Kennedy
    Reference is made to your memorandum of January 14, 1964 instructing that you be informed the details as to the circumstances under which we secured copy of original color film taken by Abraham Zapruder, which original film was purchased by Life Magazine.
    Just as soon as the President, Vice President Johnson and Texas Governor Connally were in the Parkland Hospital, Dallas, Texas, at approximately 12:45 P.M., November 22, 1963, I proceeded to Texas School Book Depository Building for the purpose of trying to locate witnesses. Some witnesses were located and were taken to the Sheriff's office which is across the street from the above named building in order that written statements might be obtained from them. While I was in the Sheriff's office, Harry McCormack, a reporter for the Dallas Morning News, contacted me and informed me that he had located a man who had made some movies that he thought we would be interested in. He then took me to the office of Mr. Abraham Zapruder, dress manufacturer, Jennifer Juniors, Inc., 501 Elm St., Dallas, Tex., who was introduced to me by Mr. McCormack. Mr. Zapruder was emotionally upset at the time as he had personally seen President Kennedy shot while taking movies of the President in the motorcade from Houston and Elm Streets to the underpass west of the Texas School Book Depository Building. Mr. Zapruder agreed to furnish me with a copy of this film with the understanding that it was strictly for official use of the Secret Service and that it would not be shown or given to any newspapers or magazines as he expected to sell the film for as high a price as he could get for it. Mr. McCormack was also interested in the film and had offered Mr. Zapruder $1,000.00 for it, but there were others that were also interested. Accompanied by Mr. McCormack we took Mr. Zapruder to the Dallas Morning News and to their radio station offices in an effort to get the film developed, however, they were not equipped to do so, but did ascertain that Eastman Kodak Company in Dallas could develop the film immediately. We then took Mr. Zapruder to the Eastman

Kodak Company where he made arrangements to have the film developed and also copies made of same. Later I went to Mr. Zapruder's office and he gave to me two copies of this film, one copy of which was immediately airmailed to Chief and one copy was retained by me. At the time Mr. Zapruder gave me the copies of the film he again specified that the film was for government use and that I was not to let either copy get in the hands of any newspaper or magazine company.

The following day Inspector Kelley obtained the retained copy of the film from me which he loaned to the FBI and which was subsequently returned to Inspector Kelley who gave the film to me and it is now in the Dallas office.

NUMBER 2.
Chief of Secret Service James Rowley's history of film to *Life*, January 27, 1964

James J. Rowley, chief of the Secret Service, related to Life's Henry Suydam the disposition of its two copies of the film in agency hands. Copy from National Archives.

Office of the Chief   January 27, 1964
Mr. Henry Suydam
LIFE Bureau Chief
1120 Connecticut Avenue, N.W.
Washington, D.C.
Dear Henry:

Reference is made to your letter of January 7, 1964, concerning the two copies of the Zapruder assassination film now in the hands of the Secret Service.

I find that Mr. Sorrels of our Dallas office, after learning of the existence of the film, called upon Mr. Zapruder in his office, at which time Mr. Zapruder agreed to furnish him with a copy of the film with the understanding that it was strictly for official use of the Secret Service and that it would not be shown or given to any newspapers or magazines, as Mr. Zapruder expected to sell the film.

Mr. Sorrels ascertained that Eastman Kodak Company in Dallas would develop the film immediately. Mr. Sorrels then took Mr. Zapruder to Eastman Kodak where arrangements were made to have the film developed and copies made. Afterward, Mr. Zapruder, in his office, furnished Mr. Sorrels two copies of the film and we received them before Mr. Zapruder had sold the original film.

We, of course, have no knowledge concerning Life's later arrangement with Mr. Zapruder; however, when we received the film from Mr. Zapruder he again specified that it was for Government use. The film has not been shown to anyone outside the Secret Service, except to members of the staff of the President's Commission on the Assassination.

Please be assured that it will not be shown by us to anyone outside the Government unless for official investigative purposes. However, we consider it part of the official Secret Service file of the investigation of the assassination of President Kennedy.

Sincerely,
/s/ James J. Rowley
James J. Rowley

NUMBER 3.
Eastman Kodak Company's affidavit on
processing original film, November 22, 1963

On the afternoon of November 22, the Eastman Kodak Company processed Abraham Zapruder's original out-of-camera film. It was 16mm double-perforated. He requested an affidavit of the work done. The process perforated identification number 0183 on the end of the film.

Eastman Kodak Company
Color Print and Processing Sales and Service
3131 Manor Way Dallas 35, Texas

Home office
Rochester 4, New York   Telephone Fleetwood 7-4654
State of Texas :
County of Dallas : SS

Mr. P. M. Chamberlain, Jr., being duly sworn deposes and says that he is employed as Production Foreman in the Kodak Film Processing Laboratory, 3131 Manor Way, Dallas 35, Texas of the Eastman Kodak Company, Rochester 4, New York.

That his department received on November 22, 1963, one 8mm Kodachrome II Film for the account of A. Zapruder, 501 Elm Street, Dallas, Texas [,] and processed the same. That the film was not cut, mutilated or altered in any manner during processing. That while the film was in the possession of the Eastman Kodak Company it was not shown to any person other than employees of said laboratory of known integrity in the ordinary course of handling the same.

And that the end of the process film and carrier strip, inside the carton, were perforated by Eastman Kodak Company at the time of processing with the following identification number:

0183

And that this film and this affidavit were returned under Kodak seal to the above-mentioned dealer for the above-mentioned customer.

/s/ P. M. Chamberlain, Jr.

Sworn to before me this
22nd day of Nov., 1963
/s/ R. T. Blain

NUMBER 4.
Jamieson Company's affidavit on making three duplicates of film,
November 22, 1963

When the Jamieson Company finished making three duplicates of the original film on 16mm double-perforated film (two 8mm side by side), Zapruder requested an affidavit attesting to the work performed. One affidavit covered all three copies.

Jamieson Film Company
3825 Bryan, Dallas, Texas, TA 3-8158
Motion Picture Producers Since 1916

Our Forty-Seventh Year

State of Texas

County of Dallas

Mr. Frank R. Sloan, being duly sworn deposes and says that he is employed as Laboratory Manager in the Jamieson Film Company, 3825 Bryan Street, Dallas, Texas.

That he received on Friday, November 22, 1963, one 8mm Kodachrome II film for the account of: A. Zapruder, 501 Elm Street, Dallas, Texas and made Three (3) duplicate copies. That the film was not cut, mutilated or altered in any manner during the printing operation. That while the film was in the possession of the Jamieson Film Company it was not shown to any person other than employees of said laboratory of known integrity in the ordinary course of handling the same.

And that the end of the processed film carried the identification number: 0183 which was printed onto the said duplicate copies.

And that the film camera original and three (3) duplicate copies were returned to the above mentioned customer and that no other than three (3) duplicate copies were made.

/s/ Frank R. Sloan

Sworn to me before this

22nd day of November, 1963

/s/ Walter Spiro

Walter Spiro, Notary Public Dallas County

NUMBER 5.
Dallas Eastman Kodak Company's affidavit on processing duplicates, November 22, 1963

In the evening of November 22, Abraham Zapruder returned to the Kodak plant from Jamieson Company with three uncut and undeveloped 16mm double-perforated copies of the film. He had them developed and two of them precision slit and assembled into a filmstrip. For each of the copies he had the Kodak production foreman swear to the work performed. Each affidavit is alike except for the identification numbers, 0185, 0186, and 0187. Number 0183 had been earlier assigned to the original film, and the normal process of "cocking," or readying, the machine for the three new films eliminated 0184.

Eastman Kodak Company

Color Print and Processing Sales and Service

3131 Manor Way Dallas 35, Texas

Home office

Rochester 4, New York   Telephone Fleetwood 7-4654

State of Texas :

County of Dallas : SS

Mr. Tom Nulty, being duly sworn deposes and says that he is employed as Production Foreman in the Kodak Film Processing Laboratory, 3131 Manor Way, Dallas 35, Texas of the Eastman Kodak Company, Rochester 4, New York.

That his department received on November 22, 1963, one 8mm Kodachrome II Film for the account of A. Zapruder, 501 Elm Street, Dallas, Texas [,] and processed the same. That the film was not cut, mutilated or altered in any manner during processing. That while the film was in the possession of the Eastman Kodak Company it was not shown to any person other than employees of said laboratory of known integrity in the ordinary course of handling the same.

And that the end of the process film and carrier strip, inside the carton, were perforated by Eastman Kodak Company at the time of processing with the following identification number:

0185

And that this film and this affidavit were returned under Kodak seal to the above-mentioned dealer for the above-mentioned customer.

/s/ Tom Nulty

Sworn to before me this
22nd day of Nov., 1963
/s/ Mrs. Kathryn Kirby

NUMBER 6.
Abraham Zapruder's contract with *Life,* November 25, 1963

Dallas, Texas
November 25th, 1963

Mr. C. D. Jackson, Publisher
Life Magazine
C/o Time, Inc.
Rockefeller Center
New York, New York
Dear Sir:

This will confirm agreement reached with your authorized representative, Richard B. Stolley, during the past few days wherein I have agreed to sell, transfer and assign to Time, Inc. all my right, title and interest (whether domestic, foreign, newsreel, television, motion picture or otherwise) in and to my original and all three (3) copies of 8 mm. color films which show the shooting of President John F. Kennedy in Dallas, Texas, on November 22nd, 1963.

You acknowledge receipt through your agent of the original and one (1) copy thereof, and it is understood that there are two (2) other copies, one (1) of which is with the Secret Service in Dallas, Texas, and one (1) copy of which is with the Secret Service in Washington, D.C. I have the assurance and agreement of the Secret Service that the copies in their possession are to be released only to me, and I agree that I shall, immediately upon receipt of same, deliver same to your office or to such of your authorized representatives as you designate, or I will agree to sign any authorization allowing same to be delivered directly to you.

It is understood and agreed that you have all rights attached to said film of any kind and character whatsoever and may use them as you see fit upon terms and conditions set forth hereinafter:

(1) You agree to pay me or my heirs the sum of $150,000.00, payable $25,000.00 cash immediately, and the balance of $125,000.00 to be paid in installments as follows:

$25,000.00 on January 3rd, 1964,

$25,000.00 on January 3rd, 1965,

$25,000.00 on January 3rd, 1966

$25,000.00 on January 3rd, 1967, and

$25,000.00 on January 3rd, 1968.

In addition to the above consideration, it is further agreed and understood that you will pay to me or my heirs a sum equal to one-half (½) of all gross receipts derived by Time, Inc., its divisions and its wholly owned subsidiaries, from any source out of the use, sale, showing, rental, leasing, licensing, or other publication of any kind or character whatsoever after you have received $150,000.00 in cash from gross receipts derived from the same sources. Gross receipts received from foreign publication or sale will mean the gross receipts less agent's commissions customarily paid by Time, Inc. under the same or similar circumstances. The proceeds of this one-half (½) of gross proceeds over $150,000.00 shall be paid to me as follows:

$25,000.00 or such lesser amount as may then be due shall be paid on January 3rd, 1969, and a similar payment of $25,000.00 or such lesser amount as may then be due annually thereafter, upon the 3rd day of January of each calendar year thereafter, until this agreement shall cease and terminate by the terms hereof.

It is, however, understood that Time, Inc. and its presently constituted divisions, as well as its wholly owned subsidiary Time-Life Broadcast, Inc., shall have unlimited free use on its own behalf of the subject matter.

(2) This contract and agreement shall last for the life of any copyrights taken out by you and/or the undersigned in connection with said film, plus any times called for by renewals. You agree to indemnify and hold me harmless of and from any claims and expenses in connection with claims arising out of your use, dissemination and distribution of the film, and further agree not to use my name in connection with any such issue or publication without my prior, written consent. You further agree that you shall furnish me with a certified audited report of the auditing firm of your company showing the total gross receipts derived from said film each calendar year or at such other times as may be agreed upon hereafter.

(3) It is further understood and agreed that in the event you shall sell or transfer all rights to this film, such sale shall be subject to the terms of this agreement and same shall be binding upon the purchaser thereof. Furthermore, should Time, Inc., transfer or assign either the print media rights, in their entirety, or the film for motion pictures, television, newsreel, etc., dissemination, publication or viewing, in their entirety, any such sale shall likewise bind the purchaser thereof to the aforementioned provisions concerning payment of one-half (½) of the gross receipts from exhibition, publication, licensing, renting, or other publication of said film.

(4) Time, Inc. further agrees that it will present said film to the public in a manner consonant with good taste and dignity and agrees to exercise its best business judgment in the presentation, sale, leasing, licensing and rental of said film consonant with your business custom and practice for the production of gross receipts therefrom.

(5) I warrant that I am the sole owner of this film and that I have not and will not grant any rights to any other person, corporation or entity, and will agree to accord to you all rights in connection with same and cooperate with you to the fullest extent to secure same.

(6) Time, Inc. agrees to obtain, at its expense, such copyright protection, domestic and foreign, as it may deem necessary or proper for its own safety and to prevent any infringement thereof, should the same be necessary.

(7) Anything to the contrary herein notwithstanding, neither I nor my heirs shall have any right to sell, transfer, assign, pledge, hypothecate, mortgagee, encumber, or in any way dispose of this contract or any of the payments specified herein or the proceeds hereof nor to receive payment at any time other than as specified herein, nor shall you have any right to make any payments in advance.

Very truly yours,

/s/Abraham Zapruder

Abraham Zapruder

ACCEPTED AND AGREED

This 25th day of November,

A.D. 1963:

TIME, INC.

By /s/ Richard B. Stolley

Richard B. Stolley

NUMBER 7.
Abraham Zapruder's statement of authenticity of original and number of copies, November 25, 1963

Dallas, Texas

November 25th, 1963

Mr. C. D. Jackson, Publisher

Life Magazine c/o Time, Inc.

Rockefeller Center

New York, New York

Dear Mr. Jackson:

This confirms the fact that I originally took the exposed roll of 8 mm. film concerning the death of President John F. Kennedy on November 22nd, 1963, in Dallas, Texas, to Eastman Kodak for developing and processing. At that time I requested Eastman to make three (3) additional copies, but was advised, firstly, that they were not equipped to reproduce these locally and that it would have to be sent to Rochester, and secondly, that Jamieson Film Co., here in Dallas was equipped to make copies, so long as the film was not split but remained in the form of 16 mm. roll. Consequently, I had Eastman Kodak in Dallas process and develop the original roll of film without splitting the same, took such processed and developed film to Jamieson Film Co., and had three (3) copies made therefrom.

The laboratory manager of Jamieson Film Co. gave me an affidavit concerning the making of the prints, the original of which is attached hereto and is self-explanatory.

I then took the three (3) copies made from the original back to Eastman Kodak for their processing and developing. I was present during the times when the film was processed at Eastman Kodak and at Jamieson Film Co. and did not at any time notice or see any circumstance that would indicate that additional copies or prints of such film were or could have been made. I did not and have not authorized either Eastman Kodak Company or Jamieson Film Co. or any one else to duplicate, reproduce or in any fashion copy any of such film or prints thereof.

I am also delivering the originals of the four affidavits I received from Eastman Kodak to you herewith.

Very truly yours

/s/ Abraham Zapruder

Abraham Zapruder

NUMBER 8.

Time Inc.'s contract on return of film to Zapruder heirs, April 9, 1975

ASSIGNMENT OF COPYRIGHT

KNOW ALL MEN BY THESE PRESENTS, that TIME INCORPORATED, a New York corporation, doing business at Rockefeller Center, in the City, County and State of New York (hereinafter called the Assignor), in consideration of One Dollar ($1.00) and other good and valuable consideration paid to it by Lillian Zapruder, of 3909 Margrette Street, Dallas, Texas, and Henry Zapruder, of 10 East Lenox, Chevy Chase, Md., and Myrna Faith Hauser, of North Jan-Mar Street, Dallas, Texas, (hereinafter called the Assignees), receipt of which is hereby acknowledged, does hereby assign to said Assignees, their executors, administrators and assigns, to their own proper use and benefit, the copyright to the Film taken by Abraham Zapruder of the assassination of President John F. Kennedy, and registered for copyright on May 15, 1967 in Class L-M under No. Mu-7813, with all its literary property, right, title and interest in any and all renewals and extensions of said copyright that may be secured under the laws, now or hereafter in force and effect in the United States of America, or in any other country or countries, together with all claims for infringement appurtenant thereto.

IN WITNESS WHEREOF, said TIME INCORPORATED, has executed this assignment on the 9th day of April, 1975.

TIME INCORPORATED

Attest: (s) [indecipherable]

By: (s) [indecipherable]

Assistant Secretary

NUMBER 9.

Time Inc.'s donation of film and slide copies to the United States, April 9, 1975

DEED OF GIFT

In furtherance of the desire of TIME INCORPORATED, a New York corporation (hereinafter called the "Donor"), to ensure the preservation of a major document recording one of the most significant events in American history, and to contribute to educational knowledge and understanding, the Donor hereby gives, grants, conveys and sets over to the National Archives and Records Service, General Services Administration, (the "Archives") acting for on behalf of the United States of America under authority of 44 U.S.C. 2101-2112, as a gift, exclusively for public purposes:

1. a first generation copy of the 8mm moving picture film showing the assassination of President John F. Kennedy, which film has come to be known as the "Zapruder" film (the "Film"); and

2. a collection of color transparency still pictures (the still pictures) comprising one transparency of each frame of the Film. Each of the above items are to be retained in perpetuity for the benefit, enlightenment and scholarship of the people of the United States. The Donor hereby expressly notifies the Archives that the copyright in and to the Film is being transferred to others and that Time cannot authorize the Archives to utilize the Film and the still pictures in any manner which would constitute infringement of that copyright or otherwise violate or invade the rights of the copyright proprietor. Accordingly, the Donor grants to the Archives only the following right:

To make the Film or copies thereof and the still pictures or copies thereof available for viewing only by individuals on the premises of the Archives provided that the Archives adopt such security procedures as will prevent the copying or removal of the Film, still pictures, or copies of either, such copyright and ownership notice as is provided by the copyright proprietor shall be included.

Dated this 9th day of April, 1975.

TIME INCORPORATED

By: (s) [indecipherable]

Attest: (s) [indecipherable]

Accepted

UNITED STATES OF AMERICA

By (s) James E. O'Neill

ARCHIVIST OF THE UNITED STATES

NUMBER 10

Zapruder heirs transfer ownership of copyright to LMH Company, April 11, 1975

ASSIGNMENT OF COPYRIGHT

KNOW ALL MEN BY THESE PRESENTS, that LILLIAN ZAPRUDER of 3809 Marquette Street, Dallas, Texas 75225, and HENRY G. ZAPRUDER of 10 East Lenox Street, Chevy Chase, Maryland 20015, and MYRNA FAITH HAUSER of 6919 Jan Mar, Dallas, Texas 75230 (hereinafter called the Assignors), in consideration of One Dollar ($1.00) and other good and valuable consideration paid to them by LMH Company, a partnership of 3909 Marquette Street, Dallas, Texas 75225 (hereinafter called the Assignee), receipt of which is hereby acknowledged, do hereby assign to said Assignee, its successors and assigns, to its own proper use and benefit, the copyright to the Film taken by Abraham Zapruder of the assassination of President John F. Kennedy, and registered for copyright on May 15, 1967 in class L-M under No. Nu-7813, with all its literary property, right, title and interest in any and all renewals and extensions of said copyright that may be secured under the laws, now or hereafter in force and effect in the United States of America, or in any other country or countries, together with all claims for infringement appurtenant thereto.

IN WITNESS WHEREOF, said Assignors have executed this assignment on the 11th day of April, 1975.

(s) Lillian Zapruder
by Henry G. Zapruder, attorney
(s) Henry G. Zapruder (s) Myrna Faith Hauser

NUMBER 11.

National Archives receipt to LMH Company on accepting original film for courtesy storage, June 29, 1978

RECEIPT

The receipt of the original 8 mm color film taken by Mr. Abraham Zapruder on November 22, 1963, showing the assassination of President John F. Kennedy (the "Film"), is hereby acknowledged this 29th day of June, 1978, by Mr. Dick Myers (for Mr. James W. Moore, Director of Audio-Visual Division, National Archives, Washington, D.C. 20408) for storage, free of charge, under secure and proper temperature and humidity conditions. Neither Mr. Myers nor Mr. Moore have any authority with regard to the Film other than storage until such time as an agreement letter from LMH Company (the owner of the Film) is received and signed by Mr. Moore.

/s/ Dick Myers
Dick Myers
(for Mr. James W. Moore,
director of Audio Visual Division
National Archives
Washington, D.C. 20408)

NUMBER 12.

National Archives memorandum for the record on accepting original film for courtesy storage, June 29, 1978

NNFJ

Original Zapruder Film

Richard Myers, NNV, delivered to me today the original 8 mm. color Zapruder film of President Kennedy's assassination. NNV has requested that the film be stored in NNFJ's security area. The film was delivered to NNV by a representative of the Zapruder family and will be formally offered to NASRS by the Zapruder family in the near future. At the moment NARS has the film on a courtesy storage basis. NNFJ will hold the film and await farther [sic] information from NNV.

/initialed/

Clarence F. Lyons, Jr.

Chief

Judicial and Fiscal Branch

Civil Archives Division

NUMBER 13.
Katzenbach memorandum, November 25, 1963

Harold Weisberg received this typed copy of the handwritten draft of the previous day as a result of a request for Department of Justice records. 129-11 is the Department's filing number, which appeared written along with the stamped date and place. The initials HPW stand for Warren Commission staff counsel Howard P. Willens. Later, copies were discovered in other record releases.

November 25, 1963

MEMORANDUM FOR Mr. Moyers

It is important that all of the facts surrounding President Kennedy's Assassination be made public in a way which will satisfy people in the United States and abroad that all the facts have been told and that a statement to this effect be made now.

1. The public must be satisfied that Oswald was the assassin; that he did not have confederates who are still at large; and that the evidence was such that he would have been convicted at trial.

2. Speculation about Oswald's motivation ought to be cut off, and we should have some basis for rebutting thought that this was a Communist conspiracy or (as the Iron Curtain press is saying) a right-wing conspiracy to blame it on the Communists. Unfortunately the facts on Oswald seem about too pat—too obvious (Marxist, Cuba, Russian wife, etc.). The Dallas police have put out statements on the Communist conspiracy theory, and it was they who were in charge when he was shot and thus silenced.

3. The matter has been handled thus far with neither dignity nor conviction. Facts have been mixed with rumour and speculation. We can scarcely let the world see us totally in the image of the Dallas police when our President is murdered.

I think this objective may be satisfied by making public as soon as possible a complete and thorough FBI report on Oswald and the assassination. This may run into the difficulty of pointing to inconsistencies between this report and statements by Dallas police officials. But the reputation of the Bureau is such that it may do the whole job.

The only other step would be the appointment of a Presidential Commission of unimpeachable personnel to review and examine the evidence and announce its conclusions. This has both advantages and disadvantages. I think it can await publication of the FBI report and public reaction to it here and abroad.

I think, however, that a statement that all the facts will be made public property in an orderly and responsible way should be made now. We need something to head off public speculation or Congressional hearings of the wrong sort.

Nicholas deB. Katzenbach
Deputy Attorney General

129-11. Department of Justice, 21 May 1965, Records Branch. File HPW

NUMBER 14.
Melvin Eisenberg's memorandum on Chief Justice Earl Warren's stated reasons for chairing President's Commission, February 17, 1964

Melvin A. Eisenberg was an assistant counsel of the Warren Commission. He left a memorandum for the record on Earl Warren's first staff conference, where he gave his reasons for accepting the chairmanship of the Commission.

MEMORANDUM   February 17, 1964

TO: Files

FROM: Melvin A. Eisenberg

SUBJECT: First Staff Conference (January 20, 1964)

On January 20, 1964, Chief Justice Warren met with the staff. After brief introductions, the Chief Justice discussed the circumstances under which he had accepted the chairmanship of the Commission.

When the position had first been offered to him he declined it, as the principle that Supreme Court Justices should not take this kind of role. His associate justices concurred in this decision. At this point, however, President Johnson called him. The President stated that rumors of the most exagerrated [sic] kind were circulating in this country and overseas. Some rumors went as far as attributing the assassination to a faction within the Government wishing to see the Presidency assumed by President Johnson. Others, if not quenched, could conceivably lead the country into a war which could cost 40 million lives. No one could refuse to do something which might help to present such a possibility. The President convinced him that his was an occasion on which actual conditions had to override general principles.

The Chief Justice then discussed the role of the Commission. He placed emphasis on the importance of quenching rumors, and precluding future speculation such as that which has surrounded the death of Lincoln. He emphasized that the Commission had to determine the truth, whatever that might be.

NUMBER 15.
Total information on the murder of JFK found in the FBI report of December 9, 1963

On December 9, 1963, the Federal Bureau of Investigation issued a five-volume report on its investigation of the assassination, finding Lee Harvey Oswald alone and unaided killed President John F. Kennedy. It contains 140 words on the evidence itself; the rest is consumed with Oswald's background and unrelated information. It omits JFK's anterior throat wound, the slight wounding of James Tague, who stood near the triple underpass, and does not describe JFK's head wound. The report became the first of the Commission documents and functioned as the blueprint for the Warren Commission's inquiry and conclusions. The following is the entire account. The first paragraph is from volume 1, page 1; the second is from volume 1, page 18 (source: Commission Document No. 1, National Archives).

As the motorcade was traveling through downtown Dallas on Elm Street about fifty yards west of the intersection with Houston Street (Exhibit 1), three shots rang out.

Two bullets struck President Kennedy, and one wounded Governor Connally. The President, who slumped forward in the car, was rushed to Parkland Memorial Hospital, where he was pronounced dead at 1:30 P.M.

Immediately after President Kennedy and Governor Connally were admitted to Parkland Memorial Hospital, a bullet was found on one of the stretchers. Medical examination of the President's body revealed that to the right of the spinal column at an angle of 45 to 50 degrees downward, that there was no point of exit, and that the bullet was not in the body. An examination of this bullet by the FBI Laboratory determined that it had been fired from the rifle owned by Oswald. (Exhibit 23)

NUMBER 16.

Damage control tickler of FBI on how it investigated the assassination, no date

This FBI damage control tickler outline illustrates the decision of the agency not to investigate the assassination of President John F. Kennedy, but, in accordance with the principles embodied in the Katzenbach memorandum, to fasten the crime on Lee Harvey Oswald. It has neither date nor title but was drawn up apparently in the 1970s in anticipation of an undefined possible need for a defense of its investigation. It outlines the areas in which the FBI might face problems. A lawsuit by JFK critic Mark Allen directed by his attorney, James Lesar, disclosed it along with other records. It bears no filing mark because it was a tickler.

From its content, it is apparent the FBI knew it had done wrong. Among many notable points are its preparation of dossiers on the Warren Commission members and staff, on the staff after the Report was out, and sex dossiers on critics, all part of the bureau's control apparatus.

Capitalization and punctuation are as in the original; interlined written notations are in brackets.

The Federal Bureau of Investigation
1. Early Bureau Response to the President's Assassination
    A. November 22–23, 1963
        1. Early teletypes; instructions to field; Hoover, Sullivan, Belmont memos; 80 agents to Dallas
        2. Jenkins memo of Nov. 24; Hoover says Oswald alone did it, Bureau must "convince the public Oswald is the real assassin."
        3. Hoover memo on Nov. 26; "wrap up investigation; seems to me we have the basic facts now"
        4. Hoover memo on Nov. 29; "hope to have investigation wrapped up by next week"
    B. Lee Harvey Oswald
        1. Establishing chain of evidence, bullet to gun, etc.
        2. November 23 memo; basic facts, yet contradictions on Oswald in Mexico; [redacted] photo not him.
        3. Hosty note destruction; handling by Bureau on Nov 24 and effect in subsequent days
        4. Interviews of Oswald associates, Marina wiretap [m=marines, etc.]

    C. Jack Ruby
       1. Basic facts, early memo
       2. Hoover suspicion of basement entry and assistance
       3. extensive teletypes and reports on organized crime connections, also Hoover's own memos
       4. contacts in 1959 as F. D. I - for use as informer on criminal element in Dallas
  2. *Structure and Methods of the Bureau Investigation*
    A. Basic Organization and Jurisdiction
       1. Legal basis of FBI involvement in probe, statutes.
       2. Hoover and Belmont memos
       3. Organization chart
    B. General Investigative Division [GID.]
       1. Rosen testimony on "ancillary nature" of probe; lack of meetings; assignment to bank robbery desk
       2. Supervisors Senate testimony on physical evidence chain
       3. Sullivan on lack of communication with Domestic Intelligence - the Division running the probe of LHO [lack of coordination between Div 5 & 6]
       4. Rosen characterization of FBI "standing with pockets open waiting for evidence to drop in"
       5. Supervisors testimony on LHO not being included in G. I. D. probe other than in relation to physical evidence
       6. Rosen didn't know of "Cale Report" which found deficiencies in Bureau coverage of Oswald [DID no initial it.]
    C. Domestic Intelligence Division [D.I.D. Div. 5]
       1. LHO background established, prior coverage
       2. Sullivan testimony on chaotic process, lack of input
       3. Soviet experts handled Oswald investigation
       4. Secret disciplining of DID officials who handled pre-assassination investigation of Oswald
       5. Incident of Sullivan's people copying CID files
       6. Hosty note destruction; Sullivan lack of knowledge
       7. Assignment of Ruby probe to Civil Rights Division - outside of DID jurisdiction, thus not a part of general Oswald investigation.
    D. Investigation of Potential Cuban Aspects
       1. Cancellation of orders to contact Cuban sources on Nov 23
       2. [redacted]
       3. Deletion of [redacted] from memo provided to Commission
       4. Cuban experts and supervisors excluded from investigation
       5. Church Committee findings on narrow Cuban focus
       6. [redacted]

E. Investigation of Potential Organized Crime Aspects
    1. Hoover memos and teletypes on Ruby connections
    2. Ruby phone records
    3. Justice Dept. interest in probing O. C. aspects
    4. Chicago interviews with Ruby associates
    5. Evans and Staffeld (and Danahy and Stanley) statements on not being consulted
    6. Use of Ruby as informant on Dallas criminal element
    7. LC[N?] sources available at time
3. Bureau Relationship with Warren Commission
  A. Formation of Warren Commission
    1. Hoover opposition: memo and Jenkins memo
    2. Katzenbach testimony and Sullivan statement
    3. Early memos - adversary relationship
    4. Hoover blocking Warren's choice for general counsel
    5. Preparation of dossiers on staff and members.
  B. Assistance to Warren Commission
    1. Basic scope of official relationship
    2. Early friction over informant allegation (LHO)
    3. Withholding of Hosty name from Oswald notebook
    4. Hoover instructions to agents not to volunteer info. to WC
    5. Destruction of Hosty note: implications
    6. Withholding of secret "Cale Report" on Bureau mistakes in earlier Oswald probe; disciplining of officials
    7. Hoover instructions ordering that no Bureau official attend earliest WC session, despite Katzenbach request
    8. Delay in sending information to Commission regarding Bureau's past nine contacts with Ruby
    9. Apparent withholding of "Oswald imposter" memos of 1960–1961
    10. Handling of information pertaining to Oswald-Kostikov contact
    11. Handling of Ruby polygraph
  C. Related Bureau Actions and Activities
    1. Preparation of dossiers on WC staff *after* the Report was out [Sept. 24, 64]
    2. Hoover's leaking of early FBI report (Sullivan statement)
    3. Hoover views on Communism and Oswald (Kronheim letter)
    4. Sullivan relationship [redacted] pre-arranging of answers to Commission questions.
    5. Secret plan to distribute Oswald-Marxist posters in Bureau plan to discredit Communist Party; prejudicial aspects
    6. Hoover reaction to Warren Report
    7. Subsequent preparation of sex dossiers on critics of probe
    8. Questions regarding FBI's continual pledge that "case will remain open for all time;" actual designation of it as "closed" in internal Bureau files.

NOTES

Introduction

1. John F. Kennedy, *Profiles in Courage* (New York: Harper and Brothers, 1955), flyleaf.

Chapter 1.
Abraham Zapruder Films the Assassination

1. Richard Stolley, interview by the Sixth Floor Museum at Dealey Plaza in Dallas, video (1996); Erwin Schwartz, interview by the Sixth Floor Museum, video (1994); *Image of an Assassination: A New Look at the Zapruder Film* (Orland Park, Ill.: MPI Video, 1998).

2. Schwartz interview. He was born in 1928.

3. "A. Zapruder Dies," *Dallas Morning News*, August 31, 1970; Richard B. Trask, *Pictures of the Pain: Photography and the Assassination of President Kennedy* (Danvers, Mass.: Yeoman Press, 1994), 57–58.

4. Ruth A. Brodsky, "A Man and His Camera," *Dallas Jewish Life* (November 1994), 11, a 1964 interview of Lillian and Abraham Zapruder printed after the death of Lillian in December 1993.

5. Ibid.; "Abraham Zapruder Dies; Filmed Kennedy Death: Footage of Tragedy in Dallas Had Role in Shaw Trial and Warren Commission Report," *New York Times*, August 31, 1970.

6. Abraham Zapruder testimony before the Warren Commission, *Hearings before the President's Commission on the Assassination of President Kennedy*, vol. 7 (Washington, D.C.: GPO, 1964), 570; hereinafter cited as 7H570.

7. Ibid.

8. 7H570; Richard B. Stolley, "What Happened Next . . . ," *Esquire*, November 1973, 134; Stolley interview.

9. Stolley, "What Happened Next," 134; 7H570; Myrna Reis interview by the Sixth Floor Museum, video (1997).

10. Reis and Stolley interviews; 7H570; Marilyn Sitzman, interview by the Sixth Floor Museum, video (1993).

11. Lawrence Howe, Vice President, Bell & Howell, to Lawson Knott, Administrator of General Services, December 12, 1966, reproduced in Harold Weisberg, *Photographic Whitewash* (Hyattstown, Md.: by the author, 1967), 151; Roland Zavada, *Analysis of Selected Motion Picture Photographic Evidence*, Kodak Technical Report (Rochester, N.Y.: Eastman Kodak, 1998), and its Study 4, "The Bell & Howell 414PD 8mm Camera Image Capture Characteristics." "P" represents power zoom; D, dual electric eye.

12. See Trask, *Pictures of the Pain*, 58, whose history of the film is on pages 57–153; Zavada, *Analysis of Selected*, study 4, part 2, "Optical/Image Characteristics."

13. It is not found in the official records and publications.

14. Patent for "Film Advancing Mechanism for Motion Picture Apparatus," Rochester, Eastman Kodak. Pat. No. 2,153,642, April 4, 1939; discussed and reproduced in Zavada, *Analysis of Selected*, study 4, part 1, "Mechanical-Camera Mechanism."

15. *Instructional Booklet: Bell & Howell Director Series, 8 mm Movie Camera, Model 414-414P* (Rochester, N.Y.: Eastman Kodak, n.d.).

16. Described in Zavada, *Analysis of Selected*, "Tutorial for Camera for the National Archives."

17. Zavada, *Analysis of Selected*, study 4, "The Bell & Howell 414PD."

18. Philip Chamberlain, interview by the Sixth Floor Museum, video (1994); *Image of an Assassination.*

19. Zapruder film; Chamberlain interview; Zavada, *Analysis of Selected*, study 4, "The Bell & Howell 414PD"; 7H570–571.

20. The film edge printed on black-and-white copies of Zapruder frames in 18H1–80. The issue was discussed thirty-five years later by Zavada, where the film is determined to be Kodachrome II; Zavada, *Analysis of Selected*, study 1, "Edge Print Analysis," and study 3, part 1, "Chronology of Events."

21. Stolley, "What"; 7H570.

22. 7H570.

23. Ibid. He testified in the office of the U.S. attorney at 301 Post Office Building, Bryan and Ervay Streets.

24. The Zapruder film; Sitzman video interview; *Image of an Assassination*; 7H571; Sitzman audio interview by Josiah Thompson, deposited in Assassination Archives and Records Collections, Washington, D.C.; Charles Hester, affidavit for the Sheriff, November 22, 1963, 19H476, on his actions on the knoll right after the shooting.

25. 7H571.

26. Sitzman video interview.

27. Ibid.

28. Ibid.

29. Blueprint of Dealey Plaza, provided by Boston architect Robert Cutler from the Dallas surveyor's office.

30. Sitzman video interview.

31. Approximate distances.

32. Patent, "Zoom Lens," Pat. no. 3,059,533, October 23, 1962, in Zavada, *Analysis of Selected*; *Optical Engineering Laboratory. Project Report Resolving Power of 8 mm Lens. Optical division. Bell & Howell* (Chicago: Bell & Howell, n.d.), as printed in Zavada, *Analysis of Selected*, study 4, part 2, "Optical/Image Characteristics."

33. *Report of the President's Commission on the Assassination of President John F. Kennedy* (Washington, D.C.: GPO, 1964), 31–32, 39, 48–50.

34. Commission Exhibit 876 is a photographic overview of the plaza; *Report*, 33; 17HCE876.

35. He describes this in his testimony before the Warren Commission, 7H569–575; also see the interviews of Sitzman and Stolley previously cited.

36. 7H571.

37. Sitzman video interview relates his intention was to do so.

38. Sitzman video interview.

39. Darwin Payne, interview by the Sixth Floor Museum, video (1996); *Dallas Times Herald* reporter telephoned notes, tear sheets, November 22, 1963, the Sixth Floor Museum.

40. Sitzman audio interview as also cited by Josiah Thompson in his *Six Seconds in Dallas: A Micro-Study of the Kennedy Assassination* (New York: Bernard Geis Associates, 1967), 102. Thirty years later Sitzman said she heard no shot sounds coming from behind her and had no knowledge of shots from there; Sitzman video interview.

41. See the Zapruder frames in 18H1-80 as well as, for example, the discussion in *Report*, 98–105.

42. *Report*, 98, 112.

43. Commission Exhibit 902, "Photograph through Rifle Scope," 18HCE902.

44. *Report*, 109.

45. *Dallas Times Herald* tear sheets.

46. Harry McCormick, "Account of JFK," *Dallas Morning News* journalists' accounts of the assassination, DMN, CD-ROM, 2002, copy in the Sixth Floor Museum.

47. WFAA-TV footage of interview at the Sixth Floor Museum.

48. Ibid.

49. Ibid.

50. Ibid.

51. Jack Harrison, interview by the Sixth Floor Museum, video (1993).

52. Time is given by Schwartz in his interview and roughly coordinates with the time of Phillips's memorandum.

53. Max Phillips, United States Secret Service, Dallas, to [U.S.S.S. Washington], Covering Memorandum, November 22, 1963, 9:55 P.M., Commission Document 87, copy, Harold Weisberg Archives, Frederick, Maryland.

54. *Report*, 61–117.

55. 7H571.

56. Liebeler's harsh and incomplete examination of him incensed Zapruder, who expressed his disgust afterward to Schwartz; Schwartz interview.

57. 7H571.

58. Ibid., 7H572.

59. Sitzman, audio interview; Trask, *Pictures of the Pain*, 76.

60. The words of Sitzman in Stolley, "What Happened," 135.

61. 7H571.

62. Schwartz interview; he does not mention the clerk and states he "ran into" Zapruder.

63. McCormick, "Account."

64. Stolley interview.

65. Schwartz interview; 7H571–72.

66. Ibid.; "Abraham Zapruder Dies," *New York Times*.

67. Sitzman and Schwartz video interviews.

68. Schwartz interview.

69. Ibid.

70. Darwin Payne, interview by the Sixth Floor Museum, video (1993).

71. Payne interview.

72. Ibid.

73. He thought it was around 1:00 P.M., but this appears to be too late; Sorrels testimony, 5H347-48.

74. Secret Service agent Forrest Sorrels to Inspector Kelley, memorandum, January 22, 1964, CO 2-34-030, Records of the President's Commission on the Assassination of President Kennedy, in the President John F. Kennedy Assassination Records Collection, National Archives.

75. Sorrels testimony, 5H352.

76. Ibid.

77. Ibid.

78. Dan Rather's account in *The Camera Never Blinks: Adventures of a TV Journalist* (New York: William Morrow, 1977), 125, is too hurriedly drawn, for it is factually incorrect in almost every detail.

79. Schwartz interview. He had been on the "other side" of Dallas at lunch with friends when he heard of the assassination.

80. Ibid.

81. Sorrels memorandum.

82. Sorrels testimony, 7H352.

83. Ibid.

84. Sorrels memorandum.

85. Stolley, "What," 135.

86. Thirty years after the fact, Schwartz in his video interview recalled it as "Channel 8 can do it," but this has to be a memory skip, for they went to the *Dallas Morning News*. The reporter probably said the *News*. Sorrels testimony, 7H352 reinforces my observations, as does McCormick's "Account."

87. McCormick, "Account."

88. Schwartz interview.

89. Payne interview.

90. Described in Schwartz interview.

Chapter 2.
Development and
Sale of the Film

1. Secret Service Agent Forrest Sorrels to Inspector Kelley, memorandum, January 22, 1964, CO 2-34-030, Records of the President's Commission on the Assassination of President Kennedy, in the President John F. Kennedy Assassination Records Collection, National Archives. Harry McCormick, "Account of JFK," *Dallas Morning News* journalists' accounts of the assassination, DMN, CD-ROM, 2002, copy in the Sixth Floor Museum at Dealey Plaza in Dallas.

2. Erwin Schwartz, interview by the Sixth Floor Museum, video (1993); Secret Service agent Forrest Sorrels, May 7, 1964, testimony before the President's Commission on the Assassination of President John F. Kennedy, *Hearings before the President's Commission on the Assassination of President Kennedy*, vol. 7 (Washington, D.C.: GPO, 1964), 352; hereinafter cited as 7H352.

3. 7H352.

4. "Legacy Event, November 22, 1996," interviews by the Sixth Floor Museum, video (1996), in printed transcript. Interview with Bert Shipp. The strange account of processing and brash credit for it given to his CBS station in Dan Rather with Mickey Herskowitz, *The Camera Never Blinks: Adventures of a TV Journalist* (New York: William Morrow, 1977), 132, on every point does not conform to the facts, apparently a victim of hasty proofreading.

5. Shipp interview; Jack Harrison,

interview by the Sixth Floor Museum, video (1994).

6. Schwartz interview; Harrison interview; Sorrels, 7H751.

7. WFAA-TV footage of interview at the Sixth Floor Museum.

8. Schwartz interview.

9. Ibid. Philip Chamberlain Jr., "The Zapruder Film," ms. (1977), copy in appendix of Roland Zavada, *Analysis of Selected*, Kodak Technical Report (Rochester, N.Y.: Eastman Kodak, 1998), says 2:30.

10. Chamberlain, "Zapruder Film."

11. Blair to Zavada, 1997, e-mail section, in Zavada, *Analysis of Selected*.

12. Ibid.

13. Ibid.; notes of telephone conversation, June 20, 1997, with Dick Blair, in Roland Zavada, "Compendious Notes of Telephone Conversation with Dallas Processing Laboratory Personnel," Zavada, *Analysis of Selected*, study 1 attachments.

14. Notes of telephone conversation, August 10, 1997, with Tom Nulty, in Zavada, *Analysis of Selected*.

15. Blair notes.

16. Ibid.

17. Ibid.

18. Sorrels testimony, 7H352; 7H569–576; and Schwartz interview.

19. Blair notes. Another employee, John Kenneth Anderson, stated in a memorandum of June 24, 1997, to Roland Zavada of the Kodak technical investigation, "The roll was never out of the secret service agent's sight and the roll was hand walked through the entire process. Davis, the agent and myself stayed in the darkroom until the film entered the dry cabinet. The agent and I then went to the dry alley. . . . When the roll of film reached take off I removed it and gave it to the agent. No film was

removed from the roll at the processing operation." Zavada, *Analysis of Selected*, study 1, attachments.

20. Abraham Zapruder to C. D. Jackson, Publisher Life Magazine, November 25, 1963, JFK Collection, National Archives.

21. Zavada, *Analysis of Selected*, study 1, part 3, "Processing Laboratory Identification . . ."

22. Schwartz interview.

23. Ibid.

24. McCormick, "Account."

25. Myrna Ries, interview by the Sixth Floor Museum, video (1997).

26. Chamberlain, "Zapruder Film."

27. Ibid.

28. Schwartz, Chamberlain, Harrison, and Stolley interviews.

29. Chamberlain interview.

30. Ibid.

31. Zapruder to Jackson, November 25, 1963.

32. Affidavit of P. M. Chamberlain Jr., November 22, 1963, in Zavada, *Analysis of Selected*, study 1, appendix.

33. Don Hewitt, interview by the Sixth Floor Museum, video (2002).

34. Rather, *Camera Never Blinks*, 132.

35. Schwartz interview.

36. Ibid.

37. Ibid.

38. Zavada, *Analysis of Selected*, study 3, "Initial Motion Picture Printing of the Zapruder 8mm Original Movie Film."

39. Zapruder to Jackson.

40. Zavada, *Analysis of Selected*, study 3.

41. Ibid.; Bruce Jamieson, interview by the Sixth Floor Museum, video (2000).

42. Affidavit of Frank R. Sloan, November 22, 1963, in Zavada, *Analysis of Selected*, study 1, appendix.

43. Zavada, *Analysis of Selected*, study 3. In study 1, attachments, is a memorandum from Doug Horne of the Archives to David Maxwell and Jeremy Gunn of the Assassination Records Review Board, April 9, 1997, which states that at Jamieson the perforated 0183 on the original "was photographically printed during the copying process."

44. Ibid.

45. Ibid., study 1, Blair notes; Chamberlain and Jamieson interviews.

46. Chamberlain interview.

47. Schwartz interview; Zapruder to C. D. Jackson; Zavada, *Analysis of Selected*, study 1, appendix.

48. Tom Nulty affidavits 0185, 0186, and 0187, November 22, 1963, JFK Records, National Archives. Also in Zavada, *Analysis of Selected*, appendix. The number 0184 was not used. The jump to 0185 came from the mechanical nature of the machine; Zavada, *Analysis of Selected*, study 1, part 3, "Processing Laboratory Identification."

49. Reis interview.

50. Stolley interview.

51. Schwartz and Chamberlain interviews.

52. Chamberlain telephone interview, January 23, 2003.

53. Ibid.; Chamberlain video interview. He is adamant on this.

54. Roland Zavada inspected them in Dallas and so stated.

55. They are in a Time Inc. paper film box, with the printed address Allied Film Laboratory, 306 W. Jackson, Chicago, and the typed label "Reversal black and white positive."

56. Ibid.

57. Ibid.

58. Ibid.; this is the only account of a drive to the police station.

59. Ibid.

60. Zavada, *Analysis of Selected*, study 1,

"Edge Print Analysis of . . ."; Schwartz interview.

61. Max Phillips, United States Secret Service, Dallas, to [U.S.S.S., Washington], Covering Memorandum November 23, 1963, 9:55 P.M., Commission Document 87; copy in Harold Weisberg Archives, Frederick, Maryland; first published in Weisberg, *Whitewash II* (Hyattstown, Md.: by the author, 1966), 141.

62. Schwartz interview; Stolley interview; Zapruder to Jackson, November 25, 1963.

63. Schwartz interview.

64. Stolley interview and his signing sales contract of November 23, 1963.

65. Zapruder's affidavits from Jamieson and Kodak; Zapruder to Jackson, November 25, 1963, in JFK Records, National Archives; Zavada, *Analysis of Selected*, study 1, appendix; Richard Stolley, interview by the Sixth Floor Museum, video (1996).

66. Zavada, *Analysis of Selected*, study 1.

67. Ibid.

68. *Air Force One* required about two hours and fifteen minutes to transport JFK's body to Washington.

69. Interview with Dino Brugioni, May 12, 2003.

70. By 4:00 EST on the afternoon of the assassination, J. Edgar Hoover, director of the FBI, had declared that Lee Harvey Oswald killed the president alone and unaided, and imposed this explanation on all who contacted him. He recorded his actions in a series of memoranda for the record. See Hoover memoranda, November 22, 1963, 4:01 EST, 62-109060-59, and 5:15 EST, 62-109060-57, FBI.

71. Early in the afternoon of November 22, FBI investigative clerk Robert G. Renfro prepared a memo for Gordon Shanklin, SAC Dallas Field Office, on a lead phoned in by the Richardson Police Department on a possible suspect in the murder of JFK. "Jimmy George Robinson and members of the National States Rights Party should be considered possible suspects" in the assassination. On the memo is written, "Not necessary to cover as true subject located." This was before Oswald had been identified or charged with the killing of President Kennedy. Renfro to Shanklin, November 22, 1963, serial 89-43-84.

72. An FBI tickler demonstrates this. It possesses no header or date, and it is titled "Federal Bureau of Investigation." Attorney Mark Allen's lawsuit forced it out. Bearing no date, it would appear the bureau prepared it in the 1970s as a damage control tickler against the possibility of a congressional inquiry into the FBI's investigation into the assassination of JFK. It acknowledges that the FBI impeded and controlled the Warren Commission and performed no true investigation. In the quoted words of a key FBI official, Alex Rosen, the "FBI stood around with its pockets open waiting for evidence to drop in." Copy in Weisberg archives. No serial number, referral document stamp, FOI/PA no. 20,326.

73. See, generally, Harold Weisberg *Whitewash* (Hyattstown, Md.: by the author, 1965); Sylvia Meagher, *Accessories after the Fact* (Indianapolis: Bobbs-Merrill, 1967); Howard Roffman, *Presumed Guilty: Lee Harvey Oswald in the Assassination of President Kennedy* (Rutherford, N.J.: Fairleigh Dickinson University Press, 1975). This is illustrated by the Federal Bureau of Investigation, *Investigation of Assassination of President John F. Kennedy, November 22, 1963*, 5 vols. (Washington, D.C.: FBI,

1963). It is Commission Document 1 (CD1) in the unpublished Records of the President's Commission, National Archives. The report does not discuss the evidentiary base of the assassination or examine the Zapruder film. It is, rather, a report on Lee Harvey Oswald as the asserted assassin, his background, career, and associates. The five volumes contain only six sentences on the assassination itself.

74. FBI Headquarters internal memorandum, C. DeLoach to Mohr, November 23, 1963, serial 62-109060-453. Zapruder's name was spelled as "Zapruber" throughout, indicating unfamiliarity with the film.

75. Memorandum, Robert M. Barrett and Ivan D. Lee, SAs FBI, to SAC Dallas, November 29, 1963, serial 89-43-1410; Sorrels memorandum.

76. C. D. DeLoach to Mohr, LMH, November 23, 1963, serial 62-109060-68.

77. Ibid.; Memorandum, FBI agents Robert M. Barrett and Ivan D. Lee, to SAC Gordon Shanklin, Dallas, November 29, 1963, serial 89-43-1410.

78. Barrett and Lee Memorandum.

79. Ibid.; cover sheet of package, November 23, 1963, serial 89-43-1A81.

80. SAC to Director FBI, LMH, November 23, 1963, serial 62-109060-1094.

81. Lyle G. Clark, ASAC, to SAC Dallas, LMH, November 25, 1963, serial 89-43-542.

82. Ibid.

83. Barrett and Lee Memorandum, November 29, 1963.

84. Director to SAC, Dallas, December 3, 1963, serial 62-109060-1094.

85. In 1975, just after Weisberg had lectured on a college campus, a member of the audience came up to him and told him what happened at her home; she was an adult child of an FBI agent outraged at her father's behavior; Weisberg interview, 1999.

86. Director to SAC, Dallas, December 6, 1963, serial 89-43-2659.

87. The Sixth Floor Museum at Dealey Plaza in Dallas possesses the radio tape; Gary Mack, Dallas, has a dub of the TV tape

88. Schwartz interview.

89. Stolley interview.

90. Loudon Wainwright, *The Great American Magazine: An Inside History of Life* (New York: Knopf, 1986), 364.

91. Stolley interview; *Image of an Assassination: A New Look at the Zapruder Film* (Orland Park, Ill.: MPI Video, 1998).

92. Patsy Swank, interview by the Sixth Floor Museum, video (1994); Stolley interview. It was not the police station, as sometimes reported.

93. Stolley interview.

94. Ibid.

95. Ibid.; Richard Stolley, "What Happened Next . . . ," *Esquire*, November 1973, 134.

96. Stolley interview.

97. Ibid.

98. Both Stolley and Schwartz interviews stress the uncouth nature of the press.

99. Richard B. Stolley, "Shots Seen round the World," *Entertainment Weekly*, January 17, 1992, 23.

100. Schwartz interview.

101. Ibid. The hastily written account in Rather, *Camera Never Blinks*, 132–133, does not reflect what occurred.

102. Stolley, "Shots Seen round the World," 23–24.

103. Ibid.; Schwartz interview.

104. Stolley interview.

105. Ibid.

106. Stolley and Schwartz interviews.

107. Stolley interview. He states in the video interview that the opening bid was $5,000, but this appears to be incorrect.

108. Stolley, "What Happened Next . . ."; Stolley interview; Richard J. B. Johnston, "Movie Amateur Filmed Attack: Sequence Is Sold to Magazine," *New York Times*, November 24, 1963, 5.

109. The two witness signatures are not on my poor copy of the original and are added in brackets to reflect Schwartz interview.

110. Schwartz interview.

111. Stolley interview.

112. Wainwright, *Great American Magazine*, 369, 376.

113. *Image of an Assassination*; Stolley interview.

114. Quite visible in the poor black-and-white copy in 18H19.

115. Ibid.

116. Stolley interview; Wainwright, *Great American Magazine*, 369.

117. Based on Stolley interview.

118. Stolley, "What," 136.

119. Ibid., 135.

120. Ibid.; the account in Rather, *Camera Never Blinks*, 132–133, is confused and mixes November 23 with the twenty-fifth.

121. Copy of contract, Zapruder file, Audiovisual Division of National Archives.

122. "Abraham Zapruder Dies," *New York Times*, August 31, 1970.

123. Stolley, "What," 262.

124. A typical expression of this public fiction is "Tippitt's [sic] Widow Gets $25,000 Paid for Assassination Movies," *New York Times*, November 28, 1963.

125. Wainwright, *Great American Magazine*, 370; Stolley and Schwartz, interviews; Stolley, "What," 262.

126. Stolley interview.

127. Ibid. Tippit's widow eventually received tax-free donations totaling $647,679, see "Widow of 2d Oswald Victim Wed," *New York Times*, January 30, 1967.

128. "Tippitt's [sic] Widow Gets $25,000."

Chapter 3.
The Film

1. Executive Order 11130, reprinted in *Report of the President's Commission on the Assassination of President John F. Kennedy* (Washington, D.C.: GPO, 1964), 471. The commissioners were Chief Justice of the United States Earl Warren, Senator Richard B. Russell, Senator John Sherman Cooper, Congressman Hale Boggs, Congressman Gerald R. Ford, former head of the Central Intelligence Agency Allen W. Dulles, and John J. McCloy.

2. Executive session transcripts of the President's Commission, December 5, 1963, to January 27, 1964, especially the January 22, 1964, session; copies in Weisberg Archives; Sylvia Meagher, *Accessories after the Fact* (Indianapolis: Bobbs-Merrill, 1967), 316–326; Harold Weisberg, *Whitewash* (Hyattstown, Md.: by the author, 1965), 8. See also *Report of the President's Commission*, 147. This is known as the Warren Report.

3. The organizational structure is set forth in the Warren Report introduction and in biographical information on the assistant counsels. See *Report of the President's Commission*, 475–482. The Report itself demonstrates this reliance on the bureau by its massive use of FBI experts

for its facts and conclusions. See its index under Federal Bureau of Investigation.

4. Executive session transcript, January 22, 1964, contains the best single illustration of this clash.

5. *Report of the President's Commission*, 98; *Hearings before the President's Commission on the Assassination of President Kennedy*, vol. 5 (Washington, D.C.: GPO, 1964), 138–139; hereinafter cited as 5H138–139.

6. 5H139.

7. Roland Zavada, *Analysis of Selected Motion Picture Photographic Evidence*, Kodak Technical Report (Rochester, N.Y.: Eastman Kodak, 1998), study 4, "The Bell & Howell 414PD 8mm Camera Image Capture Characteristics"; Shaneyfelt, 5H153–154; Lawrence Howe, Vice President, Bell & Howe Company, "Certificate of Gift," for the record, December 12, 1966, reproduced in Harold Weisberg, *Photographic Whitewash*, 2d ed. (Frederick, Md.: by the author, 1976), 148–150.

8. *Report of the President's Commission*, 97, citing the testimony of Agent Shaneyfelt, 5H153–154.

9. Ibid., 98, 108–109.

10. Ibid., 97–109.

11. Ibid., 81–85, 118–137.

12. Ibid., 115; 5H153–154.

13. 3H403.

14. 3H402.

15. 3H405.

16. 3H407.

17. 3H410.

18. 5H153–154. The testimony was hearsay, Agent Shaneyfelt reporting what the agents who made the tests had told him, a frequently encountered device by the Commission staff in taking crucial information.

19. 3H402–406.

20. FBI firearms expert Robert Frazier's testimony, 3H405–409, CE555. The telescopic scope would not adjust, and screws were "changed to move the crosshairs." Among other defects, the spring mounting of the scope did not stabilize, the ring blade adjuster shifted, and elevation and windage could not be maintained; Harold Weisberg, *Never Again* (New York: Carroll and Graf, 1995), 302.

21. Testimony of Ronald Simmons, Chief of the Infantry Weapons Evaluation Branch of the Ballistics Research Laboratory, March 31, 1964, 3H443–451; CE576–578.

22. Weisberg, *Never Again*, 303; Simmons, 3H446–447.

23. Lt. Col. A. G. Folson Jr., U.S. Marine Corps, Head, Records Branch. Personnel Department, by Direction of the Commandant of the Marine Corps, to J. Lee Rankin, General Counsel, President's Commission, June 8, 1964, Anderson Exhibit No. 1, 19H16–18.

24. *Report of the President's Commission*, 97.

25. For example, ibid., 111.

26. Ibid., 19.

27. Ibid., 110–111.

28. Ibid., 98; 5H150–151, 159.

29. *Report of the President's Commission*, 97–109, especially 105.

30. Ibid., 98.

31. Ibid., 112.

32. Ibid., 19.

33. Ibid., 92–96.

34. CE 902; *Report of the President's Commission*, 110.

35. *Report of the President's Commission*, 109.

36. 19HCE902.

37. Patrolman L. L. Hill called it in over his radio: "I have one guy that was

possibly hit by a ricochet from the bullet off the concrete"; *Report of the President's Commission*, 116. Deputy Sheriff Eddy R. Walthers examined the area (7H547, 553). Two newsmen photographed the spot, James Underwood, television movie (Commission Document 1395, 34, Warren Commission records, National Archives), and Tom C. Dillard, *Dallas Morning News* photographer (ibid., 35).

38. *Report of the President's Commission*, 116.

39. Ibid., 111–117.

40. See, for example, Weisberg, *Whitewash*; Meagher, *Accessories*; and, Howard Roffman, *Presumed Guilty: Lee Harvey Oswald in the Assassination of President Kennedy* (Rutherford, N.J.: Fairleigh Dickinson University Press, 1975).

41. 5H70.

42. 3H439; CE 399, which is the whole bullet recovered at the hospital and now in the JFK Collection in the National Archives.

43. *Report of the President's Commission*, 555; 3H399.

44. Ibid., 43–45.

45. Ibid., 44, prints Commission Exhibit 346.

46. Randy Mason, "Three Special Lincolns," *Henry Ford Museum and Greenwich Village Herald* 11, no. 1 (1981).

47. 4H114, 128.

48. Weisberg, *Photographic Whitewash*, 145, where he reproduces J. Edgar Hoover's letter to "Dear Miss," December 14, 1965; the director without blush blames the falsifying FBI exhibit on the printers.

49. 18H1-80.

50. J. Edgar Hoover to Lee Rankin, June 22, 1964, serial 62-109060-3540.

51. JFK, Warner Studios, 1991; Oliver Stone and Zachary Sklar, *JFK: The Book of the Film* (New York: Applause, 1992).

Chapter 4.
Ownership, Copyright, and the Zapruder Film

1. Loudon Wainwright, *Life: The Great American Magazine* (New York: Knopf, 1986); Richard B. Stolley, "What Happened Next . . . ," *Esquire*, November 1973, 134–135, 262–263; Stolley interview by the Sixth Floor Museum, video (1994); Theodore H. White, *In Search of History* (New York: Harper and Row, 1978); Thomas Thompson, *Celebrity* (Garden City, N.Y.: Doubleday, 1982); *Life* magazine issues November 29, 1963–1967.

2. The published volumes connected with the two major investigations of the murder do not discuss the issue. See the President's Commission on the Assassination of President John F. Kennedy, *Report*, and 26 volumes of *Hearings before the President's Commission*, all published by the GPO in 1964, and the U.S. Congress, House, Select Committee on Assassinations, *Report*, and twelve volumes of *Hearings before the Select Committee on Assassinations*, 95th Cong., 2d sess., 1979. After extensive review of JFK assassination materials, the Assassination Records Review Board did not address the issue; *Final Report of the Assassinations Records Review Board* (Washington, D.C.: GPO, 1998).

3. No mention appears in the Warren Commission executive session transcripts, December 1963 through September 1964, or in volumes 1–15 of its hearings, *Hearings before the President's Commission on the Assassination of President Kennedy* (Washington, D.C.: GPO, 1964). The publications of two members of the Commission and two assistant counsels of its staff do not address the subject: commissioner Earl Warren, *The Memoirs of Earl*

Warren (Garden City, N.Y.: Doubleday, 1977); commissioner Gerald R. Ford, *Portrait of the Assassin* (New York: Simon and Schuster, 1965); counsel David W. Belin, *November 22, 1963: You Are the Jury* (New York: New York Times, 1973); and counsel Arlen Specter, *Passion for Truth* (New York: William Morrow, 2000).

4. Discussion with Ray Marcus, Los Angeles.

5. Wainwright, *Life*, 359–363, describes the scene.

6. Ibid., 357–359.

7. Ibid., 376.

8. Ibid.

9. Presumably a color copy; Richard Levine, "Film of Kennedy Torn, 'Life' Says," *Baltimore Sun*, December 22, 1966, Weisberg Archives, Frederick, Maryland. Levine's article was based on Weisberg's tutoring and upon his use of Weisberg's archives, neither mentioned in the article. Weisberg would also be the source of and tutoring for Levine's several other articles on the JFK assassination.

10. Ibid.

11. Richard Warren Lewis and Lawrence Schiller, *The Scavengers and Critics of the Warren Report: The Endless Paradox* (New York: Delacorte Press, 1967), 127.

12. Ibid.

13. *Hearings before*, vol. 5, 19; hereinafter cited as 18H19.

14. 18H20.

15. 5H138.

16. That day Assistant Counsel Specter took the testimony of four individuals, Thomas J. Kelley, then an inspector for the Secret Service (5H129–134, 175–176); Robert Frazier, FBI firearms expert (5H165–175); Lyndal Shaneyfelt, FBI photographic expert (5H138–165, 176–178); and Leo Gauthier, FBI models and displays expert (135–138).

17. 5H139.

18. J. Edgar Hoover to J. Lee Rankin, General Counsel, President's Commission, April 21, 1964, Commission records, copy in Zapruder file, Weisberg Archives, Frederick, Maryland.

19. 5H139. The printed transcript of the hearing contains an obvious typographical error of 434 for 334.

20. One set to the Commission, one to the Secret Service, and one to the FBI. Hoover's letter to Rankin recognizes "169 slides" were received.

21. 5H138–139.

22. Robert H. Bahmer, Archivist of the United States, to Harold Weisberg, Hyattstown, Maryland, March 3, 1967, Zapruder file, Weisberg Archives, states that 169 slides were received.

23. 18H1–80.

24. There was no technical or financial reason the frames could not have been printed in color, one to a page on clay-coated stock. The Government Printing Office regularly printed books in color.

25. It was not until a month and a half later that Specter laid the basis in testimony about the film from Zapruder and the plaza, making this June 4 questioning and testimony of an expert as well as viewing the film quite at odds with conventional legal principles.

26. 5H178.

27. 5H177.

28. Ibid.

29. 5H178.

30. Zapruder file, Weisberg Archives; interview with Weisberg; Harold Weisberg, *Whitewash II* (Hyattstown, Md.: by the author, 1966), 213.

31. Based on a reading of the Commission executive session minutes and the 26 volumes, previous cited. On Spec-

ter's role, see Weisberg, *Specter v. Specter* (Frederick, Md.: by the author, CD-ROM, 2001), copy in author's files.

32. *Report of the President's Commission.* Commission Exhibit 893 appears on page 102, which includes a photograph of frame 210, "Photograph from the Zapruder Film," as well as two other photographs, one of a May 1964 reenactment, as well as a brief panel of statistical information.

33. 18H19.

34. Harold Weisberg, *Photographic Whitewash*, 2d ed. (Frederick, Md.: by the author, 1976), 19–21, discusses the *Life* reaction.

35. Mark Lane, *Rush to Judgment* (New York: Holt, Rinehart and Winston, 1966); Penn Jones Jr., *Forgive My Grief* (Midlothian, Tex.: Midlothian Mirror, 1966); Sylvia Meagher, *Accessories after the Fact* (Indianapolis: Bobbs-Merrill, 1967); Leo Sauvage, *The Oswald Affair* (Cleveland: World Publishing, 1966); Edward Jay Epstein, *Inquest: The Warren Commission and the Establishment of Truth* (New York: Viking Press, 1966); Richard Popkin, *The Second Oswald* (New York: Avon, 1966); Raymond Marcus, *The Bastard Bullet: A Search for Legitimacy for Commission Exhibit 399* (Los Angeles: Rendell Publications, 1966); Weisberg, *Whitewash II.*

36. William Manchester, *The Death of a President, November 20–November 25, 1963* (New York: Harper and Row, 1967).

37. Barbara Garson, *Mac Bird* (Berkeley, Calif.: Grassy Knoll Press, 1966); Eliot Fremont-Smith, "Books of the Times: Experiments and Fashions," *New York Times*, December 12, 1966, 45; Victor S. Navasky, "One Angel Tests His Wings with 'Mac Bird,'" *New York Times*, December 18, 1966, 7D; Dan Sullivan, 'M' Bird'

Gets Off to Flying Start: It Will 'Open' Tonight after a Profitable Month," *New York Times*, February 22, 1967, 22; "Mac Bird: A Play by Barbara Garson; Songs and Music by John Duffy," 33 rpm recording (New York: Evergreen EVE-004, 1967).

38. Peter Kihss, "4 Critics and 2 Defenders Debate Warren Report on Television," *New York Times*, November 13, 1966, 80; Jack Gould, "TV: Warren Commission Foes Get 3 Hours: 'A Minority Report,'" *New York Times*, 83; and "Lawyers Clash on Warren Panel: Aides of Commission Debate Mark Lane and Author," *New York Times*, November 18, 1966, 26, illustrate the phenomenon. Across the nation numerous programs took place on local talk radio; the White collection of audiotapes at the University of Wisconsin–Stevens Point contains recordings of some.

39. Meagher, in *Accessories after the Fact*, 34–35, notes several articles of the period. *The Minority of One*, a monthly journal of opinion, published numerous articles from 1964 to 1969, as did the *Texas Observer, Los Angeles Free Press*, and others.

40. "A Matter of Reasonable Doubt," *Life*, November 25, 1966; Peter Kihss, "*Life* Magazine Urges 2d Inquiry into Kennedy Killing: Holds Doubts Exist That Oswald Was Sole Assassin. [Senator] Hart Would Oppose Inquiry," *New York Times*, November 21, 1966, 18.

41. Martin Waldron, "Connally Backs the Warren Report: Text of Governor Connally's Statement. Lane Replies," *New York Times*, November 24, 1966, 58.

42. Meagher, *Accessories after the Fact*, 34.

43. Harold Weisberg, *Whitewash*

(Hyattstown, Md.: by the author, 1965), 45.

44. Weisberg, *Whitewash II*, 131–141.

45. Weisberg interview.

46. Levine, "Film of Kennedy Torn."

47. Ibid.

48. "*Life* to Release Today Part of Kennedy Film," *New York Times*, January 30, 1967, 22.

49. Hunt statement as published verbatim in Josiah Thompson, *Six Seconds in Dallas: A Micro-Study of the Kennedy Assassination* (New York: Bernard Geis Associates, 1967), 218.

50. "*Life* to Release Today Part of Kennedy Film."

51. Weisberg, *Photographic Whitewash*, 22.

52. Ibid.; 5H138.

53. Weisberg, *Photographic Whitewash*, 22; 5H138–178.

54. Weisberg, *Photographic Whitewash*, 22–23.

55. Ibid., 23.

56. Ibid.

57. Thompson, *Six Seconds*, 216.

58. Some were also printed as Commission exhibits in the Warren Report.

59. 5H574.

60. House Select Committee on Assassinations, *Investigation of the Assassination of President John F. Kennedy: Appendix to Hearings before the Select Committee on Assassinations*, 95th Cong., 2d sess. 1979, vol. II, 143.

61. Dan Rather, with Mickey Herskowitz, *The Camera Never Blinks: Adventures of a TV Journalist* (New York: William Morrow, 1977), 127–128.

62. Weisberg, *Whitewash*, 206.

63. Weisberg interview.

64. Interviews with Jim Garrison and Penn Jones Jr. Garrison was explicit

when asked if he did so, "Hell, yes, I did!"

65. Interview with Penn Jones Jr.; lectures of his attended by author.

66. This is based on numerous sources, including my personal experiences speaking, lecturing, and being present at the showing of the film at scores of colleges and hundreds of private gatherings over a period of ten years, including University of Wisconsin at Stevens Point, Eau Claire, Whitewater, and Madison, public libraries, high schools, Wives of Lawyers Association, polka bars, and student assassination conferences in Washington, Maryland, and elsewhere. Of the several hundred students active in the era, two suffice to illustrate this point: Dennis MacDonald, now a professor at Anselm College in Manchester, New Hampshire; and George Leopold, now a newspaper reporter in the Washington, D.C., area. Also, interviews with College Park, University of Maryland, Who Killed Kennedy chapter students that functioned as a committee without a leader. Interviews and conversations with numerous individuals, including Hal Verb of San Francisco, Mae Brussells of Los Angeles, Sylvia Meagher of New York City, Harold Weisberg of Frederick, Maryland, and Jim Garrison of New Orleans. In the Jim and Jenifer White Collection at Stevens Point are several audiotapes of San Francisco area meetings and interviews with those who showed the film.

67. *Statutes at Large* 79 (1965): 580–581, made the murder of the president a federal crime. See, too, U.S. House Committee on the Judiciary, *Providing Penalties for Assassination of the President*, 89th Cong., 1st sess., 1965, H. Rept. 488; U.S.

Senate Committee on the Judiciary, *Providing Penalties for Assassination of the President*, 89th Cong., 1st sess., 1965, S. Rept. 498.

68. *Congressional Record*, 89th Cong., 2d sess., September 7, 1965, 111, pt. 17: 23003.

69. Ibid.

70. *USA v. One 6.5 mm. Mannlicher-Carcano*, 250 FSupp 410 (1966); *John L. King v. USA*, 364 F2d 235 (1966); *John L. King v. USA*, 292 FSupp 767; *USA v. One 6.5 mm. Mannlicher-Carcano*, 406 F2d 1170 (1969).

71. *Marina Oswald Porter v. USA*, 273 F2d 1329 (1965); *Marina Oswald Porter v. USA*, 335 FSupp 498 (1973).

72. *King v. USA*, 292 FSupp 767 (1968).

73. U.S. House Committee on the Judiciary, *Preserving Evidence Pertaining to the Assassination of President Kennedy*, 89th Cong., 1st sess., 1965, H. Rept. 813; U.S. Senate Committee on the Judiciary, *Preserving Evidence Pertaining to the Assassination of President Kennedy*, 89th Cong., 1st sess., 1965, S. Rept. 851.

74. House Committee, *Preserving Evidence*, 5.

75. Ibid.

76. *Congressional Record*, 89th Cong., 2d sess., September 7, 1965, 111, pt. 17: 23002.

77. Ibid.

78. Ibid., 23003. Mathias had read the manuscript of fellow Frederick, Maryland, resident Harold Weisberg's *Whitewash* and had been positively influenced by that "important book." He also attempted to have the influential Democratic congressman Manny Celler from New York read it. The famed New Dealer would have nothing to do with the subject. Mathias also had attempted

to get someone on the *Washington Post* to read the manuscript, but to no avail; Mathias correspondence, Weisberg archives.

79. *Congressional Record*, 89th Cong., 2d sess., September 7, 1965, 111, pt. 17: 23004.

80. Ibid., September 8, 23104.

81. Ibid., 89th Cong., 2d sess., October 4, 111, pt. 19: 25873.

82. Ibid., October 13, 111, pt. 20: 26827.

83. Ibid., October 15, 111, pt. 20: 27075.

84. Ibid., October 16, 111, pt. 20: 27263.

85. Ibid., 27262–27263.

86. Ibid., October 20, 27784.

87. Ibid., October 21, 111, pt. 21: 27907.

88. Ibid., November 2, 28657.

89. *Statutes at Large* 79 (1965): 1185.

90. Ibid.

91. Department of Justice, Office of Attorney General, Notices, "The Acquisition and Preservation by the United States of Items of Evidence Pertaining to the Assassination of President John F. Kennedy," *Federal Register* 31, no. 212, pt. 2 (November 1, 1966): 13968–13974.

92. Ibid.

93. Robert Groden, "A New Look at the Zapruder Film," *Rolling Stone*, April 24, 1975, 24–36; William Shawcross, "The Day of the Conspirator: The Groden Theory," *Sunday Times Magazine* (London), July 27, 1975, 19–23; F. Peter Model and Robert J. Groden, *JFK: The Case for Conspiracy* (New York: Manor Books, 1976).

94. Richard B. Trask, *Pictures of the Pain* (Danvers, Mass.: Yeoman Press, 1994), 118.

95. Ibid., 118–119.

Chapter 5.
Control and Profits,
1975–1997

1. Interviews with Harold Weisberg, attorney James Lesar, and Jerry Policoff.

2. Lesar interview; FOIA disclosures of records and CTIA files in Assassination Archives Records Center, Washington.

3. Interview with Robert Groden, 2003.

4. The author was in attendance and witnessed the affair; Policoff, Groden, and Lesar interviews.

5. FOIA disclosures and CTIA files; Angus MacKenzie, *Secrets: The CIA's War at Home* (Berkeley: University of California Press, 1997).

6. Groden interview.

7. Commission on CIA Activities within the United States, *Report to the President* (Washington, D.C.: GPO, 1975), 257–267; Rockefeller Commission file, Weisberg archives, Frederick, Maryland; Groden interview.

8. Thomas N. Downing, memorandum for the record, January 1976, printed in Groden and Model, JFK, front matter.

9. Liz Smith column, undated clipping, *Los Angeles Times*.

10. Meyer H. Fishbein, October 15, 1974, memorandum to NNA, set of Zapruder documents, ms., Audiovisual Archives Division, National Archives.

11. Ibid.

12. Memorandum of James W. Moore, Director, Audiovisual Archives Division, to Archivist of the United States, April 8, 1975, Audiovisual Division, National Archives.

13. Ibid.

14. Ibid.

15. William Gildea, "Time Inc. Giving Up JFK Film," April 10, 1975, no paper given on clipping, Audiovisual Division.

16. Ibid.

17. Deed of Gift, Audiovisual Division.

18. April 11, 1975, Assignment of Copyright, Audiovisual Division.

19. Memorandum, April 16, 1975, J. Moore to Director of Archives, Audiovisual Division.

20. James E. O'Neill to James R. Shepley, April 24, 1975, Audiovisual Division.

21. James W. Moore, Final Report on Transfer, April 29, 1975, Audiovisual Division.

22. Change of Holdings Report, May 12, 1975, James W. Moore, Audiovisual Division.

23. Robert M. Trien, to James O'Neill, May 13, 1975, Audiovisual Division.

24. Moore to Trien, June 3, 1975, Audiovisual Division.

25. Receipt, Dick Myers, June 29, 1978, Audiovisual Division.

Chapter 6.
Profits First

1. Harold Weisberg, *Whitewash* (Hyattstown, Md.: by the author, 1965), and *Whitewash II* (Hyattstown, Md.: by the author, 1966); Edward Jay Epstein, *Inquest: The Warren Commission and the Establishment of Truth* (New York: Viking Press, 1966); Mark Lane, *Rush to Judgment: A Critique of the Warren Commission's Inquiry into the Murder of President John F. Kennedy, Officer J. D. Tippit, and Lee Harvey Oswald* (New York: Holt, Rinehart and Winston, 1966).

2. Josiah Thompson, *Six Seconds in Dallas: A Micro-Study of the Kennedy Assassination* (New York: Bernard Geis Associates, 1967), xv–xvi.

3. Ibid., 17.

4. *Time Incorporated v. Bernard Geis Associates, Bernard Geis, Josiah Thompson, and Random House, Inc.*, No. 67 Civ. 4736. 293 FSupp 130 (S. Dist. N.Y. 1967).

5. Loudon Wainwright, "Editorial," *Life*, October 7, 1967.

6. Thompson, *Six Seconds*, xvi.

7. *Time v. Geis*, 135.

8. Thompson, *Six Seconds*, 17.

9. *Time v. Geis*, 135.

10. Meeting of Assassination Records Review Board, April 2, 1997, transcript in JFK Collection, National Archives.

11. *Time v Geis*, 135.

12. Thompson, *Six Seconds*, 8.

13. *Time v Geis*, 136.

14. Ibid.

15. Ibid.

16. Ibid.

17. Minutes, Assassination Records Review Board; Lesar interview.

18. Minutes, Assassination Records Review Board, National Archives.

Chapter 7.
A Student, a Scholar, and the Zapruder Film

1. *Gerard Alexander Selby, Jr., and Harold Weisberg, plaintiffs, v. Henry G. Zapruder and the LMH Company, defendants*, DC Cir., case number 88-3043.

2. *New York Times*, October 26, 1988.

3. *Selby v. Zapruder*, plaintiff's brief.

4. Ibid.

5. See also Harold Weisberg, *Post Mortem* (Frederick, Md.: by the author, 1975), 55–56, 91, 503–504.

6. *Selby v. Zapruder*.

7. Sources who prefer to remain anonymous.

8. *Selby v. Zapruder*.

9. Ibid.

10. James H. Lesar to William Murphy, Chief, Motion Picture Sound and Video Branch, National Archives and Records Administration, November 19, 1987, *Selby v. Zapruder*.

11. Leslie Waffen, National Archives, to James Lesar, December 4, 1987, *Selby v. Zapruder*.

12. James H. Lesar to Henry Zapruder, January 21, 1988, *Selby v. Zapruder*.

13. Henry Zapruder to James H. Lesar, March 2, 1988, *Selby v. Zapruder*.

14. Lesar to Zapruder, March 4, 1988, *Selby v. Zapruder*.

15. Ibid., May 27.

16. Ibid.

17. Robert Groden and F. Peter Model, *JFK: The Case for Conspiracy* (New York: Manor Books, 1976).

18. *Selby v. Zapruder*.

19. *Reasonable Doubt* (Laurel, Md.: CS Films, 1988).

20. David Magolick, "At the Bar," *New York Times*, November 25, 1988.

21. Melville B. Nimmer, *Nimmer on Freedom of Speech: A Treatise on the Theory of the First Amendment* (New York: Matthew Bender, 1984), together with a Supplement by Rodney A. Smolla (New York: Matthew Bender, 1992). Separate pagination.

22. Nimmer, *Nimmer on Freedom of Speech*, Supplement, 74.

23. The other was the My Lai incident in the Vietnam War.

24. Nimmer, *Nimmer on Freedom of Speech*, 2-74–75.

25. Ibid., 2-78.

Chapter 8.
Prisoners of Preconception

1. I attended two of his lectures.

2. See Harold Weisberg, *Picturing the Corruption of the JFK Assassination: Robert Groden*, unpublished ms. (Frederick, Md.: by the author, CD-ROM, 1996).

3. *Hearings before the Select Committee on Assassinations*, vol. 1 (Washington, D.C.: GPO, 1979), 111–112; hereinafter cited as IH111-112. Also IVH414–415; VH420–421; VIH131–138.

4. Robert B. Cutler, *The Umbrella Man: Evidence of Conspiracy* (Beverly Farms, Mass.: R. B. Cutler, 1975); Cutler, *The Day of the Umbrella Man* (Beverly Farms, Mass.: R. B. Cutler, 1980).

5. Diagram of fléchette in umbrella is in IVH433.

6. IH113–115; IVH428–453.

7. IVH439.

8. IVH452–453.

9. I viewed the Rather overlay several times at various JFK conferences in the 1970s.

10. Dan Rather, with Mickey Herskowitz, *The Camera Never Blinks: Adventures of a TV Journalist* (New York: William Morrow, 1977), 128.

11. Ibid., 125.

12. Ibid., 128.

13. Harold Weisberg, *Whitewash* (Hyattstown, Md.: by the author, 1965), 104–105.

14. Harold Weisberg, *Whitewash II* (Hyattstown, Md.: by the author, 1966), 213–214.

15. Ibid., 214.

16. *Hearings before the President's Commission on the Assassination of President Kennedy*, vol. 7 (Washington, D.C.: GPO, 1964), 575; hereinafter cited as 7H575.

17. 5H155.

18. Alvarez file, Weisberg archives.

19. George Greenstein, "Luis's Gadgets," *American Scholar* 61 (winter 1992): 90–98; Luis W. Alvarez, "A Physicist Examines the Kennedy Assassination Film," *American Journal of Physics* 44, no. 9 (September 1976): 813–827.

20. Alvarez records obtained under FOIA request by Harold Weisberg, in Alvarez file, Weisberg archives.

21. Greenstein, "Luis's Gadgets," 90.

22. IH430–434, 440–441; IIH4–5, 8–15, 123, 130–137, 144, 173; VIH15, 19–32, 43.

23. See a critique of Alvarez's science in Michael A. Stroscio, "More Physical Insight into the Assassination of President Kennedy," *Physics and Society* 25, no. 4 (October 1996): 7–8: "It [is] extremely difficult to use Alvarez's method to support the Warren Commission's single gunman, three bullet theory and their conclusion that there was no conspiracy." Physicists A. E. Snyder and Margaret M. Snyder, in "The Alvarez Analysis of the Zapruder Film," *Dateline: Dallas*, summer 1992, 20–23, examined the Alvarez experiments and found "the evidence is only marginally consistent with the theory." They concluded that more experiments were needed to resolve the problems they found in it. Assassination critic Douglas DeSalles, M.D., carefully replicated Alvarez's melon shooting on thirty melons, videotaped his shots, and found "no significant motion of the target"; see Douglas DeSalles, "Follow-Up and Continuation to First Shot/First Hit Circa Z-190," *Kennedy Assassination Chronicles* 5, no. 3 (fall 1999): 20–23.

24. Hoover to Rankin, December 4, 1964, copy printed in Harold Weisberg, *Photographic Whitewash*, 2d ed. (Frederick, Md.: by the author, 1976), 143.

25. Weisberg files, private information.

26. CIA and Zapruder film file, Weisberg archives.

27. President's Commission on CIA Activities within the United States, *Report to the President by the Commission on CIA*

Activities within the United States (Washington, D.C.: GPO, 1975).

28. Discussed in the new matter in Weisberg, Photographic Whitewash, epilogue.

29. Weisberg, Photographic Whitewash, 303, reproduces the chart.

30. Ibid.

31. Ibid. The times, number, and sequence were incompatible with the official findings and required another rifleman or riflemen to have fired the shots..

32. Weisberg, Photographic Whitewash, 302.

33. Belin never refers to them. See President's Commission on CIA Activities, Report to the President.

34. Conversation with Jim Garrison, 1974.

35. Based on interviews with Weisberg, who was in New Orleans at the time; VIIH172, 200, 254, 264, 288–289.

36. John K. Lattimer, Kennedy and Lincoln. Medical and Ballistic Comparisons of Their Assassinations (New York: Harcourt Brace Jovanovich, 1980), 242.

37. Ibid., 169, 174, 243–246.

38. VIIH289.

39. Ibid., 200.

40. Harold Weisberg, Post Mortem (Frederick, Md.: by the author, 1975), 386–402.

41. The Warren Report, for example, depicts Oswald as essentially procommunist. See Report of the President's Commission on the Assassination of President John F. Kennedy (Washington, D.C.: GPO, 1964), 375–422.

42. For an account of Oswald's anticommunist writings and activities, see 16H243; his writings 16H283–434, 442;

Commission Exhibit 97, 16H422–423, Report of the President's Commission, 399.

43. VIIH200.

44. Weisberg, Post Mortem, 594.

45. Ibid., 357–358, 375–378.

46. Edward Jay Epstein, Inquest: The Warren Commission and the Establishment of Truth (New York: Viking Press, 1966), 55, 58.

47. Lattimer, Kennedy and Lincoln, 204.

48. Ibid., 205.

49. Josiah Thompson, Six Seconds in Dallas: A Micro-Study of the Kennedy Assassination (New York: Bernard Geis Associates, 1967), 248, back jacket cover.

50. Ibid., 223. Willis, it will be recalled, snapped the photograph in reaction to hearing a shot, which could make the first shot at or just before frame 190.

51. CE1024, 18H722–802.

52. Report of the President's Commission, 111; CE39717H29–48. Harold Weisberg, Never Again (New York: Carroll and Graf, 1995), is a discussion of the documentary basis of the medical evidence.

53. William Manchester, The Death of a President: November 20–November 25, 1963 (New York: Harper and Row, 1967). Of the numerous articles on the subject, the following illustrates the promotional activity. R. S. Collins, "Kennedy vs. Look, Manchester Harper & Row: An Informal Glossary of Press Relations Techniques," Public Relations Journal 23 (April 1967): 13–15.

54. Bennett Arnold, Jackie, Bobby and Manchester (New York: Bee Line Books, 1967); John Corry, The Manchester Affair (New York: Putnam, 1967); Lawrence Van Gelder, The Untold Story: Why the Kennedys Lost the Book Battle (New York: Award Books, 1967).

55. "Can It Hit One Million?" *Business Week*, April 1, 1967, 28; "Booksellers Assay Sales of Manchester Book," *Publisher's Weekly*, March 13, 1967, 51; *Publisher's Weekly*, March 27, 1967, 52; "People," *Time*, June 28, 1968, 31; Harry Gilroy, "Manchester Book Has Big Advance: Orders Indicate Work Will Be One of Great Sellers," *New York Times*, January 27, 1967, 42.

56. See Sylvia Meagher, "After the Battle, the Book," *The Minority of One* 9 (June 1967): 25–27; Leo Sauvage, "Reviews . . . ," *Ramparts*, June 1967, 51–56; Jake Jacobsen, "Analysis," [Rebuttal to Manchester Book], LBJ Library, Austin; Ronnie Dugger, "William Manchester and Texas," *Texas Observer*, January 20, 1967, 18–19; Dugger, "William Manchester and Texas," *Texas Observer*, February 3, 1967, 10; Dugger, "Manchestered," *Texas Observer*, February 17, 1967, 14–15; Dugger, "The Death of a President: The Book Slanted Morbid, Sentimental, and Valuable; Confusion about LBJ and Youngblood," *Texas Observer*, April 14, 1967, 4–5; Luther A. Huston, "Three Reporters Correct Manchester's Story," *Editor and Publisher*, February 4, 1967, 14; John H. Fenton, "Photo Rebuts Manchester on Johnson Swearing-In," *New York Times*, February 10, 1967, 15; Allan Nevins, "Gargantuan, Honest and Useful, but So Exasperating," *Panorama Magazine*, *Chicago Daily News*, April 8, 1967, 2–3; J. H. Plumb, "The Private Grief of Public Figures," *Saturday Review*, January 21, 1967, 42–45; Richard H. Rovere, "Books: A Question of Taste and Something More," *New Yorker*, April 8, 1967, 172–176; Arthur Schlesinger, "On the Writing of Contemporary History," *Atlantic Monthly*, March 1967, 69–74; and, Garry Wills, "Books-

Arts-Manners: The Lachrymose Mr. Manchester," *National Review*, May 30, 1967, 591–592.

57. Interview with Harold Weisberg, who worked in the archives during that period; Barbara Tuchman, "The Historian's Opportunity," *Saturday Review*, February 25, 1967, 27, 31, 71.

58. Manchester, *Death of a President*, 154, 157.

59. 7H569–576.

60. 7H573.

61. Ibid.

62. 7H571.

63. John Kaplan, "The Assassins," *American Scholar* 36 (spring 1967): 271–306.

64. John Kaplan, "The Assassins," *Stanford Law Review* 19 (1967): 1110–1151.

65. Kaplan, "The Assassins," *American Scholar*, 272.

66. Robin Winks, ed., *The Historian as Detective: Essays on Evidence* (New York: Harper and Row, [1969]).

67. Ibid., 371–419, quotation on 371.

68. Ibid., 419.

69. Charles Roberts, *The Truth about the Assassination* (New York: Grosset and Dunlap, 1967), quotation on cover.

70. Ibid., 102.

71. *Report of the President's Commission*, 105.

72. Ibid., 97.

73. 5H139.

74. *Report of the President's Commission*, 101.

75. Josiah Thompson, *Six Seconds in Dallas: A Micro-Study of the Kennedy Assassination* (New York: Bernard Geis Associates, 1967), 57. Bickel played a major role in supporting the Commission. Alexander M. Bickel, "The Failure of the Warren Report," *Commentary* 12 (October 1966):

31–39; "Leo Sauvage and the Warren Commission," *New Leader*, November 21, 1966, 19–21; "Re-examining the Warren Report," *New Republic*, January 7, 1967, 25–28; "Return to Dallas," *New Republic*, December 23, 1967, 34; "Back to the Attack," *New Republic*, June 22, 1968, 28–29; "CBS on the Warren Report: How Many Bullets?" *New Republic*, pt. 1, July 15, 1967, 29–30, and "CBS on the Warren Report: How Many Bullets?" *New Republic*, pt. 2, August 19, 1967, 30–34; Leo Sauvage, "Professor Bickel and the Warren Report," *New Leader*, November 7, 1966, 16–19; "Letters from Readers: The Warren Report [Bickel reply to critics]," *Commentary* 63 (April 1967): 4–20.

76. Stephen White, *Should We Now Believe the Warren Report?* (New York: Macmillan, 1968), contains the script of the four shows plus commentary.

77. Ibid., 231.

78. Ibid., 73–78.

79. Ibid., 202–203.

80. Ibid.

81. *Report of the President's Commission*, 101.

82. CE1312, 22H485. Positioned on the boxes and firing from them, the evidence is he would have to have fired through the double panes of glass.

83. *Report of the President's Commission*, 99, which is CE887, a photograph showing the window open.

84. Douglas DeSalles, "Follow-Up and Continuation to First Shot/First Hit Circa Z-190," *Kennedy Assassination Chronicles* 5, no. 3 (fall 1999): 22.

85. George C. Thomson, *The Quest for Truth: (A Quizzical Look at the Warren Report) or How President Kennedy Really Was Assassinated* (Glendale, Calif.: G. C. Thomson Engineering, 1964).

86. George C. Thomson, *The Quest for Truth*, pt. 5, *The Third Man in the Car!!* (Glendale, Calif.: G. C. Thomson Engineering, 1966).

87. *Lindsey K. Springer v. United States, Secret Service, Secret Service Agent William "Bill" Greer, Secret Service Agent, Roy Kellerman, The 1963–1964 Warren Commission,* USDC ND Oklahoma. 96CV 893K.

88. Gerald Posner, *Case Closed: Lee Harvey Oswald and the Assassination of JFK* (New York: Random House, 1993).

89. Harold Weisberg, *Hoax*, unpublished ms. (Frederick, Md.: by the author, 1994), on Posner, examining its factual basis; Weisberg, *Case Open* (New York: Carroll and Graf, 1994), printed about 25 percent of the manuscript. There is an extensive literature on the factual errors in Posner's effort.

90. *Report of the President's Commission*, 112.

91. Ibid., 112–113.

92. Sylvia Meagher, *Accessories after the Fact* (Indianapolis: Bobbs-Merrill, 1967), 27–35; quotation from Dr. Shaw, 4H115–116.

93. Posner, *Case Closed*, 329–330.

94. Oliver Stone and Zachary Sklar, *JFK: The Book of the Film: The Documented Screenplay* (New York: Applause Books, 1992).

95. Jim Garrison, *On the Trail of the Assassins: My Investigation and Prosecution of the Murder of President Kennedy* (New York: Sheridan Press, 1988); Jim Marrs, *Crossfire: The Plot That Killed Kennedy* (New York: Carroll and Graf, 1989).

96. See the extensive Oliver Stone JFK files, Weisberg archives, Frederick, Maryland.

97. George Lardner Jr., "Haggling over History; Zapruders, U.S. Far apart on Price of Zapruder Film," *Washington Post*, June 13, 1998.

98. George Lardner Jr., "Zapruder Film Set for August Video Release; Footage of JFK Assassination Likely to Restart Debate," *Washington Post*, June 26, 1998.

Chapter 9.
Altered Evidence, Altered States

1. Philip H. Melanson, "Hidden Exposure: Cover-Up and Intrigue in the CIA's Secret Possession of the Zapruder Film," *The Third Decade*, November 1984, 13–21.

2. James H. Fetzer, ed., *Assassination Science: Experts Speak Out on the Death of JFK* (Chicago: Catfeet Press, 1997).

3. Harold Weisberg, *Badly Reasoned*, unpublished ms. (Frederick, Md.: By the author, CD-ROM, 1998).

4. Fetzer, *Assassination Science*, 200–211.

5. Ibid., 221–238.

6. Ibid., 249–262.

7. Ibid., 263–344.

8. Ibid., 345–348, 362–366.

9. Roland Zavada, *Analysis of Selected Motion Picture Photographic Evidence*, Kodak Technical Report (Rochester, N.Y.: Eastman Kodak, 1998).

10. Harold Weisberg, *Whitewash* (Hyattstown, Md.: by the author, 1965), 26; Weisberg, *Never Again* (New York: Carroll and Graf, 1995), 301–305.

11. Raymond Marcus, *The Bastard Bullet: A Search for Legitimacy for Commission Exhibit 399* (Los Angeles: Rendell Publications, 1966).

12. Elijah Jordan, "The Role of Philosophy in Social Crisis," *Ethics* 51 (1941): 279–391.

13. Roger Bruce Feinman, *Between the Signal and the Noise: The "Best Evidence" Hoax and David Lifton's War against the Critics of the Warren Commission*, *www.boston.quik.com/amash/etcetera.htm*. I have not utilized attorney Feinman's work.

14. Josiah Thompson, "Why the Zapruder Film *Is* Authentic," *JFK/Deep Politics Quarterly* 4, no. 3 (April 1999): 2.

15. Ibid., 3–10.

16. Hal Verb, "Fetzer's Follies Continued: A Reply," *The Fourth Decade* 5, no. 5 (July 1998): 23–34.

17. Ibid., 34.

18. Erwin Schwartz, interview by the Sixth Floor Museum at Dealey Plaza in Dallas, video (1994).

19. Affidavits of P. M. Chamberlain Jr., Frank R. Sloan, and Tom Nulty, November 22, 1963, in Zavada, *Analysis of Selected*, appendix.

20. Schwartz interview.

21. Harold Weisberg, *Whitewash II* (Hyattstown, Md.: by the author, 1966), 19, 141; Schwartz, interview. Pincher and Schaffer, "The Case," 224–225, do not realize that Phillips was in the Dallas Secret Service office of Presidential Security. They put him in Washington, D.C., in order to cobble together their alleged plot.

22. Thompson, "Why the Zapruder Film," 7.

23. Ibid.

24. Schwartz interview; Myrna Ries, interview by the Sixth Floor Museum, video (1997).

25. Richard Stolley, "What Happened Next . . . ," *Esquire*, November 1973, 134; Richard Stolley, interview by the Sixth Floor Museum, video (1994); Schwartz, interview; Loudon Wainwright, *The Great American Magazine: An Inside History of Life* (New York: Knopf, 1986), 364.

26. Stolley interview.

27. Ibid.

28. 7H352.

29. Schwartz interview.

30. Memorandum of Secret Service agent Max Phillips to [illegible], Novem-

ber 22, 1963, on the receipt of the film from Zapruder. Reprinted in Harold Weisberg, *Photographic Whitewash*, 2d ed. (Frederick, Md.: by the author, 1976), 15.

31. There are few references to films and photographs in the evidentiary base for November 22.

32. Headquarters internal memorandum, C. D. DeLoach to Mohr, November 23, 1963, serial 62-109060-453.

33. Memorandum, FBI agents Robert M. Barrett and Ivan D. Lee, to SAC Gordon Shanklin, Dallas, November 29, 1963, serial 89-43-1410.

34. Bronson snapped Leica still photographs and an 8mm Kodachrome film of the assassination scene. The Dallas FBI office, after having been notified of the film by Eastman Kodak, viewed it. Agent Milton Newson reported, "Film did not depict the President's car at the precise time shots were fired; however, the pictures were not sufficiently clear for identification purposes"; serial 89-43-493, Newson to SAC Dallas, November 25, 1963. When critics discovered the film in 1978, it showed the Texas School Book Depository and windows at the time of the assassination, while the still photograph captured JFK at the time of the assassination. See *Dallas Morning News*, November 26, 1978, 1. See discussion in Weisberg, *Never Again*, 29–31, 344; Weisberg, *Whitewash II*, 142–149, 195–206; Bronson file, Weisberg archives.

35. Weisberg, *Photographic Whitewash*, concerns this point. See FBI SAC Dallas Gordon Shanklin to Headquarters, December 19, 1963, in serial 100-10461-1478a, where he notes agents are not going to acquire film from the professional photographers in the motorcade.

36. Edward Fetzer, ed., *Murder in Dealey Plaza* (Chicago: Catfeet Press, 2000), 319.

37. Noel Twyman, *Bloody Treason: On Solving History's Greatest Murder Mystery: The Assassination of John F. Kennedy* (Rancho Santa Fe, Calif.: Laurel Publishing, 1997).

38. Harold Weisberg, *Badly Reasoned*, unpublished ms. (Frederick, Md.: by the author, 1998).

39. Twyman, *Bloody Treason*, 117–121.

40. Ibid., 122–166.

41. Ibid., 141.

42. Ibid., 134.

43. Ibid., 142.

44. Ibid., 143.

45. Ibid., 134–149, 545–561.

46. Ibid., 141; Dick Russell, *The Man Who Knew Too Much* (New York: Carroll and Graf, 1992). Russell's book has no merit.

47. Twyman, *Bloody Treason*, 141.

48. Weisberg interview; Rothermel files, Weisberg archives.

49. Twyman, *Bloody Treason*, 118–119.

50. Ibid., 118.

51. Ibid., 119.

52. Ibid., 203.

53. 6H373.

54. 6H374.

55. 6H373.

56. Ibid.

57. Twyman, *Bloody Treason*, 146.

58. Weisberg, *Whitewash*, 119–134.

59. 16H283–434.

60. *Report of the President's Commission*, 399.

61. Following Weisberg, *Badly Reasoned*, 184.

62. David S. Lifton, *Best Evidence. Disguise and Deception in the Assassination of John F. Kennedy* (New York: Macmillan, 1980).

63. Ibid., 555–557. See, for critique, Feinman, *Between the Signal and the Noise;* Harold Weisberg, *Autopsy of a JFK Assassination Best Seller: Best Evidence as Bad Evidence,* unpublished ms. (Frederick, Md.: by the author, CD-ROM, 2000).

64. Weisberg, *Autopsy of a JFK Assassination Best Seller,* 356.

65. Weisberg interview.

66. Harold Weisberg, *Photographic Whitewash,* 2d ed. (Frederick, Md.: by the author, 1976), 297–304.

67. Lifton, *Best Evidence,* 555–556.

68. Ibid.

69. Untitled, undated, briefing board, Central Intelligence Agency, in Weisberg, *Photographic Whitewash,* 303.

70. See a description in William Manchester, *The Death of a President, November 20–November 25, 1963* (New York: Harper and Row, 1967), as well as the Parkland nurses' account before the Warren Commission: Nelson, previously cited; Margaret M. Henchliffe, 6H139–143; and Diana Bowron, 6H134–139.

71. 6H146.

72. CE1024, 18H771, 779; Rufus Youngblood, *Twenty Years in the Secret Service: My Life with Five Presidents* (New York: Simon and Schuster, 1973), 129.

73. CE1024, 779.

74. Ibid., 677.

75. Godfrey McHugh, "Letter to the Editor," *Time,* February 17, 1981.

76. Kenneth P. O'Donnell and David R. Powers, *"Johnny We Hardly Knew Ye!": Memories of John Fitzgerald Kennedy* (Boston: Little, Brown, 1972); and Lawrence F. O'Brien, *No Final Victory: A Life in Politics* (Garden City, N.Y.: Doubleday, 1974), are memoirs of three aides.

77. Lifton, *Best Evidence,* 678, excludes the majority of Kennedy's staff from his discussion.

78. Jake Jacobsen, "Analysis," ms., Lyndon Johnson Library, unpaginated.

79. Agent Roy Kellerman Report to Chief Rowley, February 17, 1964, JFK Collection, National Archives.

80. Mentioned by Lifton, *Best Evidence,* 677–678.

81. Manchester, *Death of a President,* 321.

82. Lifton, *Best Evidence,* 681–683.

83. Manchester, *Death of a President,* 383.

84. Weisberg file of his Freedom of Information Act request for copies of Lifton's FOIA requests for the Military District of Washington records, Weisberg archives; Lifton, *Best Evidence,* 393–394.

85. Lifton, *Best Evidence,* 579.

86. Interview with Colonel Russell Madison, Frederick, Maryland; Weisberg interview.

87. McHugh letter to *Time;* Manchester, *Death of a President,* 399.

88. James W. Sibert and Francis X. O'Neill Jr., "Results of Autopsy on John F. Kennedy," November 26, 1963, serial 89-30; reprinted in Harold Weisberg, *Post Mortem* (Frederick, Md.: by the author, 1975), 532–536.

In early 1966, Weisberg discovered the report in the records of the Warren Commission in the National Archives. Later in the year he assisted Viking Press in its publicity for Edward Jay Epstein's *Inquest: The Warren Commission and the Establishment of the Truth* (New York: Viking Press, 1966) by suggesting that the report be reproduced and distributed with the publicity packets. This the publisher did. Lifton states that his first knowledge of the report was from Epstein's book.

89. 6H137.

90. 6H141.

91. Staff interview of James W. Sibert, August 29, 1977, House Select Committee on Assassinations, doc. 002191, President John F. Kennedy Assassination Records Collection, National Archives, copy in Weisberg archives.

92. James Fox X rays of JFK, Weisberg archives.

93. Twyman, *Bloody Treason*, xi.

94. Fetzer, *Assassination Science*, 461.

95. Anthony Summers, *Conspiracy* (New York: Paragon House, 1989), 477–486.

Chapter 10.
Official Federal Policy:
Do Not Investigate

1. "Telephone Conversation between Bill Moyers and Dean Rostow, Yale Law School," November 24, 1963, transcript, LBJ library; Moyers was LBJ's principal assistant.

2. Biographies of Johnson include Robert Dallek, *Lone Star Rising: Lyndon Johnson and His Times, 1908–1960* (New York: Norton, 1991), and *Flawed Giant: Lyndon Johnson and His Times, 1961–1973* (New York: Oxford University Press, 1998). See also Eric F. Goldman, *The Tragedy of Lyndon Johnson* (New York: Knopf, 1969). Critical books include Ronald Dugger, *Politician: The Life and Times of Lyndon Johnson: The Drive for Power, from the Frontier to the Master of the Senate* (New York: Norton, 1975); Robert Sherrill, *Accidental President* (New York: Grossman, 1967); J. Everts Haley, *A Texan Looks at Lyndon: A Study in Illegitimate Power* (Canyon, Tex.: Palo Duro, 1964); Robert Caro, *The Years of Lyndon Johnson*, 2 vols. (New York: Knopf, 1982).

3. The literature on the subject includes the following: Donald Janson and Bernard Eismann, *The Far Right* (New York: McGraw-Hill, 1963); David Caute, *The Great Fear: The Anti-Communist Purge under Truman and Eisenhower* (New York: Simon and Schuster, 1978); William Albertson, *The Trucks Act: Michigan's Blueprint for a Fascist State* (New York: New Century, 1952); James Aronson, *The Press and the Cold War* (Indianapolis: Bobbs-Merrill, 1970); Eleanor Bontecou, *The Federal Loyalty-Security Program* (Ithaca, N.Y.: Cornell University Press, 1953); Frank J. Donner, *The Un-Americans* (New York: Ballantine, 1961); Harvey Matusow, *False Witness* (New York Cameron and Kahn, 1955); Richard H. Rovere, *The American Establishment* (New York: Harcourt, Brace, 1962); Albert E. Kahn, *Matusow Affair: Memoir of a National Scandal* (Mt. Kisco, N.Y.: Moyer Bell Limited, 1987); Carl Beck, *Contempt of Congress: A Study of the Prosecutions Initiated by the Committee on Un-American Activities, 1945–1957* (New York: Da Capo, 1974); John Major, *The Oppenheimer Hearing* (New York: Stein and Day, 1971); Robert C. Williams, *Klaus Fuchs: Atom Spy* (Cambridge: Harvard University Press, 1987); Walter Schneir and Miriam Schneir, *Invitation to an Inquest* (Garden City, N.Y.: Doubleday, 1965), and *New York Review of Books*, September 29, 1983; Roger Anberg, "The Rosenberg Case Revisited," *American Historical Review* 81 (April 1978): 388–400; I. F. Stone, *The Truman Era: 1945–1952* (New York: Monthly Review, 1953); Stone, *The Hidden History of the Korean War: 1950–1951* (New York: Monthly Review, 1952); Stone, *The Haunted Fifties: 1953–1963* (Boston: Little, Brown, 1988); and Ellen W. Schrecker, *No Ivory Tower: McCarthyism and the Universities* (New York: Oxford University Press, 1986).

4. James Bamford, *Body of Secrets:*

Anatomy of the Ultra-secret National Security Agency (New York: Doubleday, 2001), 64–91.

5. Among the books on Hoover are J. Fred Cook, The FBI Nobody Knows (New York: Macmillan, 1964); Max Lowenthal, The Federal Bureau of Investigation (New York: William Sloane, 1950); H. Montgomery Hyde, Room 3603 (New York: Farrar, Straus and Cudahy, 1963); Donald Downes, The Scarlet Thread (New York: British Book Centre, 1953); Herbert Mitgang, Dangerous Dossiers: Exposing the Secret War against America's Greatest Authors (New York: D. I. Fine, 1988); Cedric Belfrage, The Frightened Giant (London: Secker and Warburg, 1957); Cedric Belfrage, American Inquisition, 1945–1960 (Indianapolis: Bobbs-Merrill, 1973); Cedric Belfrage and James Aronson, Something to Guard: The Stormy Life of the National Guardian, 1948–1967 (New York: Columbia University Press, 1978); Len De Caux, Labor Radical: From the Wobblies to the C.I.O. (Boston: Beacon Press, 1970); David R. Shannon, The Decline of American Communism: A History of the Communist Party of the United States since 1945 (New York: Harcourt, Brace, 1959).

Athan G. Theoharis and John Stuart Cox, Boss: J. Edgar Hoover and the Great American Inquisition (Philadelphia: Temple University Press, 1988); William C. Sullivan, The Bureau: My Thirty Years in Hoover's FBI (New York: Norton, 1979); Kenneth O'Reilly, Hoover and the Un-Americans: The FBI, HUAC, and the Red Menace (Philadelphia: Temple University Press, 1983); U.S. Congress, House, Committee on Government Operation, "Inquiry into the Destruction of Former FBI Director J. Edgar Hoover's Files and FBI Record," Hearings 94th Cong., 1st sess., December 1, 1975; Athan G. Theoharis, J. Edgar

Hoover, Sex, and Crime: An Historical Antidote (Chicago: Ivan Dee, 1995); Ralph de Toledano, J. Edgar Hoover: The Man in His Time (New Rochelle, N.Y.: Arlington House, 1973); Donald Cruse Ferber, "J. Edgar Hoover's Concept of Academic Freedom and Its Impact on Scientists during the McCarthy Era" (Ph.D. diss., University of Maryland, 1986); Hank Messick, John Edgar Hoover: An Inquiry into the Life and Times of J. Edgar Hoover, and His Relationship to the Continuing Partnership of Crime, Business, and Politics (New York: McKay, 1972); William W. Keller, The Liberals and J. Edgar Hoover: Rise and Fall of a Domestic Intelligence State (Princeton, N.J.: Princeton University Press, 1989); J. L. Schott, No Left Turns (New York: Praeger Press, 1975); Anthony Summers, Official and Confidential: The Secret Life of J. Edgar Hoover (New York: Putnam, 1993); Richard Gid Power, Secrecy and Power: The Life of J. Edgar Hoover (New York: Free Press, 1986); Claire Bond Potter, War on Crime: Bandits, G-Men, and the Politics of Mass Culture (New Brunswick, N.J.: Rutgers University Press, 1998); Allan Theoharis, Chasing Spies: How the FBI Failed in Counterintelligence but Promoted the Politics of McCarthyism in the Cold War Years (Chicago: Ivan Dee, 2002)

6. Of the books I have read supporting the official conclusions, none mention the Katzenbach memorandum. Specifically I recall these: Gerald Posner, Case Closed: Lee Harvey Oswald and the Assassination of JFK (New York: Random House, 1993); William Manchester, The Death of a President, November 20–November 25, 1963 (New York: Harper and Row, 1967); Edward Jay Epstein, Legend: The Secret World of Lee Harvey Oswald (New York: McGraw-Hill, 1978); Jim Bishop, The Day Kennedy Was Shot (New York: Funk and

Wagnalls, 1968); Gerald Ford, *Portrait of the Assassin* (New York: Simon and Schuster, 1965); Jean Davison, *Oswald's Game* (New York: Norton, 1983); Priscilla Johnson McMillan, *Marina and Lee* (New York: Harper and Row, 1977); Arlen Specter, *Passion for Truth* (New York: Morrow, 2000); David W. Belin, *November 22, 1963: You Are the Jury* (New York: New York Times, 1973).

7. Belmont to Tolson, November 24, 1964, 4:15 P.M.. serial 105-82555-95.

8. Ibid.

9. FBI liaison to the Department of Justice, Assistant Director Courtney A. Evans, to Alan H. Belmont, FBI Headquarters, November 25, 1963, serial 62-109060-1399.

10. Belmont to Sullivan, November 25, 1963, serial 105-82555-243.

11. Secret Service logs of LBJ, LBJ Library.

12. Hoover memorandum for the record, 4:01 P.M., November 22, 1963, 62-109060-59.

13. Ibid., 5:15 P.M., 62-109060-56, and no time, 62-109060-58. There is nothing encountered in the massive record base of the assassination that reveals anyone other than Oswald was ever considered an assassin.

14. Memorandum, November 22, 1963, Investigative Clerk Robert G. Renfro to SAC Gordon Shanklin, DFO, serial 89-43-84.

15. C. DeLoach to Mohr, November 23, 1963, 62-109060-453.

16. DJ129-11 (a Department of Justice file number). It was first released to critic Harold Weisberg, who filed a request with the Department of Justice for records. Before he had to sue to force them out, the department released them. In them was this copy, which bore the stamped date of May 21, 1965, and was initialed HPW, the initials of Howard Willens who was the department's representative to the Warren Commission staff. Willens kept the memo out of the files for eighteen months. The next copy Weisberg obtained came from his FOIA suit for the FBI Headquarters file, 62-109060-1399, as cited in a previous note.

17. The communication routing in the FBI headquarters copy found in 62-109060-1399.

18. Melvin A. Eisenberg, Memorandum, February 17, 1964, Commission records, copy in Weisberg archives.

19. *Hearings before the Select Committee on Assassinations of the House of Representatives*, vol. 9 (Washington, D.C.: GPO, 1979), 162–163.

20. *Investigation of Assassination of President John F. Kennedy, November 22, 1963*, 5 vols. (Washington, D.C.: FBI, 1963).

21. CD1, JFK Collection, National Archives.

22. November 1, 1966, *Federal Register*, vol. 31, number 212, 13968–13975, lists Oswald's books; 8H254–255.

23. *Report of the President's Commission on the Assassination of President John F. Kennedy* (Washington, D.C.: GPO, 1964), 439; *Hearings before the President's Commission on the Assassination of President Kennedy*, vol. 4 (Washington, D.C.: GPO, 1964), 453–454; hereinafter cited as 4H453–454.

24. 16H243.

25. 16H283–434.

26. *Report of the President's Commission*, 399; 16H442.

27. Yuri Nosenko file, Weisberg archives.

28. 1H93.

29. *Report of the President's Commission*,

19, 21–22, 122, 244, 287–292, 301–302, 312–313, 315, 326, 331, 342–344, 390, 402, 404, 406–408, 410–413, 419, 435–436, 441–442, 567, 578, 661, 728–732, 734, 739, 744.

30. XIH158.

31. John T. McNaughton to Nicholas Katzenbach, December 16, 1963, Department of Justice file 129-11, Harold Weisberg FOIA suit, McNaughton file, Weisberg archives (courtesy of Clay Ogilvie); L. Niederlehner, Acting General Counsel, DOD, to Frank Wizencraft, Assistant Attorney General, DOJ, September 7, 1967, ibid.

32. Commission records, JFK Collection, National Archives; Howard Roffman, *Presumed Guilty: Lee Harvey Oswald in the Assassination of President Kennedy* (Rutherford, N.J.: Fairleigh Dickinson University Press, 1975), 356–362, prints the document.

33. Department of Justice file 128-11, Harold Weisberg Willens and Katzenbach files, Weisberg archives; Katzenbach file, author's files.

34. *Report of the President's Commission*, ix–xiii.

35. Executive Order 11130, November 30, 1963; reproduced in *Report of the President's Commission*, 471.

36. Ibid.

37. Public Law 202, 88th Cong., 2d sess., December 13, 1963; reproduced in *Report of the President's Commission*, 473–474.

38. Executive Order 11130.

39. Sylvia Meagher, *Accessories after the Fact* (Indianapolis: Bobbs-Merrill, 1967), 458, and generally 458–464.

40. While this is based partially on my own list, the following discuss the number: Richard B. Trask, *Pictures of the Pain: Photography and the Assassination of*

President Kennedy (Danvers, Mass.: Yeoman Press, 1994); Richard E. Sprague, "The Assassination of President John F. Kennedy: The Application of Computers to the Photographic Evidence," *Computers and Automation* 19 (May 1970): 29–60; Harold Weisberg, *Photographic Whitewash*, 2d ed. (Frederick, Md.: by the author, 1976).

41. See Trask, *Pictures of the Pain*; George Lardner Jr., "Film in JFK Assassination Reissued," *Washington Post*, November 11, 1978; "New Clue in JFK Slaying," *San Francisco Bulletin*, November 26, 1978; Wendall Rawls Jr., "New Film Suggests an Oswald Cohort," *New York Times*, November 27, 1978; Earl Golz, "JFK Film May Record Two Gunmen," *Dallas Morning News*, November 26, 1978.

42. FBI Agent Milton Newsom to SAC, 11/25/63, serial 62-109060-456.

43. Ibid.

44. Trask, *Pictures of the Pain*, 278–304, is a history of the film.

45. Newsom to SAC, 11/25/63, serial 89-43-493.

46. Weisberg interview.

47. Trask, *Pictures of the Pain*, 262–277.

48. Ibid.

49. Robert M. Barrett, November 26, 1963, FBI memorandum, serial 100-10461-[755?]; Weisberg, *Photographic Whitewash*, 125–130, 132–133, 278–281, 283.

50. FBI Exhibit 29, *Investigation of Assassination*, 19–20; Commission Document 1 (CD1).

51. Trask, *Pictures of the Pain*, 269, citing 62-109060-1899, 12/13/63, FBI lab report.

52. FBI Exhibit 29.

53. Thomas G. Buchanan, *Who Killed*

Kennedy? (New York: Putnam, 1964) 96–97; and in CE2585, 25H858.96–97.

54. J. Edgar Hoover to J. Lee Rankin, July 27, 1964, in CE2585, 857–862; *Report of the President's Commission*, 644.

55. 7H352.

56. U.S. Secret Service, Forrest Sorrels to Inspector Kelley, memorandum, January 22, 1964; CO 2-34-030; Records of the President's Commission on the Assassination of President Kennedy, National Archives; 7H347–348, 352.

57. WFAA-TV tape, the Sixth Floor Museum at Dealey Plaza in Dallas.

58. As discussed in a previous chapter; Loudon Wainwright, *The Great American Magazine: An Inside History of Life* (New York: Knopf, 1986), 368–369.

59. KRLD-TV and radio tapes, the Sixth Floor Museum; Dan Rather, with Mickey Herskowitz, *The Camera Never Blinks: Adventures of a TV Journalist* (New York: William Morrow, 1977), 125. What he described as occurring on November 23 actually occurred two days later.

60. *Life*, November 29, 1963.

61. For example, Anthony Lewis, "Panel to Reject Theories of Plot in Kennedy Death: Warren Inquiry Is Expected to Dispel Doubts in Europe That Oswald Acted Alone," *New York Times*, June 2, 1964.

62. Interview with Harold Weisberg, who waged a difficult FOIA suit for records connected to the Tague shot; Dillard deposition, 6H162–167; and Weisberg, *Post Mortem* (Frederick, Md.: by the author, 1975), 454–460, 475–487, 608–609.

63. 21H472.

64. Roffman, *Presumed Guilty*, 66–71.

65. 3H405.

66. 17H241.

67. Harold Weisberg, *Never Again* (New York: Carroll and Graf, 1995), 302.

68. 3H447–449.

69. 1H96, 325–327.

70. 19H16–18.

71. Testimony of Dean Andrews, 11H330–331.

72. Testimony of Robert Oswald, 1H325–327; Roffman, *Presumed Guilty*, 225–247.

73. Testimony of Marina Oswald, 1H96.

74. 2H466; 1H327–328.

75. *Report of the President's Commission*, 116.

76. 7H547, 553.

77. Henry Hurt file containing engineer reports, Weisberg archives.

78. 21H475–477.

79. 21H483.

80. 7H469.

81. 7H558–565.

82. 7H563.

83. 7H507–515.

84. 7H508.

85. Baker Exhibit No. 1, 19H112.

86. 7H515–525.

87. CE900, 18H93.

88. 7H569–576.

89. 7H492–497.

90. 7H498–499.

91. 7H499–506.

92. 7H506.

93. 7H525–530.

94. 7H552–558.

95. 7H544–552.

96. 7H531.

97. 7H565–569.

98. 7H577–589.

99. 6H400–427.

100. 2H253–262, 292–294; 6H428–434.

101. 2H262–292.

102. 7H573.

103. *Report of the President's Commission*, 586–591.

104. Weisberg, *Whitewash*, 103–104.

105. 7H573.

106. Ibid.

107. 18H10–12.

108. 7H576.

109. 18H1–80.

110. 18H55.

111. Weisberg, *Post Mortem*, 80.

112. J. Edgar Hoover, quoting an FBI interview with Altgens; J. Edgar Hoover to J. Lee Rankin, June 5, 1964, CD1088, JFK Collection, National Archives.

113. Original (1), color frames (2), black-and-white copies in album (3), color to black-and-white (4), and printed (5).

114. *Report of the President's Commission*, 49.

115. Ibid., 98.

116. Ibid., 98, 115, 109–110.

117. Ibid., 112.

118. Ibid., 63.

119. Ibid., 453.

120. Ibid., 100, 101, 102, 103, 108, 114.

121. Ibid., 99.

Chapter 11.
The Man in the Doorway

1. *Hearings before the President's Commission on the Assassination of President Kennedy*, vol. 7 (Washington, D.C.: GPO, 1964), 515–525; hereinafter cited as 7H515-525; Commission Exhibit 900, 18H93; *Washington Post*, November 23, 1963.

2. *Report of the President's Commission on the Assassination of President John F. Kennedy* (Washington, D.C.: GPO, 1964), 644.

3. Ibid., 112; 5H158.

4. Altgens, Oswald, Lovelady, Richter, Adams, and Baker files, Weisberg archives; Weisberg interviews.

5. *Report of the President's Commission*, 149–155.

6. Ibid., 151.

7. 3H225.

8. *Report of the President's Commission*, 152–153.

9. See Howard Roffman, *Presumed Guilty: Lee Harvey Oswald in the Assassination of President Kennedy* (Rutherford, N.J.: Fairleigh Dickinson University Press, 1975), 201–224; Harold Weisberg, *Whitewash* (Hyattstown, Md.: by the author, 1965), 36–39.

10. *Report of the President's Commission*, 137–156, sets forth the official allegations about the sixth-floor sniper's perch.

11. 3H231–232; 7H163; 6H347–349; 7H185.

12. 3H241–270.

13. 7H592; 3H253.

14. 3H254.

15. *Hearings before the President's Commission*, 159; 3H144.

16. *Report of the President's Commission*, 122–124.

17. 3H293.

18. 3H179; 3H181.

19. Weisberg, *Whitewash*, 32, 35–36, 89; Roffman, *Presumed Guilty*, 151–174; Sylvia Meagher, *Accessories after the Fact* (Indianapolis: Bobbs-Merrill, 1967), 39–45; testimony of Eugene Boone, 3H291–295, Seymour Weitzman, 7H105–109, Carl Day, 4H257–259, Weitzman Exhibits D, E, F; CE 718, 719.

20. 7H105–109.

21. 3H291–295.

22. 7H107.

23. Ibid.

24. Weitzman Exhibit F.

25. *CBS News Inquiry:* "The Warren Report," parts I–IV, June 25–28, 1967, Typescript, I, 9, CBS file, Weisberg archives.

26. 4H258; Meagher, *Accessories after the Fact*, 44.

27. *Report of the President's Commission*, 153; 6H380–381; Weisberg, *Whitewash*, 39.

28. Adams testimony, 6H386–393. Styles and two other fellow fourth-floor workers were never called as witnesses nor interviewed about the stairs. On Adams's credibility, see Meagher, *Accessories after the Fact*, xxv–xxvi, 70, 72–74; Adams file, Weisberg archives.

29. Testimony of Baker, 3H242–270, Truly, 3H212–241, 7H380–386. See Roffman, *Presumed Guilty*, 201–224; Weisberg, *Whitewash*, 36–39; Meagher, *Accessories after the Fact*, 43–44, 70–75, 80, 88, 226–227.

30. *Report of the President's Commission*, 152.

31. The Malcolm Couch film. See Roffman, *Presumed Guilty*, 203–209.

32. 3H252.

33. 3H221; 3H250–251; 3H224–225.

34. 3H223–224.

35. 7H591.

36. Roffman, *Presumed Guilty*, 209.

37. See 24H199, 227, 307; and Commission files 87, number 491, 1526, and 1546, from the Warren Commission records in the National Archives in Baker file, Weisberg archives; Harold Weisberg, *Whitewash II* (Hyattstown, Md.: by the author, 1966), 40, and see 40–45.

38. 3H256; CE497.

39. Roffman, *Presumed Guilty*, 214.

40. Floor plan diagram, CE497; Roffman, *Presumed Guilty*, 218–219.

41. *Report of the President's Commission*, 600, 605–606.

42. CE497; 3H274–279.

43. SA Kyle Clark to SAC, November 23, 1963, serial 89-43-800; Supervisor Robert Gemberling to SAC, September 24, 1964, serial 100-10461-8075.

44. Clark to SAC, 89-43-800.

45. *Report of the President's Commission*, 561.

46. FBI Lab Report, March 6, 1964, 105-82555-2384.

47. Ibid.

48. Inspector J. Malley to SAC, December 11, 1963, serial 44-1639-2142; R. Jevons to Mr. Conrad, November 27, 1963, serial 62-109060-427.

49. *Weisberg v. ERDA and the Department of Justice*, Civil Action 75-226, a voluminous file.

50. Paraffin test records, 75-226 file, Weisberg Archives.

51. *Report of the President's Commission*, 605, 626.

52. Roffman, *Presumed Guilty*, 184.

53. Harold Weisberg, *Photographic Whitewash*, 2d ed. (Frederick, Md.: by the author, 1976), 74, 210–211.

54. CD5, 41; reprinted in Roffman, *Presumed Guilty*, 276–277. Anthony Summers's account in *Conspiracy* (New York: Paragon House, 1989), 77–80, suffers from possible confabulation and must be discounted.

55. CD706 (d).

56. Arnold files, Weisberg archives.

57. Ibid.

58. 22H635.

59. Robert MacNeil, *The Right Place at the Right Time* (Boston: Little, Brown, 1982), 358–361, 368–369.

60. Ibid., 359.

61. CD354.

62. Ibid.

63. Ibid.

64. Ibid.

65. 20H156; 21H781–182.

66. 16H515; *Report of the President's Commission*, 113. The generations are original (1), *Saturday Evening Post* (2), FBI reproduction (3), Warren Commission

printing (4). The original negative was readily available.

67. *New York Herald Tribune*, May 24, 1964, 22H793–794.

68. "Federal Bureau of Investigation" tickler, no date, no serial, Weisberg files. Released to Mark Allen under FOIA. Developed in the 1970s by the FBI as an outline of the bureau's investigation of the assassination, apparently for defense purposes in case of an investigation of its role.

69. Weisberg, *Photographic Whitewash*, 294.

70. Ibid., 149.

71. 22H794.

72. 6H327–334, esp. 328.

73. 22H673; Meagher, *Accessories after the Fact*, 362.

74. 2H242; 6H338; CE369; Meagher, *Accessories after the Fact*, 363.

75. Gerald Ford, *Portrait of the Assassin* (New York: Simon and Schuster, 1965), 443.

76. Meagher, *Accessories after the Fact*, 225; Roffman, *Presumed Guilty*, 184.

Chapter 12.
The Head Shot and Zapruder
Frames 337 and 338

1. These two frames have been largely ignored by theorists.

2. Testimony of FBI special agent Lyndal L. Shaneyfelt, a photographic expert who analyzed the Zapruder film, President's Commission on the Assassination of President John F. Kennedy, *Hearings before the President's Commission on the Assassination of President Kennedy*, vol. 5 (Washington, D.C.: GPO, 1964), 138–139; hereinafter cited as 5H138-139. There is a typographical error in the printed testimony of 434 for 343. There is no information in the documentary

record on why frames before 171 and after 343 were not also requested by authorities. Frames 208–211, as previously discussed, were missing.

3. 5H139.

4. J. Edgar Hoover to J. Lee Rankin, December 14, 1964, Commission Document 858, printed in Harold Weisberg, *Photographic Whitewash*, 2d ed. (Frederick, Md.: by the author, 1976), 144.

5. Commission Exhibit 885, 18H1–80.

6. Ibid.

7. Ibid.

8. *Report of the President's Commission on the Assassination of President John F. Kennedy* (Washington, D.C.: GPO, 1964), 86.

9. 2H373; Humes's testimony.

10. Ibid. This was first discussed by Weisberg, *Photographic Whitewash*, 183–194. See also his *Never Again* (New York: Carroll and Graf, 1995), 72–78, 81–84, 87, 103–109.

11. Autopsy report, National Archives; Harold Weisberg, *Post Mortem* (Frederick, Md.: by the author, 1975), 236–237, 509–510, 515, 517, 521–523.

12. Autopsy report, page 7, National Archives; reprinted in Weisberg, *Post Mortem*, 515.

13. KRLD-TV, tape 9, Sixth Floor Museum. The audio also appeared on radio station KLIF's "The Fateful Hour," produced in the 1960s.

14. FBI Special Agent Raymond Lecter, interview of James A. Chaney, December 12, 1963. Commission Document 4, 682, JFK Collection, National Archives; FBI Special Agent C. Brown to James Adams, Deputy Associate Director, FBI, September 4, 1975, serial number 109060-7256.

15. FBIHQ FD302, serial 62-109060-7369; Jackson file, Weisberg archives.

16. *Hearings before the Commission,* Decker Exhibit 5323, 472.

17. Ibid., 471.

18. Ibid., 486.

19. Ibid., 489.

20. Ibid., 490.

21. A shot from the rear hitting the side of his head was physically impossible. Following the curve of Elm Street, the limousine had turned slightly to its left as it began to dip under the triple underpass, exposing the right side of JFK to the pergola and the wooded hill to his right.

22. CD 5, 30, National Archives, which is an FBI interview of November 26.

23. November 22, 1963, *Dallas Times Herald* tear sheets, typed by rewrite desk editor from notes phoned in from the field in the Sixth Floor Museum.

24. Interview by Josiah Thompson, Assassination Archives Research Center, Washington, D.C.

25. *Dallas Times Herald* tear sheets.

26. Tip O'Neill with William Novak, *Man of the House: The Life and Political Memoirs of Speaker Tip O'Neill* (New York: Random House, 1987), 211, on the basis of his discussions with the two men; Gary Mack, Powers interview, 1980.

27. Statement of Paul E. Landis Jr., November 30, 1963, 18H755, 759.

28. FBI Investigative Clerk Joe Pearce to Special Agent in Charge, Dallas, November 22, 1963, serial number 89-43-37.

29. Dr. Richard Bernabei files, Weisberg archives; the autopsy authority and forensic pathologist, recognized by the House Committee on Assassinations, Dr. Michael Baden, *Unnatural Death: Confessions of a Medical Examiner* (New York: Random House, 1989), 8.

30. Testimony of the autopsy surgeon J. J. Humes reading the X rays for the Commission, 2H353.

31. Prof. Richard Bernabei files, Weisberg archives. Bernabei was an amateur student of ballistics.

32. Gary L. Aquilar, "The Converging Medical Case for Conspiracy in the Death of JFK," in *Assassination Science: Experts Speak Out on the Death of JFK,* ed. James H. Fetzer (Chicago: Catfeet Press, 1997), 175–238.

Chapter 13.
Photographic Proof
of Conspiracy

1. *Report of the President's Commission on the Assassination of President John F. Kennedy* (Washington, D.C.: GPO, 1964), 137–149, 195.

2. Ibid., 423–424.

3. Ibid., 111.

4. Ibid., 111–117.

5. Ibid.

6. Ibid., 111.

7. Ibid., 48.

8. Ibid., 60.

9. Ibid., 88.

10. Ibid., 89–90.

11. Ibid., 92–96.

12. Ibid., 109.

13. Ibid., 108, 110.

14. Ibid., 116.

15. Ibid., 63.

16. Ibid., 140.

17. Ibid., 61–117.

18. Ibid., 97. Live oaks bear evergreen leaves that are elliptical or oblong, from two to five inches long and one-half inch to two inches wide that do not drop from the tree until spring.

19. Ibid., 98.

20. Ibid.

21. Ibid.

22. Ibid., 61–117.

23. See for examples of staunch defenders of the Report: William Manchester, *The Death of a President, November 20–November 25, 1963* (New York: Harper and Row, 1967); Jim Bishop, *The Day Kennedy Was Shot* (New York: Funk and Wagnalls, 1968); Gerald Ford, *Portrait of the Assassin* (New York: Simon and Schuster, 1965); Arlen Specter, *Passion for Truth* (New York: William Morrow, 2000); David W. Belin, *November 22, 1963: You Are the Jury* (New York: New York Times, 1973); and Gerald Posner, *Case Closed: Lee Harvey Oswald and the Assassination of JFK* (New York: Random House, 1993).

24. Following Willis's testimony in *Hearings before the President's Commission on the Assassination of President Kennedy*, vol. 7 (Washington, D.C.: GPO, 1964), 492–497; hereinafter cited as 7H492–497.

25. Ibid.

26. Ibid.

27. *Report of the President's Commission*, 651.

28. Hudson Exhibit 1, 20H183.

29. Ibid.

30. 7H493.

31. Weisberg interview.

32. *Report of the President's Commission*, 97.

33. 7H492–497.

34. Quoted by Richard B. Trask, *Pictures of the Pain* (Danvers, Mass.: Yeoman Press, 1994), 180.

35. FBI Special Agent A. Raymond Switzer, June 19, 1964, report, no serial on copy, in Weisberg archives, reproduced in Harold Weisberg, *Whitewash II* (Hyattstown, Md.: by the author, 1966), 206.

36. Willis files, Weisberg archives; also in Trask, *Pictures of the Pain*, 180.

37. Interview of Harold Weisberg, who had interviewed the Willises in 1965.

38. 7H495.

39. Ibid.

40. 5H135–138.

41. 5H136–137.

42. 7H562–563.

43. 15H686–702.

44. Interview with Weisberg, who had seen and held the original in the National Archives; 21H471.

45. Harold Weisberg, *Whitewash* (Hyattstown, Md.: by the author, 1965), 46.

46. 15H696.

47. 15H697.

48. Ibid., 195–202.

49. 18H1–80.

50. Barb Junkkarinen, "First Shot/First Hit Circa Z-190," *Kennedy Assassination Chronicles* 5, no. 2 (summer 1999): 23–27; Doug DeSalles, "Follow-Up and Continuation to First Shot/First Hit Circa Z-190," *Kennedy Assassination Chronicles* 5, no. 3 (fall 1999): 20–23.

51. U.S. House Select Committee on Assassinations, *Investigation of the Assassination*, vol. 2 (Washington, D.C.: GPO, 1979), 15.

52. Ibid., 183; Hal Verb, "The First Shot in the John F. Kennedy Assassination Was *Not* the Missed Shot" (paper presented at Washington conference of critics, 1994), 2.

53. Hugh William Betzner Jr., affidavit to Sheriff's Department, November 22, 1963, 19H467.

54. KRLD-TV, November 22, 1963, tape 9, the Sixth Floor Museum.

55. 5H180.

56. 7H496–497.

57. 7H449.

58. 6H243.

59. The point made here does not relate to any material appearing in Bonar

Menninger, *Mortal Error: The Shot That Killed JFK* (New York: St. Martin's Press, 1992). In 1995 Hickey claimed he had been libeled by the book and sued. In *George Hickey v. St. Martin's Press et al.*, C.95-475-M, U.S. District Court D. N. H., the case was settled and the complaint dismissed. The terms were confidential. Attorneys for Hickey were James Lesar and Mark Zaid.

60. 18H762.

61. 7H388.

62. *Report of the President's Commission,* 67.

63. 7H571.

Chapter 14.
A Command Appearance

1. "An Assassination's Retroactivity," *Minority of One* 9 (October 1967): 11–12; "New 'Plot' Inquiry Reported on Kennedy Assassination," *New York Times*, February 18, 1967; "New Oswald Clue Reported Found: New Orleans Official Vows Arrests Will Be Made," *New York Times*, February 19, 1967; "Data Are Requested on Oswald Inquiry," *New York Times*, February 20, 1967.

2. *Almanac of Jim Garrison's Investigation into the Assassination of John F. Kennedy: The Crime of Silence* (Austin, Tex.: Research Publications, 1968); Milton E. Brener, *The Garrison Case: A Study in the Abuse of Power* (New York: Clarkson N. Potter, 1969); Carlos Bringuier, *Red Friday: Nov. 22nd, 1963* (Chicago: Charles Hallberg, 1969); William H. Davis, *Aiming for the Jugular in New Orleans* (Port Washington, N.Y.: Ashley Books, 1976); William Davy, *Let Justice Be Done* (Reston, Va.: Jordan, 1999); Edward Jay Epstein, *Counterplot* (New York: Viking Press, 1969); Paris Flammonde, *The Kennedy Conspiracy: An Uncommissioned Report on the Jim Garrison Inves-*tigation (New York: Meridith Press, 1969); Jim Garrison, *A Heritage of Stone* (New York: Putnam, 1970); Warren Hinckle, *If You Have a Lemon, Make Lemonade* (New York: Putnam, 1974); Rosemary James and Jack Wardlaw, *Plot or Politics? The Garrison Case and Its Cast* (New Orleans: Pelican Publishing House, 1967); Joachim Joesten, *The Garrison Enquiry: Truth and Consequences* (London: Dawnay, 1967); James Kirkwood, *American Grotesque: An Account of the Clay Shaw–Jim Garrison Affair in the City of New Orleans* (New York: Simon and Schuster, 1970); Patricia Lambert, *False Witness: The Real Story of Jim Garrison's Investigation and Oliver Stone's Film, JFK* (New York: M. Evans, 1999); Mort Sahl, *Heartland* (New York: Harcourt Brace Jovanovich, 1976); John Seigenthaler, *A Search for Justice* (Nashville, Tenn.: Aurora Publishers, 1970); Harold Weisberg, *Oswald in New Orleans: Case for Conspiracy with the CIA,* foreword by Jim Garrison (New York: Canyon Books, 1967).

3. Brener, *The Garrison Case,* 61

4. Jim Garrison, *On the Trail of the Assassins: My Investigation and Prosecution of the Murder of President Kennedy* (New York: Sheridan Press, 1988), 207–208.

5. Raymond Marcus, *The Bastard Bullet: A Search for Legitimacy for Commission Exhibit 399* (Los Angeles: Rendell Publications, 1966). See also his *Addendum to the HSCA, the Zapruder film, and the Single-Bullet Theory* (Los Angeles: Rendell, 1995); and *The HSCA, the Zapruder film, and the Single-Bullet Theory* (Los Angeles: Rendell, 1992).

6. Orleans Parish Grand Jury Special Investigations, May 11, 1967, transcript of Ray Marcus, 140 numbered pages, with no page number for 6, 17, and 18, Marcus archives.

7. Copy of in Weisberg archives.

8. Abraham Zapruder testimony, *State of Louisiana v. Clay L. Shaw*, Criminal District Court Parish of Orleans, State of Louisiana, No. 198-059, 1426 (30), Section C, February 13, 1969, Transcript, JFK Collection, National Archives.

9. Zapruder, transcript, 80–81.

10. "Of Demonologists and Eunuchs," *Minority of One* 10 (September 1968): 8–9.

11. Epstein, *Counterplot*.

12. Ibid.; Epstein, *Inquest: The Warren Commission and the Establishment of Truth* (New York: Viking Press, 1966).

13. Epstein, *Counterplot*, 121–122.

14. Ibid., 122.

15. William DeLaney, "Film of JFK Slaying Is Being Bootlegged," *Star*, November 26, 1969.

Chapter 15.
Official Allegation

1. *Report of the President's Commission on the Assassination of President John F. Kennedy* (Washington, D.C.: GPO, 1964), 111.

2. Ibid., 61–117.

3. Ibid., 108–110.

4. Ibid., 116; Sylvia Meagher, *Accessories after the Fact* (Indianapolis: Bobbs-Merrill, 1967), 5–8.

5. CE399, in *Hearings before the President's Commission on the Assassination of President Kennedy*, vol. 17 (Washington, D.C.: GPO, 1964), 49; *Report of the President's Commission*, 85 n. 142.

6. *Report of the President's Commission*, 87–92.

7. Ibid., 81.

8. Among the defenders of the Commission who embrace the single-bullet theory are Gerald Posner, *Case Closed: Lee Harvey Oswald and the Assassination of JFK* (New York: Random House, 1993); William Manchester, *The Death of a President, November 20–November 25, 1963* (New York: Harper and Row, 1967); Edward Jay Epstein, *Legend: The Secret World of Lee Harvey Oswald* (New York: McGraw-Hill, 1978); Jim Bishop, *The Day Kennedy Was Shot* (New York: Funk and Wagnalls, 1968); Gerald Ford, *Portrait of the Assassin* (New York: Simon and Schuster, 1965); Jean Davison, *Oswald's Game* (New York: Norton, 1983); Priscilla Johnson McMillan, *Marina and Lee* (New York: Harper and Row, 1977); Arlen Specter, *Passion for Truth* (New York: Morrow, 2000); David W. Belin, *November 22, 1963: You Are the Jury* (New York: New York Times, 1973).

9. Critics who discuss the single-bullet theory include Harold Weisberg's several volumes, especially *Whitewash* (Hyattstown, Md.: by the author, 1965); *Whitewash II* (Hyattstown, Md.: by the author, 1966); and *Post Mortem* (Frederick, Md.: by the author, 1975); Howard Roffman, *Presumed Guilty: Lee Harvey Oswald in the Assassination of President Kennedy* (Rutherford, N.J.: Fairleigh Dickinson University Press, 1975); Sylvia Meagher, *Accessories after the Fact* (Indianapolis: Bobbs-Merrill, 1967); Chip Selby, *Reasonable Doubt*, video (Laurel, Md.: CS Films, 1988); Raymond Marcus's volumes, *The Bastard Bullet: A Search for Legitimacy for Commission Exhibit 399* (Los Angeles: Rendell, 1966); *The HSCA, the Zapruder Film, and the Single-Bullet Theory* (Los Angeles: Rendell, 1992); and *Addendum to the HSCA, the Zapruder film and the Single-Bullet Theory* (Los Angeles: Rendell, 1995).

10. *Report of the President's Commission*, 97.

11. Ibid., 97, 106.

12. Ibid., 102, 106.

13. Ibid., 106.

14. Ibid., 79.

15. Ibid., 81.

16. Ibid., 557.

17. CE399, JFK Collection, National Archives.

18. *Report of the President's Commission,* 587.

19. Ibid., 87.

20. Ibid., 87–88.

21. Ibid., 19, 87.

22. Ibid., 88.

23. Ibid., 92.

24. Ibid.

25. Ibid., 88.

26. Ibid., 89.

27. Ibid., 91.

28. Ibid., 92.

29. Ibid.

30. Ibid., 107.

31. Ibid., 89.

32. Ibid.

33. Ibid., 92.

34. Ibid., 93, 531.

35. Ibid. 93.

36. Ibid.

37. Ibid.

38. Ibid.

39. Ibid.

40. Ibid.

41. Ibid., 95.

42. Ibid., 93.

43. Ibid., 95.

44. Ibid.

45. Ibid., 109.

46. Ibid., 105.

47. Ibid.

48. Ibid., 104; CE697, 17H354.

49. *Report of the President's Commission,* 580.

50. Ibid., 109.

51. Ibid.

52. Ibid.

53. Ibid., 583–584.

54. Ibid., 584.

55. Ibid.

56. Ibid., 96.

57. Ibid., 97.

58. Ibid.

59. Ibid.

60. Ibid.

61. Ibid., 107.

62. Ibid., 106.

63. Ibid., 107.

64. Ibid.

65. J. Edgar Hoover to J. Lee Rankin, March 18, 1964, 20H2; *Weisberg v. ERDA,* 226–275.

66. Neutron activation analysis file, Harold Weisberg archive.

67. Records and court filings of *Weisberg v. ERDA,* CA 75-226, in Weisberg archives, as well as his neutron activation analysis file.

68. Attorney James Lesar, "Summary of 75-226," Lesar file, author's collection; see also R. Jevons to Conrad, August 24, 1964, serial [?62-109060 indistinct]-4829, where concern over possible knowledge of the tests becoming public is discussed, in neutron activation analysis file, Weisberg archives.

69. Essential discussion of CE399 is found in the following: Marcus, *The Bastard Bullet;* Meagher, *Accessories after the Fact,* 139–149, 165–177; Weisberg, *Whitewash,* 156–157, 160–166, 171–174, 193–195; Weisberg, *Whitewash II,* 67, 93–100, 103, 106–107, 125–126; and Roffman, *Presumed Guilty,* 95–150.

70. Meagher, *Accessories after the Fact,* 94–112.

71. *Report of the President's Commission,* 137–143, 173.

72. CE1301, top half of 22H479.

73. CE1302, lower half of 22H479.

74. CE509, 17H220.

75. *Report of the President's Commission,* 63.

76. Ibid., 79.

77. 3H144.

78. *Report of the President's Commission,* 149–150.

79. Ibid., 150; CE1118, 22H85.

80. *Report of the President's Commission,* 151.

81. Ibid., 152.

82. Ibid.

83. *Report of the President's Commission,* 85.

84. Interview with Harold Weisberg, who is the author of two books on the King assassination: *Frame-Up: The Martin Luther King/James Earl Ray Case* (New York: Outerbridge and Dienstfrey, 1971); and *Whoring with History: How the Gerald Posners Protect the King Assassins,* unpublished ms. (Frederick, Md.: by the author, CD-ROM, 1998).

85. Meagher, *Accessories after the Fact,* 78 n; Roffman, *Presumed Guilty,* 191, 190–198; Weisberg, *Whitewash,* 39–42.

86. *Report of the President's Commission,* 129.

87. Ibid., 130.

88. Ibid.

89. Ibid., 133.

90. Ibid., 135–137.

91. 2H245–250; 2H226.

92. *Report of the President's Commission,* 133; 6H376–377.

93. CE130s printed in *Report of the President's Commission,* 139.

94. FBI SA J. Anderson to SAC Dallas, November 29, 1963, serial 89-43-1389.

95. Ibid., serial 89-43-1390.

96. CE142, 16H513; Roffman, *Presumed Guilty,* 172, and photograph, 173.

97. 4H89–101.

98. 4H97, the testimony of James Cardigan, FBI questioned-documents expert.

99. 4H89–101.

100. J. Edgar Hoover to J. Lee Rankin, August 20, 1964, 26H455; 4H97.

101. *Report of the President's Commission,* 135.

102. 7H144.

103. 2H242; 6H356–363.

104. *Report of the President's Commission,* 135; 4H93.

105. Ibid.

106. 2H242.

107. 4H97; 3H363.

108. 3H360–362.

109. 24H209.

110. Meagher, *Accessories after the Fact,* 45–47.

111. Discussion in Joachim Joesten, *Oswald: Assassin or Fall Guy?* (New York: Marzani and Munsell, 1964), 32; Roffman, *Presumed Guilty,* 159–160; Weisberg, *Whitewash,* 21–22.

112. Copy of contact prints, Weisberg archives; date of the photographs ascertained by Daniels letter to Howard Roffman, March 19, 1970, in Roffman, *Presumed Guilty,* 260. Several of the photographs on the strip were published in various national publications, which meant federal officials were quite aware of his camera work and the information his photographs contained, but they ignored them.

113. *Report of the President's Commission,* 18.

114. 6H128–134.

115. Parkland Hospital had a basement and ground, first, second, and third floors, with the emergency room on the ground floor.

116. 6H125–128.

117. 6H129.

118. 6H131.

119. *Report of the President's Commission,* 81.

120. 6H132.

121. Ibid.

122. 6H133.

123. 6H130; Tomlinson Exhibit, 21H672.

124. 6H130.

125. Ibid.

126. 6H134.

127. *Report of the President's Commission,* 80–81.

128. 6H133.

129. 6H132.

130. 6H133.

131. 6H128–134.

132. 6H134.

133. Weisberg, *Whitewash,* 162.

134. Transcript of the broadcast in Stephen White, *Should We Now Believe the Warren Report?* (New York: Macmillan, 1968), 288–289.

135. CE1024, 18H722–802.

136. Ibid.

137. Ibid.

138. Ibid.

139. 5H449–486.

140. CE1024.

141. 2H353.

142. James Sibert and Francis O'Neill, "Results of the Autopsy on John F. Kennedy," FBI report, November 26, 1963, serial 89-30.

143. Shanklin to Director, June 20, 1964, serial 105-82555-4205.

144. CE2011, 24H411–412.

145. Ibid., 24H412.

146. Ibid.

147. Ibid.

148. Ibid.

149. *Report of the President's Commission,* 77.

150. Ibid., 557.

151. Dr. Russell S. Fisher et al., "1968 Panel Review of Photographs, X-Ray Films, Documents and Other Evidence Pertaining to the Fatal Wounding of President John F. Kennedy on November 22, 1963 in Dallas, Texas," 13, unpublished typescript; Dr. Russell S. Fisher to Harold Weisberg, March 4, 1970, Weisberg archives.

152. 2H375.

153. 2H381.

154. 2H377.

155. 4H113.

156. In a Freedom of Information Act lawsuit, *Weisberg v. ERDA,* CA 75-226, U.S. District Court of Columbia, Harold Weisberg deposed FBI Lab Special Agent John Gallagher. Gallagher stated a sample of only 1mm is adequate.

157. Trial transcript, Weisberg archives.

158. Ibid., 602.

159. 3H431.

160. Roffman interview.

161. *Weisberg v. Department of Justice,* 75-226.

162. 3H428.

163. 3H428–429.

164. 3H437.

165. Ibid.

Chapter 16.
Official Evidence

1. *Report of the President's Commission on the Assassination of President John F. Kennedy* (Washington, D.C.: GPO, 1964), 87–92.

2. Ibid., 97.

3. Ibid., 88.

4. Ibid.

5. Ibid., 92.

6. Ibid., 3.

7. Harold Weisberg, *Never Again* (New York: Carroll and Graf, 1995), 2, 74–77.

8. Ibid., 77.

9. Michael Baden, *Unnatural Death: Confessions of a Medical Examiner* (New York: Random House, 1989), 8.

10. Weisberg, *Never Again*, 217; Baden, *Unnatural Death*, 9.

11. *Report of the President's Commission*, 89.

12. Ibid., 87.

13. Weisberg, *Never Again*, 87–88.

14. Ibid., 88.

15. Ibid., 92.

16. *Hearings before the President's Commission on the Assassination of President Kennedy*, vol. 2 (Washington, D.C.: GPO, 1964), 370; hereinafter cited as 2H370.

17. January 30, 1964, Executive Session, President's Commission on the Assassination of President Kennedy, 32, JFK Collection, National Archives, copy in Weisberg archives.

18. CE385, 16H977.

19. CE386, 16H977.

20. *Report of the President's Commission*, 92–93.

21. Ibid., 92.

22. Ibid.

23. Ibid.

24. Ibid.

25. 5H60.

26. FBI Exhibit 60, *Investigation of Assassination of President John F. Kennedy, November 22, 1963*, 5 vols. (Washington, D.C.: FBI, 1963).

27. Ibid.

28. 2H81.

29. 18H740–745.

30. 2H127.

31. *Report of the President's Commission*, III.

32. James W. Sibert and Francis X. O'Neill Jr., "Results of Autopsy on John F. Kennedy," November 26, 1963, serial 89-30.

33. 2H371.

34. See Weisberg, *Never Again*, 213.

35. "Autopsy Descriptive Sheet," JFK Collection, National Archives, copy in autopsy file, Weisberg archives.

36. Ibid.

37. CE397, 17H45.

38. Weisberg, *Never Again*, 90, 98.

39. Death certificate, President John Fitzgerald Kennedy, November 23, 1963, copy from JFK Collection, National Archives.

40. Executive session, January 27, 1963, 193, JFK Collection, National Archives, copy in Weisberg archives.

41. *Report of the President's Commission*, 88. Colonel Finck is being quoted.

42. 7H508–509.

43. Weisberg, *Never Again*, 161.

44. 1968 Panel Review of Photographs, X-Ray Films, Documents and Other Evidence Pertaining to the Fatal Wounding of President John F. Kennedy on November 22, 1963, in Dallas, Texas (Washington: Department of Justice, 1968), 13, unpublished ms., copy in Weisberg archives.

45. Weisberg, *Never Again*, 205.

46. Ibid., 259.

47. *Report of the President's Commission*, 519.

48. 6H141.

49. November 22, 1963, press conference transcripts, 4, LBJ Library.

50. Ibid., 5.

51. Ibid., 6.

52. Weisberg, *Never Again*, 202.

53. Ibid., 239, 242.

54. 3H362.

55. Weisberg, *Never Again*, 239–250, especially 244–247.

56. 6H111.

57. Chip Selby, interview of Colonel Dolce, transcript, copy in Weisberg archives.

58. *Report of the President's Commission*, 583–584.

59. Weisberg interview.

60. Transcribed Johnson telephone tapes for September 18, 1964, LBJ Library.

61. The discussion of Russell's dissent is based on the following: Weisberg, *Never Again*, 221–229, 251–253, 324–325, 493–498; Weisberg, *Whitewash IV: JFK Assassination Transcript* (Frederick, Md.: by the author, 1974), 20–35, 131–132, 200–209; Weisberg, *Ex Sess*, unpublished ms. (Frederick, Md.: by the author, [1976]); *Report of the President's Commission*; Richard Russell Papers, University of Georgia, Athens; John Sherman Cooper files, William Neichter; President Lyndon B. Johnson telephone tape transcription, LBJ Library; Russell files, Weisberg archives.

62. On Russell see John A. Goldsmith, *Colleagues: Richard B. Russell and His Apprentice Lyndon B. Johnson* (Washington, D.C.: Seven Locks Press, 1993); Gilbert C. Fite, *Richard B. Russell, Jr., Senator from Georgia* (Chapel Hill: University of North Carolina Press, 1991); and Robert Mann, *The Walls of Jericho: Lyndon Johnson, Hubert Humphrey, Richard Russell, and the Struggle for Civil Rights* (New York: Harcourt, Brace, 1996). On Johnson a recent biography is Robert Dallek, *Flawed Giant: Lyndon Johnson and His Times, 1961–73* (New York: Oxford University Press, 1998).

63. Johnson telephone tape transcription.

64. "Johnson Said He Doubted Finding on Assassination," *New York Times*, April 17, 1994.

65. Cartha DeLoach Memorandum of Watson telephone conversation, April 3, 1967, April 4, 1967, serial 62-109060-5075.

66. FBI control file, especially FBI HQ file 62-109060-4250, Weisberg archives.

67. Cartha DeLoach to Clyde Tolson, April 4, 1967, serial 62-109060-5075; includes memorandum of telephone call.

68. Ibid.

69. "CBS Evening News with Walter Cronkite," April 25, 1975; "The American Assassins," CBS Reports Inquiry, November 26, 1975; Leo Janos, "The Last Days of the President," *Atlantic Monthly*, July 1973, 35–41.

70. "Johnson Feared War at Kennedy Death," *New York Times*, December 9, 1972; public television appearance by Warren, December 11, 1972.

71. Russell Papers.

72. Russell in interview with Weisberg, *Whitewash IV*, 21.

73. Ibid.

74. *Report of the President's Commission*, 19.

75. Ibid., 131–132.

76. Ibid., 21.

77. Rankin Papers, box 1, file 23, August 20, 1964, JFK Collection, National Archives.

78. Hugh Cates Oral History no. 40, John Sherman Cooper, April 29, 1971, Russell Library, University of Georgia, Athens, Georgia.

79. John Sherman Cooper, Covington & Burling Law Offices, to Edmund Johnston, Bronx, New York, February 9, 1978, Neichter Cooper papers, private collection, Louisville, Ky.

80. Russell to Scobey, December 24, 1966, Russell Library; copy provided by Chip Selby.

81. Edward Jay Epstein, *Inquest: The Warren Commission and the Establishment of Truth* (New York: Viking Press, 1966), 150.

82. Federal Bureau of Investigation, *Investigation of Assassination of President John F. Kennedy, November 22, 1963* (Washington, D.C.: FBI, 1963), I, 1.

83. Official surveyor's chart of Dealey Plaza for Secret Service, Records of the President's Commission on the Assassination of President Kennedy, National Archives. The Archives was unable to locate this chart in 2000; copy obtained from archives in Weisberg files; reproduced in Harold Weisberg, *Whitewash II* (Hyattstown, Md.: by the author, 1966), 243.

84. Commission Document 3, CD3. National Archives.

85. 3H441–451.

86. Ibid.

87. Weisberg, *Never Again*, 302–303.

88. 3H443.

89. 5H443–451.

90. 4H147.

91. 4H132.

92. Wade to Weisberg, October 10, 1968, Weisberg archives.

93. J. Edgar Hoover, memorandum, June 22, 1964, FBIHQ 62-109090-176.

94. Ibid.

Chapter 17.
Federal Purchase

1. U.S. Constitution, preamble.

2. Ibid., art. I. sec. 1.

3. Ibid., art. I. sec. 8.

4. *Hearings before the President's Commission on the Assassination of President Kennedy,* vol. 18 (Washington, D.C.: GPO, 1964), 1–80, 86–93, 95.

5. Richard Mosk to Norman Redlich, April 29, 1964, memorandum, Weisberg archives.

6. *Report of the President's Commission on the Assassination of President John F. Kennedy* (Washington, D.C.: GPO, 1964), 471–474.

7. U.S. House Committee on Judiciary, *Preserving Evidence Pertaining to Assassination of President Kennedy,* 89th Cong., 1st sess. 1965, H. Rept. 813.

8. *Congressional Record,* 89th Cong., 1st sess., 1965, 111, pt. 12: 15204.

9. Ibid., pt. 16: 21103.

10. Ibid., pt. 16: 21103–21104.

11. Ibid., pt. 17: 23002.

12. PL 89-318, Act of November 2, 1965.

13. Department of Justice, Office of Attorney General, Notices, "The Acquisition and Preservation by the United States of Items of Evidence Pertaining to the Assassination of President John F. Kennedy," *Federal Register* 31, no. 212, pt. 2 (November 1, 1966): 13968–13974.

14. *King v. USA,* 292 FSupp 767 (1967).

15. *Marina N. Oswald Porter v. USA,* 473 F2d 1329 (5th Cir 1972).

16. *Weekly Compilation of Presidential Documents,* 28 (Washington, D.C.: GPO, 1992), October 26, 2134–2135; with Presidential statement; 106 Statutes (1992) 3443.

17. See also Charles J. Sanders and Mark S. Zaid, "The Declassification of Dealey Plaza: After Thirty Years, a New Disclosure Law at Last May Help to Clarify the Facts of the Kennedy Assassination," *South Texas Law Review* 34 (1993): 408–441.

18. This follows the notes of Alan F. Lewis, Supervisory Audiovisual Specialist, in a memorandum of March 15, 1993, Zapruder file, Audiovisual Division, National Archives.

19. Ibid.

20. Ibid.

21. Ibid.

22. Ibid.

23. Memorandum, March 15, 1993, Christopher M. Runkel, Zapruder file.

24. Assassination Records Review Board, transcript of April 2, 1997, hearing, copy in Assassination Archives and Research Center, Washington, D.C.

25. Ibid., 12.

26. Ibid., 12–13.

27. Ibid., 13–14.

28. Ibid., 16.

29. Ibid., 18.

30. Ibid., 23.

31. Ibid., 24.

32. Ibid., 24–25.

33. Ibid., 26–27.

34. Ibid., 27.

35. Ibid., 33.

36. Ibid., 34.

37. Ibid., 46–60.

38. Ibid., 47.

39. Ibid.

40. Ibid., 47–48.

41. Ibid., 48–49.

42. Ibid., 49.

43. Ibid., 49–50.

44. Ibid., 50–51.

45. Ibid., 56–57.

46. Personal communication.

47. George Lardner Jr., "Zapruder Film of JFK Assassination Is Public Record, Review Board Decides," *Washington Post*, April 25, 1997.

48. ARRB press release, April 24, 1997. See also Assassination Records Review Board, *Final Report of the Assassination Records Review Board* (Washington, D.C.: GPO, 1998), 124–125.

49. George Lardner Jr., "U.S. Bids for the Zapruder Film," *Washington Post*, June 13, 1998.

50. George Lardner Jr., "Haggling over History: Zapruders, U.S. Far apart on Price of Kennedy Film," *Washington Post*, June 13, 1998.

51. David E. Rosenbaum, "Federal Government and Zapruder Family Debate the Price of History," *New York Times*, July 6, 1998.

52. Lardner, "U.S. Bids."

53. *Image of an Assassination: A New Look at the Zapruder Film* (Orlando Park, Ill.: MPI Media Group, 1998).

54. George Lardner Jr., "Zapruder Film Set for August Video Release: Footage of JFK Assassination Likely to Restart Debate," *Washington Post*, June 26, 1998; Eric L. Wise, "A Target Audience for JFK Assassination Video," *Washington Post*, July 28, 1998; James Barron, "Ideas and Trends; For Some, the Lure of Horror," *New York Times*, July 19, 1998; Frank Rich, "Journal; From Here to Zapruder," *New York Times*, July 4, 1998.

55. *Final Report of Assassination Records*, 125–126

56. Roland Zavada, *Analysis of Selected Motion Picture Photographic Evidence*, Kodak Technical report (Rochester, N.Y.: Eastman Kodak, 1998).

57. Ibid.

58. George Lardner Jr., "U.S., Zapruder Reach Deal on Assassination Film," *Washington Post*, October 17, 1998.

59. "Panel to Decide Payment for Zapruder Film," January 7, 1999, Reuters news.

60. LMH v. USA, et al. 98-CV-2569.

61. Docket, ARC.

62. ARC & Passage Productions v. LMH, 98 CV02833.

63. Deb Reichmann, "Suit Challenges Zapruder Film Purchase," AP wire story, November 24, 1998.

64. Kenneth Feinberg and Arlin M. Adams, *In the Matter of the Zapruder Film* (Washington, D.C.: Department of Justice, 1999), 13 pp., bound with Walter E. Dellinger, "Separate Statement," 7 pp.; press release, Department of Justice; Deb Reichmann, "Film of JFK Shooting Worth $16 Million," August 4, 1999, AP wire story; David Johnston, "Government Told to Pay $16 Million for Zapruder Film," *New York Times*, August 4,

1999; Will Woodward and George Lardner Jr., "Zapruder Film Nets $16 Million," *Washington Post*, August, 4, 1999.

65. *In the Matter*, 3.

66. Ibid.

67. Ibid, 4.

68. Ibid.

69. Ibid., 8–9.

70. Ibid, 4.

71. James H. Lesar to James H. Kovakas, FOIA Unit, Department of Justice, August 24, 1999, in *David R. Wrone v. U. S. Department of Justice*, complaint, U.S. District Court for the District of Columbia, case number 00CV01939.

72. Drema A. Hanshaw, FOIA Specialist, Department of Justice, to James H. Lesar, October 25, 1999, in ibid.

73. *Wrone v. Department of Justice*.

74. These will be deposited at Hood College.

75. Jim Henderson, "Zapruders Donate Film to Museum," *Houston Chronicle*, January 27, 2000.

SELECTED BIBLIOGRAPHY

Over the years, Harold Weisberg, Sylvia Meagher, Howard Roffman, and a number of other responsible citizen scholars have investigated the murder of President Kennedy. Their fundamental principle has been not to find out who shot him but to inquire into the criminal evidence and ascertain the validity of the conclusions drawn from it by officials. For that reason they deserve special mention here.

On February 15, 1965, Harold Weisberg, a commercial poultry farmer and former Senate investigator, completed Whitewash, the very first book on the assassination after the appearance of the Warren Commission Report. Based exclusively on a close analysis of the Report and its twenty-six volumes of evidence, Weisberg's study effectively demonstrates that the Commission's investigation was deeply flawed and its conclusion regarding Oswald as the lone crazed assassin wrong. The first of nine published and three dozen unpublished studies by Weisberg, Whitewash has become a "closet classic" in this controversial field, much admired by serious researchers, none of whom have ever challenged his findings.

Two years later, Sylvia Meagher (pronounced Marr), "a worker in the field of international public health both as an administrator and as a writer of analytical reports," published Accessories after the Fact (Bobbs-Merrill, 1967). Based on massive research in primary sources, devoid of speculation or special pleadings, and faithful to the facts of the evidentiary base, the book is a model of the scholarly form, with a fair presentation of the evidence and carefully drawn conclusions. Even so, her publisher did little to advertise or promote the book, most reviewers declined to review it, most bookstores did not stock it, and few mainstream or academic journals reviewed it. Yet, to this day, it remains one of the best books ever written or published on the assassination.

In 1975, Fairleigh Dickinson University Press published Howard Roffman's Presumed Guilty: Lee Harvey Oswald in the Assassination of President Kennedy, a careful, scholarly examination of the documentary base of the official investigation into the assassination. The volume, among the best books written on the assassination, effectively demonstrates that the Commission's investigation proceeded on the false assumption of Oswald's guilt, which led inevitably to the Report's false conclusions. But, like Meagher's work, Roffman's received little attention and became an orphan in the field.

Manuscript Sources

Internet sites. The thousands of JFK sites that exist are rife with theory-driven information and typically suffused with errors. Only with a solid subject matter mastery of the assassination facts possessed by few individuals can one safely navigate them. Three sites can be recommended: nara.gov/research/jfk (access to the President John F. Kennedy Assassination Records Collection in the National Archives); JFK.org (the Sixth Floor Museum at Dealey Plaza in Dallas); and History-matters.org (Warren Report, Hearings volumes—the voluminous Warren Commission executive session transcripts and other records).

Assassination Archives and Records Collection, Washington, D.C.

National Archives, Washington, D.C.
   The President John F. Kennedy Assassination Records Collection
   Records of the President's Commission on the Assassination of President
      Kennedy Record Group 272
   Orleans Parish Grand Jury Special Investigations
   State of Louisiana v. Clay L. Shaw, transcripts
Neichter, William. Louisville, Kentucky
   John Sherman Cooper files
Richard Russell Papers, University of Georgia, Athens
The Sixth Floor Museum at Dealey Plaza in Dallas
Harold Weisberg Archives, Hood College, Frederick, Maryland

General files

FBI files
   Dallas Field Office, Assassination of President Kennedy, DL 89-43, Weisberg: 2
      CD-ROMs, 2000
   Dallas Field Office, DeMohrenschildt, DL 105-632, Weisberg: 1 CD-ROM, 2000
   Dallas Field Office, Jack Ruby, DL 44-1639, Weisberg: 2 CD-ROMs, 2000
   Dallas Field Office, Lee Harvey Oswald, Main Assassination File, DL 100-10461,
      Weisberg: 4 CD-ROMs, 2000
   Headquarters, Assassination of President Kennedy, HQ 62-109060, Weisberg: 7
      CD-ROMs, 2000
   Headquarters, Jack Ruby, HQ 44-24016, Weisberg: 2 CD-ROMs, 2000
   Headquarters, Lee Harvey Oswald, HQ 105-82555, Weisberg: 5 CD-ROMs, 2000
   Headquarters, Warren Commission, Liason File, HQ 62-109090, Weisberg:
      2 CD-ROMs, 2000
   President's Commission on the Assassination of President John F. Kennedy
      Executive sessions, Weisberg: 1 CD-ROM, 2000

Government Publications

Assassination Records Review Board. *Final Report of the Assassination Records Review
   Board*. Washington, D.C.: GPO, 1998.
Congressional Record. 1965–1992.
Department of Justice. Office of Attorney General. Notices. "The Acquisition and
   Preservation by the United States of Items of Evidence Pertaining to the Assassina-
   tion of President John F. Kennedy." *Federal Register* 31, no. 212, pt. 2 (November 1,
   1966): 13968–13974.
Executive Order. "Appointing a Commission to Report upon the Assassination of
   President John F. Kennedy." *Federal Register* 28 (December 3, 1963): 12789. Signed
   November 29, 1963, dated November 30, 1963.
Federal Bureau of Investigation. *Investigation of Assassination of President John F. Kennedy,
   November 22, 1963*. 5 vols. Washington, D.C.: Federal Bureau of Investigation,
   1963. Commission Document 1.

Feinberg, Kenneth, Arlin M. Adams, and Walter E. Dellinger. *In the Matter of the Zapruder Film*. Washington, D.C.: Department of Justice, 1999.

Foreign Relations of the United States, 1961–1963. Vols. 10, 11, 14, 20, 24. Washington, D.C.: GPO, 1988–1997.

President's Commission on CIA Activities within the United States. *Report to the President by the Commission on CIA Activities within the United States*. Washington, D.C.: GPO, 1975.

President's Commission on the Assassination of President John F. Kennedy. *Hearings before the President's Commission on the Assassination of President Kennedy*. 26 vols. Washington, D.C.: GPO, 1964.

——. *Report of the President's Commission on the Assassination of President John F. Kennedy*. Washington, D.C.: GPO, 1964.

Public Papers of the Presidents of the United States. John F. Kennedy. Vols. 1961, 1962, 1963. Washington, D.C.: GPO, 1962–1964.

U.S. House Committee on the Judiciary. *Preserving Evidence Pertaining to the Assassination of President Kennedy*. 89th Cong., 1st sess., 1965. H. Rept. 813.

——. *Providing Penalties for Assassination of the President*. 89th Cong., 1st sess., 1965. H. Rept. 488.

U.S. House Government Operations Committee. Subcommittee on Legislation and National Security. "Assassination Materials Disclosure Act of 1992." *Hearings*. 102d Cong., 2d sess., 1992.

——. *Assassination Materials Disclosure Act of 1992*. 102d Cong., 2d sess., 1992. H. Rept. 102-625, pt. 1.

——. *Assassination Materials Disclosure Act of 1992*. 102d Cong., 2d sess., 1992. H. Rept. 102-625, pt. 2.

U.S. House Select Committee on Assassinations. *Investigation of the Assassination of President John F. Kennedy: Appendix to Hearings before the Select Committee on Assassinations*. 12 vols. 95th Cong., 2d sess., 1979.

U.S. Senate Committee on the Judiciary. *Preserving Evidence Pertaining to the Assassination of President Kennedy*. 89th Cong., 1st sess., 1965. S. Rept. 851.

——. *Providing Penalties for Assassination of the President*. 89th Cong., 1st sess., 1965. S. Rept. 498.

U.S. Senate Governmental Affairs Committee. "Assassination Materials Disclosure Act of 1992." 102d Cong., 2d sess., 1992.

——. *President John F. Kennedy Assassination Records Collection Act of 1992*. 102d Cong., 2d sess., 1992. S. Rept. 102-328.

Weekly Compilation of Presidential Documents. Washington, D.C.: GPO, 1992.

Laws and Executive Orders

Statutes at Large 77 (1963): 362–363.

Statutes at Large 79 (1965): 580–581.

Statutes at Large 79 (1965): 1185.

Statutes at Large 102 (1992): 3445.

Books

Almanac of Jim Garrison's Investigation into the Assassination of John F. Kennedy: The Crime of Silence. Austin: Research Publications, 1968.

Arnold, Bennett. Jackie, Bobby and Manchester. New York: Bee Line Books, 1967.

Baden, Michael. Unnatural Death: Confessions of a Medical Examiner. New York: Random House, 1989.

Belin, David W. November 22, 1963: You Are the Jury. New York: New York Times, 1973.

Bird, Kai. The Chairman. J. J. McCloy and the Making of the American Establishment. New York: Simon and Schuster, 1992.

Bishop, Jim. A Bishop's Confession. Boston: Little, Brown, 1981.

——. The Day Kennedy Was Shot. New York: Funk and Wagnalls, 1968.

Bradbury, Rex, ed. JFK Medical Evidence Archives. Ipswich, Mass.: History Matters, 1999. CD-ROM.

Brener, Milton E. The Garrison Case. A Study in the Abuse of Power. New York: Clarkson N. Potter, 1969.

Bringuier, Carlos. Red Friday: Nov. 22nd, 1963. Chicago: Charles Hallberg and Company, 1969.

Corry, John. The Manchester Affair. New York: Putnam, 1967.

Cutler, Robert B. The Day of the Umbrella Man. Beverly Farms, Mass.: R. B. Cutler, 1980.

——. The Umbrella Man: Evidence of Conspiracy. Beverly Farms, Mass.: R. B. Cutler, 1975.

Dallek, Robert. Flawed Giant: Lyndon Johnson and His Times, 1961–1973. New York: Oxford University Press, 1998.

——. Lone Star Rising: Lyndon Johnson and His Times, 1908–1960. New York: Oxford University Press, 1991.

Davis, William H. Aiming for the Jugular in New Orleans. Port Washington, N.Y.: Ashley Books, 1976.

Davison, Jean. Oswald's Game. New York: Norton, 1983.

Davy, William. Let Justice Be Done. Reston, Va.: Jordan, 1999.

Epstein, Edward Jay. Counterplot. New York: Viking Press, 1969.

——. Inquest: The Warren Commission and the Establishment of Truth. New York: Viking Press, 1966.

——. Legend: The Secret World of Lee Harvey Oswald. New York: McGraw-Hill, 1978.

Feinman, Roger Bruce. Between the Signal and the Noise. The "Best Evidence" Hoax and David Lifton's War against the Critics of the Warren Commission. 2d ed. www.boston.quik.com/amarsh/etcetera.htm.

Fetzer, James H., ed. Assassination Science: Experts Speak Out on the Death of JFK. Chicago: Catfeet Press, 1997.

——. Murder in Dealey Plaza. Chicago: Catfeet Press, 2000.

Fite, Gilbert C. Richard B. Russell, Jr., Senator from Georgia. Chapel Hill: University of North Carolina Press, 1991.

Flammonde, Paris. The Kennedy Conspiracy: An Uncommissioned Report on the Jim Garrison Investigation. New York: Meridith Press, 1969.

Garrison, Jim. A Heritage of Stone. New York: Putnam, 1970.

——. *On the Trail of the Assassins: My Investigation and Prosecution of the Murder of President Kennedy.* New York: Sheridan Press, 1988.

Goldsmith, John A. *Colleagues: Richard B. Russell and His Apprentice Lyndon B. Johnson.* Washington, D.C.: Seven Locks Press, 1993.

Instructional Booklet. Bell & Howell Director Series, 8 mm Movie Camera. Model 414-414P. Rochester, N.Y.: Eastman Kodak, n.d.

James, Rosemary, and Jack Wardlaw. *Plot or Politics? The Garrison Case and Its Cast.* New Orleans: Pelican Publishing House, 1967.

Joesten, Joachim. *The Garrison Enquiry: Truth and Consequences.* London: Dawnay, 1967.

Kennedy, John F. *Profiles in Courage.* New York: Harper and Brothers, 1955.

Kirkwood, James. *American Grotesque: An Account of the Clay Shaw–Jim Garrison Affair in the City of New Orleans.* New York: Simon and Schuster, 1970.

Lambert, Patricia. *False Witness: The Real Story of Jim Garrison's Investigation and Oliver Stone's Film, JFK.* New York: M. Evans, 1999.

Lane, Mark. *Rush to Judgment: A Critique of the Warren Commission's Inquiry into the Murder of President John F. Kennedy, Officer J. D. Tippit, and Lee Harvey Oswald.* New York: Holt, Rinehart and Winston, 1966.

Lattimer, John K. *Kennedy and Lincoln: Medical and Ballistic Comparisons of Their Assassinations.* New York: Harcourt Brace Jovanovich, 1980.

Lewis, Richard Warren, and Lawrence Schiller. *The Scavengers and Critics of the Warren Report: The Endless Paradox.* New York: Delacorte Press, 1967.

Lifton, David S. *Best Evidence: Disguise and Deception in the Assassination of John F. Kennedy.* New York: Macmillan, 1980.

MacKenzie, Angus. *Secrets: The CIA's War at Home.* Berkeley: University of California Press, 1997.

MacNeil, Robert. *The Right Place at the Right Time.* Boston: Little, Brown, 1982.

Manchester, William. *The Death of a President, November 20–November 25, 1963.* New York: Harper and Row, 1967.

Mann, Robert. *The Walls of Jericho: Lyndon Johnson, Hubert Humphrey, Richard Russell, and the Struggle for Civil Rights.* New York: Harcourt Brace, 1996.

Marcus, Raymond. *Addendum to the HSCA, the Zapruder Film, and the Single-Bullet Theory.* Los Angeles: Rendell, 1995.

——. *The Bastard Bullet: A Search for Legitimacy for Commission Exhibit 399.* Los Angeles: Rendell, 1966.

——. *The HSCA, the Zapruder Film, and the Single-Bullet Theory.* Los Angeles: Rendell, 1992.

——. *#5 Man, November 22, 1963.* Los Angeles: Rendell, 1997.

Marrs, Jim. *Crossfire: The Plot That Killed Kennedy.* New York: Carroll and Graf, 1989.

Meagher, Sylvia. *Accessories after the Fact.* Indianapolis: Bobbs-Merrill, 1967.

Meagher, Sylvia, and Gary Owen. *Master Index to the J.F.K. Assassination Investigations.* Metuchen, N.J.: Scarecrow Press, 1980.

——. *Subject Index to the Warren Report and Hearings and Exhibits.* Metuchen, N.J.: Scrarecrow Press, 1966.

Menninger, Bonar. *Mortal Error: The Shot That Killed JFK.* New York: St. Martin's Press, 1992.

Model, F. Peter, and Robert J. Groden. *JFK: The Case for Conspiracy.* New York: Manor Books, 1976.

Newman, Alfred. *The Assassination of John F. Kennedy: The Reasons Why.* New York: Potter, 1970.

Nimmer, Melville B. *Nimmer on Freedom of Speech: A Treatise on the Theory of the First Amendment.* New York: Matthew Bender, 1984. Together with Supplement by Rodney A. Smolla. New York: Matthew Bender, 1992.

O'Brien, Lawrence F. *No Final Victory: A Life in Politics.* Garden City, N.Y.: Doubleday, 1974.

O'Donnell, Kenneth P., and David R. Powers. *"Johnny We Hardly Knew Ye!": Memories of John Fitzgerald Kennedy.* Boston: Little, Brown, 1972.

Optical Engineering Laboratory. Project Report Resolving Power of 8 mm Lens. Optical Division. Bell & Howell. Chicago: Bell & Howell, n.d.

Posner, Gerald. *Case Closed: Lee Harvey Oswald and the Assassination of JFK.* New York: Random House, 1993.

Rather, Dan, with Mickey Herskowitz. *The Camera Never Blinks: Adventures of a TV Journalist.* New York: William Morrow, 1977.

Roberts, Charles. *The Truth about the Assassination.* New York: Grosset and Dunlap, 1967.

Roffman, Howard. *Presumed Guilty: Lee Harvey Oswald in the Assassination of President Kennedy.* Rutherford, N.J.: Fairleigh Dickinson University Press, 1975.

Specter, Arlen. *Passion for Truth.* New York: Morrow, 2000.

Stone, Oliver, and Zachary Sklar. *JFK: The Book of the Film: The Documented Screenplay.* New York: Applause Books, 1992.

Summers, Anthony. *Conspiracy.* New York: Paragon House, 1989.

Thompson, Josiah. *Six Seconds in Dallas: A Micro-Study of the Kennedy Assassination.* New York: Bernard Geis Associates, 1967.

Thomson, George C. *The Quest for Truth: (A Quizzical Look at the Warren Report) or How President Kennedy Really Was Assassinated.* Glendale, Calif.: G. C. Thomson Engineering, 1964.

———. *The Quest for Truth.* Pt. 5, *The Third Man in the Car!!* Glendale, Calif.: G. C. Thomson Engineering, 1966.

Trask, Richard B. *Pictures of the Pain: Photography and the Assassination of President Kennedy.* Danvers, Mass.: Yeoman Press, 1994.

Twyman, Noel. *Bloody Treason. On Solving History's Greatest Murder Mystery: The Assassination of John F. Kennedy.* Rancho Santa Fe, Calif.: Laurel Publishing, 1997.

Van Gelder, Lawrence. *The Untold Story: Why the Kennedys Lost the Book Battle.* New York: Award Books, 1967.

Wainwright, Loudon. *The Great American Magazine: An Inside History of Life.* New York: Knopf, 1986.

Weisberg, Harold. *Autopsy of a JFK Assassination Best Seller: Best Evidence as Bad Evidence.* Unpublished ms. Frederick, Md.: By the author, 2000.

——. *Badly Reasoned.* Unpublished ms. Frederick, Md.: By the author, 1998.

——. *Case Open.* New York: Carroll and Graf, 1994.

——. *Frame-Up: The Martin Luther King/James Earl Ray Case.* New York: Outerbridge and Dienstfrey, 1971.

——. *Hoax.* Unpublished ms. Frederick, Md.: By the author, 1994.

——. *The Lousiest Book on the JFK Assassination.* Unpublished ms. Frederick, Md.: By the author, 1997.

——. *Never Again.* New York: Carroll and Graf, 1995.

——. *Oswald in New Orleans: Case for Conspiracy with the CIA.* Foreword by Jim Garrison. New York: Canyon Books, 1967.

——. *Photographic Whitewash.* 2d ed. Frederick, Md.: By the author, 1976.

——. *Picturing the Corruption of the JFK Assassination: Robert Groden.* Unpublished ms. Frederick, Md.: By the author, 1996.

——. *Post Mortem.* Frederick, Md.: By the author, 1975.

——. *Whitewash.* Hyattstown, Md.: By the author, 1965.

——. *Whitewash II.* Hyattstown, Md.: By the author, 1966.

——. *Whitewash IV: JFK Assassination Transcript.* Frederick, Md.: By the author, 1974.

——. *Whoring with History: How the Gerald Posners Protect the King Assassins.* Unpublished ms. Frederick, Md.: By the author, 1998.

White, Stephen. *Should We Now Believe the Warren Report?* New York: Macmillan, 1968.

Winks, Robin. *Cloak and Gown: Scholars in the Secret War, 1939–61.* New York: Quill, 1988.

——, ed. *The Historian as Detective: Essays on Evidence* New York: Harper and Row, [1969].

Youngblood, Rufus. *Twenty Years in the Secret Service: My Life with Five Presidents.* New York: Simon and Schuster, 1973.

Zavada, Roland. *Analysis of Selected Motion Picture Photographic Evidence.* Kodak Technical Report. Rochester, N.Y.: Eastman Kodak, 1998.

Articles

"A. Zapruder Dies." *Dallas Morning News,* August 31, 1970.

"Abraham Zapruder Dies; Filmed Kennedy Death: Footage of Tragedy in Dallas Had Role in Shaw Trial and Warren Commission Report." *New York Times,* August 31, 1970.

Alvarez, Luis W. "A Physicist Eamines the Kennedy Assassination Film." *American Journal of Physics* 44, no. 9 (September 1976): 813–827.

"An Assassination's Retroactivity." *Minority of One* 9 (October 1967): 11–12.

Barron, James. "Ideas and Trends; For Some, the Lure of Horror." *New York Times,* July 19, 1998.

Bickel, Alexander M. "Back to the Attack." *New Republic,* June 22, 1968, 28–29.

——. "CBS on the Warren Report: How Many Bullets?" *New Republic,* pt. 1, July 15, 1967, 29–30.

——. "CBS on the Warren Report: How Many Bullets?" *New Republic,* pt. 2, August 19, 1967, 30–34.

——. "The Failure of the Warren Report." *Commentary* 52 (October 1966): 31–39.

——. "Leo Sauvage and the Warren Commission." *New Leader*, November 21, 1966, 19–21.

——. "Letters from Readers: The Warren Report." *Commentary* 63 (April 1967): 4–20.

——. "Re-examining the Warren Report." *New Republic*, January 7, 1967, 25–28.

——. "Return to Dallas." *New Republic*, December 23, 1967, 34.

"Booksellers Assay Sales of Manchester Book." *Publisher's Weekly*, March 13, 1967, 51.

"Booksellers Assay Sales of Manchester Book." *Publisher's Weekly*, March 27, 1967, 52.

Brodsky, Ruth A. "A Man and His Camera." *Dallas Jewish Life*, November 1994.

"Can It Hit One Million?" *Business Week*, April 1, 1967, 28.

Collins, R. S. "Kennedy vs. *Look*, Manchester Harper & Row; an Informal Glossary of Press Relations Techniques." *Public Relations Journal* 23 (April 1967): 13–15.

Daniels, Jean. "Havana: When Castro Heard the News." *New Republic*, December 7, 1963, 7–9.

——. "Two Interviews: Castro's Reply to Kennedy Comments on Cuba." *New York Times*, December 11, 1963, 1, 16.

"Data Are Requested on Oswald Inquiry." *New York Times*, February 20, 1967.

DeLaney, William. "Film of JFK Slaying Is Being Bootlegged," *Star*, November 26, 1969.

DeSalles, Douglas. "Follow-Up and Continuation to First Shot/First Hit Circa Z-190." *Kennedy Assassination Chronicles* 5, no. 3 (fall 1999): 20–23.

Dugger, Ronnie. "*The Death of a President*. The Book. Slanted, Morbid, Sentimental, and Valuable; Confusion about LBJ and Youngblood." *Texas Observer*, April 14, 1967, 4–5.

——. "Manchestered." *Texas Observer*, February 17, 1967, 14–15.

——. "William Manchester and Texas." *Texas Observer*, January 20, 1967, 18–19.

——. "William Manchester and Texas." *Texas Observer*, February 3, 1967, 10.

Fenton, John H. "Photo Rebuts Manchester on Johnson Swearing-In." *New York Times*, February, 10, 1967.

Gilroy, Harry. "Manchester Book Has Big Advance: Orders Indicate Work Will Be One of Great Sellers." *New York Times*, January 27, 1967, 42.

Golz, Earl. "JFK Film May Record Two Gunmen." *Dallas Morning News*, November 26, 1978.

Greenstein, George, "Luis's Gadgets." *American Scholar* 61 (winter 1992): 90–98.

Groden, Robert, "A New Look at the Zapruder Film." *Rolling Stone*, April 24, 1975, 24–36.

Henderson, Jim. "Zapruders Donate Film to Museum." *Houston Chronicle*, January 27, 2000.

Huston, Luther A. "Three Reporters Correct Manchester's Story." *Editor and Publisher*, February 4, 1967, 14.

"Inquiry to Be Ended by Warren Panel: Secret Service Chief Is Last of Hundreds to Testify." *New York Times*, June 19, 1964.

Janos, Leo. "The Last Days of the President." *Atlantic Monthly*, July 1973, 35–41.

"Johnson Said He Doubted Finding on Assassination." *New York Times*, April 17, 1994.

Johnston, David. "Government Told to Pay $16 Million for Zapruder Film." *New York Times*, August 4, 1999.

Johnston, Richard J. H. "Movie Amateur Filmed Attack: Sequence Is Sold to Magazine." *New York Times*, November 24, 1963.

Jordan, Elijah. "The Role of Philosophy in Social Crisis." *Ethics* 51 (1941): 279–391.

Junkkarinen, Barb. "First Shot/First Hit Circa Z-190." *Kennedy Assassination Chronicles* 5, no. 2 (summer 1999): 23–27.

Kaplan, John. "The Assassins." *American Scholar* 36 (spring 1967): 271–306.

——. "The Assassins." *Stanford Law Review* 19 (1967): 1110–1151.

Lardner, George, Jr. "Agents, Assassins, and Moles." *Washington Post*, April 23, 1978.

——. "Film in JFK Assassination Reissued." *Washington Post*, November 11, 1978.

——. "Haggling over History; Zapruders, U.S. Far Apart on Price of Zapruder Film." *Washington Post*, June 13, 1998.

——. "U.S. Bids for the Zapruder Film." *Washington Post*, June 13, 1998.

——. "U.S., Zapruder Reach Deal on Assassination Film." *Washington Post*, October 17, 1998.

——. "Zapruder Film of JFK Assassination Is Public Record." *Washington Post*, April 25, 1998.

——. "Zapruder Film Set for August Video Release; Footage of JFK Assassination Likely to Restart Debate." *Washington Post*, June 26, 1998.

Lardner, George, Jr., and Will Woodward. "Zapruder Film Nets $16 Million." *Washington Post*, August 4, 1999.

Levine, Richard. "Film of Kennedy Torn, 'Life' Says." *Baltimore Sun*, December 22, 1966.

Lewis, Anthony. "Panel to Reject Theories of Plot in Kennedy Death: Warren Inquiry Is Expected to Dispel Doubts in Europe That Oswald Acted Alone." *New York Times*, June 2, 1964.

"Life to Release Today Part of Kennedy Film." *New York Times*, January 30, 1967.

McCormick, Harry. "Account of JFK." *Dallas Morning News*, CD-ROM, 2002.

McHugh, Godfrey. "Letter to the Editor." *Time*, February 17, 1981.

Magolick, David. "At the Bar." *New York Times*, November 25, 1988.

Mason, Randy. "Three Special Lincolns." *Henry Ford Museum and Greenwich Village Herald* 11, no. 1 (1981).

Meagher, Sylvia. "After the Battle, the Book." *Minority of One* 9 (June 1967): 25–27.

——. "The Case of the Urologist Apologist." *Texas Observer*, May 26, 1972, 22–24.

——. "The Curious Testimony of Mr. Givens." *Texas Observer*, August 13, 1971, 11–12.

——. "Finishing the Commission's Unfinished Business." *Skeptic* 9 (August 1975): 31–33, 61–62.

——. "Four Books on the Warren Report: The Summer of Discontent." *Studies on the Left* 6 (September–October 1966): 72–84.

——. "How Well Did the Non-Driver Oswald Drive." *Minority of One* 8 (September 1966): 19–21.

——. "Johnny-Come-Lately to Dealey Plaza." *Texas Observer*, July 24, 1970, 11–13.

———. "The Kennedy Conspiracy, by Paris Flammonde." *Commmonweal*, March 7, 1969, 712–714.

———. "Notes for a New Investigation." *Esquire*, December 1966, 211, 335–336.

———. "On 'Closing Doors, Not Opening Them' or the Limits of the Warren Investigation." *Minority of One* 8 (July/August 1966): 29–32.

———. "Oswald—a Patsy? From Readers' Letters." *Minority of One* 7 (May 1965): 31.

———. "Oswald and the State Department." *Minority of One* 8 (October 1966): 22–27.

———. "Post-assassination Credibility Chasm." *Minority of One* 9 (March 1967): 21–22.

———. "A Psychiatrist's Retroactive 'Clairvoyance.' " *Minority of One* 8 (June 1966): 19–21.

———. "Three Assassinations." *Minority of One* 10 (September 1968): 9–10.

———. "Two Assassinations." *Minority of One* 10 (June 1968): 9–10.

———. "The Warren Commission's Private Life." *Texas Observer*, April 3, 1970, 12–15.

———. "Wheels within Deals: How the Kennedy 'Investigation' Was Organized." *Minority of One* 10 (July/August 1968): 23–27.

Melanson, Philip H. "Hidden Exposure: Cover-Up and Intrigue in the CIA's Secret Possession of the Zapruder Film." *Third Decade*, November 1984, 13–21.

Nevins, Allan. "Gargantuan, Honest and Useful, But So Exasperating." *Panorama Magazine, Chicago Daily News*, April 8, 1967, 2–3.

"New Clue in JFK Slaying." *San Francisco Bulletin*, November 26, 1978.

✓ "New Oswald Clue Reported Found: New Orleans Official Vows Arrests Will Be Made." *New York Times*, February 19, 1967.

"New 'Plot' Inquiry Reported on Kennedy Assassination." *New York Times*, February 18, 1967.

"Of Demonologists and Eunuchs." *Minority of One* 10 (September 1968): 8–9.

"Panel to Decide Payment for Zapruder Film." January 7, 1999. Reuters News Service.

"People." *Time*, June 28, 1968, 31.

Rawls, Wendall, Jr. "New Film Suggests an Oswald Cohort." *New York Times*, November 27, 1978.

Reichmann, Deb. "Film of JFK Shooting Worth $16 Million." August 3, 1999. AP wire story.

———. "Suit Challenges Zapruder Film Purchase." November 24, 1998. AP wire story.

Rich, Frank. "Journal: From Here to Zapruder." *New York Times*, July 4, 1998.

Rosenbaum, David E. "Federal Government and Zapruder Family Debate the Price of History." *New York Times*, July 6, 1998.

Rovere, Richard H. "Books: A Question of Taste and Something More." *New Yorker*, April 8, 1967, 172–176.

Sanders, Charles J., and Mark S. Zaid. "The Declassification of Dealey Plaza: After Thirty Years, a New Disclosure Law at Last May Help to Clarify the Facts of the Kennedy Assassination." *South Texas Law Review* 34 (1993): 408–441.

Sauvage, Leo. "Professor Bickel and the Warren Report." *New Leader*, November 7, 1966, 16–19.

———. "Reviews . . ." *Ramparts*, June 1967), 51–56.

Schlesinger, Arthur, Jr. "Letter." *New York Times Book Review*, December 21, 1997.

——. "On the Writing of Contemporary History." *Atlantic Monthly*, March 1967, 69–74.

Shawcross, William. "The Day of the Conspirator: The Groden Theory." *Sunday Times Magazine* (London), July 27, 1975, 19–23.

Snyder, A. E., and Margaret M. Snyder. "The Alvarez Analysis of the Zapruder Film." *Dateline: Dallas*, summer 1992, 20–23.

Sprauge, Richard E. "The Assassination of President John F. Kennedy: The Application of Computers to the Photographic Evidence." *Computers and Automation* 19 (May 1970): 29–60; 19 (June 1970): 7; 19 (July 1970): 26; 20 (March 1971): 44; 20 (May 1971): 27–29.

Stolley, Richard B. "Shots Seen Round the World." *Entertainment Weekly*, January 17, 1992.

——. "What Happened Next . . ." *Esquire*, November 1973, 134–135, 262–263.

Stroscio, Michael A. "More Physical Insight into the Assassination of President Kennedy." *Physics and Society* 25, no. 4 (October 1996): 7–8.

Thompson, Josiah. "The Cross Fire That Killed President Kennedy." *Saturday Evening Post*, December 2, 1967, 27–31, 46, 50–55.

——. "Why the Zapruder Film *Is* Authentic." *JFK/Deep Politics Quarterly* 4, no. 3 (April 1999): 2–10.

"Tippitt's [sic] Widow Gets $25,000 Paid for Assassination Movies." *New York Times*, November 28, 1963.

Tuchman, Barbara. "The Historian's Opportunity." *Saturday Review*, February 25, 1967, 27, 31, 71.

Verb, Hal. "Bloody Treason and Assassination Science." *Fourth Decade* 5, no. 2 (January 1998): 12–17.

——. "The Case *against* Alteration of the Zapruder Film." Paper presented at assassination conference, Dallas, Texas, November 1998.

——. "The Failures of the Assassination Records Review Board: A Study of (A) the Medical Evidence; (B) The Photographic Evidence; and (C) Oswald as a Possible U.S. Intelligence Agent." Paper presented at the Lancer Conference, Dallas, Texas, November 1999.

——. "Fetzer's Follies Continued: A Reply." *Fourth Decade* 5, no. 5 (July 1998): 23–34.

——. "The First Shot in the John F. Kennedy Assassination Was Not the Missed Shot." Paper presented at Washington, D.C., conference of critics, 1994.

——. "The Human Condition: The Ring of Truth." Paper presented at remembrance on Dealey Plaza, Dallas, Texas, November 22, 1999.

——. "Livingstone's Creation Science and the Zapruder Film." *Fourth Decade* 7, no. 2 (January 2000): 12–15.

——. "Looking Backward or Looking Forward." *Dealey Plaza Echo* 2, no. 2 (July 1998): 4–8.

——. "Never Again! By Harold Weisberg." *The Investigator* 16 (October 1995): 1–3.

——. "The Photographic and Ballistics Evidence: Further Comments on Litwin's 'A Conspiracy Too Big.' " *Dallas '63* (December 1995): 29–33.

——. "Solved: The Mystery of the Warren Commission's 'Top Secret' Transcript of January 22, 1964." *Assassination Chronicles*, September 1995, n.p.

——. "The Warren Commission's 'Mission: Impossible.'" *Dealey Plaza Echo* 1, no. 3 (July 1997): n.p.

——. "The Warren Commission's 'Mission: Impossible.' How It Explained the Missing Shot in President Kennedy's Assassination." Paper presented at the Coalition on Political Assassinations Conference, Washington, D.C., October 1996.

——. "Why I Do Not Believe the Zapruder Film Was Altered." Paper presented at assassination conference, Dallas, Texas, November 1998.

Wainwright, Loudon. "Editorial." *Life*, October 7, 1967.

Weis, Eric L. "A Target Audience for JFK Assassination Video." *Washington Post*, July 28, 1998.

"Widow of 2d Oswald Victim Wed." *New York Times*, January 30, 1967.

Wills, Garry. "Books-Arts-Manners: The Lachrymose Mr. Manchester." *National Review*, May 30, 1967, 591–592.

Video and Film

"The American Assassins," CBS Reports Inquiry, November 26, 1975.

"CBS Evening News with Walter Cronkite," April 25, 1975.

"The Day the Nation Cried," WFAA-TV.

Image of an Assassination. A New Look at the Zapruder Film. Orland Park, Ill.: MPI Video, 1998.

JFK. Warner Studios, 1991.

Selby, Chip. *Reasonable Doubt.* Laurel, Md.: CS Films, Inc., 1988.

INDEX

Emory, Joel F., 172
Epstein, Edward Jay, 55, 109, 203–204,
248, 277
Evidence. *See* Kennedy assassination evi-
dence
Eyewitnesses. *See* Witnesses

Farmer, Hank, 185–186
FBI (Federal Bureau of Investigation):
Dallas Field Office, 29, 30, 125, 143,
151–152, 159, 175, 229, 300n71; King
assassination investigation, 221; Oswald case file, 131; power, 147; records
on assassination critics, 68
FBI assassination investigation: autopsy
evidence ignored by, 144; Bronson
film, 150–154; bullet found at hospital, 227, 230–231; copies of Zapruder
film frames, 181–182; copy of Zapruder film acquired by, 29–31; damage
control tickler, 291–293, 300n72; evaluation of Zapruder film as evidence,
38–40, 125, 143; *Investigation of Assassination* report, 146, 147–148, 154–
155, 248, 290–291; investigation of
Tague shot, 159–160; investigatory
work for Warren Commission, 38,
229, 235, 300n72; Katzenbach memorandum and, 141, 143, 144; lack of interest in Zapruder film, 125–126; map
of Dealey Plaza, 193–194; Martin film,
175–176; in Mexico, 145; motives, 143;
photographic evidence ignored by,
126, 150–154, 176; presumption of Oswald's guilt, 143, 300nn70,71; reenactment of assassination, 115; Tague shot
ignored by, 156–157; tests of alleged
assassination weapon, 40–41, 157,
249–250; use of Zapruder film, 29;
witness interviews related to Lovelady
and Oswald, 173, 178; Zapruder film
viewed by agents, 26–27, 30, 53
FBI Laboratory: bullet found at hospital,
228; evidence testing by, 219; examina-

tion of curb hit by shot, 159; lack of
film copying equipment, 30, 125;
paraffin tests of Oswald's face, 172
Federal government: lack of control of
assassination evidence, 64, 257–258;
LMH Company lawsuits against, 270–
271, 274; seizure of Zapruder film,
255, 268–269, 272–274. *See also* Congress; Department of Justice; Official
assassination investigation
Federal Register, 64–65, 259–260
Fehner, Marie, 135
Feinberg, Kenneth R., 270
Feinman, Roger Bruce, 122
Fensterwald, Bernard "Bud," 67, 200
Fetzer, James H., 121–122, 123, 126, 137,
187–188
Finck, Pierre, 233–234, 238
First Amendment, 90
First shot, timing of: CIA analysis, 105,
249; evidence in Zapruder film, 48,
103, 112, 113–114, 120, 189, 195–198,
242; eyewitness accounts, 12, 196–198;
inconsistencies between witness ac-
counts and official findings, 12; re-
enactment of, 114, 115–116, 166;
Shaneyfelt's conclusions, 194–195;
tree blocking view from Texas School
Book Depository window, 12, 41, 48,
190; Warren Commission allegations,
12, 39, 41–42, 45, 165–166, 190, 211;
Willis photograph 5 and, 112, 119–120,
191; Zapruder's testimony, 15, 111, 164.
See also Kennedy assassination, nonfa-
tal wounds
Fishbein, Meyer H., 70
Fisher, Russell, 108, 239
Folsom, A. G., Jr., 158
Ford, Gerald R., 54, 64, 149, 179
Ford, Terry, 172, 173–174
Ford Company, 44
Frazier, Buell Wesley, 162, 174, 178–179,
222–223, 224
Frazier, Linnie Mae, 222

P. 172
P. 107